Hometown
SANTA
MONICA

The Bay Cities Book

Writers
Jenn Garbee
Nancy Gottesman
Stephanie "Tippy" Helper
Margery L. Schwartz

Editor
Colleen Dunn Bates

Prospect Park Books

PROSPECT
·PARK·
BOOKS

Published by Prospect Park Books
969 S. Raymond Ave.
Pasadena, California 91105
www.prospectparkbooks.com

Special Sales
Bulk purchase (10+ copies) of *Hometown Santa Monica* is available to companies, colleges, organizations, mail-order catalogs and nonprofits at special discounts, and large orders can be customized to suit individual needs. For more information, go to prospectparkbooks.com.

Library of Congress Control Number: 2007926344
The following is for reference only:
Bates, Colleen Dunn.
        Santa Monica / Colleen Dunn Bates
              p.cm.
        Includes index.
ISBN 978-0-9753939-2-5
        1. Santa Monica (Calif.) – Guidebooks 2. Los Angeles (Calif.) – Guidebooks.
        I. Bates, Colleen Dunn II. Title.

First Edition

Production in the United States of America.
Design by James Barkley.
Production graphics by Sally Pfeiffer. Printed by Everbest Printing Co. in China.

A People's Town
By April Smith

At one time the Santa Monica Police Department was housed in a white moderne-style building with blue trim that artfully suggested the city's twin elements, sand and sea. If you narrowed your vision to exclude the high-rises, condominiums and gangland ghettos, you would get an idea of what they saw when they built the public works project in the 1930s: a sleepy beach town sparkling with optimism in which all that would be required of the police would be the management of drunks and the occasional theft of a Packard. Inside were narrow, dimly lit hallways with old-fashioned Western signs like you'd see in a saloon. Upstairs, the detective's bullpen was a cramped island of pushed-together desks littered with outdated computers

Novelist April Smith is the author of the Santa Monica-based crime classic *North of Montana*; her most recent book is *Judas Horse*.

and debris. The wooden blinds and green walls were cop-show 1970s. All of that is gone, replaced by the $47-million Public Safety Facility, an upbeat, energy-efficient green building that is made of recycled materials and is headquarters to the police and fire departments and the 9-1-1 center.

That pretty much sums up the changes that have come to Santa Monica over the years I have worked and raised a family here. Much of the city's vintage character has been replaced by a new vision that more often than not tries to express the spirit of the undiscovered beach town I knew in the '70s: open-minded and easygoing but with a professional edge. Still, there is something about this new police facility that is not out of character with Raymond Chandler's Bay City. As a crime writer, I, too, have been attracted to the setting, which makes me wonder what it is about sleepy Santa Monica that draws the imagination toward crimes of obsession and betrayal.

Unlike the super-freeways and monolithic housing developments that blanket most of Southern California, Santa Monica is still a people's town, with walkable streets and the centerpiece Palisades Park. This puts human beings in scale with the expanse of beach and ocean and sky that forms the spectacular western front of the city. It is the human size of things that makes this place timeless, Anytown, USA, with a California spin. Something is at stake here. It feels like the last stop – or the first – for ambition, criminal or otherwise. The pursuit of money and beauty, and an escape from the past, are classic elements of noir storytelling that still collide here. From the Promenade and the Venice canals to the Malibu beaches and the TV-network and internet-company headquarters that are based here, Santa Monica and her neighbor towns are very much alive with passions of every sort.

I have found the Bay Cities' unique mix of ethnicities and social classes, and the undercurrent of mystery associated with the uncertain nature of living beside the sea, to inspire a modern fiction grounded in a sense of place but actually more concerned with what lies beneath. With its eclectic vibe, Santa Monica gives the writer, the resident and the visitor opportunities to discover a particular kind of freedom that some, maybe even Raymond Chandler in a mellow mood, might describe as romantic. In a land of perpetual sunshine, darkness becomes quite interesting.

Contents

Santa Monica is...

About *Hometown Santa Monica*

This is not a guidebook. At least not in the conventional sense – that is, a resource to guide visitors to tourist attractions, fun activities and good restaurants. Okay, okay – so maybe you will find that in the pages that follow. But *Hometown Santa Monica* is something different, something more.

The *Hometown* concept began in 2006 with the publication of *Hometown Pasadena,* which was written by a team of five locals and which met with immediate and continuing success. The goal was to reflect the community we knew – not just the weekend-visitor highlights, but the real community: its neighborhoods, its people, its culture, its quirks, its foibles. Based on the community's response, we achieved that goal. Now it's Santa Monica's turn – and I can think of no better place to celebrate. For one thing, it's a true hometown, with established neighborhoods, walkable downtowns, strong educational and cultural institutions, great architecture and a fascinating history. For another, it's a damn fine place to spend a Sunday, whether you're paddling out at Surfrider, shopping the Main Street farmer's market, taking part in the Venice drum circle or sipping a latte on Montana Avenue.

To create this book, I assembled a team of passionate, savvy local writers, including some of my longtime friends. We had a wonderful time interviewing our local heroes, uncovering new favorite places and working together to produce a book that (we hope) will both make locals proud and inspire visitors to go beyond the obvious and get to know the best of Santa Monica and her sister communities.

As with any proper guidebook, you can flip and search for that one bit of information you crave: a good sushi bar, perhaps, or a quiet beach for a Sunday stroll. But unlike other guidebooks, *Hometown Santa Monica* goes inside, revealing the character of our communities and introducing you to some of the people who matter. We hope you get to know those people, and then seek out more like them. We hope you read the *Reaching Out* chapter and find a way to make a difference here. And we hope you learn enough about Santa Monica to make it your hometown, if only for a while.

Colleen Dunn Bates
Editor

P.S. The More Things Change...
Please forgive us if a business has closed, if prices have been raised, or if your experience does not match ours. We labored mightily to verify every scrap of information in this book, but some places will close, change or misbehave, and we can't do a thing about it.

Santa Monica is...

Seven Towns in Search of One

When it comes to understanding Santa Monica and the six smaller hometowns that surround her, it's all about the geography. Underlying the beauty, appeal, wealth and challenges of this coastal region is the splendid setting: miles of sand beaches, spectacular views of the Pacific, unending burnt-orange sunsets, a majestic mountain range and cleansing ocean breezes.

At the center of it all is the city of Santa Monica, the hub for Venice and Marina del Rey to the south, Pacific Palisades, Topanga and Malibu to the north, and Brentwood to the northeast. In these pages, you'll get to know each of these towns: their founders, libraries, dog parks, hangouts, famous residents (more than could fill a month's worth of *People* magazines) and even embarrassing facts.

Santa Monica
The Bay City

The Facts
What It Is: An 8.3-square-mile municipality along the beach, bounded by Pacific Palisades to the north, Brentwood and West L.A. to the east, and Venice to the south
Population: 96,500
Sister City: Fujinomiya, Japan
Ethnic Diversity: 78% Caucasian, 7% Asian, 4% African-American, 11% other ethnicities; within those groups, 13% are Hispanic
Median Household Income: $50,714

Key Players
Does the name Sepulveda ring a bell? Col. Robert S. Baker purchased the San Vicente and Santa Monica ranchos from José del Carmen Sepulveda and other landowners in 1872. Two years later, Baker teamed up with Sen. John Percival Jones (Nevada) to plan the town of Santa Monica.

The Name
In 1769, Gaspar de Portola sent scouts to explore the coast north of San Diego. The expedition camped at a Tongva village near two springs on what is now Wilshire Boulevard. According to legend, a padre accompanying the soldiers said the waters of the springs reminded him of the tears shed by St. Monica over her wayward son, St. Augustine, before his conversion.

Commissioned in 1934 as a public works art project, an incredibly serene art deco statue of St. Monica herself stands atop the bluffs above the bay in Palisades Park, where Wilshire ends at Ocean Avenue.

Telling Moments
In 1896, Congress chose the San Pedro Bay over Port Los Angeles (in the Santa Monica Bay) as L.A.'s official port, a blessing in disguise that allowed the city to maintain its unspoiled coastal charm. Port Los Angeles is long gone, but the Santa Monica Pier, which was built in 1909 and has gone through several reincarnations, remains the quintessential Santa Monica landmark.

Then & Now
Following the economic prosperity of the 1920s, when the city was a popular resort and filming location, Santa Monica was gravely affected by the Depression. The Douglas DC-3 airliner, which made the first coast-to-coast trips, saved the day. Assembled at a plant in Santa Monica, the plane brought jobs to the city and sat Douglas and its hometown at the top of the aviation industry for years.

In the 1970s and '80s, despite the plethora of million-dollar homes, Santa Monica was often derided as the "People's Republic of Santa Monica," for its liberal policies toward the homeless, its stringent and mind-boggling building codes and a hotly contentious renters-rights movement supported by such famous residents as Jane Fonda and Tom Hayden. The '80s also marked the gentrification of Ocean Park and a complete makeover of Main Street, now one of the region's trendiest strips. The seminal transforming event in the late 20th century, however, was the success of the wildly popular Third Street Promenade, completed in 1989.

Despite its ever-increasing wealth, Santa Monica remains as socially conscious as ever. In 2003, it became one of the first U.S. cities to adopt a sustainable city plan, committing itself to green growth and environmental responsibility. This seems to have been good for business – in recent years Yahoo, Google, Symantec, Sony, MGM and MTV have flocked here, contributing greatly to both traffic and the gentrification of downtown's north end with one architecturally compelling office building after another. Meanwhile, the addition of several swank luxury hotels along the once-raggedy southern coast has completely redefined Santa Monica as a premier vacation destination.

Our Favorite…

Library: Leave it to Santa Monica to build one of the first green libraries in the country, with solar panels, a cistern to capture runoff for irrigation and sustainability education programs; great children's room, too. 1324 5th St., 310.458.8600

Park: Palisades Park, which overlooks the Pacific and offers tantalizing sunset views

Dog Parks: Joslyn Park on Kensington Road; Rustic Canyon Park on Latimer Road is not an official dog park, just a guerrilla one. Dogs should be on a leash at all times. Really. Okay, maybe just this once…

Farmer's Markets: The mother of all farmer's markets is held every Wednesday and Saturday from 8:30 a.m. to 1:30 p.m. on Arizona between 2nd and 4th; also good is the Main Street one (featuring live music) on Sunday from 9:30 a.m. to 1 p.m., as well as the third market, at Virginia Park on Pico and Cloverfield, Saturday from 8 a.m. to 1 p.m.

Annual Event: 4th of July fireworks display at dawn off the Santa Monica Pier

Environmental Watchdogs: Heal the Bay, which monitors the health of the ocean and its forests, hands out grades from A to F for every beach (some beaches need tutors) and operates the Santa Monica Pier Aquarium, the westsider's field-trip destination of choice

Radio Station: KCRW, 89.3 FM, an NPR station on the Santa Monica College campus, with such compelling shows as *The Treatment*, *The Business* and *Which Way, L.A.?*, as well as innovative music and NPR faves

Newspaper: *The Santa Monica Daily Press* and the *Santa Monica Mirror*

Hospitals: St. John's Health Center (310.829.5511) and Santa Monica-UCLA Medical Center (310.319.4000), both world-class hospitals offering some of the best medical care in the world

Web Sites: santa-monica.org, santamonica.com, downtownsm.com

Don't Be a Lawbreaker!

The Santa Monica police are notorious for busting drunk drivers, especially on Ocean Avenue, a main thoroughfare to restaurants, bars and hotels. You stand warned.

What He Said

"At one o'clock, we will sell at public outcry to the highest bidder, the Pacific Ocean, draped with a western sky of scarlet and gold; we will sell a bay filled with white-winged ships; we will sell a southern horizon, rimmed with a choice collection of purple mountains, carved in castles and turrets and domes…."

-- From Looking at Santa Monica,
by James Lunsford, 1883,
describing Tom Fitch's sales pitch for
the first residential lots in the new town

"If we talk about environment, for example, we have to talk about environmental racism – about the fact that kids in South Central Los Angeles have a third of the lung capacity of kids in Santa Monica."

– Danny Glover

"It isn't easy being green."

– Kermit the Frog

Best Hangouts

Peet's Coffee and Tea on Montana for the best nonfat latte; the beach for a tan or a wave; Palisades Park for a walk or jog; the pier with the kids, the Viceroy Bar for a hot date, the Promenade for a movie; Bergamot Station for art; and Main Street for surf gear

Born in Santa Monica

Anjelica Huston
Sean Penn
Christina Ricci
Dave Navarro
Jack Webb
Shirley Temple
Lynette "Squeaky" Fromme
Tobey Maguire
Frank Gifford
Hot Dog on a Stick

Embarrassing Fact

In 2007, the city launched a squirrel birth-control program in hopes of reducing the burgeoning furry-rodent population in Palisades Park. The squirrels can have rabies and/or carry bubonic-plague-infected fleas, but animal-rights activists protested the previous practice of thinning the population by killing them. So now city workers capture squirrels, find the females, give them contraceptive shots, tag them, release them and hope not to come upon any more squirrel baby showers in the park.

Brentwood
Beverly Hills with Class

The Facts
What It Is: A frustratingly exclusive L.A. suburb tucked between Santa Monica to the west and south, the Santa Monica Mountains to the north, and the 405 Freeway to the east
Population: 42,791
Ethnic Diversity: 83% Caucasian, 9% Asian, 1.5% African-American, and trace amounts of other ethnicities; about 6% are Hispanic or Latino of any race
Median Household Income: $120,000

Then & Now
Brentwood isn't exactly a town – it's a section of West L.A. with the most coveted zip of all: 90049. Lush and bucolic, it was once part of the Rancho San Vicente y Santa Monica, a Spanish land grant, and was covered in bean fields and avocado groves. In 1906, the Western Pacific Development Company laid out the first subdivision, Brentwood Park.

Though Brentwood has lost some of its treasured anonymity (thanks to being the point of departure and return for a certain white Ford Bronco), it remains a country-like refuge for the rich and famous. Its secret lanes, sprawling two- and three-acre properties, canyon hideaways and oceanview hillsides attract L.A.'s most prominent entertainment, business, political and academic leaders – including the Governor Arnold, his wife, Maria Shriver, and their brood, who reside in a gated enclave off Mandeville Canyon Road.

The Name
Brentwood was originally named "Westgate" after the elegant Westgate streetcar line laid out along San Vicente Boulevard. The area was later renamed Brentwood, most likely because of the immense appeal of the new Brentwood Park subdivision.

Telling Moments
The first was in 1926, which marked the opening of a "City to Sea" highway along the foothills of Brentwood – aka Sunset Boulevard. Before long, homes appeared all over upper Brentwood, covering the scenic winding roads leading to the top of the Santa Monica Mountains. The second key moment came in 1997, when the fabulous new Getty Museum, designed by Richard Meier, opened on a Brentwood mountaintop, making the community home to one of the world's most exciting and architecturally striking museums.

Our Favorite…
Library: The Kaufman Brentwood Branch of the L.A. Public Library, on San Vicente Blvd.
Park: Crestwood Hills, a rural hideaway high up on Hanley Avenue off Kenter, and a great place for kids to run wild and have birthday parties
Dog Park: Barrington Park has a designated, fenced area just for dogs
Annual Event: Fall's Great Tastes of Brentwood, along San Vicente Blvd.; proceeds benefit the Palisades Charter Schools Foundation
Farmer's Market: Sunday 9 a.m. to 2 p.m. on Gretna Green Way at San Vicente Blvd., 818.591.8161
Web Sites: brentwoodhomeowners.com, brentwoodcountrymart.com

What He/She Said
"Not guilty."
> *– The jury forewoman at the conclusion of the O.J. Simpson trial on October 3, 1995; Brentwood resident Simpson then sold his house on Rockingham and relocated to Florida*

"I did not have a sexual affair with that woman… Miss Lewinsky."
> *– President Bill Clinton, referring to Brentwood resident Monica Lewinsky*

Best Hangouts
Belwood Bakery in Brentwood Village at Barrington and Sunset for croissants; Dutton's Brentwood Books on San Vicente for browsing and celebrity-spotting; Reddi Chick at the Brentwood Country Mart for greasy roast chicken and delectable spicy fries; the Getty for art, lunch and the best view of Los Angeles

Embarrassing Facts
Just two, but they're good ones: Monica and O.J.

Pacific Palisades
Mayberry for Movie Stars

The Facts
What It Is: A 22-square-mile part of the city of L.A. (zip code 90272) tucked between Brentwood, Malibu, Santa Monica and the Santa Monica Mountains
Population: About 27,000, with children outnumbering adults – the place is overflowing with kids
Ethnic Diversity: 91% Caucasian, 4% Hispanic and very few of other ethnicities
Median Household Income: $131,614 (gulp)

Key Players
Much of the Palisades once belonged to the powerful Marquez family, whose legacy survives in the name of a street, a neighborhood, a market and a school.

Then & Now
Pacific Palisades was once a seaside escape for wealthy entertainers and social elites, and, well, not much has changed. Goldie Hawn, Billy Crystal and Julia Louis-Dreyfus are among the scores of famous residents, most of whom keep very low profiles – because the Palisades is not about being famous, it's about raising kids. Life revolves and revolves and revolves around kids. In fact, it's a never-ending merry-go-round of family activities. Did we hear someone shout, "Stop! I want to get off!"?

Telling Moments
When Will Rogers bought a large tract of Palisades land, a long line of cultural elites followed, including Aldous Huxley, Henry Miller and, much later, Steven Spielberg. During World War II, a German exile community settled here, including Thomas Mann and Lion Feuchtwanger, a prolific German-Jewish novelist. But some say it was Ronald Reagan who put the Palisades on the map, when he moved into his all-electric GE house in the posh Riviera section in the 1960s.

Our Favorite…
Library: The stunning new library, designed by Killefer Flammang Architects, opened on the site of the original in 2003
Parks: A 9,000-acre bounty of riches, from Topanga State Park to Will Rogers State Beach
Dog Park: An unofficial gathering at Pali Rec Center between 6 and 7 a.m.; regulars are scrupulous about cleanup

Farmer's Market: Sunday from 8 a.m. to 2 p.m. at Swarthmore and Sunset
Annual Events: Fabulously dorky 4th of July parade, led by whichever celebrity mayor is in office and capped with fireworks at Pali High; Mr. & Miss Palisades contest, in which teens showcase their talent, poise and quick thinking
Newspaper: The weekly *Palisadian Post* is the *ne plus ultra* in hometown newspapers; its best part is the "Two Cents Column," in which readers complain anonymously about everything from rude people on cell phones to the sorry state of parking
Hospital: St. John's Health Center (310.829.5511) or Santa Monica-UCLA Medical Center (310.319.4000), both in Santa Monica
Web Sites: pp90272.org, palisadespost.com

Best Hangouts
Starbucks after dropping the kids at school; the bluffs for another spectacular sunset, a star-studded AA meeting at the Palisades Women's Club on Sunday mornings; the Palisades Rec Center for summertime Movies in the Park; the Pearl Dragon for a martini (it's the only place in the Palisades that serves hard liquor); and Gelson's for any reason – it's the heart of the Palisades.

What She Said
"…someone invented Pacific Palisades, where you can have Paradise, and lawns and houses and a hardware store, too. Earth become heaven, our dreams become reality."
— *Acclaimed writer and Palisades resident Carolyn See*

On Screen
The Palisades is a filming location for HBO's *Curb Your Enthusiasm* (star Larry David lives here), and, of course, *Baywatch* was shot for years at the Jetty (Tower 15).

Topanga
Trees and Horses and Hippies, Oh My!

The Facts
What It Is: An unincorporated area of L.A. County occupying about 18 square miles in Topanga Canyon northwest of Pacific Palisades and bounded on three sides by state park or conservancy lands
Population: 5,441
Ethnic Diversity: 91% Caucasian, 3% Asian, 1% African-American; of these nearly 5% are Hispanic or Latino
Median Household Income: $88,661

Key Players
In the 1950s, Topanga became a refuge for actors and writers escaping an ideologically oppressive Hollywood. Upon being blacklisted, actor Will Geer moved his family from Santa Monica to Topanga Canyon, joining with his friend Woody Guthrie in building a self-sufficient artists' colony. Following in Guthrie's footsteps, Neil Young lived in Topanga, recording most of *After the Gold Rush* in his basement studio. The Topanga Corral, believed to be the inspiration for Jim Morrison's *Roadhouse Blues,* saw performances from Taj Mahal, Emmylou Harris and Little Feat. Since the Corral was destroyed in a 1986 fire, the music scene has centered around Abuelita's Mexican Restaurant. Today, Topanga remains popular with artists and musicians, as well as equestrians (stables abound) and hardcore nature lovers – in Topanga, there will always be raccoons in the garbage, rattlesnakes in the woodpile and coyotes howling in the night.

The Name
The Tongva/Gabrielino tribe called the area Topanga, which most likely means "a place above."

Telling Moments
With steep, highly vegetated terrain and little rainfall, Topanga is a prime target for wildfires; in 2005, more than 1,000 acres burned in a single hour. On November 6, 1961, the Santa Ynez fire burned almost 20 square miles of watershed, and the November 2, 1993, Old Topanga Fire burned 42 square miles and 388 homes over ten days. Perhaps it was this risk, coupled with relentless pressure from county officials, that drove the Elysium Institute, a 30-year-old nudist colony, to sell its land in 2002.

Our Favorite…
Library: In 2005 the Board of Supervisors approved construction of a new 11,000-square-foot library, slated to open in mid-2009
Park: At more than 11,000 acres, glorious Topanga State Park is the largest state park in the country that lies within city limits
Dog Park: Dogs are barred from the state park, but they are welcome with open paws at Red Rock Canyon Park, off Old Topanga Rd.
Annual Events: The three-day Topanga Days music festival and fair on Memorial Day Weekend, and the Will Geer Theatricum Botanicum summer repertory season, featuring Shakespeare and the classics in a gorgeous outdoor amphitheater
Newspaper: *The Topanga Messenger*, a weekly paper in print for over 30 years
Hospital: St. John's Health Center (310.829.5511) or Santa Monica/UCLA Medical Center (310.319.4000), not far away in Santa Monica
Web Site: topangaonline.com

Best Hangouts
Abuelita's for music and Mexican food; the Buddha mural on the boulevard, created by local artist Kedric Wolf and the backdrop for many Topanga family holiday cards; the romantic Inn of the Seventh Ray for organic vegan cuisine, if you consider vegan food romantic

Embarrassing Fact
In June 1992, six people insisted they saw either a brilliant beam of light or three flying discs over Topanga. The claims have never been deemed credible, but talk of the strange lights in the sky lingers to this day.

Malibu
A Way of Life

The Facts
What It Is: A 27-mile strip of Pacific coastline between Santa Monica and Ventura
Population: 12,757
Ethnic Diversity: 92% Caucasian, 2.5% Asian, 1% African-American, 5.5% Hispanic or Latino
Median Household Income: $102,031

Key Players
Spanish explorer Juan Cabrillo is thought to have dropped anchor here in 1542 to collect fresh water from Malibu Creek. When the Spanish returned and set up a mission, a 13,000-acre area of land became a single tract, which was passed down intact to Frederick Hastings Rindge. He and his wife, Rhoda May, zealously guarded their paradise, hiring guards to arrest trespassers and fighting the arrival of the railroad.

The Name
The Chumash named it "Humaliwo," which means "the surf sounds loudly." As the "Hu" syllable is soft, the current name can be heard.

Telling Moment
In 1989, Malibu named Martin Sheen honorary mayor. The actor promptly declared the seaside community a "nuclear-free zone, a sanctuary for aliens and the homeless and a protected environment for all life, wild and tame."

Then & Now
The Rindge way of thinking has held on, and residents continue to ward off invaders, whether an offshore freeway or a nuclear power plant. Still, they've given some ground (or have been forced to by the Coastal Commission), and despite what many residents might have you believe, every Malibu beach is public – up to the mean high-tide line. Getting onto the beach is the challenge.

Don't Be a Lawbreaker!
In Malibu, it is against the law to laugh out loud in a movie theater.

Best Hangouts
Cross Creek shopping center for lunch, shopping and a movie; Coogie's Beach Café with the kids; and any of the glorious state beaches

Our Favorite…
Library: Malibu Library at 23519 W. Civic Center Way
Park: Malibu Creek State Park, for camping or fantastic hiking
Environmental Watchdog: The surfer-run Surfrider Foundation, named after Surfrider Beach, works to reduce ocean pollution and eliminate barriers to public beach access
Newspaper: *The Malibu Times*
Hospital: St. John's Health Center (310.829.5511) in Santa Monica is the closest
Websites: ci.malibu.ca.us, malibu.org

What He Said
"We've got a nice, quiet beach community here, and I aim to keep it nice and quiet."
– Police chief from The Big Lebowski

"I own Malibu."
– Mel Gibson when arrested for drunk driving on PCH in 2006

On Screen
Gidget was shot here, as were many other 1960s beach movies. The famous last scene of *Planet of the Apes* was filmed at Point Dume, and Jim's trailer in *The Rockford Files* was parked at Paradise Cove.

Embarrassing Fact
Sobriety is a virtue, but Malibu, with 25 rehab facilities, doesn't brag much about being the high-end detox destination of choice. Britney Spears, Charlie Sheen, Ben Affleck, Diana Ross and Matthew Perry are all graduates of the resort-like Promises residential facility.

Famous Residents
Zillions, including Pamela Anderson, Barbra Streisand, Sally Field, Ted Danson, Eli Broad and that famous sand-hoarder, David Geffen.

Venice
Bohos by the Beach

The Facts
What It Is: A funky beachside district within the city of L.A., just south of Santa Monica
Population: 37,758
Ethnic Diversity: 74% Caucasian, 4% Asian, 6% African-American; of these, 22% are Hispanic or Latino
Median Household Income: $49,017

Key Players
In 1891, tobacco magnate Abbot Kinney and his partner, Francis Ryan, bought undeveloped beach and marshland south of Santa Monica and set out to build resorts. The north end, dubbed Ocean Park, became the swankier residential district – unfortunately for Kinney, the city of Santa Monica soon annexed it. But Kinney continued to develop the south end, which he called Venice of America, building canal "streets" and installing a 1,200-foot pier with an auditorium, a restaurant and roller coasters. Only a handful of the original canals remain, and they are lovely, lined with highly desirable cottages and mini-villas.

Telling Moment
By 1920, competition between Venice's amusement pier, Ocean Park's Pickering Pier and Santa Monica's new Sunset Pier had become fierce – but then Kinney's pier burned down. Instead of giving up, he embraced the competition and rebuilt with gusto, this time with two roller coasters and many more rides and The pier was a roaring success.

Then & Now
Following the discovery of (and subsequent drilling for) oil during the Depression and into the 1950s, Venice declined in popularity as a resort, rents plummeted, and Beats and hippies moved in. A certain funkiness lives on, even though 800-square-foot houses can sell for over $1 million and boutiques sell $50 baby T-shirts. Abbot Kinney's vision of a festive, amusing escape from city life remains true to this day – eclectic (okay, bizarre) street performers, artists and vendors line one side of the oceanfront walkway, open-air cafés line the other, and Venice is the number-one tourist attraction in the entire city of Los Angeles.

Our Favorite…
Library: The snazzy Frank Gehry–designed Abbot Kinney Memorial Library, 501 S. Venice Blvd.
Park: Penmar Park, for its senior programs, community events, lighted baseball/softball field, tennis courts and 9-hole golf course
Farmer's Market: Friday from 7 to 11 a.m. in the parking lot at S. Venice Blvd. and Ocean, 310.399.6690
Newspaper: Though based in Marina del Rey, *The Argonaut* does a good job of covering Venice happenings
Hospital: Centinela Freeman Marina Hospital, 4650 Lincoln Blvd., Marina del Rey, 310.823.8911
Web Site: venicechamber.net

Best Hangouts
Abbot's Habit for coffee; Hal's Bar & Grill for Sunday jazz; the Boardwalk to shock out-of-town visitors; the amazing ad-hoc drum circle that forms every Sunday before sunset on the beach; L.A. Louver Gallery to check out new work from great artists

On Screen
Venice posed as Tijuana in the Orson Welles classic *Touch of Evil.*

Embarrassing Fact
Though the LAPD says they're both in rapid decline, two shoreline gangs, the Crips and the Venice 13, have been strong influences since the 1970s, particularly in the inland Oakwood neighborhood.

Marina del Rey

Where Singles Meet the Sea

The Facts
What It Is: The largest man-made small-boat marina in the world, located on the western edge of unincorporated L.A. County north of LAX. The 807-acre marina is home to about 7,000 boats and is surrounded by high-rise condos, hotels, apartments, restaurants and shops
Population: 8,176
Ethnic Diversity: 82% Caucasian, 8% Asian, 5% African-American, 5% Hispanic or Latino
Median Household Income: $68,447

Key Players
In 1887, real estate developer M.C. Wicks envisioned turning the Playa del Rey estuary into a commercial harbor. Using monies from the Santa Fe Railroad, Wicks invested the then-enormous sum of $300,000 into the area, and subsequently went bankrupt. Still, the resolve of the locals remained strong, and some 70 years later, Chamber of Commerce president Larry Norman worked tirelessly with the city, county, state and even federal governments to secure funding to create a useable harbor.

Then & Now
In 1936, following a decision by the county to reassess an Army Corps of Engineers report deeming the area ill-suited for a port, developers focused on turning it into a haven for smaller recreational boats. The last piece of the harbor jigsaw puzzle fell into place in 1965, with the completion of a federally funded breakwater, providing protection from waves.

To accommodate the more than 100,000 boats launched from its ramps every year, the Marina continues to grow. Apart from New York City, the marina has the highest concentration of restaurant seating within a single square mile in the country.

Our Favorite...
Library: Lloyd Taber-Marina del Rey Library, 4533 Admiralty Way, 310.821.3415
Park: Admiralty Park, with a promenade full of restaurants and shops; the coastal bike path runs through the park on its way from Pacific Palisades to Torrance
Farmer's Market: See the one in Venice

Newspaper:
The Argonaut is a good, widely distributed free-press weekly covering Marina del Rey, Venice, Playa del Rey and Westchester
Hospital: Centinela Freeman Marina Hospital is an excellent facility – just ask the Lakers, Clippers and Sparks, all of whom make it their team hospital; 4650 Lincoln Blvd., 310.823.8911
Web Site: www.visitthemarina.com

Best Hangouts
Mother's Beach with little kids; the Ritz-Carlton for Sunday brunch; free afternoon weekend concerts at Fisherman's Village on Fiji Way; picnics at Burton Chace Park. You'll be amazed at how peaceful the Marina can be, given that LAX is right around the corner

Smart
The Marina is home to USC's Information Sciences Institute, a division of the Viterbi School of Engineering. The institute (not Al Gore) was largely responsible for getting the internet going, and it continues to grapple with all things technological.

Embarrassing Fact
Since the 1970s, Marina del Rey has been the locus for the swingingest of L.A.'s divorced professionals, who flock to the large inventory of six-month leases and boat-slip rentals. Even if its singles don't swing quite as much in this post-AIDS era, the reputation lingers.

Santa Monica is…

Historic

Just as the ocean carved the landscape, so has it shaped its history. The stories of the people who have inhabited the lands surrounding the Santa Monica Bay – from the Chumash and Gabrielino Indians to the European explorers and missionaries who "colonized" them, from the Mexican rancheros to the business-minded citizens who attempted to forge the beauty of the land and sea into power and prosperity – comprise a colorful collage of inventive failures and courageous successes. Each contributed to the history of Santa Monica, a place where trends begin and the promises of living the California dream really do come true.

H. F. GILL, PHOTO.

The Ocean Park Plunge in 1908

In the Beginning...

Forging the Land

As the sea subsided after the Ice Age, erosion caused sand to come down from the mountains toward the sea. Waves ate away at the alluvial matter, cutting deeply into the land and eventually forming striking palisades bluffs overlooking a pacific bay.

Then, probably about 20,000 years ago, humans discovered the place, arriving from Asia via land bridges made from the rocky islands of the Bering Strait. They made their way down to what is now Southern California, likely feeling that they had stumbled into paradise, rich with grassy plains, wooded canyons and protective bluffs overlooking soft, sandy beaches and a sparkling blue bay.

The Gabrielinos Move In

Sometime between 2000 BC and 700 BC, another group arrived on the scene, this time from the Great Basin in the northeast. These people, called the Tongva and, later, the Gabrielinos, became a rich and culturally sophisticated society. They lived off the plentiful fruits of the land and sea, dressed in hides and plant-fiber clothing, used a seashell currency to trade with their inland neighbors, and slept in lightweight circular homes made of tule reeds and ferns on high ground above the creeks that emptied out into the sea.

Up the coast, Chumash Indians had long been living a similarly productive existence. Skeletons dating as far back as 7,000 years have been unearthed in Malibu, and many relics of an Indian settlement have been discovered in what was a large cemetery in Topanga Canyon. The Chumash named their home Humaliwo, which translates as "The surf sounds loudly," and from which "Malibu" was derived (the "hu" syllable is almost silent).

Spain Sails In & Sails Away

JUAN RODRIGUEZ CABRILLO.
Juan Rodriguez Cabrillo

On October 9, 1542, Juan Rodriguez Cabrillo, sent by the viceroy of New Spain to find the elusive passage thought to connect the Pacific and Atlantic oceans, sailed his high-decked Spanish galleon into Santa Monica Bay. He recorded in his diary: "A good port; and the country is good with many valleys and plains and trees." He recognized that it was inhabited by the smoke rising from Indian camps and named it "Bay of Smokes." The first meeting of the two cultures was a peaceful one, and Cabrillo and his men soon left. Other 16th-century Spaniards, feverishly exploring the coast in search of imagined treasures and cities of gold, followed and claimed the region as their own. But Spain left its remote New World outpost untended for two centuries, until it grew worried that Russia or England would try to gain power, and profit, from their land. In 1769 the Catholic Church moved in, built a chain of missions, and began to colonize the native people.

Thus the longtime home of the Gabrielino was changed forever.

St. Monica guards
Palisades Park.

The Naming Legend

Though it remains a mystery how Santa Monica got its name, the most popular story is this:

On an inland exploratory trip in 1769, Father Crespi, a Franciscan in Gaspar de Portola's expedition party, recorded in his diary that after Mass was said one day by a freshwater spring (purportedly at the site of University High, which, ironically, is just outside Santa Monica boundaries in West L.A.), he named the spot Las

Lagrimas de Santa Monica. The little oasis had reminded him of St. Monica, the 4th-century mother of St. Augustine, and of the tears she had shed for her bad-boy son before he became a good-boy devout Christian and major theologian.

This same naming story also has been attributed to soldiers, rather than Father Crespi. In any case, by 1820 the name was official, first appearing in print as "The place called Santa Monica" on a grazing permit.

Mexico Takes Over

Following the American and French revolutions, populist dreams of freedom circulated the globe. New political ideas were introduced, and life without the chains of monarchy or colonial rule was now possible. Mexico broke free from Spanish rule in 1821, and Alta California became a territory of Mexico by 1822.

While smugglers were using the area's coves and canyons for doing their business, Mexican rancheros set the stage for Santa Monica's future land distribution. In 1828 Don Francisco Sepulveda gained title to Rancho San Vicente y Santa Monica and used it for cattle and sheep grazing. In 1839 landowner/grape grower Ysidro Reyes and blacksmith Francisco Marquez were provisionally granted Rancho Boca de Santa Monica (Santa Monica Canyon). These boundaries, however, conflicted with those of Sepulveda's granted nine years earlier. This disagreement over ownership of Santa Monica Canyon traveled through the courts but remained unsettled during the entire 26 years of Mexican rule.

Birds Eye View of SANTA MONICA LosAngeles Co.Cal.

During this era, the ranchero way of life dominated; it was a feudal system that relied heavily on the Gabrielinos, Santa Monica's first true residents, to supply nearly all the labor.

From Rancho to Resort

In 1850 California became the 31st U.S. state, and Santa Monica and environs once again changed hands. Soon the ranchos were on the decline, taking down with them the Gabrielino culture, which under Mexican rule had suffered and would soon completely disintegrate.

Gold seekers began arriving in L.A. from the United States, Europe, Mexico and China. Many stayed, joining the Pueblo of Los Angeles's longtime black and Hispanic residents. As the city's population grew, so did a need for a recreational resort. By the 1860s, Santa Monica Canyon had become the first true Southern California resort. The Marquez and Reyes families met beachgoers and campers with great hospitality, and on warm weekends and sunny summer days, bathers and picnickers packed the beaches, and campers put up tents among the sycamore groves. Vacationers even spent time prospecting for gold along the low-tide line. Once again, feisty Santa Monica had remade itself. By the 1870s, it was a full-blown resort.

Building a City

The Santa Monica Land Rush

It was a hot, dry day, even by the sea at the base of (now) Wilshire Boulevard. At one o'clock on July 15, 1875, Tom Fitch – friend of Mark Twain, former California congressman and well-known newspaperman and orator – had the crowd mesmerized. Hundreds of San Franciscans had journeyed down the coast on side-wheel steamers, with hundreds more arriving on horse and buggy from inland for the well-advertised great land sale. The lots, selling for between $75 and $500, were bargains, considering that Santa Monica, it was widely touted, was destined to become the greatest seaport city on the Pacific coast.

Fitch promised the prospective buyers: "We will sell ... to the highest bidder the Pacific Ocean, draped with a western sky of scarlet and gold; we will sell a bay filled with white-winged ships; we will sell a southern horizon, rimmed with a choice collection of purple mountains ... we will sell a frostless, warm air braided in and out with sunshine and odored with the breath of flowers." And sell they did: more than $80,000 worth of property in two days. In a few weeks, the landscape of the now little town had changed: Houses and shops sprang out of the earth seemingly overnight.

The Long Wharf

The story of Port Los Angeles and the Great Harbor War is about a long battle over a very long pier that lived a very short life....

Railroad magnate Collis Huntington and the owners of Southern Pacific Railroad shared a dream: to help Santa Monica become a world-class commercial deep-water port. They believed that for it to reach its full potential as a city, it had to have a magnificent

The Long Wharf

port, one that could overshadow even San Pedro, the region's established port. So they built the longest wooden pier in the world, jutting into the bay from Potrero

Canyon (the first gulley northwest of Santa Monica Canyon). Port Los Angeles, or as it was commonly called, the Long Wharf, could handle both seagoing traffic and trains to service the incoming marine vessels.

The first steamer arrived at the completed port on May 11, 1893. That summer, visitors came from all over to greet the cargo, passenger and fishing ships and to walk the extraordinary pier, all 4,720 feet of it. In addition to the stunning views, at pier's end was the meeting of seven sets of train tracks – and there was still room for gigantic coal bunkers, a depot, a post office, a restaurant and a sleeping space for workers. It was only in full service for a short time, but more than 750 ships used its facilities, and it helped bring great recognition and prosperity to the area.

After a protracted battle, the Senate handed down a decision in 1896 to make San Pedro L.A.'s official harbor. Soon after, shipping activity at Port Los Angeles declined, and in 1911 landslides destroyed the approaching train tracks. In 1913 the depot building and outermost 1,600 feet of the pier were dismantled, and the carcass of the once-remarkable structure was relegated to service as a simple tourist and fishing pier. The remainder of the Long Wharf was destroyed in 1920.

Santa Monica would have become a completely different city but for that close Senate decision. Though many locals were upset, more were relieved – in fact, they were thrilled to be able to keep their residential and resort community intact and protected from big-harbor, big-city progress.

The Long Wharf became a California Historic Landmark in 1976, yet the only trace left of the colossal construction is a nearly forgotten plaque set in a boulder by the lifeguard headquarters on PCH, where, a century ago, it headed out into the bay.

Japanese fishing village north of the Long Wharf

Japanese Fishing Village

In 1899 fisherman Hatsuji Sanjo founded a residential colony immediately northwest of the Long Wharf. The area, which had been a summer vacation spot for L.A.'s Japanese business community, soon had 300 permanent residents, mostly Japanese commercial fishermen who shared the sand with a few Russian families. They built homes and a couple of hotels on land leased from the Southern Pacific Railroad, and they used the Long Wharf for unloading their catches.

On the night of May 2, 1916, a fire, caused by a local who was smoking fish, destroyed the hotels and several homes. The men joined forces to fight the blaze, while the women rushed their household items onto the beach. When it was all over, reported the *Santa Monica Outlook*, both visitors and residents combed through the ashes in search of gold, which the Japanese were rumored to have hoarded.

"The Man Who Could Walk on Water"

In 1907 Jack London met George Freeth, who he had watched surf in Waikiki waters. He wrote: "I saw him tearing in on the back of a wave standing upright with his body carelessly poised, a young god bronzed with sunburn." Because of London's reporting, railroad czar Collis Huntington invited Freeth to California to demonstrate wave riding in the young Southern California beach communities (actually to promote the Redondo-L.A. railway). Freeth held a series of demonstrations up and down the coast, successfully introducing the Hawaiian custom of riding waves while standing on a shortened version of the heavy wooden Hawaiian board.

George Freeth, waterman extraordinaire

Huntington and real estate developer Abbot Kinney were growing alarmed at the number of ocean drownings off their properties, and they hired Freeth as the first official ocean and plunge lifeguard. On December 16, 1908, Freeth led a daring rescue that saved the men on five Japanese fishing boats caught in raging seas. For his efforts he received the Congressional Medal of Honor, and Kinney organized a professional lifeguard service, naming Freeth its captain.

In his brief life – Freeth died at 35 during the influenza pandemic of 1918 and 1919 – he taught competitive swimming and water polo, founded a volunteer ocean lifesaving service and organized, trained and equipped what would become the L.A. County Lifeguard Service. He did not live to see bodysurfing arrive in the 1920s to his second-home waters.

The Life & Death of Venice of America

Abbot Kinney, the schemer and dreamer who created Venice

Tobacco millionaire (Sweet Caporal cigarettes) Abbot Kinney's first Santa Monica Bay real estate development was Ocean Park, but his dream was to build Venice of America, a seaside resort much like that of its Italian namesake. He was convinced that the marshy beach community that is today's Venice would be the perfect place, physically and culturally, for such a community. With great magnetism, he charmed local merchants into building in the architectural style of the Venetian renaissance.

Apparently Kinney was in quite a hurry. Which may explain the many engineering mistakes made while constructing all six miles of canals in a single summer, 1904. Excavation, for example, went just four feet deep. Tidal action (which keeps the canals of Italy's Venice clean) could not maintain sufficient circulation – sixteen miles of shallow ditches opened to the sea through only one narrow water gate.

The good life on a Venice canal in 1909

Nonetheless, the initial effect was successful. With multicolored lights glowing along the canal banks, and a miniature railroad and gondolas carrying visitors on a tour of the town and mile-long beach, it was a lovely and popular destination. There also were pleasure piers and such attractions as the Darkness and Dawn funhouse, Bosco Eats Them Alive reptile show, and a 30-inch-tall woman and her tiny bicycle.

In 1911 Kinney managed to change the town's official name from Ocean Park to Venice, but in 1912 the state declared the canals a menace to public health. Action was not taken, however, until the city of L.A. annexed Venice in 1925. By 1927 most of the canals were filled and paved over as streets. Kinney had died in 1920, his amusement pier had burned down six weeks later, and with Prohibition, the town's tax revenues simply drained away.

Remembering Venice's Forgotten Man

The first African-American to live in Venice, Arthur Reese arrived from New Orleans in 1905. He worked for the Kinney family as a chauffeur, lived with them and inherited the family home when the egalitarian, philanthropic Abbot Kinney died in 1920. An artist and sculptor, Reese advised Kinney in his developments and was named the town's decorator. Once he hung the entire downtown in fresh grapes; another time he staged a simulated Mardi Gras in Venice with his famous, often-imitated giant papier-mâché heads resembling celebrities of the day.

Reese convinced his cousins, the Tabor side of the family, to move west and join him. They all eventually built homes in the Oakwood section of town and were among the first residents of what became a predominantly black neighborhood and one of the few historically African-American areas in West L.A. Many believe that Venice became the town it did because of Kinney and Reese, whose position was an unusual one for a black man in the early years of the 20th century. But Venice was an unusual place. It always has been.

Gold Coast, Gambling & Murder?

Golden Sands

The 1920s were easy, breezy days in the Bay Cities. New beach clubs opened, among them the Santa Monica Athletic Club, the Deauville, the Beach Club, the Wavecrest, the Edgewater, the Breakers and the Casa del Mar. The area's resort status took a leap forward when novel safety measures were adopted, including the very first lifeguards, who were hired

Looking north on Santa Monica's Gold Coast in its heyday

by the clubs in 1925. At the Santa Monica Swimming Club, legendary lifeguards Sam Reid (who first saw surfing in Atlantic City in 1912 at a Duke Kahanamoku exhibition) and Tom Blake spent all their spare time surfing, thus helping the Hawaiian sport that George Freeth introduced to Santa Monica in 1907 take root.

The relatively carefree 1920s slipped into the more difficult 1930s, and even in Santa Monica, racial strife, intolerance, natural disasters (floods and landslides), unemployment, vice and the Depression hit hard.

Gold Coast Living

It was, of course, the gorgeous natural setting that made the Santa Monica Bay such a draw for Hollywood film shoots and film-star living. A number of early movie companies set up house as early as 1900 – among them Vitagraph, Santa Monica's first film studio; Inceville, which shot silent Westerns in Santa Monica Canyon; and Kalem Film Co., which was located at 4th and Colorado. Movie stars threw lavish parties in their homes along the Gold Coast (or Rolls-Royce Row), which ran from the Santa Monica Pier to State Beach. Conspicuous Gold Coasters included Stan Laurel, Mary Pickford and her husband, Douglas Fairbanks, Norma Shearer and her husband, Irving Thalberg, Louis B. Mayer, Charlie Chaplin and, of course, Cary Grant and Randolph Scott, who shared a "bachelor" beach pad. Thirty or so years later, resident Peter Lawford hosted his brother-in-law, President John Kennedy, who happily shook hands with Sorrento Beach volleyball regulars. (Forty years after that, President Clinton enjoyed staying at the Miramar and riding along the bike path, from which he warmly greeted joggers and cyclists.)

In 1928, for Marion Davies, William Randolph Hearst built the largest and most palatial home ever seen on local sands. The estate included a Georgian-style mansion with 118 rooms, 55 bathrooms and 37 fireplaces, a marble swimming pool, cabanas, a guesthouse and dog kennels. Many of the rooms were literally extracted from 16th-century European palaces and reassembled on the Santa Monica beach.

Murder in Castellammare?

On December 16, 1935, a maid found the blood-stained body of movie star Thelma Todd, dressed in mink and a fortune in jewels, in her chocolate-brown Lincoln Phaeton. Todd had returned in the wee hours to her home atop the sprawling 1920s Spanish colonial–style building on PCH that also housed a casino and her own posh restaurant, Thelma Todd's Sidewalk Café. To this day, no one knows how she ended up dead. The investigation involved many Hollywood names and received worldwide attention, but the mystery was never solved.

Since the early 1960s, the Thelma Todd building has been home to Paulist Productions, a Catholic film company that produces spiritually heartfelt programs. The employees apparently are undisturbed by Thelma Todd's ghost, who is purportedly a friendly presence.

All Aboard the *Rex* – or, When a Bay Is Not a Bay

The definition of "high seas" – at least three miles from the shoreline – plays an important role in this story of gambling, politics and the Santa Monica "Bay." When Tony Cornero, who had served time for violating Prohibition laws, first laid eyes on the vessel that would make him an estimated $300,000 a month (during the Depression!), she was living the lowly life of selling live bait to local fishermen. Cornero renamed her the *Rex* and spent a fortune (rumored to have come from Bugsy Siegal and George Raft) on richly paneled wood decks, a dining room headed by the chef from Victor Hugo's, a bingo parlor that seated 500 and rooms for off-track betting (racing info was secretly beamed aboard via a converted dentist's diathermy machine).

On May 5, 1938, this born-again barge anchored exactly 3.1 miles off Santa Monica beach – there was no federal statute against gambling on the "high seas." Cornero hired skywriting planes and took out splashy ads in the dailies. And though headlines in the *Santa Monica Evening Outlook* screeched "We Don't Want It!" thousands hopped onto water taxis (just like the one Philip Marlowe takes in *Farewell, My Lovely*) to reach the swanky floating casino. Cornero was a master of PR and casino operations – even the bouncers were well dressed and polite, and customers were catered to with free food and water-taxi transport (Vegas learned a lot from him). Everybody was happy – except the law.

In the summer of 1938, when the police tried to close the *Rex* down, Cornero refused to let them board. During the protracted "negotiations," water taxi captains deliberately kept their police-officer-filled boats sideways to the swells to cause maximum seasickness. Finally, Cornero realized he would have to test the *Rex*'s legality in the courts. It all came down to defining the "shoreline" – which for a bay means that a ship must be three miles beyond an imaginary line drawn between the bay's headlands (in this case, Point Dume and Point Vicente). Cornero knew his customers would not fare well so far out to sea, so he argued that the Santa Monica Bay was not really a bay but, rather, a bight (big indentation in the coastline).

Sure enough, in maps going back 50 years, it had never been referred to as a bay, and expert witnesses from the Navy agreed: The bay was no bay.

The *Rex* reopened the following year, only to be targeted again by State Attorney General Earl Warren. Again, Cornero slammed shut the ship's portals to the law, this time training a fire hose on the besiegers. A standoff ensued. Warren swore he'd starve them off the ship, and the press named it "The Battle of Santa Monica Bay." Cornero loved trading verbal jabs with the law, and Angelenos loved the shenanigans. After an eight-day standoff, Cornero finally surrendered, not because his ship needed provisions but because he needed a haircut (style meant everything to him). The police ransacked the *Rex*, tossing her gambling paraphernalia into the ocean. The State Supreme Court eventually declared that the Santa Monica Bay was indeed a bay. And the poor *Rex* went off to war, where she was captured and sunk off the coast of Africa by a Nazi submarine.

The Douglas World Cruiser made the first round-the-world flight from Santa Monica's Clover Field.

Douglas Aircraft Makes History

Santa Monica's primary World War II contribution was supplying aircraft for the United States and her allies. Thanks to the ingenious efforts of Donald Douglas, the city made world history, residents had jobs, and the Allies could fight from the skies.

The development of the airplane between the world wars ranks among the finest engineering stories in U.S. history, and Douglas was at the heart of it. The Army approached the young engineer in 1923, wanting to buy, immediately, a plane that could fly around the world. He agreed to try. In March 1924, Douglas World Cruisers took off from Clover Field (located in an abandoned film studio lot on Wilshire and Chelsea, now the site of Douglas Park), flew around the world, and returned on September 3rd.

During World War II, the Douglas plant was wildly busy building aircraft. Half its workforce were Rosie the Riveter women, and the company was the area's largest employer throughout the 1940s and 1950s. (Detective-novel fans know that Walter Moseley's Easy Rawlings worked at Douglas). General Eisenhower said the Douglas C-47 was a key weapon in the Allied victory.

To protect itself from air attacks (blackouts and brownouts were a nightly regime in Santa Monica), Douglas overlaid the roof with more than 4.5 million feet of netting ingeniously decorated with fake houses, gardens and trees, and it built an entire dummy plant nearby to further the ruse. It was considered the finest example of "protective obscurement" in the world.

War Is Ugly

On April 25, 1942, local Japanese-American citizens, mainly Venice residents, were lined up on the corner of Venice and Lincoln, with only those belongings they could carry, and sent to internment camps. There was no violence. Though released when the war was over, most of them had lost almost everything.

Fun in the Sun

P-O-P

P-O-P

To compete with the exciting new Disneyland, CBS and the Los Angeles Turf Club joined forces in 1956 to create their own mega amusement park. They leased the Ocean Park Pier, hired the finest park designers and special effects crews, and poured $10 million into construction. They called it Pacific Ocean Park, but from opening day on July 28, 1958, it was forever P-O-P. In its first six days, it beat Disneyland in attendance.

The 28-acre park remains unforgettable in the minds of kids and their parents who frequented it during its too-short life. They loved the sea-green-and-white art moderne design; the Ocean Skyway (gondolas that "flew" high above the sea to the end of the pier); the Davy Jones Locker funhouse; the pastel-pretty Sea Serpent Roller Coaster; the 1926 Looff carousel (still going round and round on the Santa Monica Pier); and perhaps the most memorable, the Whirl Pool (a centrifuge that pinned riders to the walls as the floor slowly lowered away from their feet).

The magic was not destined to last. Attendance declined, ownership changed hands, and the sea and salt air caused rapid deterioration of the equipment. The final blow came in 1965, when the city began a renewal project for the decaying Ocean Park neighborhood, which involved demolishing buildings and closing streets around the park. People simply had little access to the entrance, and soon P-O-P went into bankruptcy. It closed for good on October 6, 1967, and was a ghost park until 1973-'74, when fires and demolition took down the remains. Today not even a plaque marks its location (between Venice's Rose Avenue and Santa Monica's Ocean Park parking lots). Only a sign, proclaiming "No swimming. Possible underwater obstructions," reminds oldtimers of happy childhood days buried among the pilings.

Dogtown, USA

In the 1970s, the ruins around P-O-P, called Dogtown, became the hangout for a group of south Santa Monica and Venice surfers and skateboarders who would be immortalized 30 years later in *Dogtown and Z-Boys,* a documentary about the pioneering 1970s Zephyr skateboarding team; its success led to a feature film, *The Lords of Dogtown.* Created by an Ocean Park surf shop, the Zephyr team dominated the first major skateboarding competition, the Del Mar Nationals, in 1975, and changed the way people skated. In the documentary, filmmaker Stacy Peralta revisits his Zephyr teammates and the 1970s scene, including the drought of 1976, which forced people to drain their swimming pools. When the kids skated in an empty pool, they began making pivot turns closer and closer to the pool's top edge, until the board cleared the rim and the skater was airbound. This marked the future moment when snowboards, wakeboards and BMX bikes would also take to the air.

Brave Successes & Ingenious Failures

Pier Dreams

What happened to all the piers? Since the late 19th century, a surprising number of piers appeared and subsequently disappeared from the bay's horizon. Just in Ocean Park/Venice alone there were the Horseshoe Pier and Pavilion, Crystal, Million Dollar, Pickering Pleasure, GM Jones and Dome piers. These were pleasure piers, with rides, casinos, dance halls, theaters, saloons and exotic attractions that successfully lured crowds to the seashore for ocean-cooled excitement. Many of the early piers perished in the big 1924 fire; others, along with some fine "pier ideas," sank into the Pacific, victims of circumstances beyond their control.

▶ King among pier pleasures was the La Monica Ballroom. When it opened in 1924 on the Santa Monica Pier, 25,000 revelers, including many of the top silent-film stars of the day, came out to experience the largest ballroom in the world. Its reign was relatively short but supreme, and its setting, palatial. The interior was decorated with elaborate ornamental carving and gilt chandeliers, and its exterior Byzantine turrets created a nighttime illusion – the vast ballroom appeared to float above the moonlit ocean's surface. It was the perfect location for many early radio and TV broadcasts. Severe storms that repeatedly handicapped the pier's foundation, coupled with changing entertainment trends, led to its eventual closing in 1959.

▶ In 1931 citizens voted to approve a $69,000 bond issue to build a breakwater and yacht harbor just north of the Santa Monica Pier. It was completed in 1934, but storm damage repeatedly kept it from ever making it as an established harbor. Remnants of this failed attempt can still be seen at some very low tides.

▶ In the late 1940s, Lawrence Welk and the Champagne Music Makers played a six-week engagement at the Aragon Ballroom on Venice's Lick Pier; it turned into a ten-year TV gig. Crowds of up to 7,000 enjoyed the weekly music hour through the late 1950s, when Welk moved his show to a Hollywood studio, and the Aragon slid further and further into decline until its demolition in the 1960s.

▶ During World War II, the end of Malibu Pier served as a U.S. Coast Guard lookout station until an intense storm in the winter of 1943-44 destroyed its seaward end. Fifty years later, the 1993 El Niño storms and subsequent 1995 storms dealt the iconic pier its knockout blow, and the state shut down the historic landmark. It changed hands a few times, from state to city and eventually back to state, and reopened in 2004 following a ten-year restoration.

The North Beach Bathhouse

North Beach Bathhouse & Plunge

In the late 1800s, warm saltwater dips – and watching these "plungers" from bleachers – were all the rage. Local barons Abbot Kinney and Henry Huntington both built large saltwater plunges to give bathers the feel of swimming in the ocean sans the dangers. Just north of the Santa Monica fishing pier, Senator John Percival Jones was determined to make his North Beach Bathhouse and Plunge the area's most popular resort facility. Built in 1893, with its "strengthening" hot-saltwater bath for the "weak and exhausted" (admission was 25 cents), it was constantly busy. Its particularly attentive attendants, Pavilion Restaurant, shops, roof garden and bowling alley seemed to seal its successful fate forever. But North Beach lost its popularity after 1905, when Kinney's nearby Venice of America resort captured the public's fickle fancy, and a destructive storm damaged the bathhouse building, which was moved inland. And of course it was never the same.

Chautauquas & Uplifters Take Root

When World War I ended, two groups espousing very different philosophies came west in search of property. One was the Methodist-sponsored Camp Meeting and Chautauqua Association, which held its 1921 assembly in Rustic Canyon. While there, members noticed above them an inviting mesa overlooking the bay. They snapped up about 1,100 acres to found a community they named Pacific Palisades. Simultaneously, the Uplifters, a group of prestigious L.A. businessmen and artists (a club within the famed L.A. Athletic Club), were looking for Rustic Canyon property on which to build a clubhouse and vacation homes. When the Methodists moved up to the Palisades, the Uplifters settled in Rustic Canyon.

The Uplifters enjoyed vacations with study and lectures under groves of trees, where they staged wild costume productions and danced and slept under the stars. Rustic Canyon proved to be the perfect secluded spot for their "adventures." In 1923, when their clubhouse burned down, they replaced it with a spacious Spanish colonial revival building designed by William J. Dodd that is today's Rustic Canyon Park and co-op nursery school. For the next 30 years the members delighted in their musicals, polo matches and all-male summer outings. During Prohibition, they were nicknamed the "Cuplifters"; they always found a way to keep their celebrations "wet." The Methodists literally and figuratively looked down on the Uplifters' bucolic shenanigans.

Will Rogers, Methodist and Uplifter

On the other side of Sunset Boulevard, cowboy writer/actor Will Rogers, a member of both the Uplifters and the Methodists, purchased his own piece of property in 1926 and built a ranch. After his death in a plane crash in 1935, his wife donated the home and surrounding land to the state, and today it remains a beautiful park and equestrian center.

They Just Said No

Even in tough times, Bay Cities residents consistently refused to allow oil exploration and drilling in their backyard. No doubt they learned early on from poor Venice, where oil was discovered in 1929. By the 1930s, the lovely and fashionable beachside town was an unsightly oil field, with 450 wells dominating the landscape and drilling clogging the area's remaining waterways. (The wells produced oil into the 1970s.) Savvy Santa Monica voted in 1939 (and continued to do so throughout the century) to prohibit all oil drilling within city limits and waters off Santa Monica Bay. To this day, there's a conscious collective desire to preserve the scenic beauty and neighborhood feel of the land.

Tunnel Love

The tunnel that links the Santa Monica Freeway (the 10) to Pacific Coast Highway has been called many things and served many generations since its earliest incarnation, in 1897. Originally dug under Ocean Avenue as a railroad tunnel to bring Southern Pacific tracks to the Long Wharf, the tunnel's rail usefulness ended in the early 1930s. Later that decade, it was enlarged for highway use and finally became part of the freeway in 1967. In 1979 it was formally named the McClure Tunnel – for Robert E. McClure, the *Santa Monica Evening Outlook* publisher and a member of the state highway commission.

Sports on Sand & Sea

Santa Monica's roots as a resort playground are ingrained in its residents – or maybe it's just all that sunshine and sand and surf that keeps them active innovators. Whatever the reason, it remains a place where trends begin and radiate out into the world. Sports innovation simply is part of the history of the place.

In the 1920s, the Hawaiian sport that would come to symbolize the Southern California lifestyle was reborn on local beaches. Pioneer board designers/ lifeguards Sam Reid and Tom Blake got the word out – by example. When they weren't lifeguarding, they were surfing, for all the beach to see. Surf journalist Paul Gross wrote, "Malibu is the exact spot on earth where ancient surfing became modern surfing," when Blake and Reid first rode its waves in 1925. Both men had incredible impacts on the evolution of the sport and the accompanying lifestyle and culture. Among Reid's amazing accomplishments are the inventions of the hollow-core surfboard, the waterproof camera housing and the surfboard fin.

In the 1940s volleyball upstaged surfing as the top sport on State Beach and at the beach clubs. Players who grew up playing doubles volleyball at State and Sorrento went on to become the country's top indoor college and Olympics players. By 1976 beach tournaments were awarding cash prizes, and today the sport has reached the big time, with Olympic representation and still-climbing popularity reflected in its growing TV coverage.

Not as well remembered is the fact that Santa Monica was a hotbed for tennis champions in the early years of the 20th century. In 1904, May Sutton Bundy became the first U.S. woman to win the Wimbledon singles title, and in 1928 she and her daughter Dorothy Bundy became the first and only mother/daughter combination to be seeded at the U.S. Open.

In 1970 the polyurethane wheel was invented, which sparked a rollerskating frenzy; *Time* magazine named Venice the outdoor-rollerskating capital of the world. More significantly, it spawned a skateboard resurgence that surpassed the original '60s fad. The introduction of polyurethane wheels allowed the street surfer to cruise at higher speeds while attaining better surface traction and a smoother ride – in essence, it became simply more like surfing.

Muscle Beach Scandal

In its 1930s heyday, Muscle Beach was a hangout for luminaries of the day, including Buster Crabbe (1932 Olympic gold-medal swimmer and Paramount movie star), Kirk Douglas, Clark Gable, Tyrone Power, Jayne Mansfield, Jane Russell, Mae West and bodybuilders Jack LaLanne, Joe Gold and, of course, the various Mr. Universes. Nineteen forty-seven saw the first Miss and Mr. Muscle Beach contests, and the bodybuilding and gymnastics tricks performed on the beach just south of the Santa Monica Pier were hugely popular with spectators and regulars until 1958, when Muscle was rocked by a sex scandal involving the arrest on morals charges of several popular local bodybuilders.

The People's Republic of Prosperity

The 1960 and '70s were a time of simultaneous beachy idyll and urban decay – while surfers and volleyball players thrived and north Santa Monica and the Palisades housed prosperous neighborhoods, the local economy struggled. Venice and Ocean Park dealt with crime, drugs and low real estate values (yes, you heard that right), and parts of downtown Santa Monica had become derelict. Things began turning around in the late '70s, when merchants started reclaiming once-charming but badly neglected Main Street. When property values and therefore rents started shooting up, local liberals, led by such celebs as Tom Hayden and Jane Fonda, helped inspire the city to adopt a strict rent-control law that drew national attention. Since then, Santa Monica has remained on the progressive forefront, from its commitment to green architecture to its birth-control program for squirrels.

This ongoing era of liberalism, which led to the nickname "The People's Republic of Santa Monica," has been accompanied by astonishing prosperity. The success of Main Street's renovation in the early '80s inspired the late '80s transformation of decrepit Third Street into the hugely successful Third Street Promenade. The Santa Monica Farmer's Market may be the nation's finest. Montana Avenue remains a posh and popular commercial hub. Swank hotels compete for a rising tide of visitors. And Venice's once-shabby Abbot Kinney is the coolest place to shop and eat in L.A. And with the arrival of such new-economy, high-status employers as Google, Yahoo and Sony Computer Entertainment, the area's business cachet is skyrocketing. The only issues marring this boom are the inability of all but the rich to buy homes here, the struggle to get by for lower-income families who live in south Santa Monica and parts of Venice, and the serious challenges presented by a large and entrenched homeless population. A host of excellent nonprofits and well-meaning local government folks are attacking these issues, with varying degrees of success.

The California Heritage Museum, originally a home located on Ocean Avenue, was moved to Main Street to become a museum in 1977.

History on View

Adamson House/
Malibu Lagoon Museum
23200 Pacific Coast Hwy., Malibu
310.456.8432, adamsonhouse.org
Situated on a piece of Malibu wetlands that would make even the most successful film producer jealous, the Adamson House was the home of Rhoda Rindge Adamson, onetime owner of all of Malibu, and her husband. This is really two museums in one – the Adamson House is home to a wonderful collection of tiles manufactured by the famed Malibu Potteries between 1926 and 1932, and in the adjoining Malibu Lagoon Museum you'll find displays about local history, from the days of the Chumash and Tongva to the birth of the surfing era.

California Heritage Museum
2612 Main St., Santa Monica
310.392.8537, californiaheritagemuseum.org
Built by Sumner Hunt in 1894 as a home for Roy Jones, the son of Santa Monica founder Senator John P. Jones, this place opened to the public as a museum in 1980. It is home to American pottery and furniture in its permanent holdings and diverse rotating displays, from Depression-era glass to quilts to surfboards.

Museum of Flying
Santa Monica Airport
2772 Donald Douglas Loop N., Santa Monica
310.392.8822, museumofflying.com
Celebrating much more than the private and charter planes that now frequent this exclusive airport, the museum pays homage to Douglas Aircraft, its role in commercial and military flight history and its importance to the wartime economy of Santa Monica. It holds a lot of really cool old planes, too. After a long-awaited facelift, the museum is reopening in early 2008; it will be open to the public on weekends and to field-trip groups during the week.

Santa Monica Conservancy
Walking Tours
310.496.3146, smconservancy.org
Spend a sunny Saturday morning discovering more than 130 years of Santa Monica architectural and cultural history. Covering six blocks and lasting two hours, the tour encompasses everything from the city's early Wild West roots to the metropolis it has become. Reservations are essential, and tickets are a modest $5 to $10.

Santa Monica Historical Museum
Santa Monica Library
601 Santa Monica Blvd., Santa Monica
310.395.2290, santamonicahistory.org
A place for researchers and armchair historians alike, this museum was, at this writing, in the midst of moving to a 5,000-square-foot space on the east side of the new Santa Monica Library. (The entrance is on the 7th Street side.) The new space comprises a lobby, research library, changing gallery, permanent gallery, collections storage, and staff and volunteer work area.

An Incomplete Timeline

1542	Juan Rodriguez Cabrillo sails into Santa Monica Bay.
1769	Father Crespi (or Spanish soldiers/explorers) names the area Santa Monica after the tears St. Monica shed for her wayward son, St. Augustine.
1820	Francisco Javier Alvarado and Antonio Ignacio Machado granted grazing permit for "the place called Santa Monica."
1839	Landowner Ysidro Reyes builds Santa Monica's first house, near 7th St. and Adelaide Dr.
1875	At public land auction, Santa Monica lots sell starting at $75. Santa Monica Canyon beaches become accessible when railroad to ShooFly Landing is constructed. The 99 Steps built at the foot of Arizona Ave.
1876	*Santa Monica Outlook* begins its 123-year publication run.
1879	City founder John Percival Jones plants famous, still-standing Moreton Bay fig tree on his elegant estate, Miramar (now Fairmont Miramar hotel).
1886	City electorate votes 97 to 71 to incorporate Santa Monica. Arcadia Hotel, Santa Monica's largest structure, built.
1893	Steamer *San Mateo* is the first to use the new Long Wharf.
1894	North Beach Bathhouse opens. The Jonathan Club welcomes its first members.
1896	The Sunset Trail (California Incline) allows beach access from the bluffs, often on muleback. First electric streetcar runs from L.A. to the beach.
1904	Abbot Kinney leads dredging project to create Venice of America. May Sutton Bundy becomes first U.S. woman to win Wimbledon.
1907	Surfing born on local beaches.
1909	Santa Monica Pier dedicated, to great fanfare.
1912	"Samohi" is winner of naming contest for new high school.
1922	Pacific Palisades officially born at Founders' Oak. Prohibition rumrunners use Malibu's secluded Pirate's Cove for offloading cargo.
1924	First round-the-world flight takes off from Clover Field, returning in 190 days. The largest ballroom in the world, the La Monica, opens on Santa Monica Pier.
1925	Venice annexed to the city of L.A.
1926	Silent-movie actress Anna Q. Nillson moves to Malibu, the beginning of the celebrity invasion.
1927	Most of Venice's canals filled and paved over as streets. Riviera Country Club opens.
1929	Roosevelt Highway (now PCH) opens after 22-year court battle with reclusive Rindge family of Malibu. Santa Monica's first skyscraper, Bay Cities Guaranty Building & Loan Association, changes the skyline forever.
1932	Santa Monica Lifeguard Service founded, with wooden towers built on beaches. Eyes of the world focus on Riviera Country Club for L.A. Olympics equestrian events and on Castellammare for cycling road-race finish.
1934	Sunset Blvd. (as in "Sunset to the Sea") named.
1938	Santa Monica Canyon floods.
1939	Eight-day standoff between Tony Cornero and State Atty. Gen. Earl Warren over legality of gambling barge the *Rex*.
1942	Official dedication ceremony held for Will Rogers State Beach. Venice residents of Japanese descent sent to internment camps.
1945	Hundreds of thousands of lobsters mysteriously wash onto shore; feasting ensues.
1946	Olympic Drive-In Theatre, Southern California's first (and America's second) outdoor movie house, opens at Olympic and Bundy.
1947	First beach volleyball tournament at State Beach. First Miss and Mr. Muscle Beach crowned.
1949	Gussie Moran's lace panties pack Wimbledon's center court with record-breaking crowds.
1958	Pacific Ocean Park (P-O-P) opens.
1965	After 75 years, from funding to fruition, Marina del Rey formally dedicated.
1966	Opening Day for the last link of the Santa Monica Freeway. TV music-dance series *Where the Action Is*, hosted by Paul Revere and the Raiders, films on local beaches.
1967	P-O-P closes. One of the highest-rated shows in TV history, the final episode of *The Fugitive* (shot at P-O-P), airs.
1970	Polyurethane wheels invented, sparking a skateboarding resurgence.
1973	Santa Monica Pier becomes protected historical monument. Olympic Drive-In Theatre goes dark.
1974	J. Paul Getty Museum, a re-creation of the ancient Roman country estate Villa dei Papiri, opens on PCH.
1975	Michael Medved and David Wallechinsky publish *What Really Happened to the Class of '65?* about Pali High grads. Zephyr skateboarders dominate the country's first major skateboarding competition. Santa Monica, L.A. County and L.A. City consolidate to make world's largest lifeguarding organization.
1976	The site of the Long Wharf designated California Historic Landmark. State Beach World Championship awards first volleyball cash prizes. Cat Stevens (born Steven Demetre Georgiou and now known as Yusuf Islam) has near-death swimming experience in Malibu that leads him to embrace Islam.
1979	Pacific Palisades' Bay Theater closes its streamline moderne doors after 30 years.
1989	Third Street Promenade reopens.
1991	Malibu, long unincorporated, achieves cityhood in order to exercise local control over proposed developments, including an offshore freeway and a nuclear power plant.
1998	The *Santa Monica Evening Outlook* ends its 123-year run.
2004	Malibu Pier reopens following ten-year renovation.

Q & A: Betty Lou Young

Though she was born in Minnesota, Betty Lou Young moved to California at 11 months old and considers herself a native. She's earned it. With her son, Randy Young, she is the author of *Santa Monica Canyon: A Walk through History, Rustic Canyon and the Story of the Uplifters,* and *Pacific Palisades: From the Mountains to the Sea,* among other meticulously researched local-history books. She considers herself particularly lucky to have met many of the characters whose stories she has immortalized. Margery Schwartz spoke with Betty Lou at her Rustic Canyon home, where she's raised three kids and lived for 53 years.

How is it, working with your son?
Randy designs the books and coordinates the photographs. I do the bulk of the informational research, though he does a great deal as well. We both do the interviews – tape-recorded and video.

It's so unique, a mother-son literary partnership.
It's really very symbiotic: I write with his layout in mind, and he lays out the books mindful of the content. We've set up our own press, Casa Vieja, which has really worked out well. Despite our differences, we respect and rely on each other.

How do you manage such research-intensive books?
Much of the information has not appeared in books before. It comes from all over the place, though mainly from individuals, libraries and museums. The wonderful stories and legends about the Uplifters, for example, came from all sorts of people. The mailman who used to deliver mail down there (Rustic Canyon Park) told me that one time he heard them marching down the canyon, and then saw them all jump in the pool stark-naked. Each project has taken three years, from concept to production. And I love every minute of it. I just love card files.

What stands out as one of the biggest historical surprises you uncovered?
We learned about the Murphy Ranch and a small community of Nazi sympathizers, master racers, who built a complex in Upper Rustic, intending to wait out the war and a Nazi victory. It started out by hearing rumors and tracking down sources, but we were never quite able to authenticate it. That one was a cliffhanger.

This area, especially Santa Monica and the Palisades, has grown tremendously over the last 15 years or so. Does this growth bother you?
Yes, and the new residents aren't like the old ones. Young women on cell phones in big SUVs, the whole concept of such huge houses – why? They're so unnecessary.

Can you ever imagine living anywhere else?
No. I'll go out in a box, and most of my neighbors feel the same way.

What's your favorite street?
Latimer Road. Every time I turn the corner coming home, I see the trees and I'm just happy. Us old-timers, we're all tree worshippers.

Santa Monica is…
Beachy

It's what we've all come here for – the beach. At the edge of the continent, where the mountains meet the sea. The Mediterranean climate, 300 days of sunshine a year. Surf City, U.S.A. Here's where to find the best of our beach culture… the right waves for every kind of surfer, the wide white-sand beaches, the piers and their amusements, the bike path that connects it all, the fishing and boating and whale-watching adventures, and the surf shops that sell not just wax and boards, but the iconography of California living.

Ain't Life a Beach?

Santa Monica may still be in the throes of a wild growth spurt – over the last couple of decades the city has grown into a world-class tourist destination and a booming regional commercial center – but at its heart it remains, forever, a beach town.

It's partly the weather, of course. It's blessed with lots of sunny days, with an average summertime air temperature in the low 80s and average water temperature in the low 70s. When visitors land at LAX, the first thing they want to do is stick their toes in the Pacific. Inland Angelenos wait for warm weekends to head for their favorite spots by the shore. And residents can't wait to drive home after a steamy, smoggy day of work to get down to the beach before the sun sets into the Pacific.

The beach means different things to different people. Fortunately, there's plenty of sand and surf for everybody: the volleyball players, the sun worshippers and beach-chair readers, the sandcastle builders, the walkers and joggers, and all the surfers – board, body, skim and boogie. Regulars have their own beaches. Sometimes it's a generational thing – people "inherit" the beach their parents took them to as kids. Some choose a home beach for its regular weekend volleyball game (doubles, four-man, straight, throw), while others choose one for its surf break. Kayakers look for a stretch that offers parking and short beaches for easiest access to open water. And plenty of folks get in regular pier time – to fish, take in the view, treat the kids to an amusement-park ride cooled by sea breezes, or explore the fine aquarium museum.

Visitors and locals alike may fret about unhealthful water quality, but our ocean actually is, for the most part, healthy and teeming with sea life. L.A. County runoff still drains into the sea, causing nasty bacterial levels after rains, but Heal the Bay is on the case and reporting the facts. We still have a ways to go, but there are good signs: The dolphins are out there all the time, and the pelicans are back at work diving for fish.

All the beaches are more crowded in summer, of course, which is why locals favor the other seasons: fall's long low tides, winter's bigger waves from far-off northern storms and, year round, the surprise heat waves brought by the Santa Anas.

In the pages that follow we'll take you down the coast, north to south (and east to west in Malibu, where the coastline changes direction), down the bike path, on the pier, in and on the water and even into a surf shop or two, so you can get the essential gear for California beach living, from flip-flops to a lightweight wetsuit.

Up & Down the Coast

The low-key beach across from Malibu Seafood

From Point Dume to Palos Verdes Point, the Santa Monica Bay is rich with life. Joining the more than 5,000 species of fish, mammals, birds, plants and other wildlife are 45 million visitors each year. On particularly warm summer days, crowds can top 500,000 – on a single day!

From north to south, here is a sampling of our favorite beaches. The list is not complete – that's a book in itself – but this should be plenty to whet your appetite and inspire further exploration of the bay's many beaches.

Malibu

Its very name is synonymous with surfing – the Chumash called the area Humaliwo, which means "the surf sounds loudly." And that it does, all around the world.

Because the city's boundaries extend three miles into the ocean, in terms of land and water area, Malibu is, shockingly, one of the largest cities in the United States. (Less shockingly, its total area is 80.32 percent water.) The 27-mile strip of coastline, known apparently to all but locals as the 27-Mile Miracle, is a beachfront community with worldwide allure. In the 1960s the *Gidget* and *Beach Party* movies brought it fame as the home of the quintessential surf life, and it has long kept the world fascinated with its "colonies" of opulent homes and movie-star residents.

Malibu did give the world surfing – commercial surfing, anyway – and no one can deny all that beautiful ocean and warm sandy beaches. Even its boundaries – Topanga Canyon to the east, the Santa Monica Mountains to the north, the Pacific to the south and west – are incredibly gorgeous physical specimens. The following six beaches, from Zuma in the north to Surfrider in the south, all fall within Malibu.

Zuma Beach

Way up north (at 30000 Pacific Coast Highway, past Kanan Dune Road), Zuma has it all. At two miles long, it's L.A. County's largest beach and simply a great spot for swimming, surfing, bodysurfing, boogie boarding, fishing, basically all your water activities. Extras include lots of easy parking, plenty of facilities – restrooms, showers, volleyball courts, food – and, thanks to its open-ocean wave action, clean water. Waves and riptides can get rough, so pay attention to the lifeguards' warning flags.

Westward Beach

At the south end of Zuma lies a long, sandy stretch of Pacific shoreline separated from noisy PCH by high sandstone cliffs. More private, Westward Beach is not crowded, and it's a fine beach for swimming, surfing, fishing, even scuba diving.

Paradise Cove

This private beach (28000 block of PCH) charges $25 per car and $5 for walk-ins, but for many it's worth it. The lovely, serene cove is a perfect kid-friendly beach, and there's a nice snack stand and restaurant (if you eat at the restaurant, parking drops to $3 for four hours). Because of all this, the lot is often filled by noon on weekends. One caveat: Because it's close to the runoff at Ramirez Canyon Creek, water can have high bacterial levels on days following rainfall.

The Colony

The legendary Colony in Malibu is a stretch of beach known not for its surf (which is pretty much shorebreak) but for its residents: the rich and the movie stars who value their "famous" privacy. As is true for all California beaches, it is actually public, not private, if only below the high-tide line — but here, the high-tide line is at most residents' seawalls. So you have every legal right to enter the beach from the east end (at Malibu Lagoon State Park), walk under the fence, and stroll the beach.

Malibu Lagoon State Beach

If you're looking for marine life and shorebirds rather than rights and lefts, come explore these 22 acres of gorgeous wetlands, flower gardens and sandy beaches. Enter on PCH, south of Cross Creek Road.

Malibu Lagoon is paradise for sea birds.

A fast First Point wave at Surfrider

Malibu Pier and Surfrider Beach

In July 2004 the world-famous Malibu Pier reopened after nearly a decade of renovation work. It was famous for Alice's Restaurant, views and especially the beach just below: Surfrider. Alice's is gone, but the views and Surfrider remain. The pier is open from sunrise to sunset, and the fishing is free, no license required. More peaceful than its Santa Monica and Venice counterparts, the Malibu Pier has a natural beauty that makes it the quintessential Southern California photo op, and like so many of California's natural beauties, it has an agent – it's a popular location for filming, still-photo shoots and events. Sportfishing and whale-watching excursions are now based on the pier; by the time you read this, a restaurant, surf-and-beach-equipment stand and bait-and-tackle shop should be open.

Surfrider Beach is known for its perfect wave. This is where it all started, the points (First, Second and Third) at which surfing caught on in the 1960s and spread up and down the California coast and around the world. Always crowded, First Point, the smaller inside ride, is the most popular, with longboarders vying for the high-quality wave. This is not a good place to learn to surf – collisions happen all the time, and the experienced surfers catch all the waves. Second Point's wave is shorter and faster, a more high-performance wave that can connect to the inside "Kitty Bowl." Third Point, the farthest out, is the fastest, and has both a right and a left. In the winter, decent swells from storms generated in Alaska can make it pretty big; in late summer, Surfrider can get southern swells from hurricanes in Baja. The key to understanding this three-point surf spot is to know that, by definition, any point break is a difficult proposition when it's crowded (as it always is) – since the wave generates from that single point, everybody out there is fighting to get in the same primo spot.

Topanga

This is not a lounging beach, just a surf spot. But enter at your own risk: Topanga is known for having an unpleasant vibe, ranging from fiercely loyal to downright surly. Nevertheless, surfers (both longboarders and short-boarders) brave the attitude for the long right and the challenging sections. It's best when there's a big west swell.

Surfers rule at Topanga.

Sunset

Again, not for sunbathing, this rocky beach is great for beginning surfers – once you get past the rocks. It's a better low-tide break; there are fewer waves at high tide. And Sunset has always been a good place to watch from above – it's very pretty, with a classic surf-beach look. More aggressive shredders go elsewhere, so the vibe is more welcoming to newbies.

Will Rogers State Beach(es)

Named for the American humorist, Will Rogers State Beach runs about two miles, from just above Sunset (Gladstone's) south to where the Santa Monica beaches begin, below the Beach Club. But it's really a handful of beaches, each with its own personality and crowd. These beaches may not have great surf, but they do have friendly little waves and plenty of sand. They only get really crowded on a few sweltering summer weekend days, unlike during the heydays of the 1920s and '30s, when photos show every square inch of sand occupied. That's partially thanks to the Army Corps of Engineers, who, in the '50s, added sand, widening the

Guarding the Bay

In 1929, the L.A. County Lifeguard Service was inaugurated to patrol and protect the region's beaches, which were drawing increasing numbers. Many early guards were Olympians, and some also worked in the burgeoning film industry. By 1975, it was the largest ocean lifeguarding organization in the world (and it still is today). In 1995 the Santa Monica, L.A. County and L.A. City lifeguard services merged into the L.A. County Fire Department. Today the unit works 24 hours a day, 365 days a year to protect the beachgoing public.

The men and women charged with rescuing drowning swimmers, sinking boats and downed aircraft along the 72 miles of coastline from Zuma to the L.A. Harbor make approximately 10,000 ocean rescues a year on beaches that welcome 50 million visitors a year.

Thanks in part to the TV series *Baywatch* – conceived by local lifeguard Greg Bonann, based on the experiences of real L.A. County lifeguards, named after the service's rescue boats, using identical towers, uniforms, boats and equipment and seen by millions in 145 countries – many realize that lifeguards are the law on the beach. All they ask of beachgoers is to be careful and pay attention to ocean conditions and beach rules, including the new and bold one: No smoking on the sand.

beaches and creating plenty of room for the volleyball courts, concession stands, parking lots and bike path.

From the Bel Air Bay Club (private), at the northern end of the Temescal Canyon parking lot, south to lifeguard headquarters, there are a few small lagoonlike beaches. With calm water and short beaches close to the parking lot, they're perfect for families with little kids.

Take your pick. Call it the Jetty, Tower 15, the *Baywatch* Beach or the Babewatch Beach – what *Gidget* did for Malibu, *Baywatch* did for Santa Monica beaches, specifically for this little spot just south of the small jetty that juts out into the water below lifeguard headquarters. Not so long ago a decent right peeled off the bottom, but erosion put an end to that wave, and these days it's a beach primarily popular with Palisadian families, volleyball novices, surf gremmies and kayakers.

Moving south, the next beach (Tower 18), at the base of Chautauqua Boulevard, is the real Will Rogers State Beach, known as "State" for more than 50 years. It gave the world beach volleyball and is still a doubles-

volleyball hot spot. The many permanent courts accommodate games of all levels – you'll see pros as well as impromptu twelve-on-a-side party games. Just don't "take waiters" on the courts with the big guys; you'll know them when you see them. And stay clear of the less-than-pristine running creek, especially after rains. Of historical interest: Down near the Beach Club's green wall is a smallish stretch that has been a world-famous gay beach since the 1950s.

Past the Beach Club, the beach by Tower 4 has grown in popularity over the last decade or so. It used to be the beach of the now-gone Sand and Sea Club (the only one of the area's beach clubs that allowed Jews), and loyalists of the Back on the Beach Café and volleyball players (mostly four-man games) have since made it their home. It's a long one, so there's plenty of sand, though it is a schlep down to the water (and back up for snacks and restroom facilities). The surf is nice and easy, and there's great walking and skimboarding at low tide and beginning boogie boarding all the time.

The Pier & Muscle Beach

Just south of the Santa Monica Pier is famed Muscle Beach, though it's not the tourist attraction it once was (that honor now belongs to the Venice Beach boardwalk). The muscle-men bodybuilders, bathhouses, beach clubs,

Muscle Beach and the pier beyond

plunges and ballrooms of the past are the pricey oceanfront hotels and condos of today. The beaches on either side of the pier are generally very busy, probably the most crowded in the Santa Monica Bay – which is understandable considering the location: central to the pier, the volleyball courts (not among the more serious scenes), Chess Park (the seaside version of New York's Washington Square Park), a kids' park (with a giant sandbox, misting Viking ship and jungle gym), the carousel, the amusement park and restaurants. Not to mention the original Hot Dog on a Stick, which for many locals is synonymous with Muscle Beach. Also a short walk away is the Promenade, a chain-store and movie-theater mecca. Because of all these amusements, many Angelenos who live inland make one of the beaches flanking the pier their home beach (another plus: They're close to the McClure Tunnel, where the 10 Freeway meets the sea). Other dominant groups are packs of teenage girls and third-date young couples looking for a little beach time, some pier fun, maybe a bit of shopping at the Promenade, followed by a movie….

Bay Street

When you move south of the pier and start to see surfboards out in the water, you've reached Bay Street. This sandy-bottom beach break – rights and lefts – offers fun, short rides. With enough waves to go around, it's one of the more friendly surf spots; beginners live peaceably with regulars. Surfers dominate in the early morning and late afternoon, with boogie boarders and bodysurfers staying to their south. In the summer, as at most local beaches, lifeguards often raise the black ball (or "meatball") flag around noon (often depending on the crowd size) to indicate that all boards must get out of the water to make way for swimmers, boogie boarders and bodysurfers. As soon as the flag is taken down at the end of the day, at 5 or 6 p.m., the surfers head back out.

Venice Beach

This wide, white-sand beach often is overlooked, so potent is its boardwalk's reputation as the Coney Island of the Pacific. Known for its carnival atmosphere, with sidewalk performers, artists, street vendors, musicians, wild rollerbladers, crazy costumes, bodybuilders and bike-path crowds, it truly is a sea of sometimes-overwhelming humanity. You can take in this show on Ocean Front Walk (also known as the Venice Boardwalk) from a café or head for the fairly distant water's edge and enjoy a more pacific beach experience.

Marina del Rey/Mother's Beach

The Marina is really more of a boaty place than a beachy place. It has plenty of on-the-water stuff going on, and decent parks, but as far as beaches go, the Marina is pretty much limited to Mother's Beach, a tranquil non-ocean-facing, kid-friendly lagoon. Little ones love the calm waters, and when they get bored with their buckets and shovels, there's a play area with equipment. Not to spoil the fun, but because this is a protected cove with weak currents, bacterial levels can get high.

Wave-free Mother's Beach

Healing the Bay

Misconceptions abound about the health prospects of swimming in the Santa Monica Bay, so we are grateful for the straight shooting of Heal the Bay, the nonprofit organization that is both the bay's watchdog and advocate. Its web site, healthebay.org, answers questions about pollution, safety and efforts to keep improving our waters. Its weekly Beach Report Card is based on readings from four public agencies, including the county health department, and it accurately lists individual beach conditions.

The number-one source of near-shore pollution is urban runoff from the city's storm-drain system. Runoff from city streets is transported through the drain system to our beaches, picking up large amounts of pollutants along the way. In the summer months, a relatively new system diverts water from the highest-risk drains into sewage-treatment plants, and this system has noticeably improved water conditions. In winter, however, heavy rainfalls can overwhelm the drains, and flows can and do spill into ocean water – thus the health-department signs that warn not to swim for 72 hours after a rain. (And honor those signs, unless you want to deal with ear infections, skin rashes or respiratory infections.)

The other big problems come from sewage-related issues: spills from breakages in the system or output from treatment plants. The treatment plants themselves have been upgraded, but not the conveyance system that gets the waste to the plants. This system is 40 to 50 years old, and when overburdened, spills happen. Fortunately, an upgrading of the conveyance system is now under way. And Heal the Bay is educating the next generation of ocean-protectors via its fun and fascinating aquarium below the Santa Monica Pier.

Thanks to Heal the Bay (as well as regional government and other environmental groups, from the Surfrider Foundation to Oceana), many former sources of bay pollutants no longer pose a threat. And the signs are out there: The dolphins are back, in part because the water is cleaner than it was 40 years ago (which means more plankton, more fish and a healthier ecosystem), and so are the brown pelicans, because we stopped putting PCBs and DDTs in the ocean.

Heal the Bay and its allies are only in the infancy of this work; the next few decades are critical for the health of our local waters. But at least people are paying attention. And at least we have Heal the Bay.

Heal the Bay
Healthy Surf

A few tips from Heal the Bay:
- ▶ Wait 72 hours after a rainstorm to swim
- ▶ Avoid flowing storm drains and swim at least 100 yards away from where storm-drain flow enters the surf
- ▶ Check the weekly Beach Report Card (healthebay.org)
- ▶ Avoid enclosed beaches, where poor tidal circulation means higher bacterial levels

The Beach Clubs

The Beach Club

For many locals, all beach activities, not to mention entire social lives, revolve around membership at one of the area's three private beach clubs. And why not? Who wouldn't want to belong to a private club on the beach with great dining, hot showers, immaculate locker rooms, fab parties, and all sorts of fun activities, from clambakes to interclub paddle tennis tournaments to concerts on the sand? All of this, of course, comes at a price.

Sitting at the base of the California Incline, the Jonathan Club (or the "JC") has the biggest membership and is the most affordable, easiest to join, plus it includes membership to the elegant Town Club in downtown L.A. But it can get maddeningly crowded in the summer.

Next up the coast, just south of West Channel, is the dreamy Beach Club, whose white clapboard clubhouse looks like it was plucked off the coast of Maine, and its Hamptons-style interior that makes New Yorkers feel at home. The Beach Club limits membership to about 450 families, which means there is always a four- or five-year waiting list. Its food is known as the best on the beach, and the facilities are excellent.

Finally, just north of Temescal is the newly renovated and quite exclusive Bel Air Bay Club (BABC), which sits on the sand just yards from the shoreline. Its spectacular new oceanfront facility features a double row of highly coveted cabanas, new beach bar, state-of-the-art gym and swank dining facilities. The BABC also features an Upper Club, which is just across PCH and is the site of nonstop parties and weddings.

The Jonathan Club

To become a member of any of these clubs, one must endure a rigorous application process involving sponsors, multiple references and, oh yeah, lots of cash (initiation fees run into the tens and tens of thousands of dollars; of course clubs do not disclose such crass information). Many lives are shattered when membership is declined.

A Club for the Rest of Us

It took about nine years of intense, complicated and far-reaching legal wrangling to get the green light, but late in 2006, the city of Santa Monica started work on the first and only public beach club in the nation. Plans call for a spring 2009 opening of the Annenberg Community Beach Club of Santa Monica State Beach, at 415 Pacific Coast Highway.

In 1929, William Randolph Hearst built an estate for his mistress, Marion Davies; at the time, it was the largest house on the Southern California coast. Designed in part by Julia Morgan (Hearst Castle), it included three guesthouses, two swimming pools, dog kennels and a 100-room mansion. Entire rooms were re-creations of 16th-century European chambers, and the parties Hearst and Davies threw there are legendary. In 1937, for example, they borrowed a merry go round from Warner Bros. for a party; to make room in the home for the carousel, Hearst ordered a wall torn down and then put back. Photographs show Charlie Chaplin, long rumored to have been Davies's

THE BEACH HOME OF MARION DAVIES, SANTA MONICA, CALIFORNIA   T250

Marion Davies's beach mansion in its prime

lover, cavorting with her in the 110-foot saltwater swimming pool, which was lined with Italian marble and spanned by a Venetian marble bridge.

Some years later, the property became the Ocean House Hotel, then the Sand and Sea Club. And now, thanks in part to a grant from the Annenberg Foundation, the city will breathe new life into the five-acre beachfront site. With just one of the guesthouses and one pool remaining, the club will include the restored North House, which will be named the Marion Davies Guest House (a City of Santa Monica historic landmark), a two-story main/locker building and the original marble-tile pool, which suffered significant damage in the 1994 earthquake. When completed, the open-to-the-public "club" will comprise a beach playground, pool, poolhouse, children's water-play area, recreational courts, event rooms, snack bar (the existing Back on the Beach Café), changing and locker rooms, rec room, lounge deck, picnic area and on-site and shuttle parking. Docents also will lead tours of the garden areas and North House. Details aren't fully fleshed out, but most likely there will be advance reservations as well as walk-in availability for a reasonably priced day-at-the-beach pass.

The Bike Path

Its official name is the South Bay Bicycle Trail, but no one will know what you're talking about unless you call it simply the bike path. For our intents and purposes, we focus on the section that runs from the northern part of the Temescal Canyon parking lot to Playa del Rey. In its entirety, however, it runs 22 miles, north-south, from Will Rogers State Beach to Torrance County Beach and is the longest beach path of its kind in the world. At fourteen feet wide, it really should be called the bike-skate-jog-walk path, and it does get crowded, especially on weekends and summer days. Many locals use it only on winter weekends, early mornings or around dusk, as it can be downright hazardous.

The bike path in Venice, heading north to Santa Monica

Words of Bike Path Caution

As a walker, watch out. Walkers technically are not supposed to use the bike path, but of course they do. So stick to the edges and be ready to jump out of the way.

At the time of this writing, a few areas along the path were torn up, as work on beach parking lots labored on.

South of Venice the path loops inland around the Marina del Rey yacht basin and into Playa del Rey before returning to the ocean at Dockweiler State Beach.

Also, watch out for the Segways, the big-wheeled, upright motorized contraptions that are becoming the path's increasingly prevalent scooter monsters.

This concrete swath atop the sand is a fine way to sample the Santa Monica Bay. The trail connects it all: the beaches, the Santa Monica and Venice piers and its most popular destination, the Boardwalk (Ocean Front Walk) in Venice. The most popular stretch of the bike path is the 8.5 miles from Temescal Canyon Road to Washington Boulevard in Venice Beach.

Depending on your starting point, there are several shops and stands along the path that rent equipment – bikes, inline skates, accessories, even recumbent three-wheel bicycles, which require more leg strength. Most popular are the several strategically sited Perry's Cafés, which rent everything and can feed you, too. (Hours at all are seasonal and vary; go to perryscafe.com for locations and information.)

Fun on the Pier

Pacific Park on the Pier
380 Santa Monica Pier, Santa Monica
310.260.8744, pacpark.com
Open daily; hours vary by season (check web
site); admission free; fees for rides & games

Where Route 66 meets its western end stands the memorable arch and sign announcing the historic Santa Monica pier. At the pier's opening, on September 9, 1909, thousands showed up for the swimming races and concerts, but mostly for the thrill of walking 1,600 feet out over the Pacific. Hugely popular in the 1920s, the pier fell into decline after 1930 and wasn't saved until the 1980s, when it was decreed a National Historic Landmark. Today it is the oldest and longest wood-piling pier in the state.

Pacific Park, the West Coast's only amusement park located on a pier, now draws three million visitors annually. It boasts a nine-story-tall Ferris wheel (the first solar-powered one in the world, and named by the Auto Club as one of the 8 Great Places to Pop the Question), a dandy five-story-high steel roller coaster, spectacular views, the historic Looff Hippodrome Carousel, bumper cars (a set for tikes, and a set for their road-enraged parents), rides for the wee ones, midway games, souvenir shops, a birthday-party area, all the snacks you'd expect and even a Santa Monica Police substation.

On a warm summer's evening, dancing to live music or watching a film at one of the pier's twilight series, or feeling the speed of the roller coaster, or taking in the views from the Ferris wheel, or watching your child take her first carousel ride alone, the nostalgia is palpable. Maybe it's because we've seen so many images of the pier in movies and on TV (remember Paul Newman's character in *The Sting* even worked there?). Or maybe it's just one of those wonderful and universal human-delight moments.

Admission is free, but everything else is, well, not free. (Put your kids on a budget in advance, or they'll blow through $40 in fifteen minutes on the overpriced midway games.)

Santa Monica Pier Aquarium

1600 Ocean Front Walk, Santa Monica
310.393.6149, healthebay.org
Open Tues.-Fri. 2-6 p.m., Sat.-Sun. 12:30-6 p.m.; suggested donation $5, kids under 12 free

A touch tank sign reads: "Gentle Fingers Make for Happy Animals." And the Santa Monica Pier Aquarium, an ecologically friendly and instructional place created by UCLA and now run by Heal the Bay, makes for happy kids, which makes for happy parents. Kids are so busy touching, asking questions and looking through microscopes at the fascinating creatures that its environmental messages go down easy.

Santa Monica's underwater ecosystem is brought to shore (at beach level, just below the pier's carousel) via dozens of indigenous species of marine animals and plants. The touch tanks are manned by a young, impressively knowledgeable staff who get the more hesitant kids to get their fingers wet by asking such questions as, "Want to feel the sea urchins give you a hug?" We learn that the slimy purple mottled sea hare releases a purple ink when danger lurks. And what sweet child isn't delighted to be introduced to the "sea cucumber who throws up his guts"? A nontouching tank belongs to the sharks and rays, but though you aren't able to "feel" these guys, you can get up close and personal.

The aquarium's big tanks are just as fascinating. The Pier Tank's inhabitants are so incredibly colorful that it's difficult to believe they all live under the pier; the Kelp Forest Tank's leopard sharks cruise by creatures found in local tide pools; in the Rocky Reef Tank, courageous kids go eye-to-eye (separated by only a slice of glass) with a moray eel; and who can resist playing hide-and-seek with the camouflaging dotted octopus in the Octopus Tank?

Kids also can check out brine shrimp under a microscope, squid, stingray and octopus in a jar, and a ginormous spiny lobster in a glass cube. Short films, such as the captivating *Inky the Little Whale*, screen throughout the day. And in the Kids' Corner are books, puzzles, crafts and a sea-animal puppet theater complete with a "kelp" curtain.

On the Water

In terms of getting on the water, the place to be is Marina del Rey, the largest manmade pleasure-craft harbor in the world. From the Marina you can have just about any kind of watercraft experience: motor, sail, pedal and paddle boats (with guides and/or instruction if needed), windsurfing, whale-watching excursions (January through March), ocean-fishing getaways, corporate parties, dinner cruises, shipboard conferences, even scattering ashes at sea.

Santa Monicans are lucky to be in the path of the largest mammal migration on the planet. Once a year, gray whales make a 13,000-mile roundtrip from Siberian-Alaskan seas to Baja lagoons, where they deliver their calves and then return north. Seeing one of these 40-foot-long, 40-ton creatures on the open seas is a thrill. As for fishing trips out of Marina del Rey, many charter companies take out anglers of all experience levels. The catch can include halibut, sand and calico bass, barracuda, white sea bass, shark and yellowtail.

Here are some on-the-water outfits we recommend:

Crown Pacific Cruises (crownpacific.net) hosts private charters, corporate and family events, party cruises, birthdays, bar mitzvahs, burials at sea, Catalina trips, you name it.

Short-term rentals from **Marina Boat Rentals** (310.574.2822, boats4rent.com) include electric, power, sail, pedal, kayak and one- and two-person waverunners by the hour, half-day and full day. The Fisherman's Village location provides immediate access to the Marina.

The open-party fishing excursions with **Marina del Rey Sportfishing** (310.822.3625 or 800.822.3625, marinadelreysportfishing.com) depart mornings and afternoons. Knowledgeable guides are available, as are licenses, poles and bait. Other offerings include whale- and dolphin-watching tours and twilight fishing from May through September. These guys even clean and package your catch for you.

The fine, eco-friendly **UCLA Marina Aquatic Center** (310.823.0048) offers lessons and classes in sailing, rowing, kayaking, surfing and windsurfing, with such special outings as Birding by Kayak and the Sunset Paddle.

As for Catalina, your best bet from the Marina is **Catalina Ferries** (310.305.7250, catalinaferries.com). It's more expensive than going from San Pedro, with far fewer departures, but for locals, the convenience is often worth it.

Anglers tend to be quite loyal to their favorite fishing spots. After long closures for each of the bay's three piers, Malibu, Santa Monica and Venice, all are currently open for fishing. Given the amusement park, carousel and tourists, the Santa Monica pier is typically crowded; to fish, get there early and bring your own chair. It's open day and night and has a bait-and-tackle shop and pay parking. The Venice Pier also is crowded, particularly in the warmer months, when halibut is the big catch. The pier's wide, circular end provides lots of fishing space, and its 1,310-foot length gives access to some deeper-water species. Speaking of halibut, the Malibu Pier is one of the best for halibut fishing in the state. The optimum spot is above the shallower water near the surf line, where the halibut like to hang out between the pier pilings.

Sailboats for rent in the Marina

Surf Shops We Love

Some of the stores serving the area's surfers and skaters have been in business for more than 30 years; others jumped into the game more recently, chasing a piece of the booming market for all things surf: not just boards and wax, but clothing, skate gear, beach gear, jewelry and accessories, Not since the 1960s have we seen so much beachy-looking clothing, particularly on kids. And what kids wear, their parents soon wear, too.

Becker Surfboards
23755 W. Malibu Rd., Malibu
310.456.7155, beckersurf.com
A Malibu Colony Plaza resident for sixteen years, Becker Surfboards is best known for its excellent boards (the longboards and retro boards are particularly choice) and apparel. At least half of its customers are women, many of whom are moms coming in for both themselves and their kids. Pepperdine students, tourists and, oh yes, local surfers make up the rest. The shop's classic surf decor, Brian Bent designs and the eclectic and colorful paintings set the tone. All the "essential" brands – O'Neill, Quiksilver, Volcom, Ruca, Billabong, Roxy – are here; Rainbow's leather flip-flops are the current must-have item.

Horizons West
2011 Main St., Santa Monica
310.392.1122, dogtownskateboards.com
This is the historic home of the Z-Boys, the skateboarders who, in the 1970s, popularized skateboarding and essentially created the current punk/skater subculture. But now, alas, "Santa Monica's Oldest Hardcore Surf Shop, Established 1977" is saying its goodbyes. At least that was the case at the time of this

writing. Its lease expires in 2008, and the building is scheduled to be torn down for a new development.

But for now, the small corner establishment, Dog Shop, sells skateboard stuff and a few surfboards. Next door, in the bigger surf shop, a rock-and-tiki-garden window display promises cool merchandise inside, and it delivers: lots of hip clothes, a good selection of used boards and everything and anything surf-related.

Rip City Skates
2709 Santa Monica Blvd., Santa Monica
310.828.0388, ripcity.net
In the beginning, skateboarding was a hobby for the surfer when the waves sucked; now it's a subculture grown up. This "Home of the $99.95 complete skateboard since 1978" is the oldest pure skateboard shop in California, having hung in there for nearly 30 years. No sellout, Rip City sells only skateboarding stuff: you choose your components, deck, trucks, wheels, everything custom. Accessories include skate-related T-shirts and clothing and the treasured Nike SB, a skate shoe that's durable and lightweight, with a sole you can feel the board through; true sneakerheads salivate at its very mention.

Rip Curl

1451 3rd St. Promenade
310.656.2875, ripcurl.com
If you're on the mall and need a surfwear fix,
head to Rip Curl, one of a chain. The store
is stocked with the standard brands and
gear: boards, wetsuits (Rip Curl brand only),
skateboards, men's and women's clothing (Rip
Curl brand only) and surf accessories, from
luggage to Saint Christophers (a bargain here
at only $6.99). If you're not on the mall, you can
skip this one.

Santa Monica Surf Shop

2934 Wilshire Blvd., Santa Monica
310.315.7244,
Local boy Jon Monroy recently bought this
place, and he quickly expanded the clothing
selection, particularly the great-looking beachy
pieces for girls (but as with all surfwear, it's
pricey). In addition to boards, wetsuits and
surf accessories, we love some of the fun
surf-genre toys, like the Yo Baby Carpet Skate
(just $11.95), a quiet plastic board that young
skateboard addicts can practice on indoors.
There's also a great selection of the colorful
Saint Christopher necklaces now in vogue again
(Saint Christopher is the protector of travel, and
in the '60s, surfers wore the necklaces to protect
them while surfing – and gave them to girlfriends
to indicate they were going steady).

ZJ Boardinghouse

2619 Main St., Santa Monica
310.392.5646, zjboardinghouse.com
This is the big kahuna of local surf shops,
carrying the widest selections of the most
merchandise. Parking's not easy – this is
Main Street, after all – but it's worth it. Besides
new and used boards for surfing, skating and
snowboarding, you'll find sunglasses, T-shirts,
hats, luggage, shoes, surf and snow clothing,
bathing suits, dresses and casual wear, and all
in cool styles and prints that you just don't see
everywhere. Much of the clothing is inspired by
classic Hawaiian surfwear, but given modern
flair. Really a clump of small shops, ZJ comprises
a skateboard shop, the main surfboard shop,
another for men's and boys' surfwear, and the ZJ
Ladies Lounge, which stocks all the good lines
– O'Neill, Billabong, Roxy, Volcom – and such
fab smaller ones as Lucy Love. This is pricey
merchandise; watch for the sales.

Zuma Jay Surfboards

22775 Pacific Coast Hwy., Malibu
310.456.8044, zumajays.com
Wetsuits are Zuma Jay's bread and butter, and
for good reason – the water gets chilly up Malibu
way! But the shop, which has been owned and
run by Jefferson Wagner for nearly 35 years,
also stocks everything you need to get out
there: surfboards (shaped by the legendary
Midget Smith), boogie boards, skimboards,
kayak rentals. By summer 2008, Wagner also
should have the rental concession business on
the pier, providing beach equipment, boards
and kayaks. Across PCH from the Malibu Pier
and Surfrider Beach, Zuma Jay's is a hardcore
surf shop dedicated more to equipment than to
fashion. And the rentals are easy: $20 a day for
a board, $10 a day for a wetsuit. Check out the
entertaining web site.

Dogtown is memorialized on the door at Horizons West.

Q & A: Michael "Newmie" Newman

Michael Newman was born a water baby. His father, a member of the British national water polo team, met his mother, who would become a swim teacher to the stars, at a pool. A Junior Lifeguard, Mike swam for Pali High and UCSB, was an L.A. County lifeguard and firefighter for twenty years, and won the National Lifeguard Ironman Championship in 1996 at age 39. The world knows him as "Newmie" from the long-running TV series *Baywatch* – he was the only non-professional actor to star in the show. Mike lives in the Palisades with his wife and two kids, and he's still in the water almost every day, keeping in lifeguard/ironman shape. He talked to Pali classmate Margery Schwartz on a sunny Palisadian afternoon.

What beach do you frequent these days?
Will Rogers, near lifeguard headquarters. I train down there because I can get in the parking lot. I paddleboard, surfski (on an eighteen-foot kayak), run and swim. It's funny, I still go to the Jetty – I was a little kid on that beach, then a lifeguard on that beach, then a real lifeguard pretending to be a lifeguard (for Baywatch*) on that same beach.*

Did you go there as a kid for the social scene?
It was my first Beach Blanket Bingo experience, with all the Paul Revere Junior High kids. It's where we learned how to surf. Unfortunately, the Jetty doesn't work anymore as a surf spot – the sand moved, and there's no longer that perfect little machine right.

How did you become a "real" lifeguard?
After graduating UCSB I worked in advertising for five years. Then it struck me: Life is not about two weeks off a year. There's less money but more freedom as a lifeguard.

How did you get involved in *Baywatch*?
Because I looked the part, fellow guard Greg Bonann (the show's producer) asked me to be in a teaser tape to sell the concept. He couldn't pay me, but he promised if it went, there would be a job in it for me. It was a day in the life of a lifeguard: rescue the kids, break up the fight, meet the chick, walk off into the sunset – you know, just like real life.

Did the real-life guards call it Babewatch, too?
Oh, we called it Boobwatch and other names . . . much worse names.

Can you imagine ever living somewhere else?
Not anywhere away from an ocean. You know, I'm out in the water in the mornings and I wonder why I'm the only one. So many people who work so hard to afford to live here, and belong to the beach clubs and all, never even go in the water.

What's the longest you've ever been away from the ocean?
We always organize vacations around the ocean. I went to London for a press thing for Baywatch *once, for one week, and that was a long time ago.*

Santa Monica is…
Architectural

The white-hot center of SoCal architecture, Santa Monica and environs are home to a plethora of fabulously diverse styles – from the dreamy Monterey revival homes of the 1930s and '40s, to cutting-edge green architecture, to the controversial work of the postmodernist god, Frank Gehry. And thanks to vigorous preservation efforts, many exquisite examples of California's most revered architectural styles remain, including buildings by John Byers, Frank Lloyd Wright, Cliff May, Raymond Kappe, Charles Moore and William Pereira. From restored streamline modernes to boundary-pushing moderns – you name it, we've got it.

The Architecture of Santa Monica

The Weaver House, on beautiful Adelaide Drive

When you're talking about the evolution of architectural styles in Santa Monica and the six towns that surround her, the discussion begins where all discussions about California architecture begin: the Spanish and Mexican influences, from the first missions of the 18th century through the ranchos of the 19th century. It wasn't until the United States annexed California in 1848 that things began to change. While Spanish neoclassicism was still revered (and, in fact, endures in Southern California to this day), the adobe building method used by Mexican and Indian workers was soon replaced by fired-brick and wood-frame construction, a style much preferred by the new settlers from back east, who began pouring into the Santa Monica area by the thousands. Queen Anne–style houses and highly adorned Victorians started appearing in the early 1900s, particularly in Ocean Park, on Santa Monica's south end. At the same time, enchanting Arts & Crafts bungalows, modest and eschewing Victorian geegaw but containing a high degree of craftsmanship, were popping up on Venice's canals and beach-close walk streets, as well as on Adelaide Drive in north Santa Monica, overlooking Santa Monica Canyon.

Meanwhile, over San Vicente way, prosperous Brentwood residents were looking to Santa Monica architect John Winford Byers to provide them with gracious upper-middle-class homes on lots of an acre or more. A former French and Spanish teacher at Santa Monica High School who graduated from Harvard, Byers was a self-trained architect with an interest in and sensitivity to the Hispanic tradition. The Spanish, English, French-Norman and Anglo-colonial homes that he designed, often

Malibu Potteries tile at the Adamson House

with Edla Muir, set the standard for what beautiful, intelligently designed residential architecture should be.

In the 1930s, other architectural styles started taking hold along the coast. In 1930, Stiles Clements completed Malibu's Adamson House for Rhoda Rindge Adamson, one of Malibu's original landowners. The house is a graceful Andalusian farmhouse, but what it's really known for is the lavish use of vibrant, hand-painted ceramic tiles made by artisans at Malibu Potteries between 1926 and 1932. The Adamson House is the best place to see these tiles used in profusion, as they are extremely rare. (It is now a museum that's part of Malibu Lagoon State Beach; *see page 71 for tour information*.)

Back in Santa Monica, Hollywood's elite discovered the new Georgian Hotel (1415 Ocean Avenue), a showcase of Romanesque revival and art deco architecture. Other styles emerged, too – many lovely Spanish revival apartment buildings appeared north of Wilshire, and Santa Monicans embraced streamline modernes, including the famous eight-story Shangri-la Apartments, now a hotel, on the corner of Ocean Avenue and Arizona. Built in 1940, it was undergoing extensive renovation at press time, but not to worry – the streamline style is intact.

Not every new building of this era hewed to the deco/streamline aesthetic. In the 1930s and '40s Frank Lloyd Wright was very, very busy in the Brentwood hills, creating dramatic residences that cantilever effortlessly into lushly landscaped hillsides. And the spare, modernist works of Richard Neutra and Rudolph Schindler were becoming prevalent in Brentwood and the canyons of Santa Monica, Mandeville and the Palisades. From the 1930s through the '50s, Cliff May established a virtual enclave of his signature low-slung, rambling, U-shaped homes, which fully integrated indoor/outdoor living, in Brentwood's buçolic Sullivan Canyon. All these homes are among the most sought-after (and expensive) properties on L.A.'s westside.

In the Palisades, the Eames House on lower Chautauqua Boulevard, the Entenza House next door and the Bailey House up the block represent three extraordinary examples of John Entenza's landmark Case Study House

Malibu's historic and lovely Adamson House

program (1945-1960), which promoted affordable housing for ordinary Americans – and, by the way, the architecture is anything but ordinary.

As for Malibu, by the 1960s it was pretty cool to have a house on the sand designed by a hot architect. Soon the coast was crammed with one spectacular house after another, designed by such luminaries as John Lautner, Craig Ellwood, Melinda Gray and Frank Lloyd Wright. One that is open to the public, if extensively altered since its construction in 1950, is the former Holiday House Motel, designed by Richard Neutra. It's now home to the date-night restaurant Geoffrey's (27400 Pacific Coast Highway), with condos above.

And then in 1967 a man named Frank O. Gehry, a graduate of the USC School of Architecture, set up shop on Cloverfield Boulevard in Santa Monica, and the deconstructionist and

All aboard the streamline Shangri-la!

postmodern movements exploded. Soon Santa Monica was a focal point for avant-garde architecture, with homes, studios, schools, auditoriums and office buildings designed by Johannes van Tilberg, Kanner Architects and Koning Eizenberg.

According to architectural historian Robert Winter, co-author of *An Architectural Guidebook to Los Angeles*, "The greatest monument of the postmodern in the Los Angeles area is, of course, Frank Gehry's Chiat/Day/Mojo Building (1985-1991) in Venice." You know – the Binocular Building on Main Street.

Just when you thought the area could not possibly get any more architecturally rich, the end of the 20th century marked the debut of the magnificent J. Paul Getty

Frank Gehry's zany Chiat/Day/Mojo Building

Originally a motel, this Richard Neutra modern is now home to Geoffrey's, a view-blessed restaurant.

Center for the Arts, designed by Richard Meier, landscaped by Robert Irwin and perched majestically atop eastern Brentwood. The travertine-clad buildings are vast and beautiful, in hues of cream and white, and the views from downtown to the ocean are jaw-dropping.

But that's not all! On Pacific Coast Highway in Pacific Palisades, on the Malibu border, the newly renovated Getty Villa (the "original" Getty), houses ancient treasures in a fabulous location overlooking the ocean. Originally constructed in the 1970s (and met with derision from many locals at the time), the villa reopened in 2006 after a seven-year renovation, designed by Salvetti and Machado, which kept the museum's original style, modeled after the ancient Roman Villa dei Papiri. It's really the antithesis of the Getty Center, but it works.

All this architectural history inspired many of California's leading architects, including Thom Mayne, Steven Ehrlich and Mike Rotundi, to locate their offices in Santa Monica. And now the city is leading the charge for the new era, addressing the urgent issues of climate change, pollution and energy shortages. Such architects as Pugh + Scarpa and David Hertz are designing buildings that are rich in natural light and fresh air but light on energy and water consumption. Moore Ruble Yudell's smashing new Santa Monica Library is a fine example of the next generation of green building that is keeping Santa Monica and its neighbors at the forefront of international design.

The sustainably built Santa Monica Library

Crenshaw House, designed by John Byers

9 Great Architectural Walks (& Drives)

Santa Monica is filled with so many notable buildings and so many quirky, fun, architecturally significant neighborhoods that we cannot possibly do it all justice. But we'll try nonetheless. In the pages that follow, we'll take you on walks (and two drives) that feature not only compelling, interesting structures but also beautiful geography, including luscious canyons and breathtaking ocean views.

A note of gratitude: We could never have compiled this section without the help of L.A.'s building bible: *An Architectural Guidebook to Los Angeles*, by David Gebhard and Robert Winter. It's a superb guide to not only L.A.'s beach communities but to the entire Los Angeles area, and it's an essential companion to *Hometown Santa Monica.*

John Byers Extravaganza

La Mesa Drive, Santa Monica

During the period between the world wars, John Winford Byers made more of an impact on Santa Monica homes than any other architect. All of his dreamy-looking residences reflect his fascination with native California architecture and its Mexican and Spanish roots. He often used old-world craftsmen to create the tile, adobe brick and wrought iron so prominent in his work. On this lovely, easy walk along Rustic Canyon's La Mesa Drive (the street where Byers himself lived), you'll get a real sense of the man's vision, talent and significance.

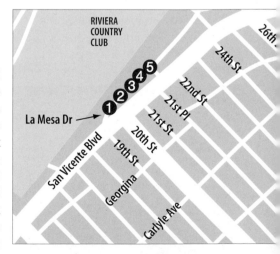

❶ Crenshaw House (1925-26)
1923 La Mesa Dr., Rustic Canyon
This gracefully proportioned Spanish-style home represents the romance of 1920s California living.

❷ Byers House (1924)
2034 La Mesa Dr.
This balconied Monterey revival–style home was Byers's second residence in Santa Monica and within walking distance of his office.

❸ Zimmer House (1924)
2101 La Mesa Dr.
Simple stucco walls and a low-pitched roof define this one-story residence.

❹ Bundy House (1925)
2153 La Mesa Dr.
This house displays heavy Spanish and Mexican influences.

❺ Tinglof House (1925-26)
2210 La Mesa Dr.
Another good example of Byers's Hispanic vision.

Craftsman Atop the Canyon
Adelaide Drive, Santa Monica

Adelaide Drive, one of the most scenic and historic streets in Southern California, is lined with many fine examples of early-20th-century architecture. Perched above Santa Monica Canyon, it affords spectacular views of the ocean and the mountains and is famous for being at the top of the Santa Monica Stairs, the workout spot of choice for preening fitness fanatics. They (and their cars) jam the short blocks, especially on weekends.

To begin this walk, start at the western end of Adelaide, which begins at Ocean Avenue just north of San Vicente. You may want to park on Ocean or San Vicente and stroll over. Most of the houses on this very short walk are designated historic landmarks.

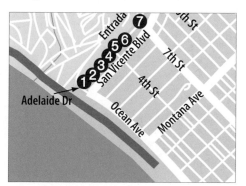

Milbank House was designed by the same firm that did Grauman's Chinese Theatre in Hollywood.

❶ Second Roy Jones House (1907)
130 Adelaide Dr.
Prominent banker Roy Jones, son of Santa Monica founder John P. Jones, built this fine example of an Anglo-colonial revival. His first home was originally on Ocean Avenue and much later was moved to Main Street; it now houses the California Heritage Museum.

❷ Weaver House (1910-11)
142 Adelaide Dr.
Constructed by the Milwaukee Building Company, this home is a lovely Japanese-style Craftsman that echoes the work of Greene and Greene. After the Santa Monica earthquake in 1984, it was restored to perfection by the firm Meyer and Holler, and it's listed on the National Register of Historic Places.

❸ Milbank House (1911)
236 Adelaide Dr.
Another Milwaukee Building Company Craftsman with a strong Asian influence, this house is situated amid a lovely garden. It was built as a vacation home for wealthy L.A. industrialist Isaac Milbank.

❹ Gorham-Holliday House (1923-24)
326 Adelaide Dr.
One of John Byer's most distinctive Andalusian-style residences, with a Monterey-style balcony overlooking the backyard garden and pool.

❺ Gorham House (1910)
336 Adelaide Dr.
Designed by Robert Farquhar, this one-story stucco home combines an Arts & Crafts aesthetic with such Spanish touches as a red-tile roof.

❻ Gillis House (1905)
406 Adelaide Dr.
Built by famed L.A. architects Myron Hunt and Elmer Grey for real estate developer and onetime *Evening Outlook* owner Robert Gillis, this stately two-story Craftsman is one of the prettiest on the street; it looks to have been extensively renovated. Adelaide Drive was named for Gillis's daughter.

❼ Worrel House (1926)
710 Adelaide Pl.
Designed by Robert Stacy-Judd in the highly ornamental style that became known as "Zuni" architecture, this residence was described as a "Pueblo-Revival Maya fantasy" by architectural scholar Robert Winter.

All Aboard!
Streamline Modernes in North Santa Monica

The Voss Apartments

One of the more enduring and whimsical styles of architecture is the streamline moderne, which followed the art deco movement of the 1930s. Its sleek, curved, nautical style was ideally suited to beach-town development in the 1930s and '40s, so fine examples abound. The first four are all located north of Wilshire.

❶ Roosevelt Elementary School (1935)
801 Montana Ave.
Not too many curves to this structure, but moderne it is – and a fine school, too.

❷ Voss Apartments (1937- 47)
945-953 11th St.
This multi-unit building is a perfect representation of an authentic streamline moderne, but it looks a bit distressed (read "ripe for development"), so you better hurry if you want to see it.

❸ 1123 12th St.
This is a neat-as-a-pin, tidied-up apartment building.

❹ 1021-1023 17th St.
Again, another completely fab streamline moderne apartment building with curved walls, portal windows and other romantic features.

❺ 741 Franklin St.
An exceptionally well-preserved and exquisite moderne house at the eastern end of Santa Monica; it's best visited by car.

Hidden Beauties

Strolling Rustic Canyon

Once belonging to the Uplifters Club, a private retreat for a subgroup of members of the Los Angeles Athletic Club, this hidden Rustic Canyon neighborhood now features a dazzling diversity of architectural styles, from rustic log cabins to cutting-edge moderns. Also home to an enchanting public park with tennis courts, pool, playground, nursery school and the Uplifters' original Spanish revival clubhouse, this is one of the most bucolic secret neighborhoods in Southern California.

The view up Latimer Road in Rustic Canyon

❶ Kappe House (1968)
715 Brooktree Rd.
This was architect Raymond Kappe's own residence, a virtual treehouse perched over a steep hillside. It's a wood-and-glass beauty with a Craftsman influence but a modern style. We want it!

❷ Emmons House (1954)
661 Brooktree Rd.
Designed by Jones and Emmons, this is a simple post-and-beam modern that still looks pretty darn good.

❸ Elton House (1951)
635 Hightree Rd.
Craig Ellwood's open house is a nod to Mies van der Rohe, whom he greatly admired.

❹ Uplifters Club (1923)
Haldeman Rd. at Latimer Rd.
William J. Dodd designed this muted Spanish-style structure, which now serves as Rustic Canyon Park's recreation center.

❺ Marco Hellman Cabin (1923)
38 Haldeman Rd.
The story goes that Uplifter Marco Hellman found this cabin on a movie set and had it moved here; it was fixed up by noted L.A. and Pasadena architect Alfred Heineman, who also designed bank buildings for the wealthy Hellman.

❻ Abel House (1978)
747 Latimer Rd.
Charles W. Moore, Ron Frank and Robert Yudell are credited with designing this home, but it's clearly a work by Moore. It's a wonderful example of a modern design commingling exquisitely with a rustic site.

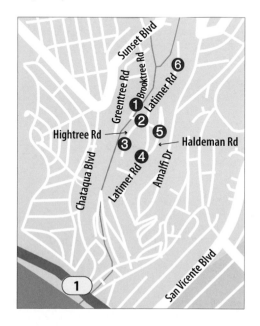

Frank Gehry's Santa Monica home

Frank O. Gehry – Oh, My!

A Driving Tour of Santa Monica & Venice

Gehry, Gehry, Gehry! Haven't you all had it up to here with Frank Gehry? If you haven't, you'll be happy to discover that his work is all over the Bay Cities, from Venice to Malibu. The Pritzker Prize–winning superstar architect set up shop in 1967 on Cloverfield Avenue, and soon his wild, deconstructionist, postmodern buildings, which you either love or hate, began to appear. This outing requires a car or a pair of exceptionally sturdy legs.

❶ Gehry House (1978)
22nd St. & Washington Ave., Santa Monica
The house started out as a Dutch colonial but was tortured into submission by Gehry's inimitable vision. His 1978 remodel features slanted metal walls, a chain-link fence and windows facing the sky; more recent landscaping has helped soften it a bit.

❷ Santa Monica Place (1979-81)
315 Broadway, Santa Monica
This shopping mall, which by the dawn of the new century had become rather sad and shabby, is now being renovated. It is a more subdued and rational Gehry design.

❸ Edgemar (1984-88)
2415-2437 Main St., Santa Monica
Formerly the site of the Edgemar Farms Dairy, this commercial development is an interesting assemblage of sculpture-like buildings that house several businesses and the Edgemar Center for the Arts. It also got the first Ben & Jerry's west of Chicago. It's still a hit.

❹ Chiat/Day/Mojo Building (1985-91)
340 Main St., Venice
Built for a well-known ad agency (which has since changed its name and moved), this seminal office building is famed for its entrance, which is set in a massive pair of binoculars designed by artists Claes Oldenburg and Coosje van Bruggen. Half of the building is an homage to International Style, and the other half is a big rusty slab of steel. It's so very Gehry.

❺ Spiller House (1980)
39 Horizon Ave., Venice
This three-level townhouse covered in galvanized metal and plywood is definitely worth a look-see, at the very least, to understand where Gehry was headed as the '80s dawned.

❻ Norton House (1982-84)
2509 Ocean Front Walk, Venice
The main feature of this beach house is a viewing room that looks like a box on a pole, it's wacky.

❼ Abbot Kinney Memorial Library (1991)
501 S. Venice Blvd., Venice
The library carries Gehry's signature postmodern style (in this case with a Craftsman feel), but it has a more toned-down municipal feel than he usually exhibits.

It's Not Easy Being Green

Santa Monica's Sustainable Buildings

In 1994 the city of Santa Monica was one of the first in the nation to adopt the Sustainable City Program, which was later updated to the Sustainable City Plan and adopted by the City Council in 2003. Today Santa Monica has the nation's highest number per capita of LEED-certified buildings. (LEED stands for Leadership in Energy and Environmental Design, which is overseen by the U.S. Green Building Council.) "Sustainable" here means to conserve local resources and have as little impact on the environment as possible during construction. The following buildings are LEED-certified, and more are expected to follow.

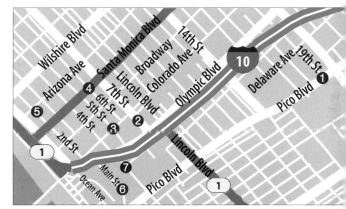

❶ Santa Monica College Liberal Arts Buildings I and II
1900 Pico Blvd.
Part of this green project was still under construction at press time, but it already had warranted LEED attention.

❷ Big Blue Bus Building
1660 7th St.
A more recent addition to the green-building landscape.

❸ Colorado Court
502 Colorado Ave.
This pioneering low-Income housing project was designed by Pugh + Scarpa Architects.

❹ Santa Monica Public Library
601 Santa Monica Blvd.
Designed by Moore Ruble Yudell, this has become the city's newest pride and joy.

❺ National Resources Defense Council Building
1314 2nd St.
Pasadena's new-urbanist architects Moule & Polyzoides designed this major rehab of a 1920s building near the Third Street Promenade.

❻ RAND Corporation Headquarters
1776 Main St.
This sleek, sustainable building by DMJM Design houses America's preeminent think tank.

❼ Public Safety Facility
Olympic Blvd. & 4th St.
The city's police and fire departments are based in this ultramodern, environmentally sound building by Cannon Design.

Solar panels became a design element of the Colorado Court building.

The Eames House is now an architectural museum of sorts.

Modern Elegance

The Eames House

This is not really a walk (though if you need a workout, you can power all the way up Chautauqua), but we're including it because it is worth a trip of its own – plus, you can stroll the property.

❶ The Eames House (1947- 49)
203 Chautauqua Blvd., Pacific Palisades

More than a dozen addresses in Pacific Palisades have official status from the city of Los Angeles as historic cultural monuments, with many more deserving the designation. Architects such as Richard Neutra, Eero Saarinen, John Byers, Craig Ellwood and Raymond Kappe all designed homes in Pacific Palisades. But one house stands out like no other: the internationally renowned Eames House, also known as Case Study House #8. Charles and Ray Eames designed it as part of John Entenza's landmark Case Study House program, which yielded incredible (and at the time, incredibly affordable) contemporary architecture throughout the greater L.A. area – but the heart of the program was in Pacific Palisades. Composed of two steel boxes, the Eames House is a light, airy, graceful structure made from standard industrial materials. Situated 150 feet above the ocean and set against a eucalyptus-covered hillside, it is the ultimate statement of modern elegance achieved through basic materials. You can tour the Eames House by appointment; call 310.459.9663 or visit eamesfoundation.org.

Homes You'd Marry the Wrong Man For

Dream Houses in Brentwood Park

There's an old saying, "When a man buys a house, soon follows a spouse." Well, there's no better place to be that spouse than in Brentwood Park, perched above Santa Monica Canyon and arguably the most luxurious neighborhood on L.A.'s westside. It was laid out north and south of Sunset Boulevard in 1906 by Western Pacific Development and features huge lots, meandering streets and lots of restrictions, which helped it retain its charm and beauty. Here are some of our favorite romantic houses in a neighborhood that's great for walking. These are not name-architect places – just beautiful homes. And they are private, so please keep your distance.

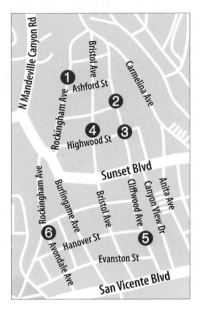

❶ 457 N. Rockingham Ave.
This Georgian colonial mansion comes complete with long brick driveway, a guesthouse over the garage, columns defining the entrance and an absolutely flawless design inside and out.

❷ 306 N. Cliffwood Dr.
Another dreamy property, this one is Spanish, dripping in vines.

❸ 211 N. Cliffwood Dr.
What a beautiful country English estate! It's situated far from the street and boasts an elegant combination of dark-chocolate wood and stone. The long drive up is cobbled, of course.

❹ 220 N. Bristol Ave.
This sprawling Monterey colonial mansion in hues of cream and dark green is so dark it's almost black. We wouldn't be surprised if John Byers designed it, but we can't find any proof.

❺ 324 S. Cliffwood Dr.
Getting a bit more serious, this gorgeous Mediterranean estate is notable for its sophisticated, intricate ironwork on the gate and balcony.

❻ 221 S. Avondale Ave.
If you like Tudors, you'll love this one.

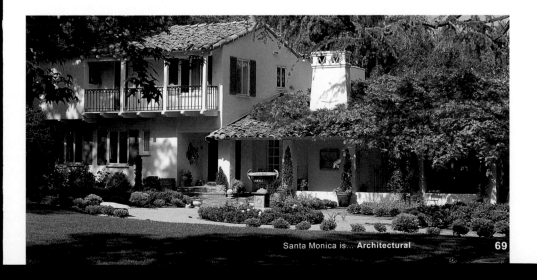

The Doumani House, designed by sculptor Robert Graham

On the Waterfront

Ocean Front Walk, Venice & the Marina

There's something about building a house on the beach, where everyone can see it, that makes people want to make a statement. Here are five oceanfront houses that make such statements. The first house is best seen when you're in central Santa Monica; the others are all within walking distance of one another.

❶ Israel House (1990)
1273 Palisades Beach Rd. (PCH), Santa Monica
Steven Erhlich Architects created this tall beach house, which doesn't look like it could accommodate many fat people.

❷ Beach House (1990)
2311 Ocean Front Walk, Venice
Another Steven Ehrlich, this is a fine example of modern beach-house design, incorporating concrete, glass, and stucco.

❸ Snipper House (1988)
2511 Ocean Front Walk, Venice
Designed by Miguel Angelo Flores and Associates, this modular framed box made of stucco and glass brick sits next door to the

wacky-looking Norton House (by Frank Gehry), so it gives the viewer two very different examples of modern residential architecture.

❹ Stone Condominiums (1973)
3815 Ocean Front Walk, Marina del Rey
This sleek, beautiful wood, stone and glass building, designed by Kahn, Kappe and Lotery, has held up well over the past three decades.

❺ Doumani House (1982)
Southwest corner of Ocean Front Walk & Yawl St., Marina del Rey
Designed by the sculptor Robert Graham, this beautiful white stucco beach house on a fabulous corner lot gives a nod to the art deco aesthetic; its dramatic step-pattern windows can open wide to the sun and the salt air.

Sneak a Peek: Home Tours, Walks & Shows

Adamson House Garden Tour
23200 Pacific Coast Hwy., Malibu
310.457.8185, adamsonhouse.org
Tour Fri. 10 a.m.
This walking tour showcases the beautifully
preserved landmark gardens, which date
from the 1930s, and include the pool, several
gorgeous tiled fountains and flagstone walkways.

Adamson House Tour
23200 Pacific Coast Hwy., Malibu
310.457.8185, adamsonhouse.org
Tours Wed.-Sat. 11 a.m.-3 p.m.
(last tour begins at 2 p.m.)
Trained docents relate the history of this
fabulous Spanish colonial revival house, as well
as details about the architecture, interior design
and the famous Malibu Potteries tiles that fill the
place with color. The adjoining Malibu Lagoon
Museum contains artifacts and rare photographs
depicting the history of Malibu.

**CA/BOOM (West Coast Independent
Design Show)**
Barker Hangar, Santa Monica Airport
3021 Airport Ave., Santa Monica
310.394.8600, caboomshow.com
This design and architecture extravaganza
is now an annual spring event at the Santa
Monica Airport, the perfect venue to showcase
everything from tabletop accessories to prefab
housing. Architectural tours of neighborhoods in
Santa Monica, Venice and the Marina take place
throughout the four-day event.

The Getty Villa
17985 Pacific Coast Hwy., Pacific Palisades
310.440.7300, getty.edu/visit
Tours Thurs.-Mon.; times vary
The Getty Villa is modeled after a first-century
Roman country house, the Villa dei Papiri, in
Herculaneum, which was buried by the eruption
of Mt. Vesuvius in AD 79. Docent-led tours
include the worthwhile 45-minute Getty Villa
Architecture and Gardens Tour.

The Green Gardens Tour
Various locations, Santa Monica
310.264.4224, VirginiaAvenueProject.org
This annual spring garden event is a celebration
of what is beautiful, sustainable and ecologically
sound (did we mention this is in Santa Monica?).

The tour benefits the Virginia Avenue Project, a
terrific arts program for local kids.

Malibu Garden Tour
Various locations, Malibu
310.455.1558, malibugardenclub.com
Each May, members of this half-century-old
garden club lead walking tours of extraordinary
private gardens.

**Pacific Palisades Junior Women's Club
Holiday Home Tour**
Various locations, Pacific Palisades
310.285.3218, ppjwc.com
Always popular and crowded, this tour includes
three to six fabulous Palisades homes, as
well as a holiday boutique, and it benefits
community-improvement projects.

Ramirez Canyon Park
5750 Ramirez Canyon Rd., Malibu
310.589.2850, lamountains.com
Tours by appt. only
Not many people know that Barbra Streisand's
22.5-acre estate, which she donated to the
Santa Monica Mountains Conservancy in
1993, is open to the public, and it's well worth a
visit. It comprises four gorgeous ("like buttah")
structures: Barwood, a Craftsman post-and-
beam house; the Barn, a whimsical vine-draped
building that was Babs's first and favorite house
on the property; the Mediterranean-style Peach
House, which served as a guest house; and the
Deco House, which has been described as an
art deco temple. The gardens and meadows can
be explored as well.

Venice Art Walk
Various locations, Venice
310.392.9255, venicefamilyclinic.org
An annual spring event, the Venice Art Walk &
Auctions is a tremendously popular celebration
of art, architecture, music and food. All proceeds
benefit the Venice Family Clinic.

Venice Garden & Home Tour
Various locations, Venice
310.821.1857, venicegardentour.org
A self-guided spring walking tour, this event has
the rep of being inspiring and rewarding. And it
benefits the Las Doradas Children's Center.

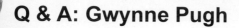

Q & A: Gwynne Pugh

Gwynne Pugh, an architect and engineer at Pugh + Scarpa in Bergamot Station, has been at the forefront of green architecture since 1984. All of his firm's projects integrate modern design, sustainability and materials and methods that have as little impact as possible on the environment. Now the chair of Santa Monica's Planning Commission, Pugh spends a lot of time thinking about incorporating sustainability into every new city project. He also has a few ideas about solving the city's traffic problems. Tippy Helper met with Gwynne at his office, where she discovered that he talks as fast as he thinks.

What led you to pursue environmentally sound architecture?
Architecture is inherently about environment, and I've always looked for ways to use materials and sources in the most efficient ways possible. Sustainability should be a factor in any building plan – it's as important as structure and finance.

One of your first green buildings, Colorado Court, won international acclaim and a Leadership in Energy and Environmental Design (LEED) gold rating, which is like the getting the green Academy Award. What's so green about that building?
Santa Monica adopted its Sustainable City Policy in the early '90s – one of the first cities to do so. It commissioned our firm to build Colorado Court, which is low-income housing, as a showcase property for green building. They challenged us to go all out. It's practically ostentatious in its sustainability and "green-ness."
We changed the original drawings and reoriented the building to capture the ocean breezes so it would never need air conditioning. We installed two kinds of solar panels to generate electricity and heat the water. We achieved 85 percent efficiency, and we used local materials with almost no impact on the environment.

Why is Santa Monica such a leader in green architecture?
Because it has the motivation, the wealth, the climate and the interest, and it's always been at the forefront of new ideas and progressive thought.

This is such a hip place to work, but with awful traffic. Do you have any solutions?
Yes! Let it get unbearable! Then people will finally do something – they'll get rid of their cars. We need to offer pedestrian walkways, a good bike route, a light-rail system and buses. I'm not looking to get rid of cars, but let's use them more judiciously.

So how green are you at home?
My wife drives a Prius, and I drive a motorcycle, which is a good way to avoid traffic. My house has solar panels, and all my windows are double-glazed.

What brought you to Santa Monica in the first place?
After I got my engineering degree in London, UCLA offered me a scholarship to study architecture. The first place I lived was on Wadsworth in Ocean Park, across the street from Jane Fonda and Tom Hayden. I met my wife on that street. I sent my son and daughter to the public schools. I like everything about the place.

Santa Monica is…
Smart

The Bay Cities house so much brainpower it boggles the mind. At RAND, great thinkers solve the weightiest issues of the day. Marina del Rey is home to USC's Information Sciences Institute, which helped invent the internet. Google and Yahoo set up huge offices here. The Getty Center boasts one of the top art-research libraries in the world. On hilltops bracketing the bay are two excellent universities, Pepperdine on the north and Loyola Marymount on the south. And in between lies Santa Monica College, one of the most thriving community colleges in the nation. Read on to learn more about our smart side.

Thinking Hard at the Think Tanks

Santa Monica is home to not one but two significant institutions devoted to thinking about – and solving – the world's most pressing problems. The most famous is RAND (a semi-acronym for Research and Development), which started at Douglas Aircraft during World War II to conduct technological R&D. It separated from

RAND's sleek, environmentally sound headquarters

Douglas in 1948, incorporated as a nonprofit, and in no time flat built a world-class team of researchers, experts and thinkers to tackle a remarkable diversity of issues, from teenage drug abuse to bioterrorism prevention. It has always remained nonpartisan, and its current and former roster of staff is positively thick with Nobel laureates. RAND is headquartered on Main Street in Santa Monica (in a sleek, circa 2004 building that earned Gold LEED certification for its environmental friendliness) but has five more offices around the world, and a total staff of 1,600. Current areas of focus include obesity in America, climate change, hot-button countries (including China, Afghanistan, Iran and Iraq), access to health care, stability in the Middle East and global HIV/AIDS.

Much newer in the thinking game, but quite ambitious, is the Milken Institute, which was endowed by philanthropist and former junk-bond king Michael Milken and his brother in 1991. Its focus is strictly economic – projects include researching

RAND

models for creating capital and jobs in America's low-income communities; measuring the capacity of each state's technology base; and examining access to capital by minority and women entrepreneurs. It is best known for its annual Global Conference, which attracts 3,000 economists, politicians, business leaders and journalists to the L.A./ Santa Monica area.

Two Think Tankers on Thinking

Chloe Bird

To find out what people who are paid to sit around and think all day really think about thinking, we went to the nation's preeminent think tank, Santa Monica's own RAND. Here's what two of their finest had to say about using their noggins.

Chloe Bird, Ph.D., is a senior sociologist at RAND, professor of sociology at RAND Graduate School, chair of Medical Sociology at the American Sociological Association – *and* the vice chair of the Santa Monica Housing Commission. She researches social disparities in health and health care and thinks about ways to address them. Her husband, Allen Fremont, M.D., Ph.D., is also a sociologist at RAND. They (and their young sons) live in Sunset Park.

Natalie Crawford moved to Santa Monica as a teenager, graduated from Santa Monica High, and went on to do advanced research in engineering and mathematics at UCLA. Now a Malibu resident, she's a senior fellow at RAND, the director of RAND's Project AIR FORCE and an expert in such things as tactical aircraft, electronic combat, space systems and aircraft survivability.

How do you define "think"?
Bird: It's the process of considering and organizing information and developing new ideas. What is amazing to me is how nonlinear this process can be.
Crawford: First you have to know you have a problem. Then you have to define the problem, break it down into solvable parts, solve those parts, and rebuild it again. That is the essence of critical thinking.

What are different kinds of thinking?
Bird: You can consider existing options or think about how to create entirely new options. More imaginative problem-solving often requires you to question the assumptions and even consider whether you are asking the right questions.

Who is your favorite thinker, today or in history?
Bird: Today, I'd say Thich Nhat Hanh, the Vietnamese Buddhist monk and peace activist. In history, I think of the most curious and inventive people, such as Benjamin Franklin, who worked in science, diplomacy and social policy.

Natalie Crawford

Crawford: I would have to say my late husband, Robert C. Crawford. He was one of the best teachers of mathematics I have ever seen, he owned a class-C baseball team, he was a champion chess player, he medaled in golf in college, and he owned part of a patent in earthquake construction. He believed that to be a real problem-solver you had to have hands-on experience in as many things as possible. Besides him, I would say Richard Feynman at Caltech – he was a great thinker who could communicate with everybody.

How do you know when you've had a great thought?
Bird: You realize you've had a new way of looking at an issue that might lead to new solutions. Then you try it out, either by using your new approach or by explaining it to others. Sometimes the point is to elaborate on a new idea; other times it's to try to shoot holes in it and see how well it holds up.

When is it best to not think at all?
Crawford: When you need to make a decision so quickly that if you thought about it, the results could be catastrophic – for instance, if you're reacting in the face of a possible car accident. You actually are thinking, but it's subconscious and at warp speed. And you can't carefully analyze the situation.

Can a person think too much?
Crawford: Yes, if you've reached a point where you feel like you've exhausted every approach to solving a problem. Sometimes you just have to step away – you can dig a hole only so deeply. When you come back to it, your mind might be ready to see another approach.

Is it possible to not think?
Bird: We all do some things without thinking, like driving the same route home from work every day. But typically you're listening to the radio, talking with someone in the car, or thinking about what you need to do when you get home. Truly not thinking is much harder – like with some forms of meditation. It's easy enough to learn how to quiet your mind or just acknowledge thoughts as they come and go. But few develop the discipline and skill to actually clear one's mind and not think.

Do you need to be a great thinker to be a great leader?
Crawford: No – but I need to define that. Take a great thinker like Albert Einstein. Could he have led a huge corporation like Intel? Probably not. A political leader certainly has to have intelligence, but a great thinker might not have the patience for the political process. Sometimes they merge, though. Churchill was a great thinker and leader. Reagan and JFK were good thinkers and problem-solvers. They didn't have Ph.D.s, but they had a lot of common sense, and you need common sense to be a good thinker.

Headquarters of USC's Information Sciences Institute in Marina del Rey

High-Tech Hideaway

Marina del Rey is best known for its pleasure craft and pleasure-seeking singles, but few people know that it's also the working home of some extremely smart people, those at USC's Information Sciences Institute. Since 1972 the institute's researchers have pushed the envelope of computer technology. It was a major player in creating ARPANET (the predecessor to the internet), as well as the internet, and it's done groundbreaking work on artificial intelligence. Today, its staff of 300 is working on everything from robotics and artificial intelligence to natural-language technology and electronic commerce.

Basketball is huge at LMU.

The College Tour

The thousands of students who pursue their education in the Bay Cities are smart *and* lucky. While working to become a teacher, lawyer, theologian, pastry chef or digital filmmaker, students can surf in the Pacific Ocean, hike in the Santa Monica Mountains, walk the Venice Boardwalk and check out great art any day of the week. Here's what you need to know about the institutions of higher learning in and around Santa Monica.

The Art Institute of California – Los Angeles
2900 31st St., Santa Monica
310.752.4700, artinstitutes.edu/losangeles

Princeton it ain't, but at this unique institution one can get an associates degree in culinary arts, graphic design, interactive media design or video production. Bachelor of science degrees are offered in audio production, culinary management and game art and design, among other practical fields. The school describes itself as "an institution for career preparation in the visual and culinary fields." The goal is to acquire a real skill that will result in a real job. The school opened its Santa Monica location in 1997, with a faculty composed mostly of working professionals.

Loyola Marymount University
1 LMU Dr., Westchester
310.338.2700, lmu.edu

Atop a hill a stone's throw from the Marina, LMU is one of 28 Jesuit universities in the United States. It's blessed with a beautiful and private campus that boasts sweeping vistas of L.A. in one direction and the Pacific Ocean in the other.

Originally a men's college called Loyola, it was founded in 1918, moved to this location in 1929 and, in 1973, merged with Marymount College, a women's college founded in 1923 by the sisters of the Sacred Heart of Mary. Today it educates 5,000 undergraduates and 3,000 graduate students; some of these grad students are at the excellent Loyola Law School in downtown L.A. Known in particular for its business, education, film, theater arts and engineering programs, it offers more than 80 majors in four colleges: Bellarmine College of Liberal Arts, College of Business Administration, College of Communication and Fine Arts, and the Frank R. Seaver College of Science and Engineering. Robert Winter, co-author of *An Architectural Guidebook to Los Angeles*, identifies four significant buildings on the campus: Sacred Heart Chapel (1953, Barker and Ott), a good example of a postwar Spanish Revival; Loyola University Theater (1963, Edward Stone), with a façade in the style of a stone Palladian villa; the solidly modernist Library (1977, Richard C. Martin); and the University Gymnasium, Athletic and Recreational Complex (1978-80, Kappe, Lottery and Baccato), which uses a unique cable-hung suspension system. It's a Division I force in basketball, swimming, water polo and volleyball, with Malibu's Pepperdine as its chief rival.

Mount St. Mary's College, Chalon Campus
12001 Chalon Rd., Brentwood
310.954.4000, msmc.la.edu

Situated in the shadow of the Getty Center, but with its own spectacular views of the city and ocean, Mount St. Mary's occupies 56 acres of prime Brentwood real estate. Primarily a college for women (who make up 95 percent of the undergraduate population), it is an independent Catholic liberal arts college with 22 majors, from American studies to philosophy to nursing. The graduate division offers degrees in education, psychology, religious studies and physical therapy, among others. The college was founded in 1925 by the Sisters of St. Joseph of Carondelet, whose vision of empowering young women endures today. It educates some 2,500 students, including graduate students, at this campus and at the historic Doheny Campus in Los Angeles near USC.

Mount St. Mary's hilltop campus is a Moorish-Spanish beauty.

Pepperdine has one of the choicest hunks of collegiate real estate in the nation.

Pepperdine University
24255 Pacific Coast Hwy., Malibu
310.506.4000, pepperdine.edu

Nestled in the undulating foothills of the Santa Monica Mountains, the 830-acre Malibu campus of Pepperdine University commands a majestic view of the Pacific Ocean. It's got a killer volleyball team, too. Founded by auto-supply millionaire George Pepperdine in 1937, Pepperdine was first located in South-Central Los Angeles. The Malibu campus opened in 1972 and remains a relatively conservative university committed to Christian values; it is affiliated with the Churches of Christ, though it is nonsectarian and free from any church control. Pepperdine is home to approximately 8,300 students in five colleges and schools: Seaver College, the Pepperdine School of Law, the Graduate School of Education and Psychology, the Graziadio School of Business and Management and the School of Public Policy. It's a great school, with some acclaimed professors and exemplary athletic facilities and teams, but it's pricey: Tuition, room and board for 2007-08 was $44,510.

Santa Monica College

1900 Pico Blvd., Santa Monica
310.434.4000, smc.edu

Outside the science building at SMC

Santa Monica College is a 38-acre, state-of-the-art, two-year community college less than two miles from the beach. It's not nicknamed "Harvard by the Sea" for nothing – it is the leader among California's 109 community colleges in transferring students to the University of California, USC and other first-rate four-year campuses. It's so affordable (tuition is $20 per unit) and exceptional that many westside parents of very bright children have figured out (duh!) that they can cut their college bills *in half* by sending their kids to SMC for the first two years. If they get decent grades, admission to UCLA or USC is practically guaranteed. SMC is also terrifically popular with continuing-ed adults who want to learn French, bookkeeping, web design or sculpture.

Opening in 1929 with just 153 students, SMC has evolved into a flourishing campus, with 30,000 full- and part-time students, including some 2,500 students from other countries, and courses in more than 80 fields of study. On the campus you'll find the John Derescher Planetarium and the Academy of Entertainment & Technology, as well as computer labs, performing- and visual-arts spaces and athletic facilities, including a really cool new swim center that's open to the community. The SMC Library recently completed a multimillion-dollar expansion and modernization, and the new Theatre Arts Building features an impressive 264-seat theater with a "black box" performance space, classrooms and more. Many of the newer campus buildings, which were built after the 1994 Northridge earthquake destroyed some older structures, are now sustainable and green, in true Santa Monica fashion.

One of SMC's most meaningful contributions is its radio station, the award-winning KCRW (89.9 FM), which brings the best of NPR, as well as great music and regional programming, to all of Southern California.

The Private-School Polka

The Bay Cities have loads of highly exclusive private schools, and getting into them is like applying to Yale – you need killer grades, off-the-chart test scores, zillions of activities and one special skill that no one else in the world possesses, like helping to develop a vaccine for avian flu or playing violin with Midori Goto in Prague. A sizeable cash gift from the grandparents never hurts either. While most westsiders are happy with Santa Monica public schools or LAUSD (which runs the schools in Brentwood, Venice and the Palisades) for elementary school, when junior high looms, parents panic and start the competitive jostling for a spot in the most coveted middle and high schools. These include the power crowd's favorite, the Brentwood School (where some of Arnold's kids go), the passionately all-girls Archer School in Brentwood, the star-studded and progressive Crossroads School in Santa Monica and the newer New Roads, which some call "the poor man's Crossroads," also in Santa Monica. Other elite schools include Harvard-Westlake in Studio City (it's far, but they have buses), which some say is the best ticket to the Ivy League; Windward, a fine, more progressive choice in nearby Palms; Marymount, an excellent Catholic girls' school just across the 405 in Westwood; and Concord, a tiny high school in an office building on Wilshire that offers only AP courses. Most of these schools charge more than $25,000 per year; for your investment, you get small class sizes, many teachers and administrators with Ph.D.s, and such extras as state-of-the-art science labs and phenomenal theater programs. Each new school year brings thousands of applicants for very few openings.

Suffice it to say, lives are ruined and dreams of Stanford are dashed upon rejection from these schools. Parents go to great lengths to gain an advantage: hiring a multitude of tutors, using "application coaches," wrangling recommendation letters out of powerful alums and pushing their children to excel in as many activities as possible. When the acceptance/rejection letters arrive in mid-March, some people leave town while others walk around looking smug. The happy ones get to pay well more than $100,000 over the next four years for their kid to go to high school!

The Archer School for Girls, an elite academy in Brentwood

3 Great Libraries

Getty Research Library
The Getty Center, 1200 Getty Center Dr., Brentwood
310.440.7300, getty.edu/research
Mon.-Sat. 9 a.m.-6 p.m.

Within the Getty Center lies the Getty Research Institute, which aims "to advance understanding of the visual arts in their widest possible significance." And so the institute's library focuses on the history of art, architecture and archaeology, with collections spanning from the prehistoric to the contemporary. The library is most robust in the history of Western European art, but it recently has expanded to include most other regions of the world, including Asia, Eastern Europe and Latin America. The general collections include almost 900,000 books, periodicals and auction catalogs; special collections contain rare books, prints, maps, photographs, optical devices, manuscripts and archival collections. There is a rich Photo Study Collection, and the library also holds a copy of the Princeton Index of Christian Art. It also supports its own conservation laboratory, which preserves its collections as well as those of the Getty Institutional Archives. The general public is welcome to use the Plaza level of the library, which includes art-reference materials, Getty Trust publications, periodicals and a Los Angeles collection; the more in-depth areas are limited to scholars and researchers with credentials – and appointments.

Santa Monica Library, Main Branch
601 Santa Monica Blvd., Santa Monica
310.458.8600, smpl.org
Mon.-Thurs. 10 a.m.-9 p.m., Fri.-Sat. 10 a.m.-5:30 p.m., Sun. 1-5 p.m.

This new, green library was unveiled in December 2006 and is the recipient of the prestigious LEED Gold Rating from the U.S. Green Building Council. Designed by the Santa Monica firm Moore Ruble Yudell (MRY), the new library presents a strong, streamlined contemporary presence in the heart of downtown Santa Monica, with multiple entrances, garden spaces and window walls that soak patrons in abundant natural light. The first floor features activity areas for kids and teens, the fiction and popular collections, a grand reading room, 150 public computers (61 with internet access), the Bookmark Café and the Friends of the Library Bookstore. The Martin Luther King Jr. Auditorium and the new home of the Santa Monica Historical Society Museum are also on the first floor. The second floor is dedicated to nonfiction, reference, periodicals, the Santa Monica Collections, study rooms, a quiet reading room and community meeting groups. You have to pay to park in the structure, but it's well worth it to spend time in this fantastic place, where you can easily pass an entire day. Also, take note: In this new era in which libraries tend to be noisy social centers, this library is quiet.

The reading room at the new Santa Monica Library

Venice-Abbot Kinney Memorial Branch Library
501 S. Venice Blvd., Venice
310.821.1769, lapl.org
Mon.-Wed. 10 a.m.-8 p.m., Tues.-Thurs. noon-8 p.m., Fri.-Sat. 10 a.m.-6 p.m.

Part of the Los Angeles Public Library system, the Venice branch was designed by Frank Gehry (natch) and opened in 1991. In addition to its fiction and nonfiction collections, it offers computer workstations with wireless access to the internet and all of LAPL's databases, plus a large collection of historic documents and photographs. Extras include reading programs for preschoolers, teens, adults and senior citizens. The popular summer reading program, for all ages, uses incentives and activities to keep everyone's nose in a book.

More Libraries to Explore

Malibu Library
23519 W. Civic Center Way, Malibu
310.456.6438, colapublib.org
Mon.-Tues. 10 a.m.-8 p.m., Wed.-Thurs.
10 a.m.-6 p.m., Fri.-Sat. 10 a.m.-5 p.m.

Until the late 1960s, a bookmobile provided the only library service to the entire Malibu community, including Topanga Canyon. And then, in 1970, this branch of the county library system came along. It houses 92,466 books, 82 magazines and newspapers, computers with wireless internet access, and three special collections: the Arkel Erb Memorial Mountaineering Collection, the Peter A. Horn Senior Citizen Collection, and the Sean Matthews Collection for children.

Ocean Park Branch Library
2601 Main St., Santa Monica
310.392.3804, smpl.org
Mon.-Thurs. noon-9 p.m., Sat., 10 a.m.-5:30 p.m.

Do check out this tiny library on Main Street. A Santa Monica Landmark, it was built in 1917 with a $12,500 Carnegie Grant and is one of the few remaining Carnegie Foundation Libraries operating in California.

Palisades Branch Library
861 Alma Real Dr., Pacific Palisades
310.459.2754, lapl.org
Mon. & Wed. 10 a.m.-8 p.m., Tues. & Thurs. noon-8 p.m., Fri.-Sat. 10 a.m.-6 p.m.

The great thing about this library is its newness and its architecture. Designed by Killefer Flammang Architects, it's a beautiful combination of glass, stone and wood skillfully integrated into a sylvan setting at the entrance to the Palisades Rec Center. Part of the Los Angeles Public Library system, the branch provides computer access to the main library's information network, as well as all sorts of programs for kids, teens and adults, from storytimes to book clubs.

Q & A: Karen Gunn

Organizational psychologist Karen S. Gunn, Ph.D., has been a tenured professor of psychology at Santa Monica College since 1985. She also runs Gunn Consulting Group, which provides institutions and corporations with strategies to create flourishing workplaces; clients include Venice Family Clinic and the L.A. Department of Health. A Detroit native, she earned her doctorate from the University of Michigan, Ann Arbor, and now lives in Santa Monica. Tippy Helper met Karen in her SMC office. Just the previous weekend, the prof had run the L.A. Marathon for the first time. She finished!

Wow, the L.A. Marathon is a very big deal. How did you train?
I joined a track club for the first time in my life last year. I never gave the marathon a moment's thought. I just wanted to get into shape. But the more I ran, the more empowered I felt. And here I am, a marathon runner!

Did your work as a psychologist help you prepare?
When it comes to athletics, which I'm new to, I've learned that your attitude is key. You have to believe you can do it. You have to stay positive.

What exactly is an "organizational" psychologist?
It's an offshoot of what was known as "industrial psychology." My dad has a Ph.D. in that, and his biggest client was Ford in Detroit. He dealt with psychological issues on the assembly line, like keeping morale up in workers dealing with machines. Organizational psychology is an evolution of that – it's the planning, growth, development and education of a particular work environment.

How smart is Santa Monica?
Santa Monica is so smart because the city's leaders have the vision to take a stand on some very difficult issues, like homelessness, mental health, green building, protecting the bay and youth violence. We're ahead of the game because our citizens are bright enough and courageous enough to make important, humane decisions on matters other cities wish would just go away.

You've lived in both Venice and Santa Monica. How do they differ?
When I first moved here, I lived in Venice and it was perfect. I love its bohemian flair, the great diversity in the arts and music, and the quirky restaurants. In Santa Monica, I love the eye candy: the ocean, the mountains, the clean air.

What do you like to do on weekends?
Usually I'm training with my track club, but after that I like to go to the Venice Boardwalk and find good bargains – I love a bargain! Favorite restaurants are Hama Sushi in Venice, Chez Jay in Santa Monica and Hal's in Venice. Catching a movie at the NuWilshire is also a treat.

I notice you have a beautiful tattoo – what's the story there?
I finally reached a point in life where I wanted to spread my wings. So I got this butterfly tattoo after all those years in school and working hard. I wanted a permanent symbol for the next phase of my life, where I wanted to soar.

Santa Monica is…
Famous

Around here celebrities are ubiquitous. And when the limos descend upon our streets for the Academy Awards, it's not just the movie stars they're picking up; it's also the producers, composers, special-effects wizards and film editors. Aside from the high-wattage star quotient, we're also famous for things that have nothing to do with celebrities: the spectacular, mind-bending views; the countless movie and TV locations; the scandals and unsolved crimes; and two of the top tourist attractions in Southern California, the Venice Boardwalk and the Santa Monica Pier. You'll get to know the famous side of the Bay Cities in the pages ahead.

Life Among the Rich & Famous:
The Four Cardinal Rules

Santa Monica and environs are famous for their famous people. Literally thousands of celebrities have chosen to live here during the decades past and present. They pop in and out of our lives like the blinding flashbulbs on a paparazzo's camera, drenching us briefly in their hot, celestial light.

Pervasive though they may be, one must nonetheless abide by the Four Cardinal Rules of Life Among the Rich and Famous, lest you run the risk of having a restraining order slapped on you. Here are the rules:

Rule # 1: Leave the celebrity alone. That's right, even though Julia Louis-Dreyfus is right in front of you at the Gelson's checkout line, and even though you only want to give her a good ol' shove like Elaine does to Jerry, leave her be. She just wants to get her groceries bagged and get home. The same principle applies when you see Tom Hanks at your son's flag football game. Do not stare (or cry), and do not ask for his autograph. Which leads us to:

Rule # 2: Never, ever ask for an autograph, unless the celebrity in question is proceeding down a red carpet. The only other exception is if the person is a sad has-been who is clearly seeking attention: Carrot Top, say, holding court on the Third Street Promenade. Otherwise, when you ask for an autograph, you are acknowledging the star's fame and being intrusive. Steven Spielberg and Kate Capshaw do not want their fame acknowledged at the local community theater; they just want to sit quietly and watch their little girl in a play. And just because Owen Wilson is skateboarding down Santa Monica Canyon looking really cute does not mean you should slam on the brakes and ask him to sign your chest. And even if your brother really did date (once) Reese Witherspoon in high school, don't rush up to her outside the Ivy at the Shore to remind her of this fact. She won't care. Besides, the line between fan and stalker is often impossible for celebrities to determine. That said, it is possible to become friends with a celebrity, as explained in:

Rule # 3: You can make friends with a famous person, but only if it happens in a natural way. For example, if your son plays ice hockey with Goldie and Kurt's kid and you give him a ride to the rink, or if your good friend's brother marries Julia Roberts and "JR" invites you to New York to see her play, or if you're chairing the school auction with Maria Shriver and you go to her lavish estate for a meeting, or if you're at a poetry reading at Dutton's and Dustin Hoffman, who practically lives there, gets a huge crush on you, or if you work out next to Amber Tamblyn at Pilates and discover you share a passion for Bright Eyes, or if you go to an extravagant toddler birthday party in Malibu and Courtney Cox is there with Coco, and Coco and your Anastasia become BFFs. The possibilities are endless. In fact, you can even marry a celebrity – it does happen. Longtime Palisadian Anthony Hopkins not so long ago married an ordinary middle-age woman who worked in a Palisades antiques shop. And they're very happy!

A red canopy serves as a red carpet at celeb-stuffed Nobu Malibu.

Rule # 4: Don't get too attached, because celebrities come and go. Just when you think your 5-year-old son and Maddox are really hitting it off, the Jolie-Pitts up and take off again. So much for hanging out with Brangelina. The truth is, celebs often don't stick around in one place for long. They not only jump around our own Bay Cities a lot (it's stunning how many live in, say, the Palisades and have yet another house next door in Malibu), but they're constantly traveling to premieres, film festivals, movie locations, charity events with Bono and international conferences with Bill.

So whatever you do and wherever you go in and around Santa Monica, remember that at any moment you could have an electrifying chance encounter with a high-wattage star. Just remember the Four Cardinal Rules and you'll be just fine.

Star Spotting

You might well find yourself sitting next to Tobey Maguire at a Wilshire Boulevard traffic light or bumping into Jamie Lee Curtis at the dry cleaners, but if you want to increase your odds of spotting a famous person, hang around these places.

Malibu
Broad Beach
Malibu Seafood
Nobu Malibu
Malibu Country Mart

Palisades
Gelson's
Pearl Dragon
Palisades Rec Center
Sunday farmer's market

Santa Monica
Giorgio's (aka Il Ristorante di Giorgio Baldi)
Whole Foods
Locanda Portofino
Café Montana
Aura Boutique
Ivy at the Shore
Chinois on Main
Wednesday farmer's market

Brentwood
Toscana
Katsuya
Vicente Foods
Whole Foods
Dutton's Brentwood Books
Shopping in Brentwood Gardens

Venice
Hama Sushi
Hal's Bar & Grill
Shopping on Abbot Kinney
Axe
Chaya Venice

Indelible Moments of Infamy

▶ At 10 a.m. on December 16, 1935, Thelma Todd's lifeless body was found by her maid in the front seat of her Lincoln Phaeton. The car was parked in the garage above her swank restaurant and home on PCH. Todd, the blonde bombshell du jour who appeared in the original 1931 version of *The Maltese Falcon*, was last seen the night before at a dinner party. Rumors of a murder were rampant,

Thelma Todd was found dead in 1935 above her home in Castellammare.

and she had, in fact, expressed fears about gangsters that very night. To this day, however, her death remains a mystery – though officially it was deemed an accident or suicide.

▶ Members of Charles Manson's "family" began their murder spree on July 31, 1969, by torturing and killing Topanga resident Gary Hinman, a music teacher who opened his home to many who needed a place to crash. Manson had lived in Topanga for a short while, where he befriended musicians Neil Young and Brian Wilson.

▶ Nicole Brown Simpson and Ronald Lyle Goldman were stabbed to death during the evening of June 12, 1994, outside Nicole's Brentwood condominium on Bundy Drive. On June 17, Simpson's ex-husband, O.J. Simpson, was charged with the double murder. The arrest came after a bizarre car chase throughout Southern California in Simpson's white Ford Bronco. The chase concluded on live TV in the driveway of Simpson's posh mansion on Rockingham in Brentwood. On October 3, 1995, a jury acquitted Simpson of the murder charges, but few believe he's innocent. He now resides in Florida.

▶ High-powered record promoter and Malibu fixture "Good Time Charlie" Minor was famous for boosting the careers of such artists as Sting, Janet Jackson and Bryan Adams. The good times ended for Charlie in 1995 after he met Suzette McClure, a laid-off aerospace worker turned stripper. When she found him in bed with his new girlfriend, she shot him dead.

Remnants of the TV show "M*A*S*H*" at Malibu Creek State Park.

- When Robert Downey Jr. was stopped in Malibu for drunk driving, he was found to be in possession of black-tar heroin, crack and powder cocaine and an unloaded .357 Magnum revolver. This arrest marked the beginning of a long downward spiral for this talented actor. However, after several more arrests and some jail time, Downey turned things around and reclaimed his life and his career.

- The arrest of megastar Mel Gibson in July 2006 marked a new low in celebrity DUIs. Gibson, a longtime Malibu resident, had been cavorting with regular folks and fans at Moonshadows on PCH until the wee hours, drinking, chatting and posing for pix. Just after leaving the restaurant/bar, he was clocked at 87 miles per hour on PCH and had an open bottle of tequila in the car. Upon his arrest, Gibson let forth with a toxic, anti-Semitic rant while L.A. County Sheriffs were attempting to transport him to the station. His words shocked the world and sparked a debate about the seriousness of such diatribes made by the severely inebriated.

- And then there's Brentwood's hometown girl, former D.C. intern Monica Lewinsky, who almost single-handedly brought down the presidency of William Jefferson Clinton. Their affair started after she flashed her thong (who would *do* that?!). "I did not have a sexual affair with that woman … Miss Lewinsky," Clinton famously declared during a nationally televised press conference. It all depends on how you define "sexual."

Lights, Camera, Action!

So many movies and television shows have been shot around here it would take days to name them all. Here are just some of the most memorable:

Venice

Films
Grease
The Falcon and the Snowman
White Men Can't Jump
Speed
Dogtown and Z-Boys
Million Dollar Baby
Touch of Evil (the canals)

TV Shows
Simon & Simon
The A-Team
24: Season Six

Santa Monica

Films
It's a Mad, Mad, Mad, Mad World (1963)
The Lords of Dogtown
Going My Way (St. Monica's Catholic Church)
They Shoot Horses, Don't They? (Santa Monica Pier)
Titanic (Santa Monica Pier)
The Sting (Santa Monica Pier)

TV Show
Three's Company

Brentwood

Films
Grand Canyon
Murder, My Sweet
The Player
American Beauty
Crash

Pacific Palisades

Films
Beethoven
Freaky Friday

TV Shows
Baywatch
Curb Your Enthusiasm

Malibu

Films
Gidget
Planet of the Apes

TV Shows
The Rockford Files (Paradise Cove)
M*A*S*H* (Malibu Creek State Park)

The famed Santa Monica Pier

The Pier & the Boardwalk

We all have relatives who live elsewhere, let's say Cleveland, and the first thing they want to do when they visit is… that's right, go immediately to the **Venice Boardwalk**. And that's why it's the number-one tourist destination in L.A. County. Why do they want to go there so badly? Because in Cleveland, there is nothing even remotely so magical, spontaneous, odd and even creepy. In fact, nowhere else in the country can one find such a daily assortment of wild characters, from street performers juggling chainsaws, to tarot card readers who don't seem to shower, to gorgeous bikini-clad girls blissfully roller skating. The entertainment continues on every block, featuring jugglers, singers, magicians, prophets, mimes, artists and just plain crazy people. There are also super-fab bargain-hunting opportunities; outdoor vendors offering trashy T-shirts, "smoke shop" items, sunglasses galore, cheap socks… you name it, they have it. If you're hungry, don't miss Jody Maroni's famous sausages (yum!). If you want to relax and have a Bloody Mary, grab a spot at On the Waterfront Café. The boardwalk action is found from Rose Avenue on the north to Venice Boulevard on the south.

The very famous and historic **Santa Monica Pier** (at the end of Colorado Boulevard) is just as colorful but much more family oriented. It features a fabulous vintage merry-go-round with the most fanciful handcrafted horses imaginable, beautifully restored by the city in 1990. It's housed in the Looff Hippodrome Carousel Building, a National Historic Landmark. You'll also find vendors selling fast food, cheap trinkets and bait – lots of people, believe it or not, catch their dinner off the pier. The pier also is home to Pacific Park, which has rides and games that kids can't get enough of, including the 135-foot-high Pacific Wheel, a giant Ferris wheel perched over the ocean. Riding it is almost surreal – it feels like it might drop you right into the bay. At night the experience becomes almost hallucinogenic, with the wheel's 6,000 multicolored lights, which can be seen from Venice to Malibu. Finally, environmental watchdog Heal the Bay operates the Santa Monica Pier Aquarium under the carousel; this interactive marine-science center offers a closeup look at our ocean habitats and is home to dozens of species of marine animals and plants. Check the web site for more info: healthebay.org.

7 Majestic Views,
from Malibu to the Marina

Just a portion of the dazzling view from Malibu's Point Dume

Many of us who live here say, "Forget the celebrities, we'll take the geography!" The real stars are the mesas, canyons, mountains and coastline that have captivated people all over the world for centuries. From always-funky Venice, to wealthy Brentwood, to the 27 miles of stunning coastline that define Malibu, one is never far from a Pacific panorama or a mountain vista. Here are our favorites:

▶ "The Queen's Necklace" – named for the twinkling lights that line the curved shoreline from the Santa Monica Pier to the beach at Topanga Canyon – is one of the most romantic views on the West Coast. You can see it from almost anywhere: the pier (especially atop the Ferris wheel), Palisades Park, the bluffs and hills of the Palisades, and the coast of Malibu looking south. The lights sparkle and shimmer in an extravagant, joyous dance.

▶ The Getty Center in Brentwood provides hands-down the most expansive and intoxicating views of Los Angeles, from downtown to the Santa Monica Bay. On a clear day, of which we have many, we simply cannot get enough of this almost-overwhelming vista.

▶ Another awe-inspiring view is from the top of the Temescal Ridge Trail in Temescal Canyon Park. Take the short way up, a hardcore 30-minute workout. But once you reach the top, drenched with sweat, you will be rewarded by cool ocean breezes and spectacular views of the mountains and the bay. You literally feel like you're on top of the world, and in a way you are. The walk down, thankfully, is a piece of cake.

▶ At the end of Via de la Paz at Via de las Olas in a residential neighborhood of the Palisades is an extraordinary three-way view of Palos Verdes and Santa Monica Pier to the south, Catalina straight ahead and the Malibu coastline to the north. At night PCH is dramatically lit up from car headlights.

▶ Malibu's Point Dume is one of the most beautiful seaside residential neighborhoods in the world, with great big lots and sprawling mansions. Some of the houses are perched on the cliffs above Zuma Beach, and they have the best views of all – a vast expanse of ocean stretching to the furthest reaches of the horizon. Those of us who don't live there enjoy an equally magnificent vista by taking Heathercliff (off PCH) to Dume Drive until it ends at Point Dume State Preserve. Bring a picnic and your bathing suit, and after enjoying the views, you can head down the long staircase to one of the prettiest beaches in California.

▶ To feel like you're on vacation, take a stroll on the paved walkway on Marina del Rey's North Jetty. You'll enjoy the ocean air while you watch boats of all shapes and sizes cruise in and out of the Marina. It's peaceful and beautiful. Sometimes you can get really lucky and spy dolphins frolicking in the sea. Follow Speedway till it ends and you're there.

▶ There's something sad and haunting about the Venice Pier, found at the end of Washington Boulevard. Maybe it's the dramatic expanse of ocean with only seagulls and boats to break up the view. The 1,300-foot-long pier was built in 1963 and completely restored in 1997. It's been an important location for scores of movies, including the unfortunate demise

Q & A: Mary Steenburgen

Oscar-winning actress Mary Steenburgen has lived in Malibu since she married actor Ted Danson in 1995. (They also have a home in Ojai.) In 2006, she joined with Santa Barbara interior designers Jami and Eric Voulgaris to launch Rooms & Gardens, a wonderfully eclectic home design store on Montana Avenue. Tippy Helper met with Mary (while Ted sat nearby) in the store to talk about what it's like to be famous in this community.

How have you managed to have a normal family life as a famous person married to a famous person?
Ted and I have four children between us, and we've worked very hard to stay grounded. Our family is extremely close. Laughter is key, and we adore each other's children, siblings and extended family. We both come from really strong families. We're so compatible; I would sign up for a hundred more lifetimes with this man!

What are some of the perks of being famous?
Getting a good table at a restaurant! But really, being from Arkansas, I really don't look at fame as a way of getting perks. I look at it as a way to make a positive difference in the world by calling attention to someone less fortunate or adding to someone's life in a positive way.

As a kid in Arkansas, did you imagine you'd be friends with other famous Arkansans – like the Clintons?
Well, one of the bizarre things about this latest presidential race is that it's the third person I know to run for president! First was Bill, then General Wesley Clark, whose wife used to work with my mom in a bank in Little Rock, and now Hillary. She's not really from Arkansas, but she was the first lady of our state for a long time.

Do you think winning the Oscar for *Melvin and Howard* (1980) ensured your place in the annals of the famous for all eternity?
Winning the Oscar means I get to sit between Spacek and Streep at those luncheons the Academy arranges for past winners, which is really fun. But it was thrilling to win. I look at my Academy Award as a very "pure" win, because the film had no budget, so there was no marketing campaign whatsoever. It was because film critics across the country loved the film and praised my performance. Without them, I don't think I would have won.

What inspired you to launch Rooms & Gardens here on Montana?
I have been visiting Jami and Eric's stores in Santa Barbara and Summerland for years. I approached them about the Montana store, and they were game. It's so much fun, and it's turned into a big success.

Is it hard to find acting work at this stage of your life?
I'm working more in my 50s than I ever did in my 40s. I'll keep going until they stop hiring me.

Santa Monica is…
Artistic

Maybe it's the light. Maybe it's the vast canvas of the Pacific. Whatever the reason, Santa Monica and her neighbors (especially Venice and now, with the Getty, Brentwood) have long been serious players in the art world, from the early 1960s Venice culture that fueled such rising artists as Ed Moses and Ed Ruscha, to the beach-inspired paintings of Diebenkorn and Hockney, to today's acclaimed galleries, public art and museums. Santa Monica is blessed with the soul of an artist.

3 World-Class Museums

The Getty Center
1200 Getty Center Dr., Brentwood
310.440.7300, getty.edu
Open Tues.-Thurs. & Sun. 10 a.m.-6 p.m., Fri.-Sat. 10 a.m.-9 p.m.; admission free; parking $8; no reservations needed

If you still haven't been to the Getty, shame on you. If you have, there are plenty of reasons to go back. And not just for the spectacular views. (Tip: The second-floor terrace outside the West Pavilion touts the best view with the fewest tourists.) Despite rumors to the contrary, the Getty really does have must-see art. And there's always a worthwhile concert, family program or lecture to attend.

Whether its permanent collection is revolutionary may be debatable, but the Getty really shines at creating intimate, original rotating exhibitions and large-scale special exhibitions. The hidden gems here are the small, frequently changing shows organized by the curators of individual departments: manuscripts, drawings, photography or, occasionally, paintings. It's a treat to explore these singular subjects: French neoclassical sketchbooks in the drawings gallery, or "The Hours of Louis XII" in manuscripts, or the architectural work of Julius Shulman in photography. And that's just one season's treasures.

Wading your way through the Richard Meier-designed compound can be daunting, but so was building this behemoth, a process that took ten long years, primarily due to its location on a hilltop in the Santa Monica Mountains. Atop the hill are the Getty Research Institute, the Getty Conservation Institute, the Getty Grant Program, the Getty Trust and the Getty Museum. Once you get there, the views are so grand, the white travertine so pristine, and the gardens so lush, that it's hard to break away and actually venture inside a gallery.

No matter, there's plenty to see and do outside the galleries. Installation artist Robert Irwin's Central Garden is worth a walk-through, with its 500 continuously rotating plant varieties. Follow the zigzag pathway up to the Garden Terrace Café, settle in with a glass of wine and enjoy. Steer clear

Light, space and art inside the Getty Center

The travertine-and-glass Getty Center

of the much larger Café at the Getty Center, a ho-hum cafeteria-style restaurant with a wider selection of California fare but lacking the outrageous outdoor views. Bigger spenders should reserve a table for lunch or dinner at the restaurant, with its own noteworthy view and surprisingly thoughtful chef-prepared creations.

If the kids are in tow, pick up the Art Detective Cards and become a family of Sherlocks as you explore the galleries. You also can sign up to study a single work of art together in the Family Art Stops or take a fanciful storytelling tour on Sundays with a guide. The biggest family lures are the festivals that entice thousands to celebrate exhibition-themed art making, music, storytelling and performances. They're free, but the timed tickets disappear quickly, so sign up online early.

Leave the kids at home for the springtime Selected Shorts programs, old-school book readings by big names; Jane Kaczmarek and Bradley Whitford are regular readers. The monthly "Friday Nights off the 405" are a good way to take the edge off traffic woes and loosen up with live music before heading home. The more formal Friday Nights at the Getty, free performances featuring music, dance, theater and the like, have become wildly popular. If you don't have a ticket, don't bother showing up – you'll never even make it to the tram.

Speaking of the tram, it's a rare irritant in an otherwise bucolic environment. After your first visit, the novelty of riding up the mountain in a sideways elevator wears off, or maybe it's simply the realization after 20 minutes in line with droves of visitors that you could have walked up the hill faster. Even still, it's not quite as annoying as forking over $8 to park in a Getty-owned lot when you're about to visit a museum worth billions that flamboyantly touts its "free admission" policy. Maybe instead of "free" it should admit that admission cost varies, depending on how many people you can stuff into a car.

The Getty Villa

17985 Pacific Coast Hwy.,
Pacific Palisades
310.440.7300, getty.edu
Open Thurs.-Mon. 10 a.m.-5 p.m.;
admission free but advance ticket
reservations required; parking $8

We waited for years, through the neighborhood bickering and international looting debacles, in anticipation of the second coming of the Getty Villa. It's here, and, thankfully, it really was worth the wait.

Sure, there are scholarly conferences and very serious lectures exploring the finer

Greek classicism at the Getty Villa

points of the 44,000 Greek, Roman and Etruscan antiquities dating from 6,500 B.C. in the Getty's collection. But there's plenty of fun to be had, too. You can, for instance, take in a modernized Greek comedy in the 450-seat outdoor classical theater, the very source of the neighborly bickering that delayed the Villa's opening for so long (if the decibel level of Greek theater ever soars high enough to disturb the neighbors, some sleepy audience members would be grateful). Or spend a Saturday sculpting clay figures from a live model under the tutelage of seasoned instructors. And come back on Sunday with the kids for the Art Odyssey tour, a clever game that sends the whole family on a treasure hunt through the museum complex.

Activities aside, what makes a day at the Villa so relaxing and worthwhile is simply strolling through the property on a sunny afternoon. The audio tour (this one is good, we promise) takes you through the open-air entry pavilion, the outdoor theater and the numerous Roman-style gardens – all before getting to the museum itself. And you'll discover why (and how) J. Paul Getty re-created the Villa dei Papiri, a first-century Roman country house in Herculaneum, on the northern edge of the Palisades (the museum claims it's in Malibu, but technically it resides in Pacific Palisades).

Inside the museum, galleries are arranged by theme rather than chronologically, so you can choose to peruse based on the subject matter and your mood. If you're feeling aggressive, check out the artwork related to stories of the Trojan War; if love is more your speed, try the gallery of gods and goddesses. Just don't miss the Getty's prized *Statue of a Victorious Youth*, aka the famous Getty Bronze, dating from 300–100 B.C. It's one of the few surviving life-size Greek bronzes from that era, a true treasure.

Afterward, grab a lunch box to go from the café and enjoy it as the Greeks would have – alfresco, taking in the ocean breezes and the California sunshine.

Santa Monica Museum of Art
Bergamot Station, Bldg. G1, 2525 Michigan Ave., Santa Monica
310.586.6488, smmoa.org
Open Tues.-Fri. 11 a.m.-6 p.m., Sat. 11 a.m.-8 p.m.; suggested donation $3-$5

With so many contemporary art galleries to cherry-pick from in Bergamot Station, why bother stepping foot into a museum that showcases the exact same genre? For good reason: After a day of gallery hopping, a museum exhibition is a welcome respite, the curator having already shuffled through the good, the bad and the even worse for you.

The SMMoA is a chameleon, not a collector – it focuses its dollars on exhibitions rather than acquiring a permanent collection. That gives it wiggle room to feature a broad range of exhibitions, from artists' series to innovative group or thematic shows developed in-house or borrowed from other institutions. Contemporary art is decidedly the focus, but occasionally a modernist slips into the mix, for those who prefer their art two dimensional and in a traditional medium.

If you think kids don't get contemporary art, head here, where young art lovers are nurtured. They can participate in studio art classes led by contemporary artists, a far cry from the craft-project workshops at many other museums. Who knows? Your budding Picasso's work might even make an appearance at SMMoA's Neighborhood Outreach Gallery in the Santa Monica Place mall. We also recommend joining the museum and taking the kids to the members-only opening-night parties, which are usually torture for kids – but here, they have fun making art in workshops while you ponder the finer points of the art *du jour*.

Our favorite SMMoA event is the annual fundraiser, Incognito, held each spring. The highlight is the sale of hundreds of works by well-known and emerging international artists, which always includes plenty of hot names, from Raymond Pettibon to Alison Saar to Yoko Ono. But unlike other auctions, the pieces are created on identical 8x10 formats and are all priced at $250. They're signed on the back, but the artist's identity is not revealed until after you buy a piece, so you have to trust your instincts. What a novel concept... buying art that you like! For those of us who can't afford a $250 piece, even if it's a steal, there's plenty of free art to ponder, and make, at the Santa Monica Museum of Art.

The Santa Monica Museum of Art

Going Public:
The Murals of Venice & Santa Monica

R. CRONK. 2004

Take a close look and you'll see painted murals all over the Bay Cities – under bridges, on brick-walled buildings, even on public parking structures. Since it was founded in 1982, the Santa Monica Arts Commission has funded dozens of these wall-bound wonders. Others are private works, part of a mural movement that began decades ago and gained momentum in the 1970s.

In 1939 Stanton MacDonald-Wright painted two of the earliest, *Recreation* and *Colonial Spanish* (Santa Monica City Hall). An avant-garde abstract painter and key player in the early Los Angeles art scene, MacDonald-Wright founded the first modern art exposition here and later became director of the Works Project Administration in Southern California.

Other artists, such as Art Mortimer, have made a living by painting murals. In 1971 Mortimer painted a scene on the side of the Venice home where he lived, and he never stopped. His 1998 Santa Monica city commission *Santa Monica Beach* (Parking Structure 1 on Fourth Street) is a whimsical collage of beachfront snapshots, one of 100 murals he's painted throughout Los Angeles.

Some murals double as a social, political or environmental commentary, such as Ann Thierman's 1983 *History of the Pico Neighborhood* (Stewart Street at Virginia Avenue), which depicts the struggle of neighbors on both sides of the Santa Monica Freeway to remain united, or Eva Cockcroft's sprawling 1996 piece *Recycle, Renew, Restore and Repair* on the Santa Monica City Yards's external wall (Michigan Avenue across from Bergamot Station), which details a day in the life of a public works facility. Other murals are just plain fun, such as Daniel Alonzo's 1983 *Whale of a Mural* (Ocean Park Boulevard at Fourth Street), which features – you guessed it – whales.

So next time you speed past what looks like a painting on the side of a building, muttering curses about graffiti, slow down and take a good look. You might well be in for a treat.

Artists in Paradise

Before the haute galleries, public art commissions and fancy museums came to town, the beach towns were (and still are) a magnet for the artists who made it all possible. Hundreds of international artists have lived and worked here, some lifelong residents, others merely thumbing rides through town.

In the 1950s, Billy Al Bengston and Ken Price, surfer buddies turned artists, rented a studio in a slummy nook of Venice for reportedly $30 a month (rumor has it they were the only residents on the block peddling art, not drugs). Thus the beachside artist community was born.

The 1960s brought a barrage of hipper-than-hip artists. Andy Warhol visited Venice allegedly at the urging of friend and resident actor/artist Dennis Hopper, whose own work has seen the insides of the glitziest galleries. Warhol didn't stay long, but isn't that a bit of west-coast sunshine in his vibrant pop-art portraits? As for Hopper, he still lives in a Venice building designed by Frank Gehry and Brian Murphy. Dubbed the Art Barn, it triples as his home, art studio and private museum (stocked with $8 million of contemporary art).

Other '60s Venice residents include European artists Jean Tinguely and Nikki de Saint-Phalle, who named their studio the Zinc-Zinc Company; Laddie John Dill, a Santa Monica High School grad; sculptor Robert Graham; consumer pop painter Ed Ruscha; abstract painter Ed Moses; Peter Alexander, known for his conceptual studies of light and space (hey, maybe that sunshine did have something to do with it); and countless others. Some of them, such as Ruscha, Moses and Alexander, still live and work in Venice.

Don't worry – we didn't forget David Hockney and Richard Diebenkorn, who both lived in Santa Monica in the '60s. Hockney arrived fresh from England via Manhattan, a wide-eyed, eager young man keen on beach babes (okay, muscle men); Diebenkorn was a seasoned mid-career artist who moved to Los Angeles to teach at UCLA. For Hockney, Santa Monica was a playground where he could hang out at the Santa Monica Pier, the Venice Boardwalk or at Malibu pool parties (ever wonder about the inspiration for his famous *Swimming Pool* series?). Diebenkorn was equally enthralled by Santa Monica's light, color and ocean, but he kept to himself, painting in the sunshine. His most famous series of 140-plus paintings, *Ocean Park*, was named after the Ocean Park neighborhood outside his studio window.

Jean-Michel Basquiat was here, too, on the graffiti-art beat in Venice. Up next was a parade of westside mural artists, such as Art Mortimer *(see page 99)*.

Today, you'll see artists everywhere: strolling the boardwalk, in lofts and in restaurants, from Hal's in Venice to Michael's in Santa Monica. At Michael's, co-owner Kim McCarty is a talented portraitist whose work is in galleries and museums nationwide. She and her husband, the eponymous Michael, also have amassed an impressive collection of contemporary art – including pieces by Diebenkorn and Hockney – that they display in the restaurant in rotating exhibitions. Food and art, all in one stop. How's that for local flavor?

Arts Organizations That Matter

Broad Art Foundation

3355 Barnard Way, Santa Monica
No phone; broadartfoundation.org

Scan the donor wall at any major contemporary arts institution in the United States and you'll likely find the names Eli and Edythe Broad. Back home, they've set up base camp for their continuously expanding collection of contemporary art at the Broad Art Foundation in Santa Monica. Not to be confused with the Broad Foundation in Westwood, which doles out hundreds of millions in grants to arts and educational pursuits, the Art Foundation is an art warehouse and study center that's lent work to hundreds of museums nationwide. Don't expect to take a tour – the foundation opens its doors to art scholars and collectors only. But you can view much of the collection in the top-notch online catalog, and if you read wall labels carefully, probably at a museum near you.

18th Street Arts Center

1639 18th St., Santa Monica
310.453.3711, 18thstreet.org

At 18th Street Arts Center, you can literally watch art unfold before your eyes. Local and international artists accepted to the highly competitive artist-in-residency program live and work at this appealingly funky compound across the street from Crossroads School's athletic facilities. Some stay for a few months on scholarship, while others live here for years at reduced rents. For those of us with less talent but plenty of interest, 18th Street offers free public programs and exhibitions. Check out the quarterly ArtNight festival, a bohemian evening of exhibitions, live music and a peek inside several artists' studios.

Santa Monica Arts Commission

1685 Main St., Santa Monica
310.458.8350, arts.santa-monica.org

A government that supports the arts? We're not dreaming – they really do still exist. The Santa Monica Arts Commission, founded in 1982, funds public art and provides grants for local artists and organizations that encourage public participation in the arts. Ever wonder why there are so many galleries in Santa Monica? The commission encourages galleries and artists to set up shop here by fighting for affordable rental rates. It's also amassed an impressive collection of more than 50 public murals and sculptures by pairing artists with architects and landscapers. And then there's the Fresh Art program for emerging artists, many of whom have never shown their work in public – it places site-specific sculptures in Santa Monica parks each fall. Kudos to the city for making itself a dynamic, visually interesting place to live – and visit.

Santa Monica's mural-art tradition continues at 18th Street Arts.

Bergamot & Beyond: Our Favorite Galleries

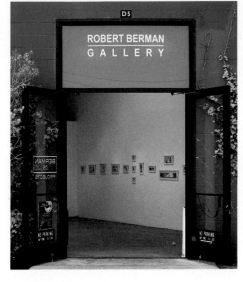

Like Soho, the Santa Monica area has more than its share of galleries – more than 70, in fact. Bergamot Station in particular has become the magnet for the biggest names in the contemporary art scene, but there are plenty of other areas to check out, too. Try to go with the flow – inevitably a few are closed for an exhibition installation, lunch or no apparent reason at all.

Bergamot Station
2525 Michigan Ave., Santa Monica
bergamotstation.com
Hours vary by gallery, but most are open Tues.-Fri. 10 a.m.-6 p.m., Sat. 11 a.m.-5:30 p.m.

Bergamot Station calls itself an art-gallery complex, and with good reason. The sprawling warehouse spaces are home to more than 30 galleries and arts organizations, as well as the Santa Monica Museum of Art and several shops. The compound, named after the 1875 Red Line trolley stop once located on this site, has housed a celery-packing facility, an ice-making plant and a water-heater factory since the demise of the trolley in 1953. After the city of Santa Monica scrapped its plans to build a light-rail system there, Wayne Blank, the developer behind the Santa Monica Airport's hangar-based art studios, turned it into a visual arts center. With so many high-end galleries here and so many long-standing dealers wooed from other parts of L.A., it's hard to believe that Bergamot has been open only since 1994.

Galleries are independently owned, so you'll find a wide range of styles, media and prices, although most fall under the vast domain of contemporary art. Heavy hitters include Shoshana Wayne Gallery (works by Kiki Smith and Jeanne Silverthorne, among others), Patrick Painter Gallery (Andy Warhol, Georg Baselitz), Bobbie Greenfield Gallery (Roy Lichtenstein, Frank Gehry, Robert Motherwell), Ikon Ltd. Contemporary Art (Damien Hirst, David Hockney, Ellsworth Kelly) and Berman Turner Projects, a collaboration between prominent L.A. dealers William Turner and Robert Berman, each of whom also runs his own gallery.

Be forewarned: Except at Frank Pictures Gallery, where we've always gotten a friendly hello, count yourself lucky if a gallery assistant lifts an eyebrow to acknowledge your presence. But with more than 600,000 gawking visitors flocking to Bergamot each year, precious few of them serious buyers, we'll give the stone-faced gallery staff a bit of a break. Besides, it means you can make a guilt-free beeline for the door if a particular gallery isn't your speed.

If you're keen on tracking down the next great artist, check out artists' cooperative F.I.G. (Southern California art), Hunsaker/Schlesinger Fine Art (California painters and sculptors), Patricia Correia Gallery (Mexican-American and Chicano art) and Rosamund Felson (socially charged art). Or if photographs are more your thing, head to Rose Gallery (contemporary photographs), Gallery Luisotti (contemporary photographs) and Peter Fetterman Gallery (19th- and 20th-century prints and photographs).

To refuel, head over to Bergamot Café. It doesn't look like much, just patio tables and a takeout counter, but the food is fresh and the coffee is good. And if you're lucky, you might see one of the espresso-sipping gallery assistants crack a smile.

Afterward, visit Frank Lloyd Gallery, where the age-old art of pottery making has morphed into wildly creative contemporary wall hangings, vessels and freestanding sculptures. And for a taste of the bizarre, check out Copro/Nason Fine Art, where Hieronymous Bosch meets techno-geeks in oddly entertaining hipster paintings.

What to do when the thrill of finding your inner critic wanes? Head over to Suzanne Felson, a boutique jewelry shop with artfully simple designs bedecked with brilliant gemstones. If you're treating someone special, wrap that necklace in hand-printed papers from Hiromi Paper International next door, and throw in an edgy, limited-edition artist-designed T-shirt from the Santa Monica Museum of Art, which sells surely the coolest museum T-shirts in town.

More shopping awaits at Lois Lambert Gallery, whose namesake owner has turned half the gallery into the not-to-miss Gallery of Functional Art (a fancy name for really cute shop). Lambert has an eye for design, stocking her store with artsy gifts, from $15 mod desk accessories and handmade bracelets to $375 undulating Colin Schleeh vases and $1,500 wine-cork chairs.

Before you leave, get a museum-worthy haircut (yes, haircut) at Frank Studio, where you can sip martinis and ponder the Andy Warhols while hip designers fuss over your locks. If you're lucky, Track 16 will be hosting one of its free evenings of film, music and readings, at which you can show off your new look.

Bergamot Galleries & Shops

Our favorites are listed below in walking order, starting at Warehouse A on the east and ending at Warehouse T.

Mark Moore Gallery
Bldg. A1, 310.453.3031, markmooregallery.com
Mixed media contemporary

Gallery Luisotti/RAM Publications
Bldg. A2, 310.453.0043
Contemporary photography and publishers of art publications

Bergamot Café
Bldg. A3, 310.828.4001, bergamotcafe.com

Frank Pictures/Off Main
Bldg. A5, 310.828.0211, frankpicturesgallery.com
Mixed media contemporary

Peter Fetterman Gallery
Bldg. A7, 310.453.6463, peterfetterman.com
19th- and 20th-century photography

Patrick Painter Gallery
Bldg. A8 & B2, 310.264.5988, patrickpainter.com
Mixed media contemporary

Shoshana Wayne Gallery
Bldg. B1, 310.453.7535, shoshanawayne.com
Mixed media contemporary

Craig Krull Gallery
Bldg. B3, 310.828.6410
Mixed media contemporary

Rosamund Felsen Gallery
Bldg. B4, 310.828.8488, rosamundfelsen.com
Mixed media contemporary

Gail Harvey Gallery
Bldg. B5, 310.829.9125
Mixed media contemporary

Richard Heller Gallery
Bldg. B5-A, 310.453.9191,
richardhellergallery.com
Mixed media contemporary

Frank Lloyd Gallery
Bldg. B5-B, 310.264.3866, franklloyd.com
Contemporary ceramics

Bobbie Greenfield Gallery
Bldg. B6, 310.264.0640,
bobbiegreenfieldgallery.com
Contemporary works on paper

Patricia Faure Gallery
Bldg. B7, 310.449.1479, patriciafauregallery.com
Mixed media contemporary

Track 16 Gallery & Smart Art Press
Bldg. C1, 310.264.4678, track16.com
Mixed media contemporary

**Robert Berman Gallery &
Santa Monica Auctions**
Bldg. C2 & D5, 310.315.1937,
robertbermangallery.com
Mixed media contemporary

**William Turner Gallery &
Berman Turner Projects**
Bldg. E1, 310.453.0909, williamturnergallery.com,
bermanturnerprojects.com
Mixed media contemporary

Patricia Correia Gallery
Bldg. E2, 310.264.1760, correiagallery.com
Mixed media Mexican-American and Chicano
contemporary

**Lois Lambert Gallery &
the Gallery of Functional Art**
Bldg. E3, 310.829.6990,
galleryoffunctionalart.com
Mixed media contemporary and adjacent store

Schomburg Gallery
Bldg. E3A, 310.453.5757
Mixed media 20th- and 21st-century art

**Art Concepts –
Custom Framing & Gallery**
Bldg. F2, 310.315.9772
Framing and prints

**Santa Monica Museum of Art
& Museum Store**
Bldg. G1, 310.586.6488, smmoa.org
*See discussion in 3 World-Class Museums,
page 94*

Ruth Bachofner Gallery
Bldg. G2, 310.829.3300,
ruthbachofnergallery.com
Mixed media contemporary

Suzanne Felson
Bldg. G3, 310.315.1972, suzannefelson.com
Fine jewelry

Ikon Ltd/Kay Richards
Bldg. G4, 310.828.6629, ikonltd.com
Modern and contemporary works on paper

Rose Gallery
Bldg. G5, 310.264.8440, rosegallery.net
Contemporary photography

F.I.G. (First Independent Gallery)
Bldg. G6, 310.829.0345, figgallery.com
Mixed media contemporary; artist cooperative

Grey McGear Modern
Bldg. G7, 310.315.0925
Mixed media contemporary

Hiromi Paper International
Bldg. G9, 310.998.0098, hiromipaper.com
Handmade Japanese papers

Frank Studio
Bldg. J1, 310.998.1920, frankstudios.com
Hair salon

Sarah Lee Artworks & Projects
Bldg. T1, 310.829.4938, sarahleeartworks.com
Mixed media contemporary art and photographs

Hunsaker/Schlesinger Fine Art
Bldg. T3, 310.828.1133
California painting and sculpture

Copro/Nason Gallery &
Fine Art Publishing
Bldg. T5, 310.829.2156, copronason.com
Outsider art

Other Galleries to Explore

Angel's Attic
Check web site for reopening date & new
address, Santa Monica
310.394.8331, angelsattic.com
It's worth a trip to this quirky doll and miniature
museum to tour the fully restored 1895 Victorian
home, one of the only surviving examples of this
era in Santa Monica. But you'll have to wait. It's
moving, Victorian home and all, to a new Santa
Monica location, where it will reopen with an
expanded mission that includes art and music
therapy programs for children and seniors.

Christopher Grimes Gallery
916 Colorado Ave., Santa Monica
310.587.3373, cgrimes.com
Open Tues.-Sat. 10 a.m.-5:30 p.m.
Serious art galleries with museum-quality
standards really do exist outside of Bergamot
Station. Christopher Grimes delivers
contemplative, cutting-edge work by established
and emerging international artists. Come
with an open mind and a fat wallet – this is
investment-worthy art that's sure to spark many
an interesting dinner conversation.

Hamilton Galleries
1431 Ocean Ave., Santa Monica
310.451.9983, hamiltongalleries.com
Open Tues.-Sun. noon-7 p.m.
Paintings by Southern California artists with
such titles as *Cannonball Pigs* (cannonballs
of the swimming, not military, persuasion) and
Stampeding Dachshunds are as whimsical
and refreshingly free of political and social
commentary as they sound. Swing by for a fitting
end to a day of fun at the beach.

L.A. Louver Gallery
45 N. Venice Blvd., Venice
310.822.4955, lalouver.com
Open Tues.-Sat. 10 a.m.-6 p.m.
Unless you have deep pockets – we're talking
oil-rig deep – don't expect to find something
for your living room at this 30-year mainstay in
the international gallery scene. But you should
stop by every few months to check out the latest
museum-quality contemporary art exhibitions
(after all, it's free to browse), mostly new work
from such artists as Richard Deacon, David
Hockney, Edward and Nancy Kienholz, Alison
Saar, Sean Scully and just about every other
big-name contemporary artist you can rattle off.
Even the Frederick Fisher–designed building is
worth a peek, with its minimalist cement walls,
museum-like interior spaces, multiple galleries
spanning two floors, research library and
rooftop exhibition space dubbed the Skyroom.
Top-notch publications, occasionally produced
in partnership with museums, are a welcome
change from the usual ho-hum gallery tear
sheets. The catch: They're not free. But once
you flip through the color photos and curatorial
intros, you'll understand why.

The Lowe Gallery

2034 Broadway, Santa Monica
310.449.0184, lowegallery.com
Open Tues.-Fri. 10 a.m.-5:30 p.m.,
Sat. 11 a.m.-5:30 p.m.
Atlanta gallery owner Bill Lowe opened this west coast outpost in 2002 with the same diverse range of user-friendly art, from Dale Chihuly's contemporary blown-glass sculptures to African tribal art. The ambitious exhibition schedule rotates frequently, so there's always something new to discover.

M. Hanks Gallery

3008 Main St., Santa Monica
310.392.8820, mhanksgallery.com
Thurs.-Sat. noon-5 p.m. & by appt.
Since 1988, David Driskell, a retired professor and leading scholar of African-American art, has been exhibiting and selling 20th-century African-American paintings, sculpture and drawings at his Santa Monica gallery. With annual seminars on art appreciation and the history of African-American art, a fund-raiser in conjunction with Martin Luther King Day and Driskell's enthusiastic emphasis on art education, it's hard to leave here without learning, and appreciating, something new.

Obsolete Gallery

222 Main St., Venice
310.399.0024, obsoleteinc.com
Open Wed.-Mon. 11 a.m.-6 p.m.
Part treasure trove of quirky antique collectibles, part art gallery, Obsolete specializes in the bizarrely beautiful, from historic wooden artists' models to folk art figures and religious relics. The artists represented here share a similar penchant for the odd, such as Ron Pippin's collages made from animal skeletons and Tricia Cline's haunting porcelain figures.

Santa Monica Art Studios

3026 Airport Ave., Santa Monica
310.397.7449, santamonicaartstudios.com
Arena 1 Gallery open Wed.-Sat. noon-6 p.m.
In 2004, Santa Monica artist Yossi Govrin and gallery owner Sherry Frumkin converted this sprawling 22,000-square-foot space in the historic airport hangar into private studios and an experimental-art exhibition space. Satiate your burning desire to peek into the mind of an artist at Santa Monica Art Walks, an all-day open house of on-site studios.

Santa Monica Public Library

601 Santa Monica Blvd., Santa Monica
310.458.8600, smpl.org
Open Mon.-Thurs. 10 a.m.-9 p.m.,
Fri.-Sat. 10 a.m.-5:30 p.m., Sun. 1 p.m.-5 p.m.
Even if you're not the library type, the gorgeous new Main Library in Santa Monica, flooded with natural light and vibrant spaces, is worth an afternoon's wandering. Before hitting the books, procrastinators can take in one of the oft-changing exhibitions, like the recent survey of Nordic furniture design, which was reminiscent of the library's own furniture aesthetic.

Sherry Frumkin Gallery

3026 Airport Ave., Studio 21, Santa Monica
310.397.7493, frumkingallery.com
Open Wed.-Sat. noon-6 p.m.
You're likely to have a love/hate reaction to the art here, and that's exactly the point. A pioneer in the Santa Monica gallery scene for more than fifteen years, Frumkin is best known for her support of female artists who create politically and socially charged pieces using unconventional materials. In 2004, the gallery moved to Santa Monica Art Studios, the airport hangar turned affordable studio space that she developed with partner Yossi Govrin.

TAG (The Artists' Gallery)

2903 Santa Monica Blvd., Santa Monica
310.829.9556, TAGtheArtistsGallery.com
Open Tues.-Sat. 11 a.m.-5 p.m.
A cooperative gallery run by and for artists, TAG sits unassumingly on a nondescript corner of Santa Monica Boulevard. Inside you'll find a wide range of artwork – most, for better or worse, easily digestible – selected from paying members of the cooperative. Prices start at a few hundred dollars, so it's a good stop for first-time buyers who want to ease into the collecting scene.

Art Your Way

Brentwood Art Center
13031 Montana Ave., Brentwood
310.451.5657, brentwoodart.com
Since 1971, Brentwood Art Center has been
providing westsiders with some of the best
classical painting, drawing and sculpture
courses outside a university setting. Most are
multi-week series led by practicing artists and
professional art teachers. Adult classes range
from figure drawing to plein-air painting and
everything in between; kids and teen offerings
include classical technique courses, cartooning
and fashion drawing. You can also enroll the kids
in summer drawing camp while you set up your
easel in the Italian countryside during the annual
three-week studio class abroad.

Earthstone Gallery
2651 Main St., Santa Monica
310.452.2126, home.earthlink.net/~antaras
If an intimate one-on-one wheel throwing or
hand-building pottery lesson is more your speed,
Earthstone is for you. The outdoor patio studio
is barely big enough for two students, and that's
exactly what makes it so charming.

Farthingales Los Angeles
3306 Pico Blvd., Santa Monica
310.392.1787, farthingalesla.com
Displaced Victorian-era ladies living modern
beachfront lives can learn to make their own
corsets, complete with ribbon waist cinchers, at
this corset and costume-supply shop. Men-
only Edwardian corset classes (yes, men wore
corsets) are also available. Less adventuresome
sorts can sign up for sewing classes.

Jennifer Joyce Ceramics
3028 Pico Blvd., Santa Monica
310.392.4626, jenniferjoyce.com
Ceramist Jennifer Joyce's roomy working studio
has been a popular after-school and evening
stop since 1997. Students of all ages learn
classic hand-building techniques, including
coils, slab and press molding. An on-site
gallery exhibiting work by guest artists provides
inspiration for the creatively challenged.

Ritual Adornments
2708 Main St., Santa Monica
310.452.4044, ritualadornments.com
If you want to turn Grandma's overflowing
bead collection into mod jewelry, head to Ritual
Adornments. Everything you need is here, from
stringing wire to instructional classes. Intro
classes teach beginners basic wire wrapping
and stringing techniques, while more advanced
bauble makers can sign up for decorative
knotting and bead looming. The store also
boasts a staggering collection of beads, stones,
shells and other small, stringable objects.

Rustic Canyon Recreation Center
601 Latimer Rd., Santa Monica
310.454.5734, laparks.org
There's something for everyone at this lush,
oak-lined park. Take a picnic to enjoy after your
ceramics class or outdoor drawing class. If the
rest of your family isn't as keen on art classes,
sign them up for a soccer clinic, guitar lesson or
dance class while you're busy painting.

Santa Monica College
1900 Pico Blvd., Santa Monica
310.434.4000, commed.smc.edu
Continuing-education classes offer a wide
menu of visual art classes, from Chinese brush
painting to creating comic strips. Budding
photographers can improve their snapshot skills,
and those just looking for a little fun can take up
knitting, crocheting or flower arranging.

Santa Monica Museum of Art
Bergamot Station, Bldg. G1, 2525 Michigan
Ave., Santa Monica
310.586.6488, smmoa.org
Creating art is almost as big at the SMMoA
as seeing it. At the Emerging Artist Family
Workshops, a contemporary artist leads the
charge, encouraging burgeoning artists to
channel their inner creativity. Other art-making
events tend toward the crafty, all the better to
garner the youngest participants' attention.

Wildfiber
1453 E. 14th St., Santa Monica
310.458.2748, wildfiber.com
Wildfiber is a knitter's paradise – yarns in every
color, texture and fiber overflow from wall bins.
Novice knitters can take a private lesson or join
one of the group classes; experienced weavers
can hone their skills in a multi-course clinic.

Q & A: Ethel Fisher

Painter Ethel Fisher and her art historian husband, Seymour Kott, have lived in their 1926 Spanish-colonial home in the Palisades since 1971. The house boasts terrific light and smashing views of the ocean, mountains and treetops. Ethel has captured many variations of these views in the strong, vibrant paintings she creates in her second-floor studio. Mostly oil on canvas, her work includes portraits, still lifes and landscapes and has been exhibited in museums and galleries around the world. Ethel talked with her neighbor Tippy Helper on a sunny Saturday afternoon.

What brought you to the Palisades?
Seymour and I had been living in New York; we wanted to get out of there and relocate to L.A. So we started looking and saw this house. We bought it for the great wall space, the great light, and the clincher was the view of rooftops and the ocean. We can see as far as Palos Verdes and Catalina some days. Plus, there was a great space for my studio here.

How has living here affected your work?
When we first moved here, I was still doing paintings based on architectural themes, very geometric work. After a trip to Greece, I went back to figurative art, and then I started doing landscapes – all I had to do was look out the window and see the most extraordinary vistas.

I heard you dined with the great painter Francis Bacon many years ago in London.
Yes, that's true. I was visiting my daughter Sandra and she had the pop artist Richard Hamilton and his wife, as well as Francis Bacon, over for dinner. Sonia Orwell, the widow of the writer George Orwell, was also there. Sandra wanted to prepare an authentic American dinner, so she made fried chicken and baked beans. He didn't like the fried chicken and asked for his chicken broiled. Other than that, it was a fun evening.

Do you consider yourself a California or New York artist?
I got my start in New York. I studied at the Art Students League with Morris Kantor and Will Barnett, and I've shown in many galleries there. But I would have to say I am a California artist. I've been painting the California landscape and California people – family, friends and some of my collectors – for all these years.

What is your favorite part about living in the Palisades?
I love living in the hills but still being close to the village. I like going to the farmer's market on Sunday, and to the library, and the people are very nice usually. I also like to check out garage sales. I once found a 19th-century Chinese porcelain lamp, which is really beautiful. A Chinese antiques dealer told me it was valuable.

How has the Palisades changed over the years?
It used to be just a sleepy little beach town, kind of square, and most people thought it was just too far from any cultural events. But all that has changed. It's gotten crowded, particularly the traffic.

Literary

Perhaps it was because Santa Monica was once, as Christopher Isherwood wrote, L.A.'s "backyard washed by waves," far enough away from the power centers to allow for artistic freedom. Perhaps it had something to do with the salt air. Whatever the reason, Santa Monica and her neighbors, especially Venice, Malibu and the Palisades, have long been as much havens for literary artists as for visual artists. This is a writing community and a reading community, as you'll see in the pages that follow.

The Words

Great and good writers have lived in, or passed through, Santa Monica and her sister towns, and we could fill volumes with the words they've written about these towns. But for now we'll fill these two pages.

On the beaches of the Pacific that display was indeed superb, Mack Sennett Bathing Beauties by the hundred. They gambolled all around us, as we walked up and down in the windy sunlight along the sands. Frisking temptations. But we were three St. Anthonies – Charlie Chaplin and Robert Nichols and I – three grave theologians of art, too deeply absorbed in discussing the ways of cinematographic salvation to be able to bestow more than the most casual attention to the Sirens, however plumply deserving.

– Los Angeles, A Rhapsody
Aldous Huxley, 1926

Montemar Vista [Malibu] was a few dozen houses of various sizes and shapes hanging by their teeth and eyebrows to a spur of mountain and looking as if a good sneeze would drop them down among the box lunches on the beach.

– Farewell, My Lovely
Raymond Chandler, 1940

[Santa Monica] Canyon is our western Greenwich Village, overrun now by various types of outsiders, but still maintaining an atmosphere of Bohemianism and unpretentious artiness.

– The Shore
Christopher Isherwood, 1952

This evening we're dining in a canyon that opens onto the sea and where a whole colony of artists or would-be artists lives. There are little cafés vaguely reminiscent of old Montparnasse.

– America Day by Day
Simone de Beauvoir, 1948

Venice U.S.A., Venice West, a horizontal, jerry-built slum by the sea, warm under a semitropical Pacific sun on a Sunday afternoon.

– The Holy Barbarians
Lawrence Lipton, 1959

I drove with the kids one dreadful morning into the San Fernando Valley and felt that if there had to be a nuclear war, certainly it might do some good in this area. I drove through Topanga Canyon, fifteen miles from the Valley to the coast (like Switzerland after the A-bomb, some friend of mine had said years before), hands sweating on the steering wheel as I took the curves, and had to think that maybe I wasn't ready for the Canyon; maybe I just didn't have the nerve. I braked at the Pacific, knowing that Malibu was north and no way could I afford it yet. I turned south, looking for Venice ... and headed – like a gerbil in a cage – back downtown.

– Golden Days
Carolyn See, 1986

There was still a large stretch of farmland between Los Angeles and Santa Monica in those days. The Japanese farmers grew artichokes, lettuce and strawberries along the sides of the road. That night the fields were dark under the slight moon and the air was chill but not cold.

I was unhappy about going to meet Mr. Albright because I wasn't used to going into white communities, like Santa Monica, to conduct business. The plant I worked at, Champion Aircraft, was in Santa Monica but I'd drive out there in the daytime, do my work, and go home. I never loitered anywhere except among my own people, in my own neighborhood.

– Devil in a Blue Dress
Walter Moseley, 1990

Venice is a quiet, shabby little place at the edge of an oil field which extends for a mile or two along the shore. But you can still see the hotel where Sarah Bernhardt stayed. You can still live at an address on the Grand Canal (though a garbage raft will float past your window instead of a gondola); you can

still admire the pure curve of a bridge which would not disgrace Italy, except that it stands among oil derricks, is made of wood and plaster and is apt to fall down soon.
— *The Shore*
Christopher Isherwood, 1952

Malibu tends to astonish and disappoint those who have never before seen it, and yet its very name remains, in the imagination of people all over the world, a kind of shorthand for the easy life. I had not before 1971 and will probably not again live in a place with a Chevrolet named after it.
— *Quiet Days in Malibu*
Joan Didion, 1979

The Santa Monica Freeway is traditionally the scene of every form of automotive folly known to man. It is not white and well-bred like the San Diego, nor as treacherously engineered as the Pasadena, nor quite as ghetto-suicidal as the Harbor. No, one hesitates to say it, but the Santa Monica is a freeway for freaks, and they are all out today.
— *Gravity's Rainbow*
Thomas Pynchon, 1973

"Trouble," he said, still softly, "is something our little city don't know much about, Mr. Marlowe. Our city is small but very, very clean. I look out of my western windows and I see the Pacific Ocean. Nothing cleaner than that, is there?" He didn't mention the two gambling ships that were hull down on the brass waves just outside the three-mile limit.
— The Bay City (Santa Monica) police chief speaking in *Farewell, My Lovely*
Raymond Chandler, 1940

There is Muscle Beach, where the barbell kings lift and jerk, and the tumblers build their human towers. Tumbling makes you lithe and graceful. Barbells make you formidable, imposing and, ultimately, grotesque. Our culture has preferred barbells.
— *The Shore*
Christopher Isherwood, 1952

Alas, the lovely garden, placed high above the coast
   Is built on crumbling rock. Landslides
   Drag parts of it into the depths without warning. Seemingly
   There is not much time left in which to complete it.
— *Garden in Progress*
Bertolt Brecht, 1944

Last night, because I was bored, I found myself doing what I would least have expected – hunting up Tennessee Williams. I located him, after some search, at a very squalid rooming house called The Palisades, at the other end of town [Ocean Park] – sitting typing a film story in a yachting cap, amidst a litter of dirty coffee cups, crumpled bed linen and old newspapers.... We had supper together on the pier and I drank quite a lot of beer and talked about sex the entire evening.
— *Diaries*
Christopher Isherwood, 1943

They'll ... wander hand-in-hand into the booming shadows of Palisades Park, which Olga knows like a favorite book never tired of. All along that enormously tall cliff, under royal palms and over the Pacific, are little summer houses and trellised arbors with benches where sudden acquaintances burst into prodigal flower.
— *The Mattress by the Tomato Patch*
Tennessee Williams, 1954

What I like best is the ocean end of town, the side toward the beach, the cliffs that break off like a cookie so you can see what the earth is like, before the highway takes over at the bottom. And then the bike path, and then the sand, and then the water.
— *Making History*
Carolyn See, 1992

I am attached to the particular curve of coastline as one leaves the tunnel at the end of the Santa Monica Freeway to drive north on the Pacific Coast Highway. I am attached equally to the glories of the place and to its flaws, its faults, its occasional revelations of psychic and physical slippage, its beauties and its betrayals.
   It is the end of the line.
   It is the last stop.
   Eureka!
   I love it.
— *Eureka!*
John Gregory Dunne, 1978

Bookish by the Bay

Will Rogers, the great wordsmith of the Palisades

A man only learns in two ways. One by reading, and the other by association with smarter people.

– Will Rogers

In Santa Monica, Will Rogers had plenty of opportunity for both. In the early part of the last century, the beach town's bohemian, off-the-beaten-track charm enticed plenty of "smarter people," many of them writers. Rogers himself, perhaps America's most populist writer-humorist since Mark Twain, bought 186 acres overlooking the Pacific in the 1920s and developed the land into a ranch and home, which is now Will Rogers State Park. (The area is now part of Pacific Palisades.)

In later decades, other illustrious writers followed Rogers's lead. Playwright Bertolt Brecht fled from the Nazis and relocated in Santa Monica for most of the 1940s. He described his house at 1063 26th Street in a 1942 diary entry: "One of the oldest, [it] is about 30 years old, California clapboard, whitewashed, with an upper floor with four bedrooms. I have a long workroom (almost seven meters), which we immediately whitewashed and equipped with four tables. There are old trees in the garden (a pepper-tree and a fig-tree). Rent is $60 per month, $12.50 more than in 25th street." Brecht's fellow German writers-in-exile Lion Feuchtwanger and Thomas Mann also moved to the Santa Monica-Palisades area in the '40s. What's not known, however, is whether Feuchtwanger or Mann managed to snag as good a deal on rent.

Even though such celebrity writers as Rogers, Brecht and Mann took up residence here, the writer most associated with Santa Monica is Christopher Isherwood, who lived in Santa Monica Canyon from 1939 until he died in 1986. His home, which he shared with companion and painter Don Bachardy (who lives there still), was very close to Will Rogers Beach and the bars on West Channel Road, which attracted a primarily gay clientele (the beach was even called Ginger Rogers – and sometimes still is). Isherwood wrote about the colorful, arty life of Santa Monica Canyon in his novel *A Single Man*, sometimes in lurid detail. Here's how he described the Starboard Side, a fictional bar doubling for the real-life S.S. Friendship, a gay hangout on West Channel Road that closed in 2006: "He sees the round green porthole lights of the Starboard Side,

Santa Monica's acclaimed man of letters, Christopher Isherwood, as drawn by Don Bachardy

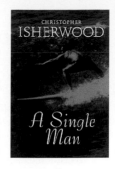

down on the corner of the Ocean Highway across from the beach, shining to welcome him. The Starboard Side has been here since the earliest days of the colony. Its bar, formerly a lunch counter, served the neighbors with their first post-Prohibition beers.... But its finest hours came later. That summer of 1945! The war was as good as over. The blackout no more than an excuse for keeping the lights out at a gangbang." Wow. (By the way, you can still see the porthole lights – the building's ship façade was not changed when the Friendship changed ownership.)

Also setting up shop by the beach in the '40s was Tennessee Williams, who wrote *The Glass Menagerie* in a rather seedy two-room apartment at 1647 Ocean Avenue. Writers who put down roots here in later years included Joan Didion and John Gregory Dunne (Malibu), Carolyn See (Topanga and now Pacific Palisades), her daughter Lisa See (the Palisades and now Brentwood) and a host of acclaimed screenwriters, including Callie Khouri, Steven Zallian, Robert Towne, Robin Swicord and James L. Brooks.

Today, "smarter" folk are still drawn to the area. Though astonishing real estate prices mean that it's no longer the "western Greenwich Village" Isherwood called it in a 1952 *Harper's Bazaar* essay, the region appeals to both writers and readers with a proliferation of bookstores, literary events and publications. To wit:

- A wealth of community newspapers: the *Corsair* (the student paper at Santa Monica College); the *Santa Monica Daily Press*; the *Santa Monica Mirror* and the *Santa Monica Observer,* both weeklies; the monthly *Santa Monica Sun*; and, elsewhere in the Bay Cities, the adored *Palisadian-Post*, the weekly *Argonaut*, which serves Venice and the Marina, and a few papers in Malibu, including the *Malibu.*
- 36 bookstores, according to directory listings (which include used bookstores, newsstands and coffeehouses that sell books) – and that's just in Santa Monica proper.
- Poetry readings or literary events practically every night of the week (see poetryflash.org) – the most popular of which are held at Beyond Baroque

Literary Arts Center (681 Venice Blvd., Venice, 310.822.3006), a gathering place for writers since 1969.
- An annual Citywide Reads book club sponsored by the Santa Monica Public Library, at which residents and visitors receive a free book then come together to talk about it at scheduled discussions and author events. Past selections have included *The Kite Runner* by Khaled Hosseini, *The Time Traveler's Wife* by Audrey Niffenegger, *The Berlin Stories* by Christopher Isherwood and *Balzac and the Little Chinese Seamstress* by Dai Sijie.
- A literary arts journal, *Santa Monica Review*, featuring first-time and established local writers, that's published twice yearly by Santa Monica College and distributed nationally.

Santa Monica is a literary town, without doubt. The infamous diarist and Lost Generation party girl Anais Nin lived in Hollywood but felt such a connection to Santa Monica that her ashes were scattered over the bay. But she may have fared even better as a writer had she moved to Santa Monica while she still had a pulse. As Will Rogers quipped, "In Hollywood the woods are full of people that learned to write but evidently can't read. If they could read their stuff, they'd stop writing." Or move to Santa Monica.

Bookstores to Prowl

Above the Fold Newsstand
1257 3rd St. Promenade, Santa Monica
310.393.2690
A good newsstand is as essential to readers as a good bookstore, and this one fits the bill just fine. The selection is broad, and the location – in a train-car-like kiosk in the middle of the Promenade – is handy.

Angel City Bookstore & Gallery
218 Pier Ave., Santa Monica
310.399.8767, angelcitybooks.com
Quoting from the store's manifesto: "We are more than a bookstore, we are a philosophy. We believe that selling literature is not like selling hardware, and that the current trend of superstore is an inappropriate method for the handling of literature precisely because there is no distinction between the great and the mundane." The stock is large and primarily used, though you will find choice new books; it also carries new and used classical CDs and work from local artists. A book-lover's place, run by book lovers.

Arcana Books on the Arts
1229 3rd St. Promenade, Santa Monica
310.458.1499, arcanabooks.com
Specializing in rare and out-of-print books on 20th-century art, Arcana covers such subjects as African-American art, art theory, conceptual art and Viggo Mortensen's photography (yep, he's an accomplished photographer). A serious place for serious collectors.

Barnes & Noble
1201 3rd St. Promenade, Santa Monica
310.260.9110, barnesandnoble.com
13400 Maxella Ave., Marina del Rey
310.306.3213, barnesandnoble.com
These two big-box bookstores, one on the Promenade and another in a Marina mall, have good all-around selections and friendly staffs.

Borders Books & Music
1415 3rd St. Promenade, Santa Monica
310.393.9290, borders.com
What Barnes & Noble would be complete without an adjacent Borders? This is a good one, with a popular café, a great CD area and, by the front door, a fine selection of local-interest books, from Santa Monica history books to, well, this one.

Gene de Chene Books
11556 Santa Monica Blvd., West L.A.
310.477.8734, gdcbooks.com
WWII vet Gene de Chene opened this store selling "people's books" in 1968, stocking it with a jumble of used and new books; for many years the only part of the store that was alphabetized was the war section. A westside intellectual haven, it also has supplied large quantities of "books in browns and dark reds" to Hollywood set designers for years.

Diesel, a Bookstore
3890 Cross Creek Rd., Malibu
310.456.9961, dieselbookstore.com
Malibu is pretty darn excited to at last have its own bookstore – and to have one this stylish is just frosting. The first offshoot of the fine Diesel in Oakland, this is an all-around collection, with an intelligent and artfully displayed mix of new and used titles. For such a small store, it gets terrific authors to come in for signings.

Dutton's Brentwood Bookstore
11975 San Vicente Blvd., Brentwood
310.476.6263, duttonsbrentwood.com
Recently spared by billionaire landlord Charlie Munger, who'd planned to build condos here, Dutton's will have a shiny new home on this site – but not for a couple of years. Part bookstore, part community center, Dutton's is a warren of cluttered but inviting rooms wrapping around a flagstone courtyard. You can start in the west wing with literature and fiction, then work your way through doorways and around piles of books into biography, history, politics, travel, science and children's books, with stops for periodicals, wrapping paper, gifts and, finally, the coffeehouse in the east wing. Even though Dutton's is on the east end of the Bay Cities, it's at the literary center.

Equator Books

1103 Abbot Kinney Blvd., Venice
310.399.5544, equatorbooks.com
This bookstore-as-gallery showcases a small,
hand-picked selection of some new but mostly
used books, sold in collectible condition, often
cleaned and wrapped in archival covers. The
collection of surf and skate books is amazing;
other specialties are such kooky ones as
circus freaks and call girls. The high-ceilinged,
3,500-square-foot space also features a gallery
wall with monthly exhibits of original artwork.
Make sure to check out the new adjacent store
featuring used vinyl, especially jazz, blues, old
rock, reggae and country.

Hennessey + Ingalls

214 Wilshire Blvd., Santa Monica
310.458.9074, hennesseyingalls.com
A destination bookstore, this airy, neatly
organized shrine carries just about every book
out there on architecture, design, graphics, art,
fashion, horticulture, photography, transportation
and furniture – mostly new, but also rare and
out-of-print. It's tremendously fun to wander
through for an hour or three – this is a visually
dynamic collection of visually captivating
books. There's a good selection of arts-based
periodicals, too, and a swell roster of local-
interest books near the front door. Hennessey +
Ingalls also publishes an extensive line of high-
end architecture and design books.

Books piled on books at Dutton's

Hi De Ho Comics & Books

525 Santa Monica Blvd., Santa Monica
310.394.2820, hideho.com
One of the premier providers of comic books
(new and old), magazines, books, toys, posters,
trading cards and fantasy items in the greater
Los Angeles area.

Sam Johnson's Bookshop

12310 Venice Blvd., West L.A.
310.391.5047, abebooks.com/home/bobklein
No description can equal that of Popula.com
writer Maria Bustillos, who wrote in a profile
of owner Robert Klein, "The great elegance
of Sam's lies in its modesty and utility, and in
the delicate, eclectic taste with which its plain
wooden shelves are stocked; here are no dusty
paperback bodice-rippers, nor yet the mincing
superiority of virginal, gilded first editions still

Hennessey + Ingalls = architecture and design heaven.

and quiet under glass; mostly, there are good, comfortable reading copies of the classics of English literature; heavy cloth bindings, thick and scented with age, type that you can feel sunk into creamy paper, sculpting it like Braille." Ah, heaven....

Kenneth Karmiole Bookseller
1239-A 3rd St. Promenade, Santa Monica
310.451.4342, abebooks.com/home/karmbooks
Open by appt. only
A rare-book collector's dream, specializing in works printed before 1800. Come here for that original printing of Ben Franklin's autobiography that your collection is still somehow lacking.

Barry R. Levin Science Fiction & Fantasy Literature
720 Santa Monica Blvd., Santa Monica
310.458.6111, raresf.com
In business since 1973, this small bookstore complete with oak shelving and a reading lounge fit for the most discriminating literati specializes in, you guessed it, science fiction, fantasy and horror, with a strong emphasis on rare editions, autographs, correspondence and literary art.

Novel Café
212 Pier Ave., Santa Monica
310.396.8566, novelcafe.com
This casual coastal coffeehouse doubles as a used bookstore and village square, where locals come to type, talk, nosh or read without being bothered by the Main Street masses. Secluded nooks in the loft offer enough peace and quiet for readers to read and writers to freely commune with their muses.

Santa Monica College Bookstore
1900 Pico Blvd., Santa Monica
310.434.4258, smc.edu/bookstore
Here's where you can pick up that Biology 101 textbook you've been dreaming of. Make sure to get the sixth edition, because, we're not sure if you heard the news, but this year they're calling it the Golgi *Body*.

Small World Books
1407 Ocean Front Walk, Venice
310.399.2360, smallworldbooks.com
When you need to get out of the sun or away from the wackos, veer off the boardwalk and into this friendly store with a surprisingly good selection of fiction, nonfiction, biography and bestsellers from both big houses and small presses. An excellent neighborhood bookstore.

Katie O'Laughlin at Village Books

Thunderbolt Books
512 Santa Monica Blvd., Santa Monica
310.899.9279
Sacred ground for westside seekers of truth, this store specializes in books on the world's religions, as well as New Age and self-improvement topics and music that puts one in the mood for a spiritual quest. The Buddha statues welcome even the cynics among us.

Village Books
1049 Swarthmore Ave., Pacific Palisades
310.454.4063, palivillagebooks.com
In perfect keeping with that particular Palisadian small-town charm, Village Books's motto says it all: "Big enough to serve you, small enough to know you." Owner Katie O'Laughlin and her staff hand-sell books the old-fashioned way, by reading them and finding the right fit for their customers. Despite its small size, it hosts big-time author signings, poetry readings and children's events.

Wilshire Books
3018 Wilshire Blvd., Santa Monica
310.828.3115,
sprezzatura.editthispage.com/wilshirebooks
This used bookstore is supplied with reviewers' copies of new titles, so brand-new books often appear here a few days before reviews hit the newspapers. It's a small room – if you enter in search of a particular title, you may be disappointed, but if you enter looking for something interesting, you'll find plenty.

Libraries
The Santa Monica area is blessed with several superb libraries; for details, see the Smart chapter, page 82.

Writers frequent the loft in the Novel Café.

Bring Your Laptop: Where to Write

You'll find free WIFI at these hot zones and coffeehouses (all are in Santa Monica unless noted):

- ▶ Bergamot Café (in Bergamot Station), 2525 Michigan Ave., 310.828.4001
- ▶ Cafe Bolivar, 1741 Ocean Park Blvd., 310.581.2344
- ▶ Caffe Divine, 500 Broadway, 310.451.5796
- ▶ Infuzion Café, 1149 3rd St., 310.393.9985
- ▶ Palisades Branch Library, 861 Alma Real Dr., Pacific Palisades, 310.459.2754
- ▶ Panera Bread, 501 Wilshire Blvd., 310.566.3080
- ▶ Santa Monica Main Library, 601 Santa Monica Blvd., 310.458.8600
- ▶ Third Street Promenade, between Wilshire Blvd. and Colorado St., thirdstreetpromenade.com
- ▶ UnUrban Coffee House ("Death Before Decaf"), 3301 Pico Blvd., 310.315.0056
- ▶ Velocity Café, 2127 Lincoln Blvd., 310.314.3368
- ▶ Virginia Avenue Park, 2200 Virginia Ave., 310.458.8688

The WiFi isn't free (or even available in some cases), but you can't beat the quiet, noncommercial, writer-friendly vibe at these spots (in Santa Monica unless noted):

- ▶ Abbot's Habit, 1401 Abbot Kinney Blvd., Venice, 310.399.1171
- ▶ Dutton's Brentwood Bookstore, 11975 San Vicente Blvd., Brentwood, 310.476.6263
- ▶ 18th Street Coffeehouse, 1725 Broadway, 310.264.0662
- ▶ It's a Grind Coffee House, 602 Santa Monica Blvd., 310.260.0066
- ▶ Lazy Daisy, 2300 Pico Blvd., 310.450.9011
- ▶ Novel Café, 212 Pier St., 310.396.8566
- ▶ Rose Café, 220 Rose Ave., Venice, 310.399.0711
- ▶ Will Rogers State Park, 1501 Will Rogers Park Rd., Pacific Palisades, 310.454.8212

Q & A: Doug Dutton

Doug Dutton was born among books. His book-loving parents opened Dutton's Books in North Hollywood in 1961, and he helped sweep out the store and shelve books from the very beginning. In 1984, Doug and his brother Dave took over the old Brentwood Bookstore on San Vicente, gradually growing it into the beating literary heart of the westside. Dave moved back to the original store (now closed) years ago, so Doug is the face of Dutton's, where he chats with regulars and brings in first-rate authors. Away from the store, he plays piano, teaches music at Colburn, reads a whole lot of books and helps his youngest child with college applications. Doug sat with Colleen Bates in the bookstore's café to talk about reading, writing and the survival of the independent bookseller.

Most people around here are probably writing a screenplay – are you writing a book?
I never wanted to write a book – I've always been a reader, not a writer. But now I have an idea for a book about music. I think I have something to say that hasn't been said. But it's just something I'm fooling around with.

Are your wife and kids readers?
Our four kids are all readers, as is my wife, Penny. I met her in the North Hollywood bookstore – she was looking for a Chaim Potok book, and I'd never read him. Then we discovered we were both musicians. That was where it started, 26 years ago.

Will the independent bookstore survive the onslaught of the chains?
I think it will survive in some manifestation – but it can't go on as a repository for everything. That won't work when you can find anything online, and probably for less. But I can't imagine a world without the social aspect of the bookstore: the exchange of ideas, the recommendations, the exploring. It's part of what makes a community. The first thing I do when I'm in a new place is find a bookstore.

Even the most dedicated bookworm has to eat every now and then. Where do you go when you get hungry?
I love Pizzicotto – the food is great and you see the two women who own it working there every day. It's an authentic experience. The same thing is important in bookstores. I also love Tlapazola Grill – the food is just wonderful.

You have a lot of famous customers. How do you respect their privacy?
I've got one employee who has an encyclopedic memory of film, and he likes to tell people about movies they were in that they've completely forgotten. I don't know if they always appreciate it – sometimes they've forgotten the film for a reason! But generally, we have a policy that famous people must be afforded privacy and the ability to look at books at the same pace as everyone else. And I have had to chase away paparazzi who've come here to follow people like Ryan O'Neill or Dustin Hoffman… even O.J. Simpson.

Santa Monica is…
Reaching Out

Long reputed to be packed with bleeding-heart liberals, Santa Monica is actually quite diverse, with conservatives, libertarians, liberals and radicals living side by side. What unites them is an uncommon concern for the common good. From its churches and temples to its homeless shelters and environmental caretakers, Santa Monica and her sister communities get involved, look inward and reach out.

Nonprofits That Matter

The Boys & Girls Club is a bustling center offering everything from a skatepark to homework help.

Assistance League of Santa Monica
1453 15th St., Santa Monica
310.395.2338, santamonica.assistanceleague.org
Among the efforts supported by this long-established, socially elite group are college scholarships; Operation School Bell, which outfits needy kids with clothing, backpacks, glasses and dental work; and sponsoring kids for summer camp. Check out its thrift shop, the Bargain Bazaar, at 1453 15th Street in Santa Monica.

Boys & Girls Club of Santa Monica
1238 Lincoln Blvd., Santa Monica
310.393.9629, smbgc.org
Santa Monica Boys & Girls Club is a thriving place, a center for all kinds of kids to learn academic and personal skills, get help with homework, play sports, acquire leadership skills, find mentors and much more – including using the terrific skatepark. It also runs programs at eight local schools, and it has many volunteer opportunities, including ones for teens. A cornerstone of Santa Monica life.

Catholic Charities
211 3rd Ave., Venice
310.392.8701, catholiccharitiesla.org
A branch of the national organization devoted to social justice, Catholic-style, this group provides all sorts of help for immigrants, refugees, job seekers, runaway youth, the homeless and those in need of professional counseling to deal with such issues as domestic violence and marital strife. This branch helps people throughout the westside.

Center for Healthy Aging
2125 Arizona Ave., Santa Monica
1527 4th St., Santa Monica
310.576.2550, centerforhealthyaging.org
This marvelous organization delivers a rich array of services for older people: peer-to-peer counseling, professional referrals, health screening and education, money management, visits to the homebound, bereavement groups, caregiver support and more; it also does a fine job of educating the public about the challenges of aging. The center always needs donations, as well as volunteers to conduct home visits and to help seniors with money and medication management.

Chrysalis
1853 Lincoln Blvd., Santa Monica
310.401.9400, changelives.org
Teaching people how to fish, instead of giving them fish, is the mission of this long-standing nonprofit, which also has centers in downtown L.A. and Pacoima. The homeless and unemployed learn work, job-hunting and basic computer skills, as well as interview strategies; practical counseling helps the newly employed stay employed. It has particularly rewarding ways to help, from conducting mock interviews to employing a graduate of the program.

18th Street Arts Center
1639 18th St., Santa Monica
310.453.3711, 18thstreet.org
The only residential arts program of its kind in Southern California, 18th Street is all about using art to foster community and diversity. Mid-career artists (some from around the world) get to live and work in this quiet, low-slung campus across the street from the Crossroads School's sports facilities. It sends artists of all kinds (dance, music, theater, visual art, new media) to schools, and it frequently hosts art shows and performances.

Family Service of Santa Monica
1533 Euclid St., Santa Monica
310.451.9747, vistadelmar.org/fssm.html
This fine group goes back to Depression-era Santa Monica. It helps families in need with counseling, trauma recovery, parenting issues and infant and child development; it also works with local preschools and elementary schools to identify and address developmental, learning and social issues.

Heal the Bay
1444 9th St., Santa Monica
310.451.1500, healthebay.org
Santa Monica's very own environmental watchdog has grown to have statewide, even national importance in the struggle to keep our oceans clean. It analyzes, rates and reports on the cleanliness of local waters; works to improve sewage-treatment systems; organizes beach cleanups; lobbies to limit ocean dumping; educates the public on the risks of runoff; and operates the very fine aquarium underneath the Santa Monica Pier. Its fundraisers are celebrity love fests, and it offers lots of ways to get involved, from picking up beach trash to donating money. The return of the dolphins to Santa Monica Bay is due in part to Heal the Bay's efforts, and for that we are eternally grateful.

The Heart Touch Project
3400 Airport Ave. #42, Santa Monica
310.391.2558, hearttouch.org
Inspired by research that shows the psychological and physical benefits of "healing touch" – i.e. massage therapy – for the seriously ill, this program trains and organizes volunteers to provide comfort-based massages for homebound seniors, terminally ill infants and children, AIDS and Alzheimers patients and people in hospice.

Inside Out Community Arts
2210 Lincoln Blvd., Venice
310.397.8820, insideoutca.org
Some see No Child Left Behind as No Arts Left Standing, and this program aims to address the depressing lack of arts programs in local middle schools. It runs workshops and field trips, sponsors festivals, conducts teacher training and, at its Venice center, operates programs aimed at rival gang kids. It's always looking for artists who are good with kids, as well as artists who can teach teachers.

Meals on Wheels
1823-A Michigan Ave., Santa Monica
310.394.5133, mealsonwheelswest.org
This branch of the venerable national organization nearly went under when the church that provided its home shut down. But it carries on in a new home, delivering two meals a day, five days a week, to the sick, disabled and elderly in Santa Monica, Malibu, the Palisades and Topanga Canyon. It always needs drivers and helpers, and the work can be tremendously rewarding.

OPCC
1453 16th St., Santa Monica
310.264.6646, opcc.net
Formerly known as the Ocean Park Community Center, this growing place now serves an area well beyond Ocean Park. Its focus is on abused women and children, the homeless, runaway

Homelessness is a significant problem in Santa Monica; some of the nonprofits (and the churches, too) in these pages work to get people fed, clothed, treated, sober, housed and employed.

The mediation garden and beach beyond at Phoenix House

youths and the mentally ill, and it helps some 8,000 people a year. OPCC uses creative programs – like the one in which at-risk teens train homeless dogs so they're adoptable – that have made a real difference; the graduates of its transitional housing program have a remarkable 90-percent success rate in staying housed for at least a year. It has a constant need for volunteers and financial and in-kind donations.

One Voice
1228 15th St., Ste. C, Santa Monica
310.458.9961, onevoice-la.org
In the early 1980s, Sue Silbert started a small outreach program as part of a sociology class she was teaching at Cal State Northridge; little did she know that it would grow to be such a significant presence. Its programs are divided into three categories, all aimed at the poor. One Voice Scholars places low-income kids in the country's finest colleges, and its graduation rate is an astonishing 95 percent. The holiday food program provides a week's worth of groceries (as well as books and toys) to more than 2,500 families. And the family-assistance division offers such things as emergency relief, a wonderful private-public school adopt-a-student program, and summer camps. This place has had a tremendous positive impact in the lives of many local children from poor homes.

Phoenix House of Venice Beach
503 Ocean Front Walk, Venice
310.392.3070, phoenixhouse.org/California
This branch of the largest nonprofit substance-abuse treatment operation in the country has a residential facility in a beautiful oceanfront location right on the Venice Boardwalk. Its program is demanding.

Pico Youth & Family Center
828 Pico Blvd., Santa Monica
310.396.7101, picoyouth.org
Founded after a series of shootings roiled the Pico neighborhood in 1998, this terrific community center gives young people important positive options. Its biggest draw is its full-fledged recording studio, which trains kids in production and gives them a wonderful creative outlet. Also offered are yoga classes, tutoring, computer training, web design, job-hunting help, leadership training and counseling.

P.S. Arts
11965 Venice Blvd., #201, West L.A.
310.586.1017, psarts.org
The research is definitive: Arts programs in schools lead to greater academic and personal success. Yet arts programs have been slashed from public schools. Enter this vibrant and growing organization, which is bringing music,

visual art, drama and dance to underfunded public schools, including several in Venice and Santa Monica. It also teaches teachers to bring the arts into their core curriculum, even if the school doesn't offer an arts program. P.S. Arts has made such an impact on local schools that it has become a national model for other arts-starved school districts. Its main need is fund-raising.

St. Joseph Center
204 Hampton Dr., Venice
310.396.6468, stjosephctr.org
Serving more than 1,000 working-poor families, this 30-year-old nonprofit gets people off the streets and above the poverty line. Programs include job training and referrals, childcare, tutoring, family activities, money-management training, crisis intervention and, of course, feeding the hungry. Its thrift store (2545 Lincoln Boulevard, Venice, 310.306.8357) always needs volunteers and donations; volunteer needs include tutors, mentors, food-service workers and home visitors for seniors.

Santa Monica Conservancy
P.O. Box 653, Santa Monica
310.496.3146, smconservancy.org
Founded in 2002, this small but growing group is working to preserve Santa Monica's diverse and historic architectural landmarks, far too many of which were destroyed in years past. Its walking tours of downtown Santa Monica and Santa Monica Canyon are terrific and very popular, so make your reservations early. And if you love architecture, consider volunteering as a docent.

Santa Monica Mountains Conservancy
5750 Ramirez Canyon Dr., Malibu
310.589.3200, smmc.ca.gov
This is a governmental agency, not a local nonprofit, but it works with groups (including Heal the Bay and TreePeople) and local governments to protect and grow public lands in the Santa Monica Mountains, one of California's great natural resources. The volunteer programs can be really fun – at this writing, for instance, they were looking for mountain bikers to help patrol the mountains. And if you're trying to figure out what to do with that 100-acre Malibu ranch you just inherited – well, they'd be happy to talk to you!

Venice Family Clinic
604 Rose Ave., Venice
310.392.8636, venicefamilyclinic.org
Started in a storefront by a couple of do-good doctors in 1970, this is now the largest free clinic in the nation, serving some 22,000 patients, including more than 5,000 children. It has made a profound difference in the lives of low-income locals. There are many ways to provide support, from joining the 2,400-person volunteer team to shopping at the annual Venice Art Walk, a wonderful community-based fund-raiser.

Virginia Avenue Project
3000 Olympic Blvd., Santa Monica
310.264.4224, virginiaavenueproject.org
In partnership with PAL (the Police Activities League), this neighborhood center sponsors free after-school performing-arts programs for kids, as well as long-term, one-on-one mentoring. The kids have to commit to the program, and the program commits to them: Together they write and produce plays, publish a literary magazine, stage performances and learn the business of the arts in an entrepreneur program. It's a vibrant, cheerful, positive place.

Westside Food Bank
1710 22nd St., Santa Monica
310.828.6016, westsidefoodbankca.org
WSFB's mission is to distribute as much nutritious food as possible to local food-assistance charities while reducing food waste – and it does a wonderful job in achieving that goal. It gets 4 million pounds of food annually from supermarket warehouses, restaurant suppliers, caterers, bakeries and others, making sure the food gets to seniors, low-income families, the homeless, veterans and people living in domestic-abuse shelters and rehab centers. It needs lots of volunteers to do everything from sort food to support the fall hunger walk.

Women in Recovery
911 Coeur D'Alene Ave., Venice
310.821.6401, womeninrecovery.com
Run by longtime Venice resident and force of nature Sr. Ada Geraghty, this live-in substance-abuse recovery center is a flower-filled place of calm and positivity. With a focus on individual care and following the twelve steps, it has enjoyed a remarkable success rate in helping women recover from alcoholism and/or drug addiction.

11 Spiritual Centers to Know

Beth Shir Sholom
1827 California Ave., Santa Monica
310.453.3361, bethshirsholom.com
Its name translates to "Home of the Song of Peace," and in honor of the name, music is paramount at this Reform temple. Services and celebrations are rich with music, as is the well-regarded Early Childhood Center, a full-service preschool. Activities and groups abound, from a choir and religious education to a book club and singles' group.

Corpus Christi Catholic Church
880 Toyopa Dr., Pacific Palisades
310.454.1328, corpuschristichurch.com
This bustling parish is the spiritual, social and educational center for many Palisadians, who call the place "Corpus." A little more conservative than rival St. Monica's, it's home to a good parochial school, a full schedule of Masses, various community events and such service projects as teen trips to Mexico to build housing for the poor.

Kehillat Israel
16019 Sunset Blvd., Pacific Palisades
310.459.2328, kehillatisrael.org
The largest Reconstructionist synagogue in the western United States, this vibrant place has more than 1,000 families in its congregation. More liberal than Reform, Reconstructionist rabbis focus on Judaism as an evolving culture experienced through art, music, study, inclusion of women, and tolerance. Commitments to the democratic process and social justice are essential to Reconstructionists.

Pacific Palisades Presbyterian
15821 Sunset Blvd., Pacific Palisades
310.454.0366, palipres.org
Pali Pres, as it's known, is a thriving community that attracts members from well beyond the Palisades. Philosophically it is more on the welcoming side than the conservative side, and it always has something going on: traditional services featuring choral music, modern services featuring Christian rock/folk, youth-group activities and trips, bible study, adult social activities and all sorts of community service; it works to support Chrysalis, the Westside Food Bank, Heifer International and the Ocean Park Community Center, among others.

Pacific Palisades Presbyterian

Saint Augustine by the Sea
1227 4th St., Santa Monica
310.395.0977, saint-augustine.org
This progressive Episcopal church dates to 1875, when the town of Santa Monica had just 1,500 residents. Today, an active congregation meets in a modern church (the original burned down decades ago) to worship, socialize, learn and get involved. It has many groups – seniors, young adults, gays and lesbians, prayer circle, youth – as well as plenty of outreach opportunities. In the current schism splitting the Episcopal church, this place comes down squarely on the side of inclusion for all (including gay priests) and social activism.

St. Matthew's
1031 Bienveneda Ave., Pacific Palisades
310.454.1358, stmatthews.com
A beautiful modern church with an acclaimed elementary school, this Episcopal community is one of the largest in the greater L.A. diocese. If you're hankering for a traditional (but not conservative) high-church service with gorgeous music, this is the place to come – its choir is superb. It offers a rich roster of retreats, social events, educational opportunities, youth programs (including Scouts and a great summer day camp) and outreach efforts.

St. Monica Catholic Community
725 California Ave., Santa Monica
310.566.1500, stmonica.net
People drive miles out of their way to attend
Mass at St. Monica's – this is not the Catholic
church of your youth. The Masses are joyous
and engaging, the choir is wonderful, and the
sermons are lively and thought provoking.
Philosophically… well, let's just say the priests
here aren't puppets of the Pope. This is a large
and busy place, with an elementary school,
an affiliated high school, and dozens of ways
to get involved. It's also a good place to spot
famous people (Arnold and Maria, for instance,
are parishioners).

Santa Monica Zen Center
1001 Colorado Ave., Santa Monica
310.393.3536, smzen.org
It's not clear whether this is a spiritual center or
a pay-as-you-go Zen training school, but it does
offer a roster of Sunday services, children's
programs, talks and instruction, so we'll call it a
spiritual center. It also offers Zazen (mindful –
or is it mindless? – sitting) every evening.

Self-Realization Fellowship Lake Shrine Temple
17190 Sunset Blvd., Pacific Palisades
310.454.4114, lakeshrine.org
If there is a heaven, it must look like this
ten-acre property overlooking the ocean, with
gardens, pathways, shrines and a spring-fed
lake. It's quite the hot tourist attraction, as
well as a place for strolling, pondering and
meditating; most popular is the lakeview
Mahatma Gandhi World Peace Memorial,
where some of the great pacifist's ashes
are enshrined. The temple is devoted to
the teachings of Paramahansa Yogananda,
which focuses on meditation, breathing and
concentration. As you can imagine, this
is a hugely popular place to get married,
although in-house ministers must perform
the weddings.

Unitarian Universalist Community Church of Santa Monica
1260 18th St., Santa Monica
310.829.5436, uusm.org
Like all good Unitarian communities, this
longstanding one (founded in 1927) is socially
active and tremendously inclusive. Minister
Judith Meyer is a dynamic leader, and the
congregation can take part in covenant groups,
religious exploration, Zen meditation, a legislative
ministry, a green sanctuary group, children's
programs, a women's alliance and more.

West Los Angeles Buddhist Temple
2003 Corinth Ave., Los Angeles
310.477.7274, wlabt.org
In the heart of Sawtelle's long-established
Japanese-American community, this house-
like temple offers services for all the important
days (spring and fall equinox, Eitaikyo, Buddha
Day, New Year's Day…), as well as weddings,
funerals, confirmations, classes, bingo, family
activities and, in July, the lovely and lively
Obon Festival.

Peace and beauty at the
Self-Realization Fellowship

Q & A: Bobby Shriver

Bobby Shriver first arrived in Santa Monica in 1977, to work as a reporter for the *L.A. Herald-Examiner.* He left from time to time – to attend Yale Law School, for instance, and to work in venture capital in New York – but he kept returning, finally for good in 1987, lured by the chance to produce the album *A Very Special Christmas,* which benefited the Special Olympics. The son of Sargent Shriver and Eunice Kennedy Shriver, Bobby was elected to the Santa Monica City Council in 2004; he's also working with the RED campaign, which fights AIDS in Africa. Bobby talked with Colleen Bates about doing good in a do-gooder's town.

Did your commitment toward doing good come from your mother?
My workaholic behavior definitely comes from her, but both my parents have been role models. They always started programs that people said couldn't be done. My mother was outraged that no summer camp existed for intellectually disabled kids – so she started one in our backyard (Maria and I attended it, too!). That became the Special Olympics. My father created many groundbreaking programs: the Peace Corps, VISTA, Head Start, Job Corps and more.

Why did you keep returning to Santa Monica?
Besides being naturally beautiful, it's a state of mind. People here are creative, artistic, educated, socially aware, politically passionate and fiercely protective of their city.

What's the single most pressing problem in Santa Monica? And is it solvable?
Everyone says the same thing: homelessness. And yes, it is solvable. The solution is no mystery: permanent supportive housing. Most homeless people suffer from addictions, mental illness or both. It is not realistic to expect a person to beat an addiction or manage mental illness while struggling to survive on the street. But if that person can move into housing with rehab services, then he or she has a good chance. This is working in many other cities. Republicans even like it, because it's cost effective. But we can't solve it alone. About 90,000 homeless people live in L.A. County – one tenth of the homeless population of the entire United States. If all 88 cities in the region accepted their proportionate share of responsibility, homelessness in the county could be eliminated.

Where do you hang out?
A lot of coffeehouses, and not just because coffee is my favorite food – the people there give me good ideas and no-nonsense performance evaluations. I have working breakfasts and lunches at Café Montana – its paper tablecloths are perfect for making to-do lists. I go to Father's Office for the excellent beers. I also like to explore Hennessey + Ingalls.

Santa Monica has been called "The People's Republic of Santa Monica" and "The Home of the Homeless." What would you suggest as a better moniker?
The motto on our city seal is Populus felix in urbe felici – *Happy people in a happy city. That calls to mind a sea of aimless yellow smiley faces. "Creative People in a Creative City" would be more accurate. Or how about "Santa Monica: What Will We Think of Next?"*

Santa Monica is…
Hungry & Thirsty

We can't think of a better place to be hungry or thirsty than Santa Monica. It's home to world-class restaurants, friendly pubs, oceanview cafés, lively bars, great burger joints, comfortable coffeehouses and the nation's most famous farmer's market. You'll find the best of them all in the pages that follow.

A User's Guide to Food & Drink

Price chart

Price symbols are based on the range of most dinner entrees, as follows (for one dinner main dish, or lunch if dinner isn't offered):

$	Less than $14
$$	$15-20
$$$	$21-29
$$$$	$30-up

A Note About Chains

Other than a few exceptions, we don't tell you about the chains in the pages that follow, because chances are you already know them. Just be aware that if you're craving Baja Fresh, California Pizza Kitchen, Cheesecake Factory, Islands, P.F. Chang's, Ruth's Chris or Souplantation, we've got 'em all. And if it's Starbucks you want, just throw a rock and you'll hit one. (But please consider trying one of our fine independent coffeehouses instead.)

The Greatest Hits

Every place in this chapter is recommended, but if you don't have time to try them all, here are our don't-miss favorites in all sorts of categories:

Bakery: A La Tarte, 154
Bar menu: Beechwood, 130, 161
Barbecue: Baby Blues BBQ, 152
Breakfast: Bread & Porridge, 144
Burger: Father's Office, 152
Cocktail lounge: Veranda, 163
Coffeehouse: 18th Street Coffee House, 158
Deli: Izzy's Deli, 145
Fine dining: Josie, 135; JiRaffe, 136; Whist, 143
French bistro: Lilly's French Café, 137
French, elegant: Mélisse, 138
Happy hour: Chaya Venice, 133, 164
Lunch: Joe's, 136
Lunch (secret spot): The Bookmark Café, 144
Italian, ristorante: Vincenti, 142
Italian, trattoria: Locanda Portofino, 138
Market: Robins Nest, 155
Mexican, modern: Tlapazola Grill, 141
Mexican, new-school Cal-Mex: Border Grill, 131

Mexican, old-school Cal-Mex: Paco's Tacos, 140
Oceanview, high end: One Pico, 132; Catch, 139
Oceanview, low end: Malibu Seafood, 138
Old Santa Monica: The Galley, 134
Outdoor café: Cora's Coffee Shoppe, 145
Pizza: Antica Pizzeria, 148
Pub: Finn McCool's Irish Pub, 160
Romantic: Chez Mimi, 133
Sandwiches: Panini Garden, 146
Seafood, elegant: Catch, 132
Seafood, lively: The Lobster, 137
Soul food: Aunt Kizzy's Back Porch, 130
Star-gazing: Nobu Malibu, 139
Sushi: Katsuya, 136
Taqueria: La Playita, 153
Thai: Cholada, 150
Unusual ethnic: Typhoon, 151
Vegetarian/vegan: Real Food Daily, 140
Wine shop: Wine Expo, 165

Good Values

The following may not charge fast-food prices, but they give good bang for the buck in their category.

Back on the Beach, 144
Bread & Porridge, 144
Cha Cha Chicken, 150
China Beach Bistro, 150
Cholada, 150
El Texate, 134
Figtree's Café, 145
Finn McCool's Irish Pub, 160
Gaby's Mediterranean, 150
Gate of India, 150
Gilbert's El Indio, 134
Hakata Sushi & Sports Bar, 134
Izzy's Deli, 145
Le Petit Café, 137
Malibu Seafood, 138
Monte Alban, 139
Paco's Tacos, 140
Panini Garden, 146
Real Food Daily, 140
Snug Harbor, 153
Tacos Por Favor, 153
Tlapazola Grill, 141
26 Beach Café, 141
Ye Olde King's Head, 160

On the Waterfront

Oceanfront elegance at Catch in Casa del Mar

It's the eternal question, asked of every California restaurant writer for decades: Where can we get a really good dinner with a view of the ocean? The answer has typically been: Nowhere! But that old dining-out axiom – great view = bad food – is only true sometimes along the Santa Monica coast. Here are our favorite oceanview restaurants in various categories:

For a lively special occasion
The Lobster
Crowded, convivial and fabulously located on the edge of the Santa Monica Pier, the Lobster also has first-rate seafood. *See page 137.*

To propose marriage
One Pico
This cottagey-Craftsmany dining room in the swank Shutters hotel boasts a beachfront location, great food and smooth service. *See page 139.*

To wow a client
Catch
Spectacular sushi and American seafood are served in a subtly elegant room with grand ocean and beach views. The neighboring lounge has equally good views. *See page 132.*

To take the family
Back on the Beach Café
Good, inexpensive coffee-shop fare is served right on the sand. *See page 144.*

For seafood on paper plates
Malibu Seafood
Order at the counter and take your fish tacos, grilled halibut or fried scallops out on one of the three oceanview terraces. *See page 138.*

A few more choices…
Geoffrey's
27400 Pacific Coast Hwy., Malibu
310.457.1519, geoffreysmalibu.com
Californian. L & D daily, BR Sun. Full bar. $$$$
Famed for its awesome location perched atop the north coast of Malibu, this is a respectable spot for a romantic dinner, with views of the Santa Monica Bay stretching all the way to the pier. Try the prosciutto-wrapped salmon or splurge on the two-pound Maine lobster.

Ocean & Vine
Loews Hotel, 1700 Ocean Ave., Santa Monica
310.576.3180, oceanandvine.com
Californian/American. B, L & D daily, BR Sun. Full bar. $$$$
For a hotel restaurant, Ocean & Vine is as hip as they come: retro lounge chairs, a backlit bar and stellar ocean views. Dinner is pricey, so we prefer cocktails or dessert – or both. Cozy up by the indoor firepit with a pomegranate margarita or vodka-spiked blueberry lemonade, then move on to an oceanfront window seat to indulge in the chocolate blood orange soufflé. Also consider Sunday brunch, when prices are more reasonable, and the view – and food – is just as good.

Paradise Cove Beach Café
28128 Pacific Coast Hwy., Malibu
310.457.2503, paradisecovemalibu.com
American. B, L & D daily. Full bar. $$-$$$
You're paying for the location – right on the sand on one of the loveliest beaches in Malibu – but that doesn't mean the food is bad. It's just not the point. Breakfast is your best bet, and after your coffee and huevos con tortillas you can hit the beach. (Beach parking is $20, but if you eat at the restaurant, it's $3 for four hours.) Lunch is fine, especially the straightforward sandwiches and salads; dinner is classic surf-and-turf, on the overpriced side, but then again, a location like this ain't cheap. Extras include a full bar, a good kids' menu and friendly waiters who are used to dealing with large family groups.

Our Favorite Restaurants

Abode Restaurant & Lounge
1541 Ocean Ave., Santa Monica
310.394.3463, aboderestaurant.com
Modern American. L Mon.-Fri., D nightly, BR
Sat.-Sun. Full bar. $$$-$$$$
This high-end new place in a hidden courtyard
across from the pier is about "sustainable fine
dining," but what exactly does that mean? For
starters, ingredients are either local or procured
sustainably – so cattle are raised on ranches,
not in factories, and produce comes directly
from farmers, not through a distributor. That's
all well and good, but at these prices, the food
better be damn good. And it is. Chef Dominique
Crenn turns out such interesting stuff as cider-
braised pork osso buco with shallot confit and
apple-blackberry compote. The desserts are
fantastic – the rum gelée with pineapple foam
and coconut sorbet is so intriguing and delicious,
we'll forget that it involves that dreaded icon
of foodie trendiness, foam. For brunch, snag a
table on the terra-cotta patio and order the short-
rib hash, one of the best brunch dishes in town:
tender braised meat speckled with diced apples
and turnips, served with fingerling potatoes and
perfectly poached eggs.

Abuelita's Mexican Restaurant
137 S. Topanga Canyon Blvd., Topanga Canyon
310.455.8788, abuelitastopanga.com
Mexican. L & D daily. Full bar. $$
If Topanga's got a hot spot, this is it. Abuelita's
offers up a full slate of Mexican classics,
including enchiladas, tamales and burritos, not
to mention a myriad of specials, from fajitas
to such Topanga-friendly dishes as the soy-
cheese quesadilla and the spinach burrito. The
live music, from hard rock to jazz, is a big draw
every Friday and Saturday night. A friendly,
small-town hangout.

Aunt Kizzy's Back Porch
4325 Glencoe Ave., Marina del Rey
310.578.1005, auntkizzys.com
Southern. L Mon.-Sat., D nightly, BR Sun.
No booze. $$
Hidden in the corner of a nondescript outdoor
mall, Aunt Kizzy's is the only place by the
beach for traditional, down-home soul food:
smothered pork chops, fried chicken, meat loaf
and jambalaya, all served with such essentials
as okra, corn, red beans and collard greens.
The food isn't as good as at places in south L.A.,
Inglewood or points east, but it is comforting and
generous, and the atmosphere is celebratory –
it seems there's always a birthday, and the
whole place regularly breaks out in singing
Stevie Wonder's "Happy Birthday." Best bets
are the mac and cheese, corn muffins, fried
catfish and peach cobbler pie.

Axe
1009 Abbot Kinney Blvd., Venice
310.664.9787, axerestaurant.com
Modern American. D Tues.-Sun.,
BR Sat.-Sun. Beer, sake & wine. $$$-$$$$
Axe doesn't refer to a hatchet, but to the
divine energy and goodwill (it's pronounced
"ah-shay") that you'll presumably receive from
eating its organic fare. The decor is minimalist –
polished concrete floors, white walls – but far
from Zen-like, given that the tables are packed
in like yoga mats at an overbooked studio. The
entrees, like the porterhouse pork chop with
a cider reduction (and little else), tend to be
overpriced, heavy on the organic hype and light
on flavor; the small plates, such as shaved baby
artichokes in lemon dressing or soy-braised
short ribs with chestnuts, are the best.

Beechwood
822 Washington Blvd., Venice
310.448.8884, beechwoodrestaurant.com
Modern American. D nightly (Mon.-Tues. in bar
only). Full bar. $$-$$$
Why every table isn't full every night is a mystery
to us: Beechwood offers as much midcentury-
modern style and quality American-chic food as
any other spot in town, but the prices are lower
and the attitude is nonexistent. And the bar menu
is rich in delicious, generously served dishes
that range from $7 to $15. After struggling and
failing to get a liquor license at their last Venice
restaurant, owner/chefs Brooke Williamson and
Nick Roberts got even with this place, in the
process creating our favorite bar in town. Over
in the more serene dining room, people sit in
deep-brown leather booths (everything is brown
here), enjoying good service and equally good
food: whole roasted artichoke with basil aioli,
grilled baramundi with a ragout of lentils and
haricots verts, and rigatoni with lamb bolognese,
Spanish sheep's-milk cheese and purple basil.
Beechwood suits the "new" Venice perfectly:
artful and stylish, appealing to foodies without
succumbing to pretension.

Bistro of Santa Monica

2301 Santa Monica Blvd., Santa Monica
310.453.5442, bistroofsantamonica.com
Italian. L & D Mon.-Fri., D Sat.-Sun.
Full bar. $$-$$$
If you think old-school neighborhood Italian restaurants only exist in New York City, get over to Bistro of Santa Monica, where regulars are greeted by name as they settle into their favorite window table in the casual, cozy dining room. The food is a hodgepodge of Italian-American hybrids, from hearty red sauces to chicken alla everything. You're better off with such handmade pastas as the chicken ravioli, a real bargain at less than $15, or the seafood classics, like the frutti di mare that's brimming with shellfish in a light tomato sauce. Be sure to stick around for an after-dinner espresso, or grab a martini at the tiny bar to enjoy the pianist or sax player who plays jazz favorites nightly.

BOA Steakhouse

101 Santa Monica Blvd., Santa Monica
310.899.4466, innovativedining.com
Steakhouse. L & D daily, BR Sun. Full bar. $$$$
Step into this sleek Ocean Avenue steakhouse and you might just forget about the droves of shorts-and-sneakers-wearing tourists outside. It's a Hollywood dealmaker setting, from the glass-enclosed wine cellar to the sleek metal bar and mysterious glow of the stoplight-red chandeliers. Some of the food – truffled nachos and Kobe beef corn dogs – can be equally over the top, with price tags to match. But such steakhouse staples as the dry-aged New York strip with garlic mashed potatoes are worth the splurge. Be sure to ask for the worthy housemade steak sauce, J-1, on the side.

Border Grill

1445 4th St., Santa Monica
310.451.1655, bordergrill.com
Mexican. L & D daily, BR Sun. Full bar. $$-$$$
Chef/owners Susan Feniger and Mary Sue Milliken are foodie rock stars in L.A. In the 1980s they were California-cuisine pioneers at their first, shoebox-size restaurant, City, which morphed into the original Border Grill when their love for Latin food became all-consuming (leading to a hit cooking show, *Two Hot Tamales*). Today their empire includes this Border Grill, another in Vegas, and downtown L.A.'s Ciudad. This is where Santa Monica meets for happy hour, to drink aged tequila or designer margaritas and mojitos while noshing on superb appetizers: shrimp ceviche, wild-mushroom quesadillas, chicken panuchos, great guacamole, and plantain empanadas stuffed with black beans, poblano and cotija

Making fresh tortillas at the Border Grill

cheese. The main courses are less rewarding (and a lot more expensive), so the savvy stick to appetizers and drinks, and come early for the happy-hour deals. As befits the food, the setting is vibrantly colorful, cheerfully festive and powerfully noisy.

Brass.-Cap. (Brasserie-Capo)

100 W. Channel Rd. (at PCH), Santa Monica
310.454.4544
French. D nightly $$$-$$$$
Bruce Marder's French bistro has everything you'd hope to find in a bistro: adorable imported chairs, a classic bar lined with shelves of pastis, petite tables topped with white butcher paper and comforting, though not mind-boggling, bistro fare. But for all its simplicity, the prices are higher than one should pay for the French version of pot roast. Still, it's charming, and it's one of the few places in these parts to enjoy a properly poured pastis.

Bravo Cucina

1319 3rd St. Promenade, Santa Monica
310.394.0374, bravocucinaeatlove.com
Italian. L & D daily. Beer & wine. $$
Sometimes even locals need to eat on the Promenade, to make a movie time or meet friends, and this is where they often end up. Unlike most Promenade restaurants, it is neither corporate nor a tourist trap; it's run with enthusiasm by two brothers whose family owns Café Ferrera in New York's Little Italy. This is a convivial place with delicious, straightforward Italian food (calamari fritti, good salads, cappellini with fresh tomato and basil, spaghetti carbonara, scampi with spaghetti), respectable wines by the glass, a kids' menu and, for those who don't want Italian, good burgers.

Brentwood Restaurant & Lounge

148 S. Barrington Ave., Brentwood
310.476.3511, brentwoodrestaurant.com
American. L& D daily. Full bar. $$$$
Yet another one of ubiquitous westside
restaurateur Bruce Marder's success stories,
this is a dark and sexy place, with provocative
art on the walls and black-leatherette booths.
It's a good second- or third-date kind of spot
for well-funded people from this well-funded
neighborhood. The menu offers all-American
comfort foods: shrimp cocktails, Kobe burgers
and fries, chicken pot pie, a $42 New York steak,
mac and cheese and a rosemary-scented apple
pie. There's a popular bar for those who are still
working on that first date.

Café del Rey

4551 Admiralty Way, Marina del Rey
310.823.6395, cafedelreymarina.com
Californian. L Mon.-Fri., D. nightly, BR Sat.-Sun.
Full bar. $$$-$$$$
In a modern space overlooking bobbing boats,
judiciously tanned regulars (boat owners,
business folk, Marina residents) sip cocktails
and dine on oysters, sushi, black spaghetti with
seafood and Alaskan halibut with braised fennel
and baby artichokes. The cooking is appealing
and consistent, though not quite worth the steep
dinnertime tab – but the view counts for a lot
here. We're bigger fans of the place at lunchtime
or, especially, for the excellent weekend prix-fixe
brunch, in which two courses run $22 and three
courses $28, including a glass of champagne or
cider. The bar is a good spot for a nightcap, and
the service is welcoming.

Café Montana

1534 Montana Ave., Santa Monica
310.829.3990
Californian. B, L & D daily. Beer & wine. $$-$$$
It's hard to believe that this longtime Montana
place was once so au courant; now it's mellowed
into a reliable neighborhood bistro, where old
friends run into each other and celebrities are
typically left alone. Breakfast (huevos rancheros,
chicken hash, waffles) is our favorite meal here,
followed by lunchtime salads (try the chicken
bella); dinner is just okay, but the diverse
menu does have something for everyone,
and the prices aren't bad, given this high-rent
neighborhood.

Capo

1810 Ocean Ave., Santa Monica
310.394.5550
Italian. D Tues.-Sat. Full bar. $$$-$$$$
Bruce Marder's restaurants are pricey, and Capo
is no exception. But the luxuriously simple, farm-
fresh fare served in this tiny, romantic, elbow-
to-elbow Italian almost hidden between the
posh Ocean Avenue hotels is worth a special-
occasion investment. Meats are Marder's
strength, so resist the handmade pastas and
dive into the steaks and chops, which are grilled
inside the wood-burning fireplace in the corner of
the dining room. For dessert, stick to the simple,
seasonal offerings, like a fresh-fruit crostata or
creamy panna cotta. The service is excellent, as
well it should be at these prices; the wine list is
good but, again, expensive.

Catch

Hotel Casa del Mar, 1910 Ocean Ave.,
Santa Monica
310.581.5503
Seafood/Modern American. L & D daily.
Full bar. $$$$
Money may be the root of all evil, but it does
allow for such profound pleasures as a meal in
Casa del Mar's dining room. If you can swing
it, stop first for a drink in the adjacent lounge,
where beautiful people soak in a dazzling view of
the bay while lounging in a subtly opulent setting
and sipping $14 cocktails. In the dining room,
high ceilings and crisp white walls lead all eyes
to the floor-to-ceiling windows that bring in the
view. Dark wooden tables are set with gleaming
silver, a serene sushi bar fills the room's center,
and professional waiters surf gracefully through
the room. Chef Michael Reardon's spent a few
years cooking at St. Helena's Tra Vigne and
Santa Barbara's posh Andalusia, and his cuisine
now seems fully realized as the perfect Southern
California fare: a little sushi and seafood crudo
(Italian-style sashimi), a few creative salads
made with things like organic wild arugula and
English peas, and gorgeous but very simple
seafood dishes. Why complicate that piece
of snapper from Thailand when it tastes so
fabulous just sautéed until crisp and placed
next to a "salad" of calamari, cannelli beans
and herbs? Reardon gets the best seafood
he can find and brings out its natural flavors,
but he doesn't show off with foams, essences
and towers of seventeen ingredients. If you
have room for dessert,
get the Meyer
lemon
tart.

Crisp-sautéed snapper from
Thailand with a salad
of calamari, cannelli
beans and tomato
at Catch.

Chaya Venice

110 Navy St. (at Main St.), Venice
310.396.1179, thechaya.com
French/Japanese. L & D daily. Full bar. $$$
For years now, Chaya Venice (along with Hal's) has been command central for Venice's artists and musicians, when they can afford it, and for the movie moguls who can always afford it. The once-pioneering east-meets-west cuisine is now found all over L.A., but we still like coming back to the source for good sushi, seaweed salads, lobster enchiladas, pastas and such French-Japanese hybrids as miso-marinated sea bass with a wasabi-tamari beurre blanc. The bar is a happening spot after a hard day's work, with one of the best happy hours in town.

Chez Jay

1657 Ocean Ave., Santa Monica
310.395.1741
Steakhouse/American. B Sat.-Sun., L Tues.-Fri. D nightly. Full bar. $$-$$$
On this strip of Ocean Avenue – with its upscale hotels and overpriced restaurants – the only place that hasn't changed in 50 years is Chez Jay. An oasis in a sea of gentrification, this tiny shack festooned with Christmas lights still manages to pack in the crowds nightly. The food is fine – not great – but regulars and tourists can't resist its midcentury appeal (the 20th, that is), peanut-shell "carpet" and celebrity-dive cachet. (Warren Beatty and Sean Penn were regulars for many years.) It's also a great place to come for a drink after dinner, when the red-leatherette booths start to empty out.

Chez Mimi

246 26th St., Santa Monica
310.393.0558, chezmimirestaurant.com
French. L Tues.-Sat., D nightly. Full bar. $$$-$$$$
Don't come here with an old flame – it's bound to get you in trouble. Romance oozes out of every candlelit corner: the brick patios, the nooks and crannies, the fireplaces, the obsequious waiters, the overpriced wine and the opulent traditional French food. Culinarily speaking, Charles de Gaulle is still president – meals begin with pâté de foie maison or endive salads, then progress to cassoulet, duck with black-cherry sauce or steak au poivre, and conclude with tarte tatin or chocolate cake. The food doesn't always live up to the setting, and it's pricey, but there are some excellent dishes: the cool vichyssoise, the pâtés, the simple salads (try the mushroom), the succulent roast chicken, the leg of lamb, and the deservedly famous tarte tatin. If only the Eiffel Tower was across the street instead of the Brentwood Country Mart…

Chinois on Main

2709 Main St., Santa Monica
310.392.9025, wolfgangpuck.com
Cal-Asian. L Wed.-Fri., D nightly. $$$-$$$$
It's been 25 years since Wolfgang Puck opened Chinois on Main, and not much has changed. Usually, that's not a good thing, but somehow it works here: the tacky, hot-pink-and-turquoise 1980s decor, those omnipresent Cal-Asian dishes (after all, he did start the craze) and such deserving menu staples as Shanghai lobster in ginger-curry sauce with paper-thin, crispy fried spinach that so mysteriously dissolves on your tongue. The downsides are the noise level, price level and cramped seating, but if you can stick it out, don't miss the desserts, especially the dim sum dessert box and the crème brûlée trio.

Divino

11714 Barrington Ct., Brentwood
310.472.0886
Italian. L & D daily. Beer & wine. $$-$$$
Italian trattorias are as plentiful in Brentwood as Guatemalan nannies, and most of them are good. One of the best, however, is one of the least known: Divino. Tucked in the back of a posh Barrington Court mini-mall, this high-ceilinged space is decorated with old black-and-white family photos of brother/owners Davor and Goran Milic, who hail from the Yugoslav side of the Adriatic, where the cooking is clearly comparable to the Italian side. Seafood is a specialty (wonderful basil-bathed orecchiette with branzino and the daily whitefish specials), as are crisp pizzas, lemony salads, light gnocchi porcini and good gelati.

Drago Ristorante

2628 Wilshire Blvd., Santa Monica
310.828.1585, celestinodrago.com
Italian. L Mon.-Fri., D nightly. Full bar. $$-$$$$
Thirty years ago, when Celestino Drago arrived in L.A. via Sicily, southern Italian cuisine was hardly on anyone's mind. Now he's built a mini Italian empire, comprising two restaurants, a bakery and a catering company. Drago remains his showpiece, one of a dying breed of L.A. restaurants that still draws a crowd dressed to dine. Everything is rich here: the elegant decor, the hearty regional dishes and, judging by the baubles, the clientele. When Celestino is in the kitchen, pretense vanishes as he strolls from table to table, grinning and chatting while guests nibble on handmade pumpkin tortelloni in sage cream and fettuccini with pheasant-morel sauce. Other nights, waiters seem more concerned with regulars than the special-occasion diner. Maybe that's why we recoil at some of the prices ($34 for the veal chop?). After all, this is simple

trattoria fare – handmade and delicious, but not inventive. Avoid the inflated wine list and pick a simpler by-the-glass wine – all the better to enjoy with the $16 venison ragu with fresh cavatelli.

El Texate
316 Pico Blvd., Santa Monica
310.399.1115, eltexate.com
Mexican. B, L & D daily. Full bar. $
To understand why Southern California is such a great place to live, head to this no-frills joint. Here you are, just a few blocks from the Pacific Ocean, eating a terrific Oaxacan meal for less than $12, and it tastes equally good whether you live in a $5 million north-of-Montana château or a rent-controlled south-of-Pico shack. The bar makes a decent margarita on the rocks, and the kitchen turns out barbecued goat tacos on handmade tortillas; hearty fried dumplings (molotes) filled with chorizo and potatoes; wonderful chicken soup with rice and avocado; and a roster of tasty moles. Kind people serve you all this on a shady patio or in a simple, often-empty dining room decorated with intensely colorful Mexican folk art.

The Galley
2442 Main St., Santa Monica
310.452.1934
Steakhouse/American. D nightly. Full bar. $$$
Santa Monica's oldest restaurant/bar has been a local treasure since it opened in 1934. Regulars love the martinis with mermaid toothpicks, steaks, littleneck clams and signature salads with the "secret-recipe" dressing (tastes like a tangy Green Goddess). A nautical decor—indoors and out front – a crooner's jukebox and dim lighting that anyone over 35 can appreciate add to the old-school steakhouse appeal.

Gilbert's El Indio
2526 Pico Blvd., Santa Monica
310.450.8057, gilbertselindio.com
Mexican. B, L & D daily. Full bar. $
Dog-eared photographs of grinning customers are tacked to the walls amid cracked vinyl booths and cramped tables at this family-owned Cal-Mexican that's been serving up simple, honest fare for more than 30 years. Everything about the place is big – the smiles, the noise, the food – except the prices. Can't decide between the chile relleno and the overstuffed burrito? Then order Fernando's Burrito, which is stuffed with a sinfully plump fried cheese relleno and all the fixins for a whopping $6.30. The food isn't fancy, but it's satisfying and refreshingly straightforward. During peak hours you'll have to wait for a table, but you can grab a beer and hang out with the regulars in the parking lot. That's right, the parking lot.

The Golden Bull Bar & Restaurant
170 W. Channel Rd., Santa Monica
310.230.0402
American/steakhouse. D nightly, BR Sun. Full bar. $$
In the 1940s, West Channel Road was a beachy boy's town (see Literary, page 112). The Golden Bull is the only establishment that remains from the era, though you'd hardly identify it as a gay restaurant. The clientele today consists of seniors enjoying the weeknight early-bird specials, sports fans watching TV and sipping martinis, and couples dining on steak, prime rib and halibut in the fireplace-lit bar room. The food is fine, nothing special, but the prices are eminently reasonable, and we love the old Santa Monica vibe.

Hakata Sushi & Sports Bar
2830 Wilshire Blvd., Santa Monica
310.828.8404
Japanese. L & D daily. Full bar. $$
Don't run when you spot the plasma TVs and beer ads hanging overhead at this quirky hybrid sushi restaurant and sports bar. Locals in the know come for sushi that's always fresh, simply prepared and reasonably priced. Steer clear of the drab teriyaki and combo plates offered in the main dining room. Instead, grab a seat at the sushi bar and get to know the chef – if you're lucky he might offer you a bonus treat, like cucumbers with salmon or a nibble of the fish he's slicing. Riki's lobster roll, stuffed with rich tempura-fried lobster and drizzled with a sweet, creamy sauce, might just be the best "unofficial" dessert in town.

Hama Sushi

213 Windward Ave., Venice
310.396.8783, hamasushi.com
Japanese/sushi. D nightly. Beer & wine.
$$$
One of the nation's first sushi restaurants, Hama has been hot since 1979, combining a flip-flops-friendly atmosphere with fresh, carefully prepared sushi, sashimi and cooked Japanese classics: spicy tuna shiso, seaweed salad, popcorn shrimp, steamed

The tropical-nautical bar at Ivy at the Shore

monkfish liver, grilled yellowtail collar with ponzu, and much more. The rolls are inventive, the chefs are exuberant, the surf videos are fun, and the Asahi and sake flow freely (this is not a place for a quiet conversation). If you stay until closing, you'll get to hear the chefs belt out "Hotel California," perhaps accompanied by a few well-served patrons. A must-visit in Venice.

Il Ristorante di Giorgio Baldi

114 W. Channel Rd., Santa Monica
310.573.1660, giorgiobaldi.com
Italian. D Tues.-Sun. Beer & wine. $$$-$$$$
While Celestino Drago was introducing the westside to southern Italian cuisine, Giorgio Baldi was busy cooking northern Italian specialties for a devoted and moneyed crowd of Santa Monica Canyon locals. Risotto specials are cooked perfectly al dente, and Tuscan classics such as tonno e fagioli (white beans with tuna) are authentically delicious. But with "real" Italian no longer a novelty, the prices seem high for such cozy, home-style fare. Unless you've got a celebrity-size wallet, you're better off picking up one of Baldi's excellent jarred tomato sauces at a local grocery store for a more reasonably priced weeknight meal.

Inn of the Seventh Ray

128 Old Topanga Canyon Rd., Topanga
310.455.1311, innoftheseventhray.com
American/vegetarian. L Mon.-Sat., D nightly, BR Sun. Beer & wine. $$$-$$$$
Although it's tempting to make fun of this 1970s-era hippie landmark, the delicious food is no joke. This beautiful, luxurious haven is a popular wedding location, thanks to its gardens, terraces, gazebos and fountains. Mind you, it does have a New Age gift shop, and the web site expresses the wish that diners "partake of the angelic vibrations of the violet ray." To help you discover those vibrations is a diverse menu of raw food (summer-squash lasagna), vegetarian dishes (agave-glazed vegan duck) and carnivore pleasers (naturally raised filet mignon with a mirepoix of asparagus). The Sunday brunch, though not cheap, is peaceful and lovely.

Ivy at the Shore

1535 Ocean Ave., Santa Monica
310.393.3113
American/Creole. L & D daily. Full bar. $$$$
Is that Rob Lowe over there? Having lunch with Tom Petty? Nah… but it certainly looks like them. In fact, most everyone here looks either famous or rich or both. And you pretty much need to be rolling in it to hang out at the Ivy, given the $20 individual pizzas and $29 lunch entrees. If eaten in a strip mall in Arcadia, the food would be worth half the price, but you're paying for a lot more than the Gulf shrimp on your pasta – you're buying the Ocean Avenue location, the almost kitschy tropical decor (it predates Tommy Bahama) and the California-dreamin' people-watching: celebrities, their agents and producers, and the tourists who feed the machine. The Key lime pie is more than worth the investment.

JiRaffe

502 Santa Monica Blvd., Santa Monica
310.917.6671, jirafferestaurant.com
Californian/French. D nightly. Full bar. $$$-$$$$
If there's one restaurant in Santa Monica that epitomizes the California bistro, it's JiRaffe, where elegant chandeliers hang above cozy tables, friendly waiters dole out first-rate service, and creative California-French cuisine is served at fair prices. Chef/owner Raphael Lunetta has added a touch of whimsy to the menu since his former partner Josiah Citrin left to open the more formal Mélisse down the street. Seafood is usually outstanding, including pancetta-wrapped tiger shrimp with lemon-harissa nage or crispy salmon with braised fennel and parsnip purée. Bargain hunters come on Monday for the $35 bistro night, a three-course set menu that's viewable online a few days beforehand. Monday Night Football or chocolate croquettes with butterscotch pudding? We'll take the croquettes.

Joe's Restaurant

1023 Abbot Kinney Blvd., Venice
310.399.5811, joesrestaurant.com
Modern American. L Tues.-Fri., D Tues.-Sun.,
BR Sat.-Sun. Beer & wine. $$$-$$$$
Before Abbot Kinney was the coolest place in
L.A., Joe Miller took a gamble and opened a
tiny restaurant here. His first-rate cooking and
the warmth of his handsome little place brought
success; he then expanded into a neighboring
space and watched Abbot Kinney gentrify
around him. Now this still-young man is a Venice
oldtimer, respected for the continuing excellence
of his food, which is served with skill in a clean-
lined, California-elegant bistro. The best deal
in town is lunch at Joe's, where for $13 to $16
you get either "soup of today" or a salad with
greens, roasted squash, caramelized walnuts
and a pomegranate vinaigrette, followed by such
main courses as grilled shrimp on saffron risotto
or roasted prime sirloin with smashed potatoes,
snap peas, carrots and a brown-butter balsamic
vinaigrette. Dinner will cost you quite a bit more,
but you won't be sorry.

Josie

2424 Pico Blvd., Santa Monica
310.581.9888, josierestaurant.com
Modern American. D nightly. Full bar. $$$-$$$$
Chef/owner Josie Le Balch has a gift for
making the inventive comfort food you dream
of whipping up at home – if only you were
a talented chef with decades of experience
and a professional kitchen at your fingertips
(learning the ropes from your father, a French
chef, wouldn't hurt either). Don't expect white-
glove service – this is a classic bistro, from the
stone hearth and simple decor to the friendly
but not exactly doting servers. Everyone these
days pays at least lip service to the notion
of farm-fresh California cuisine, but here it's
the real thing – ingredients are simple, local
and excellent, and they're thoughtfully paired:
herbed goat cheese tart with roasted beets,
grapefruit and wild arugula; skillet-cooked trout
with an asparagus and lemongrass nage; Key
lime cheesecake with brown-butter crust and
baked blueberries. It's all delicious. To get the
most out of your dollar, come for Farmer's
Market Wednesdays, when fresh pickings from
that morning's market are put to work in a $32
prix-fixe meal. (On normal evenings, dinner can
get pricey.) Meat eaters, take note: Josie spent
her formative years at Saddle Peak Lodge, so
you'll find plenty to sink your teeth into, from
Moroccan-style braised short ribs to a buffalo
burger with foie gras on brioche. The desserts
from Le Balch's longtime pastry chef Jonna
Jensen – dark-chocolate bread pudding with

vanilla bean ice cream and chocolate sauce,
warm seasonal tarts and cobblers –
are addictive, and best shared.

Katsuya

11777 San Vicente Blvd., Brentwood
310.207.8744, sbeen.com/katsuya
Japanese. L & D daily. Full bar. $$$$
This upscale, always-packed, almost manic
place is very *Lost in Translation* – lots of neon,
purple and white leather, all of it created by
famed French designer Philippe Starck. The
menu, from sushi chef Katsuya Uechi, who also
owns Sushi Katsu-ya in Studio City and Encino,
includes a wide array of inventive, meticulously
prepared cold and hot items, including seaweed
salad, scallops with kiwi in yuzu vinaigrette,
baked black cod, and very good sushi rolls.
There's also a robata bar, where chefs
grill delectable skewers of shrimp, chicken
meatballs, vegetables and steak; the cocktail bar
turns out fancy cocktails for the beautiful people.
Who knew Brentwood could be this happening?

La Botte

620 Santa Monica Blvd., Santa Monica
310.576.3072, labottesantamonica.com
Italian. L Mon.-Fri., D nightly. Full bar. $$$-$$$$
When you see the floor-to-ceiling wine racks
filled with hundreds of bottles, you might think
you're dining in a cozy private wine cellar.
Unfortunately, the wine prices befit a private
cellar as well, with only a handful under
$60, most running $150 and up. Still, it's
worth seeking out this Italian for hard-to-find
ingredients (including plenty of offal) and chef
Antonio Mure's dishes from the Veneto region:
duck prosciutto, incredible braised oxtail, fried
sweetbreads and pillowy, meltingly tender
handmade ravioli. Expensive, yes, but worth it if
you're a connoisseur of serious Italian cooking.

Lares

2909 Pico Blvd., Santa Monica
310.829.4559
Mexican. B, L & D daily. Full bar. $-$$
For 40 years, the Lares family has been
welcoming diners to their two dining rooms –
downstairs is family oriented, well lit and
homey, and upstairs is for such adult pleasures
as drinking margaritas, listening raptly to the
flamenco guitar of Gino D'Auri (he's been
performing here for years) and enjoying basic
southern Mexican dishes: chiles rellenos, steak
picado, carnitas en chile verde, even lengua
(tongue) en mole. The display of colorful folk-art
paintings by local artists (some are for sale) is
worth seeing even if you aren't hungry.

La Serenata de Garibaldi

1416 4th St., Santa Monica
310.204.5360, laserenataonline.com
Mexican/seafood. B Sat.-Sun., L & D daily.
Full bar. $$-$$$
A branch of the East L.A. foodie mecca, La Serenata occupies a colorful, candlelit storefront across the street from that other stylish Mexican, the Border Grill. Seafood is the point of this place, and you're crazy if you get anything else – shrimp cocktails, a seafood quesadilla appetizer, fisherman's soup, delicious fish enchiladas in salsa verde and seasonal fresh fish in sublime sauces: mojo de ajo (garlic), campeche (fresh spinach), salsa verde (tomatillo) and more. And the shrimp with butter, garlic and parsley is decadence defined. The margaritas are good, but the service can be a problem. After a margarita and a seafood quesadilla, however, you'll find yourself more forgiving.

Le Petit Café

2842 Colorado Ave., Santa Monica
310.829.6792
French. L Mon.-Fri, D Mon.-Sat. Beer & wine. $$
So many restaurants claim to be a neighborhood bistro these days, but it's a shock to actually find one. Le Petit Café is the real deal, with chalkboard-toting waiters, tiny bistro tables and honest bistro fare at great prices. During lunch it draws a business crowd from nearby studios; as evening rolls around the locals take over, with couples sharing plates of escargots and friends lingering long after their duck confit and steak au poivre have been cleared. Many entrees come with standard sides that have seen better days, but everything else is so good that no one seems to mind.

Lilly's French Café

1031 Abbot Kinney Blvd., Venice
310.314.0004
French. L Mon.-Sat., D nightly, BR Sun.
Beer & wine. $$-$$$
In a charming old house in the heart of Abbot Kinney lies a French café that combines Venice style with traditional bistro cooking. Terrine de canard, salade frisée aux lardons, moules frites, entrecôte grillée, soufflé au chocolat chaud – it's all here, just like at your favorite Parisian bistro, at reasonable prices in a convivial setting. The cooking isn't dazzling, just consistent and comforting, and the service is cheerful. Lilly's is also a great place to have a private party. And the $12 brunch specials are a total bargain.

Literati II

12081 Wilshire Blvd., West L.A.
310.479.3400, literati2.com
Modern American. L Mon.-Fri., D Mon.-Sat., BR Sat.-Sun. Full bar. $$$
An offshoot of Literati, a coffeehouse next door, this more ambitious restaurant showcases the sort of rustic Cal-Med fare that put Campanile on the national culinary map – which makes sense, because chef Chris Kidder was Campanile's longtime chef de cuisine, and pastry chef Kimberly Sklar (Kidder's wife) made the desserts at A.O.C. The farmer's-market-based menu changes every day, but you can usually count on some core dishes, including a delicious fritto misto of seasonal vegetables and a hefty and fantastic wood-grilled burger and steak frites. Kidder usually has an appetizer involving the ultra-fashionable burrata, perhaps paired with prosciutto, fresh plums and nectarines, and subtly spicy undressed arugula – really, a meal unto itself. All the appetizers, in fact, are hearty and best to share, as are Sklar's superb desserts – her showpiece, the amazing seven-layer chocolate cake called Carpe Diem, will satisfy four. In fact, if you order right – sharing dishes and a bottle of wine – you can eat very well at a very fair price, either on the lovely walled patio or in the reading-room-themed dining room.

The Lobster has a prime oceanview spot next to the Santa Monica Pier.

The Lobster

1602 Ocean Ave., Santa Monica
310.458.9294, thelobster.com
American/seafood. L & D daily. Full bar. $$$-$$$$
It has every right to be a tourist trap, but Allyson Thurber's pierside seafood restaurant is anything but. Always packed and always noisy, the modern concrete-and-glass space gives diners stellar views of the sea, sky and Ferris wheel – as well as a daily-changing roster of carefully prepared, high-quality fish and shellfish meals. Thurber's cooking is cosmopolitan without being

pretentious. So fat scallops may be seared and served with a simple trio of sides (grilled tomatoes, spinach and grilled asparagus); and black bass may be given Asian flair with sesame seeds, grilled shiitake mushrooms and a ginger-wasabi sauce. The namesake steamed Maine lobster will cost you, but if you've got the simoleons, it's worth it. Don't even think of coming without a reservation, and even then, you may have to wait a bit – but the bar makes good cocktails for such an occasion.

Locanda Portofino

1110 Montana Ave., Santa Monica
310.394.2070, locandaportofino.com
Italian. L Tues.-Sat., D nightly. Beer & wine. $$$
Despite its strip-mall location, Locanda Portofino is the kind of intimate, authentic trattoria you dream of finding in your own backyard: easy to get to, with seductive, garlicky odors wafting through the room and cute, heavily accented waiters just off the boat from Italy. And the food lives up to the promise, from a hearty pasta arrabbiata, with just enough zing, to a handcut grilled swordfish of a quality that's hard to find these days (the chef is so picky about the cuts of fish and meat that if the day's offerings don't meet his standards, he'll take it off the menu). The risotti and pasta are appealing, and the filet mignon is superb. It's a little place, so reservations are recommended.

Malibu Seafood

25653 Pacific Coast Hwy., Malibu
310.456.3430, malibuseafood.com
American/seafood. L & D daily.
No booze (BYOB). $
This PCH fish market has some of the best seafood on the beach, at a fraction of the prices charged at the white-tablecloth places – which is why there's usually a line out the door. You order at the counter and take your chow up to a table on the three-level outdoor patio, which has, by

There's always a crowd outside Malibu Seafood.

the way, devastating ocean views (it's often chilly, so bring a jacket). The combination crab-and-shrimp Louie (it's not on the menu – you have to ask for it) is delicious; also good are the seafood tacos, fried scallops, ahi burger and fresh grilled snapper, sea bass, swordfish and ahi. The chowder is respectable, the sourdough bread is hot, and did we mention the views? Bring a bottle of wine and make it a feast.

Mélisse

1104 Wilshire Blvd., Santa Monica
310.395.0881, melisse.com
French. D Tues.-Sat. Full bar. $$$$
In 1999, when chef/owner Josiah Citrin departed JiRaffe, the Cal-French bistro he founded with Raphael Lunetta, he left some of the Cal behind – and that's not a bad thing. Maybe it's the romantic, dimly lit space, the formal tables set with French cutlery, the occasionally haughty wait staff or the cheese cart (yes, an actual cheese cart) brimming with oozing, stinking delicacies. Whatever the reason, Mélisse is luxuriously French, with just a bit of California flair. The dry-aged côte de boeuf (for two) with potato-leek torte, wild mushrooms and braised lettuce deserves its status as a menu classic, but with so many inspired seasonal choices, it's hard to resist the four-course tasting menu. The parade of dishes might include chestnut soup with celery-apple hash and burrata cheese; sole gnocchi with horn mushrooms, spinach and truffle jus; braised veal cheeks with salsify; and a brown-butter peach tart with lemon verbena ice cream. At $95 without wine, it's an indulgence, but one you're not likely to forget.

Michael's Restaurant

1147 3rd St., Santa Monica
310.451.0843, michaelssantamonica.com
Californian. L Mon.-Fri., D Mon.-Sat.
Full bar. $$$$
In 1979, at the ripe old age of 25, chef/owner Michael McCarty opened his namesake restaurant, known for its patios, its still-amazing art collection, its wine list and its California cuisine. Goat cheese, arugula and caramelized onions were the new kids in town, and cutting-edge California restaurants like Michael's made them wildly popular. It still seems caught in that era (or maybe the chef is just tired), dishing up food that's lacking in modern flair for the price. The $25 filet mignon sandwich with caramelized onions and homemade potato chips at lunch morphs into an uninspired $42 New York steak with bordelaise sauce and pommes frites by nightfall. For Michael's to weather another decade, perhaps it's time for a little nip and tuck.

Monte Alban

11927 Santa Monica Blvd., West L.A.
310.444.7736
Mexican/Oaxacan. B, L & D daily. Beer & wine. $
A devoted following from miles around frequents
this dirt-cheap strip-mall café. Some swear
by the breakfasts – cinnamon-infused coffee,
huevos a la Mexicana – but most come for
dinner to revel in the many mole dishes (try the
mole negro tamale), guacamole, empanadas
de huitlachoche and frijoladas, a yummy mix
of beans, chicken and mole sauce. Don't limit
yourself to the black mole, even though it's
terrific – the kitchen also makes fine yellow,
green, red and colorado moles.

Musha

424 Wilshire Blvd., Santa Monica
310.576.6330
Japanese. D nightly. Beer & wine. $$
The newest of the bunch and certainly the most
fun, Musha has an eclectic menu that includes
sushi and lots of delicious and unusual cooked
dishes for those with raw-fish phobias. Don't-
miss choices include the slow-cooked pork belly,
spicy fried rice, spicy tuna dip with rice crackers,
and seared ahi salad. Crowded tables + harried
waitresses = hell, right? No: Just a leisurely
dinner with patient fellow patrons, who are
happy to sip Asahis or sakes and engage in the
art of conversation. Bring friends, and join in the
warmth of the central communal table – this is a
place to try lots of dishes family-style. Note that
they make a big fuss if it's your birthday.

One Pico

Shutters on the Beach, 1 Pico Blvd.,
Santa Monica
310.587.1717, shuttersonthebeach.com
Modern American. L & D daily. Full bar. $$$$
Hotel dining rooms used to be considered death.
But in the red-hot hotels in Santa Monica, hotel
dining (and drinking) is fashionable and, well,
fun. Echoing the cottage-Craftsman aesthetic of
this swank beachfront hotel, the dining room has
wood floors and high, wood-beamed ceilings,
but the look is beachy-light, not Craftsman-
dark. The cooking suits the sand and sea that
shimmer just beyond the vast windows: baby
greens with apples, almonds and goat cheese;
pearl pasta with English peas and shrimp; a
wonderful grilled vegetable tarte tatin; elegant
preparations of wild salmon, Alaskan halibut,
and Kobe flat-iron steak; and desserts that are
worth the calories and the cost – it's all pricey,
especially the wines, but real estate like this
doesn't come cheap.

Nobu Malibu

3835 Cross Creek Rd., Malibu
310.317.9140, nobumatsuhisa.com
Japanese. D nightly. Full bar. $$$$
It's Disneyland Malibu here – a perfectly
orchestrated miniature version of clichéed
Malibu life. Waiters expertly deliver their patter
(like the Jungle Cruise spiels without the hokey
jokes), guiding diners to the most popular
dishes. Busboys dance through the two simple,
compact rooms, whisking soiled plates away the
moment diners have set their chopsticks down.
Celebrities (Cindy Crawford, David Duchovny,
Courtney Cox, Pat Riley) are nearly always
present, dressed down and looking as if they're
just trying to have a normal dinner out, even
though they've chosen the most celebrity-filled
restaurant in L.A. to hide in. Here's a typical
Sunday-night scene: Several large tables hold
families (inspiring wonder at the number of
parents who will spend $40 to feed an 8-year-
old); in the center room, Kelsey Grammar is
strategically seated at a center table; in the
corner, two 20ish blond babes are dining with a
unshaven stud in a baseball cap and flip-flops,
but all three are so intensely focused on their
Blackberries that none of them has spoken for 20
minutes; and in the bathroom, two 40ish blond
gals loudly discuss whether one of them should
have cheek implants instead of a planned eye
job. Really, it's just too good to be true. As for the
food, it's perfectly fine – delectable black cod in
miso, basic sushi, tasty but soggy rock-shrimp
tempura, yellowtail sashimi with jalapeno – but
it has none of the excitement that the original
Matsuhisa had back in the day. Chef Matsuhisa
now has an empire of restaurants from Dallas
to London. He's got the formula down, and it's a
formula that works just fine for the Malibu locals
who've made Nobu their canteen.

Osteria Latini

11712 San Vicente Blvd., Brentwood
310.826.9222, osterialatini.com
Italian. L Mon.-Fri., D nightly. Beer & wine. $$-$$$
Of the many Italians in Brentwood, this is one
of the homiest, friendliest and most reasonably
priced. Trieste native Paolo Pasio has the
warmth required of a good trattoria owner, his
dining room is inviting and often crowded, and his
kitchen turns out very fine Italian comfort food:
beet salad, burrata with red and yellow tomatoes,
buttery whole roasted branzino, delicious lobster
risotto, excellent pastas. Our only complaints are
the weak desserts and the excessive number of
daily specials recited, which are impossible for
most diners to remember.

Paco's Tacos

4141 S Centinela Ave., West L.A.
310.391.9616
Mexican. L & D daily. Full bar. $
If you grew up in Southern California, this is the sort of restaurant you dreamt of when you went away to college. It boasts every Mexican-restaurant cliché imaginable: paintings of hokey Mexican scenes, a logo with a sombrero-wearing hombre, rustic ranchero-style leather chairs and a costumed señora making tortillas on a griddle – plus walls crammed with antlers, armor and decorations for St. Patrick's Day, Halloween and every holiday in between. As for the food, it's Cal-Mex cuisine in its best gut-busting form: outstanding carne asada, perfect fresh tortillas, a huge tostada and gooey, cheesy enchiladas with rice and beans, the comfort food of native Angelenos. Add low prices and an excellent cadillac margarita, and you'll understand why there's often a wait.

Pecorino Restaurant

11604 San Vicente Blvd., Brentwood
310.571.3800, pecorinorestaurant.com
Italian. L Mon.-Fri., D nightly. Beer & wine.
$$-$$$$
Step inside Pecorino, and you'll be greeted by a gush of warmth – brick walls, cozy bistro tables, rustic chandeliers – and exuberant host Mario Sabatini. As Sabatini hops around the small dining room doting on guests, his twin brother Raffaele cooks up dishes from their hometown of Abruzzo and beyond. The most basic pastas, such as cacao e pepe (spaghetti with pecorino, parmesan and pepper), are so satisfying you'll wonder what else they're sneaking into the bowl. When paired with an appetizer, such as house-cured carpaccio with arugula and percorino, dinner costs about the same ($30) as one meat entree. And you'll still have room for the amaretto-soaked tiramisu (it's good here, really).

Piccolo

5 Dudley Ave., Venice
310.314.3222, piccolovenice.com
Italian. D nightly. Beer & wine. $$$
Just off the Venice Boardwalk, this teeny-tiny place serves appealing Italian fare with a healthy shot of fresh sea air. The owners, chef and manager, all native Italians who also own La Botte in Santa Monica, are charming, the vibe is relaxed and romantic, and the northern Italian food is delish. Consider splurging on the five-course seasonal tasting menu, which is prepared for the entire table. No reservations, so it's best to go on weeknights to avoid a long wait.

Pizzicotto

11758 San Vicente Blvd., Brentwood
310.442.7188
Italian. L Mon.-Sat., D nightly. Beer & wine. $$
There's always a crowd at this Brentwood trattoria, so don't even think of coming without a reservation. The ceilings are high, the noise level is considerable (request an upstairs table if you want quiet) and everybody looks happy, tucking into bruschetta, panini, crisp-crusted pizzas, risotto with wild mushrooms, and the irresistible pesce cuocopazzo, fresh whitefish with a horseradish-pistachio crust and a sauce of white wine, garlic, lemon and fresh tomatoes. Service is efficient, but the owner is intense and not always welcoming – nonetheless, the crowds keep coming, drawn by the very good cooking at reasonable prices.

Primitivo Wine Bistro

1025 Abbot Kinney Blvd., Venice
310.396.5353, primitivowinebistro.com
Mediterranean. L & D Mon.-Fri., D nightly.
Beer & wine. $$
Is it a set design or a tapas bar? You be the judge. To find out, you'll have to score a small wooden table in the high-ceilinged space that's filled with columns, old stained-glass church windows, acres of linen drapes and lots of beautiful Venice folk. The by-the-glass collection of wines (divided into "old world" and "new world") is extensive and interesting, if on the costly side, and the food runs to small plates designed to share and to go well with wine. They're labeled tapas, but many are actually just small-size entrees: asparagus risotto with lemon and parmesan; paella; roasted salmon with couscous. Tapas or not, they're delicious, and those that are true tapas – marinated olives, cheeses, a platter of cured meats and olives – are satisfying.

Real Food Daily

514 Santa Monica Blvd., Santa Monica
310.451.7544, realfood.com
American/vegetarian. L & D daily. No booze. $-$$
For fifteen years, chef/owner Ann Gentry has been serving up enticing meat-free and dairy-free fare to westside vegans, vegetarians and plain old vegetable lovers in her casual café. Seasonal vegetables in wasabi vinaigrette, Yin Yang veggie salad with peanut-sesame dressing and a chunky miso soup are fresh and zippy. Avoid the sandwiches that try too hard to mimic their meat counterparts, such as the faux reuben and mock club. We opt for the Ciao Bella instead, a dish of roasted veggies with pesto on hemp bread. And we pass on the tofu cheesecake.

Shrimp enchiladas with two sauces at Tlapazola Grill

Rustic Canyon Wine Bar & Seasonal Kitchen

1119 Wilshire Blvd., Santa Monica
310.393.7050, rusticcanyonwinebar.com
Modern American. D nightly. Beer & wine. $$-$$$
The name is a bit pretentious – the restaurant is not located in Rustic Canyon, and Seasonal Kitchen is a little much – but we forgave and forgot the minute we tasted the burger. Made with Meyer beef, Niman Ranch bacon, wild greens, a brioche bun and either Point Reyes blue cheese or sharp Tillamook cheddar, it rivals the one at Father's Office. The rest of the food served in this high-ceilinged, candlelit room is excellent, too: a perfect Caesar, wild snapper ceviche and a fabulous roast chicken with caramelized baby onions. Dessert is a disappoinment – none (at least at this writing) is worth the calories. As for the wine, this is a wine bar, so you can expect pricey, small-producer varieties.

17th Street Café

1610 Montana Ave., Santa Monica
310.453.2771, montanaave.com/17thstreet/
Californian/American. B, L & D daily.
Beer & wine. $$-$$$
This charming, low-key café is where you go when you don't want to be seen. So everyone who doesn't want to be seen is seen here. Whatever. The food is consistently good – our all-time favorite is the Chinese grilled-chicken salad, but others swear by the grilled-vegetable tostada, the Thai pasta or the stir-fries. And everyone loves the sweet-potato fries.

Three on Fourth

1432-A 4th St., Santa Monica
310.395.6765, 3onfourth.com
International. L & D daily. Beer, wine & sake.
$$-$$$
Wine, beer, sake and… family friendly? Well, sort of – families come here, and maybe you can get your kids to eat sautéed gai lan. You'll probably have better luck with the addictive sweet-potato fries with garlic aioli. The latest in the seemingly endless supply of modern tapas bars, Three on Fourth has an ambitious menu of American, European and Asian small plates. The mod shotgun space is so very New York, with simple wood tables lining one wall and leather booths along the other. But the prices aren't quite so simple: With small plates topping out at $18, the dinner bill can add up quickly. The kids don't mind – they're too busy picking the wild boar bacon, arugula and gouda off their Three's Big Burger.

Tlapazola Grill

11676 Gateway, West L.A.
310.477.1577, tlapazolagrill.com
4059 Lincoln Blvd., Marina del Rey
310.822.7561
Mexican. L Tues.-Sat., D nightly.
Beer & wine. $-$$
Some Mexican food lovers disparage this place for not being authentic Oaxacan. But who cares how authentic the food is when it's this delicious? Celerino and Samuel Cruz started out with a small Oaxacan café; later, after working in such fashionable kitchens as 72 Market and Rockenwagner, they opened this place, which is more gracious than its just-south-of-Brentwood strip-mall setting suggests. Theirs is a hybrid cuisine, combining Oaxacan staples (chicken in a mole negro) with Mexican classics (carnitas with rice and black beans) and a California approach to fresh vegetables, seafood, sauces and presentation. So a shrimp-and-vegetable enchilada boasts a vividly colorful julienne of zucchini, carrots and squash and has plenty of grilled shrimp and a delicious tomatillo sauce. We're happy that the Cruzes don't feel chained to the past, and we're grateful for the cooking, the modest prices, the quality wines and the solicitous service. The cozy new offshoot on Lincoln has equally good food and service.

26 Beach Café

3100 Washington Blvd., Venice
310.823.7526
American. B, L & D daily. Full bar. $-$$$
Okay, so it's not really at the beach, though it used to be. But with food this good, at prices this reasonable, who cares? You can splurge on a somewhat expensive strip steak or wild salmon dish, but most regulars come for the very good burgers (featuring housemade buns), the burger variations (salmon, turkey, veggie), the pesto chicken sandwich and the excellent entree salads, from ceviche tostada to ginger-infused salmon with asparagus, mushrooms, greens and soy dressing. Breakfasts are also good, especially the famed french toast and the egg-and-pasta scrambles. And if they have the cheesecake, get it. The setting is flea-market cute (with a fetching covered garden), the vibe is casual, and it's usually not hard to get a table.

The Queen of Brentwood's Little Tuscany

Maureen Vincenti was one of the first modern restaurateurs to open an Italian restaurant in Brentwood, and now there are so many that it's a regular Little Tuscany. She and her husband, Mauro, owned Rex, the 1980s Italian powerhouse in downtown L.A.; she opened Vincenti as a sort of tribute to Mauro after he died, and it quickly became one of the finest Italian restaurants in the west. These days Maureen lives across the street from Vincenti and walks to work.

How did you get into the restaurant business?
Through my husband, Mauro. I was in law school when I met him, and he asked me to work at his ice cream factory for two weeks. I stayed for four years.

What brought you to Brentwood?
We were going to be leaving downtown anyway, because our lease was almost up. When Mauro got bored, which was often, he got the urge to open a new restaurant. So we started looking over here, but we weren't sure. Then he passed away, the Rex lease was up, and I jumped on this. I wanted to open something in his honor, and I love the neighborhood and the people, so it seemed like the right thing to do.

Why have so many Italian restaurants congregated in Brentwood?
I have no idea! When we moved in ten years ago, it was just us and Toscana. Then all of a sudden it was a boom. It kind of freaked me out at one point – I kept thinking it would be nice for a French bistro to move in, but no, it was more and more Italians.

What's your favorite Italian dish?
I'm in love with pasta. Anything pasta. I could say I love fish, because it's good for me, and I do love it, but really, it's pasta. Anytime. All the time.

Valentino
3115 Pico Blvd., Santa Monica
310.829.4313, pieroselvaggio.com
Italian. L Fri., D Mon.-Sat. Full bar. $$$$
It pains us to say this, because we have been longtime fans of this groundbreaking Italian restaurant and have celebrated many an anniversary here… but unless you have a foolproof system for printing $100 bills in your basement, Valentino just isn't worth the investment. Wait, we'll amend that – Valentino is worth a visit if you're a serious wine lover who knows how to find good buys in a huge, lovingly maintained list, because owner Piero Selvaggio has spent a lifetime building just such a collection of wines, some of which are quite reasonably priced, given their age and rarity. Otherwise, we'd rather eat at Vincenti. It's not that there's anything wrong with Valentino – the silver and service are impeccable, the atmosphere exudes self-satisfied wealth, and the kitchen is accomplished, turning out such delicacies as truffle-topped risotto, agnolotti filled with braised Sonoma lamb, and a garlic-rubbed veal chop served over wilted wild greens. It's all good, but it's all a bit dull and stuffy, and at well over $100 a head for dinner with wine (a lot more if you go nuts on the wine), it just doesn't light our fire.

Vincenti Ristorante
11920 San Vicente Blvd., Brentwood
310.207.0127, vincentiristorante.com
Italian. L Fri., D Mon.-Sat. Full bar. $$$$
Can one northern Italian in L.A. really be all that different than the rest? Yes it can. Owner Maureen Vincenti greets visitors at the door with cheek kisses and a contagious laugh. Inside are the obligatory wood-burning oven, racks of Italian wine and tiramisu (skip it, by the way). Then you step inside the elegant dining room, with its marble counters and slick leather banquettes, and it's clear this isn't your average homespun trattoria. Chef Nicola Mastronardi turns out gutsy cuisine, such as osso buco tortelloni with wild mushroom sauce and sliced steak with herb ravioli, endive and green peppercorn sauce. Don't miss the housemade porchetta, spit-roasted until it's a perfectly charred, juicy hunk of pure pork bliss. For dessert, avoid anything that sounds like a stateside Italian standard and try one of Mastronardi's creations: a pillowy ricotta and pear budino or a deconstructed napoleon with hazelnut and caramel creams. With such delectable fare – and Maureen doting on each guest – it's easy to forget that all good fun must come to an end. Then the check arrives: We never said a divine dinner won't cost you. But Vincenti is one Italian that's worth the price.

Violet

3221 Pico Blvd., Santa Monica
310.453.9113, violetrestaurant.com
Modern American. L Tues.-Fri., D Tues.-Sun.
Beer & wine. $$-$$$
The hippest joint in the newly hip east Pico
restaurant row, Violet plays on the edge of the
cutting edge (i.e., a host with spiky hair and
an astonishing number of tattoos) but offers
enough comfort and value to attract respectable-
looking older diners. The concept is all the
rage: reasonably priced, small tasting plates to
accompany glasses of wine. We wish some of
the dishes were a little better, but there's plenty
of good eating; try the braised short ribs and the
salmon-and-rock-shrimp cassoulet. Best of all
are the deals – Sunday is a three-course menu
with a "bottomless" glass of wine for $35, and on
weeknights seven dishes are priced at just $7 for
orders placed before 7 p.m.

Vittorio's

16646 Marquez Ave., Pacific Palisades
310.459.3755
Italian. D Tues.-Sun. Beer & wine. $$-$$$
Vittorio's has the best Italian food in the
Palisades. Period. The chicken Parmigiana is to
die for, and the second you sit down, a server
delivers a heaping plate of the irresistible mini-
rolls, drizzled in olive oil and lots of garlic. Also
exceptional is the cheesy, New York–style pizza.
The tables have red-checked cloths, and the
service is friendly and familiar.

Wabi-Sabi

1635 Abbot Kinney Blvd., Venice
310.314.2229,
Japanese/Asian. D nightly. Beer & wine. $$$
This typically Venice place isn't the cheapest
sushi joint in town, but it's one of our favorites,
thanks to its creativity and fun vibe. Lining one
wall of this impossibly narrow storefront is a sushi
bar, with tables for two lining the other wall; larger
groups get to sit in the open-air atrium in back.
Everyone eats the same good sushi, sashimi
and Asian-fusion cooked dishes: crunchy shrimp
rolls, a Korean-influenced bouillabaisse, Thai
snapper over summer beans… yum.

Whist

Viceroy Hotel, 1819 Ocean Ave., Santa Monica
310.260.7511, viceroysantamonica.com
Modern American. B, L & D daily, BR Sun.
Full bar. $$$$
Executive chef Warren Schwartz is keen on
making Whist a culinary destination first and
hotel dining room second, and he is succeeding.
The hotel attracts an international clientele,
young enough to be enticed by the bottomless

champagne at Sunday brunch but old enough
to drop $100 on dinner without flinching. A
Saddle Peak Lodge alum, Schwartz brings that
game influence here, albeit with a refreshingly
light hand. Those in the know call ahead for the
blue-foot chicken, the French bird that's taken
the culinary world by storm with its gamey, "real"
chicken flavor. He tucks a few decadent slivers of
black truffle under the skin, roasts it to a golden
brown, then presents it tableside, blue legs and
all. Some hotel-restaurant staples – a salad
with goat cheese and balsamic vinaigrette, the
same old seared ahi – are here, presumably to
please that fashionista sipping champagne in the
elegantly retro, English-inspired dining room, but
we can happily ignore those. For a celebration,
book one of the gorgeous cabanas.

Wilshire Restaurant

2454 Wilshire Blvd., Santa Monica
310.586.1707, wilshirerestaurant.com
Modern American. L Mon.-Fri., D nightly. Full bar.
$$$-$$$$
Maybe it's the too-cool country club vibe,
complete with leather club chairs, or the martini-
sipping crowd at the packed bar that made us
wary of this latest restaurant to jump on the
organic, sustainable bandwagon. But despite
the occasional disinterested server and a noise
level that surges as the evening progresses, chef
Christopher Blobaum is on his game – especially
with the main courses, such as king salmon with
braised chard, kabocha squash spaetzle and
trumpet mushrooms. Skip the appetizers and
order a main course and one – maybe two! –
of the updated comfort-food desserts, like the
maple twist doughnuts with spiced butternut
squash and a cranberry parfait.

The ultimate in romantic dining in one of
Whist's dining cabanas

Breakfast & Lunch Cafés

Back on the Beach Café
445 Pacific Coast Hwy., Santa Monica
310.393.8282
American. B & L daily. Beer & wine inside only. $
You don't come here for the food, although it's perfectly fine, and sometimes even good. You come here to pay a modest price to have breakfast or lunch on a prime piece of real estate right on the sand. Good coffee-shop fare is served promptly and pleasantly to a crowd of locals: families (whose kids can romp on the sand and swing sets without bothering anyone), cyclists, beach-walkers and volleyball players. In this era of $100-a-person beachfront restaurants, this place is a treasure. Note: If you're bothered by birds, get an inside table.

Bizou Garden Bistro
2450 Colorado Ave., Santa Monica
310.582.8203, bizougarden.com
American. L Mon.-Fri., BR Sun. Full bar. $$-$$$
Despite new owners, everything is the same at this Water Garden–adjacent bistro. At lunch it's packed with business types chattering over standard chicken Caesar salads and French dip sandwiches; by nightfall early-bird locals are noshing on well-priced bistro staples. And you can add a house salad or soup for just a buck. Sunday brunch, with solid crepes, Belgian waffles and egg dishes, is the best bet if you're looking for more than just bang for your buck.

Blue Plate
1415 Montana Ave., Santa Monica
310.260.8877
American. B, L & D daily. No booze. $-$$
This cute-as-a-button coffee shop isn't as good as we wish it would be: Service is spotty, prices are on the high side for such simple fare, and the kitchen is inconsistent. That said, it's got a good vibe, and it's a pleasant place to meet a friend for a turkey-avocado wrap or chopped salad (two of the better dishes).

The Bookmark Café
Santa Monica Main Library,
601 Santa Monica Blvd., Santa Monica
310.587.2667
American. B Mon.-Sat., L daily, D Mon.-Thurs. No booze. $
These sorts of institutional cafés in museums and libraries typically offer only premade sandwiches and salads; the surprise is that this one in the fabulous new Main Library makes food to order, including turkey burgers, panini, wraps and an amazing range of salads (chef's, Cobb, Caesar, Greek, apple-walnut…). Best of all, you eat this good food on the large, quiet, sunny courtyard in the middle of the modern library – and most everything costs less than $7. Breakfast includes omelets, pancakes and good coffee. It's the best secret café in town.

Bread & Porridge
2315 Wilshire Blvd., Santa Monica
310.453.4941, breadandporridge.com
American. B, L & D daily. No booze (license pending). $
This foodie haven was expanding as we went to press, holding out hope for a beer-and-wine license and preparing the newly acquired room next door for more seating. But at this writing, it's a retro-hip café with high wooden booths, tile work, chalkboard specials. And it's known for its all-day breakfasts (excellent omelets, pancakes and designer sausages), salads, sandwiches (try the goat cheese and roasted pepper) and homey entrees, notably the suave and tender barbecued brisket. Good service, good coffee and – rare for a popular breakfast café – you can make reservations.

Broadway Deli
1457 3rd St. Promenade, Santa Monica
310.451.0616
American. B, L & D daily (Fri.-Sat. to 1 a.m.). Full bar. $-$$
The concept is wonderful: A large, lively, all-things-to-all-people place that's part deli, part brasserie, with everything from a kids' menu to quality wine, matzo-ball soup to pizza puttanesca. It's also open early and late, reasonably priced (given the neighborhood), full of roomy booths and situated ideally on the south end of the Third Street Promenade.

Unfortunately, the service is often chaotic, and the kitchen is wildly inconsistent. It does a good business regardless, thanks to the steady tourist trade, but it's a shame that Broadway Deli doesn't live up to its considerable promise.

Café Vida
15317 Antioch St., Pacific Palisades
310.573.1335
American/Mexican. B, L & D daily. No booze (BYOB). $$
Café Vida came to the Palisades several years ago, replacing Greg's Grill (anyone remember that?), and its arrival triggered a local epiphany: "Healthy" food can be really good! It won over people with such dishes as the delicious egg-white frittata with sausage and roasted vegetables. The menu has a Mexican bent, with huevos rancheros as the locals' favorite. Get there before 11:30 a.m. for brunch or lunch and before 6 p.m. for dinner or you'll wait, wait, wait – that's how good it is. You can bring your own wine, and there's no corkage fee.

Cora's Coffee Shoppe
1802 Ocean Ave., Santa Monica
310.451.9562
American. B & L daily. No booze. $-$$
Bruce Marder, owner of the smart bistro Capo next door (among other high-end eateries), bought this miniature and adorable old diner and restored it, adding a funky but fetching bougainvillea-shaded patio furnished with marble tables and bistro chairs. That patio is the reason to come here – on a sunny day, it's lovely indeed to linger over a burrata caprese omelet or the organic rotisserie chicken. You may linger more than you care to, because the service can be spotty, and the prices are on the high side – but certainly no more than you'd expect for an outdoor café with really good food a block from the beach.

Figtree's Café
429 Oceanfront Walk, Venice
310.392.4937
American. B & L daily. Beer & wine. $
Of the parade of tourist-bait sidewalk cafés on the Venice Boardwalk, this is our favorite. We started coming here in the late 1970s, when the boardwalk wasn't nearly the zoo it is today, and when sandwiches with avocado and sprouts were still exotic. Today, Figtree's large, health-conscious, often organic menu has something for everyone, from huevos rancheros made with tofu to a gratifying turkey burger. We particularly like the egg scrambles.

Boardwalk dining at Figtree's

Izzy's Deli
1433 Wilshire Blvd., Santa Monica
310.394.1131
Delicatessen. B, L & D daily 24 hours. Beer & wine. $
To paraphrase Damon Runyon, a regular at the famed Lindy's in New York, there are two types of people in this world: those who like delis, and those you shouldn't associate with. Izzy's serves superb lox, eggs and onions, turkey on rye and matzo-ball soup, among its deli fare, and offers complimentary valet parking besides. So who are we to argue with Damon Runyon?

Lazy Daisy
2300 Pico Blvd., Santa Monica
310.450.9011
American. B & L daily. No booze. $
A funky-cute cottage across the street from Virginia Park, Lazy Daisy is emblematic of the gentrifying of the Pico neighborhood. Hipsters hang out on the ivy-shaded patio, sitting at adorable little tiled tables and eating good-to-okay egg scrambles and rosemary turkey burgers. The service is lackadaisical (maybe even lazy, as the café's name suggests), but that fits with the relaxed vibe.

Le Pain Quotidien
316 Santa Monica Blvd., Santa Monica
310.393.6800, painquotidien.com
11702 Barrington Ave., Brentwood
310.476.0969
French/American. B, L & D daily. No booze. $
New Yorkers did a jig when their favorite café arrived in California. Founded in Belgium, this fast-growing chain boasts a level of quality that's almost never seen in chains. Fresh, flavorful, often organic ingredients go into the delish open-face sandwiches (the chicken curry and egg salad are both great), quiches, salads, soups and sweets (try the lemon tart). And the bread, of course, is substantial and flavorful. Really, we don't know how they do it. And though vegans and vegetarians have excellent options,

The daily bread at Le Pain Quotidien

carnivores aren't shamed. These cafés are built around an inviting communal table, but smaller tables are also plentiful. If we could just get a glass of sauvignon blanc with our goat cheese and arugula salad, all would be right with the Quotidien world.

Literati Café
12801 Wilshire Blvd., West L.A.
310.231.7484, literaticafe.com
Modern American. B, L & D daily. No booze. $
Literati restaurant's casual sidekick is country-café cute, complete with a fireplace, bud vases on the tiny tables and a daisy-painted bench for to-go customers. The soups, salads and hot entrees are fresh and foodie-friendly. Try the carrot-ginger soup, chicken-pesto salad or grilled vegetable lasagna. The artisanal coffee is excellent, rich but not bitter, and even better with a dark chocolate–espresso brownie. Seating is tight, so keep an eye out for a table as you order at the walk-up counter, or you might end up eating your lunch on the daisy bench.

Marmalade Café
710 Montana Ave., Santa Monica
310.395.9196, marmaladecafe.com
3894 Cross Creek Rd., Malibu
310.317.4242
American/French. B, L & D daily (Santa Monica closes at 7 p.m.). No booze (wine in Malibu). $
Seating is very limited at the flagship of the Marmalade restaurant local mini-empire; up in Malibu, there's a fancier dining area. The two-salad plate is plenty, but with so many tempting choices, it's hard not to go with three: Herb chicken ravioli in pesto sauce, roasted beets with oranges and candied walnuts in rosemary vinaigrette, and tuna with dried cranberries, apples and almonds are all great. Get it to go for a day at the beach, and you'll have every PB-sandwich-toting family eyeing your Cowgirl Creamery cheeses and grilled-chicken panini.

Panini Garden
2715 Main St., Santa Monica
310.399.9939, paninigarden.com
French/American. B, L & D daily.
No booze. $
Main Street is full of restaurants, but too many of them are touristy or not worth the money. This modest café is the sleeper find on the street for lunch or an afternoon treat. Take your crisp, absolutely delicious panini sandwich (grilled vegetables, mozzarella and pesto, perhaps, or prosciutto, mozzarella and fresh basil) to the hidden rear garden, where umbrellas shade the tables, lavender lines the walk, and a fountain burbles, and you'll be in heaven. There are also lots of good salads made with organic fixings, and the sweet crepes are lovely.

Patrick's Roadhouse
106 Entrada Dr. (at PCH), Santa Monica
310.459.4544
American. B & L daily. No booze. $
What looks like an oceanside Irish pub thanks to the jolly green paint is actually a booze-free greasy spoon that's been greeting PCH passersby since 1974. Bill Fischler bought the place when it was a hot dog joint and turned it into a hearty breakfast dive, complete with flea-market antiques, worn wood tables and a hodgepodge of photos (including several of Arnold Schwarzenegger, who's been known to polish off a few rounds of scrambled eggs here). When Bill passed away a few years ago, daughter Tracie took over. She's still serving up tried-and-true classics – omelets, pancakes and scrambles – to newspaper-toting regulars.

Urth Caffe
2327 Main St., Santa Monica
310.314.7040, urthcaffe.com
American. B, L & D daily. No booze. $$
When this place first opened on Main Street, the locals thought, "What? Is this some weird vegan place?" Not so! Yes, the emphasis is most decidedly on the healthy, but not to the point of diminishing taste – so the croissants are the real thing, made with real butter, and they're wonderful. Pair one with an egg-white omelet, and you'll have cancelled out the fat. Also good are the Mediterranean platter, tortilla soup, curried chicken salad and berry layer cake. It's famed for brewing up very good homegrown organic coffees and teas.

Eat & Run: Fast Food, Pizza & Takeout

See also Burgers, Burritos & Barbecue, page 152.

Fast Food

Hot Dog on a Stick
1633 Ocean Front Walk, Santa Monica
No phone
L & D daily. Cash only.
Now found in malls across the nation, this simple, goofy chain started right here on Muscle Beach in 1946. The little red stand staffed by young people in dorky 1960s hats serves the same few things, day in and day out: corn dogs (aka batter-dipped turkey dogs on sticks), fried cheese on a stick, french fries and lemonade. It's a fun guilty pleasure.

Hungry Pocket
1725 Pico Blvd., Santa Monica
310.450.5335
L & D daily.
College kids and Sunset Park locals are well fed on a budget at this falafel stand. Skip the fancier meals and stick to the very good gyros, schwarma and falafel sandwiches, as well as the fresh-squeezed juices.

Forget the junk food on the Venice Boardwalk and head for Jody Maroni's.

Jody Maroni's
2011 Ocean Front Walk, Venice
310.822.5639, jodymaroni.com
L & D daily (closes at sunset); closed when raining. Cash only.
Jody Maroni started selling his family's fancy sausages on the Venice Boardwalk in 1979, and it remains the best fast-food place on the boardwalk. We're partial to the bratwurst with onions and peppers, but others swear by the spicy chicken andouille or the sweeter chicken-apple. All sausages are served in an onion roll, with kraut or grilled onions and peppers if you like. If you'd rather have a plain ol' hot dog, you can have that, too. A California fast-food landmark.

Neptune's Net
42505 Pacific Coast Hwy., Malibu
310.457.3095, neptunesnet.com
L & D daily (closes early). Beer & wine.
Known as a regular haunt of weekend bikers and for its outdoor location near the Ventura County Line, this fish market and order-at-the-counter joint has its pros and cons. On the one hand, the clam chowder and steamed-to-order shellfish (lobster, clams, crabs and shrimp) are terrific; on the other, the fried fish and shellfish are not so great. Food is dished out brusquely on flimsy paper plates, but you get to eat it all outdoors on picnic tables with the Pacific Ocean across PCH – and you can have a beer with your steamed shrimp. Weekends are packed with Harley riders, tourists and County Line surfers.

Reddi-Chick
Brentwood Country Mart, 225 26th St.
Santa Monica
310.393.5238
L & D daily until 7:30 p.m. No booze.
Cash only. $
See listing page 149.

Pizza

Abbot's Pizza Company
1407 Abbot Kinney Blvd., Venice
310.396.7334, abbotspizzacompany.com
1811 Pico Blvd., Santa Monica
310.314.2777
L & D daily. No booze. $
The under-30s in this ultra-cool Abbot Kinney neighborhood would starve if it weren't for the constantly replenished racks of by-the-slice bagel-crust pizza: tomato-basil, the Gypsy (spinach, mushroom, onion, tomato, ricotta, mozzarella and an olive pesto), the Meat-eaters (pepperoni, sausage and ham) and more. The slices are huge, the crust is substantial without being thick, and the ingredients are quality. You can eat your slice at a narrow counter or one of the highly prized outdoor tables. The newer outpost in Santa Monica has actual tables, but somehow it just doesn't seem quite as good.

Antica Pizzeria
Villa Marina Marketplace,13455 Maxella Ave., 2nd Fl., Marina del Rey
310.577.8182, anticapizzeria.net
L & D Tues.-Sun. Beer & wine. $
When Naples native Peppe Miele says his restaurant is a pizzeria, he really means it. Miele is the first, and one of the only, U.S. residents accepted into the Associazione Vera Pizza Napoletana, the Naples-based pizza-police force that sets strict traditional guidelines for pizza production. Among the rules: The crust must be made from flour, natural yeast and water (nope, not even salt) and baked in an oven fueled only by wood. Oh, and it has to taste *fantastico*. Not to

miss is the classic pizza Margherita, a simple but spectacular sauce-free combo of tomatoes, fresh mozzarella, Parmesan and basil. You'd be crazy to order anything other than pizza, so don't.

Bravo Pizzeria
2400 Main St., Santa Monica
310.392.7466
L & D daily. For takeout & delivery only. Beer $
Bravo makes a very good thin-crust pizza, with a richly flavorful sauce and just the right amount of cheese. Main Street revelers can stop in for a slice; locals often get a whole pie to take home. The service can be spotty, but they do deliver.

Bruno's
1652 Ocean Ave., Santa Monica
310.395.5589
L & D daily. Beer & wine. $
Had enough of the new, slick, $30-entree Santa Monica? Then head to Bruno's to recover. Bruno himself is in the kitchen, making great pizzas and comforting spaghetti and meatballs, typically served by the genial America in a reassuringly divey room filled with red-checked tablecloths. Stick to the simple stuff, especially the pizza, and get in touch with your inner Corleone. To complete the old Santa Monica experience, go to Chez Jay across the street for a drink before or after your pizza.

Vittorio's
16646 Marquez Ave., Pacific Palisades
310.459.3755
D Tues.-Sun. Beer & wine. $$
We once saw a guy from the Sopranos here. If that's not a testimony for an Italian joint, we don't know what is. Vittorio's makes great garlic rolls, a great marinara sauce and, most of all, a great New York–style pizza, with very fresh vegetables for the toppings and excellent sausage for those who eschew vegetables.

Wildflour Pizza
2807 Main St., Santa Monica
310.392.3300
L & D daily. Beer & wine. $
Before Main Street got as hip as it is today, there was Wildflour. It's a classic pizza joint in a fetchingly funky historic shack, with a wood-paneled, sawdust-floored inside room and large outdoor patio in back. Made with white or whole-wheat flour, these are large, thin-crust, New York–style pies, sold by the slice or the pie. You can have them any way imaginable, but we're partial to the simply delicious cheese pizza. There's a range of subs, pastas and chicken entrees, but that's not what you come here for. Delivery is available in the neighborhood.

Takeout

Bay Cities Italian Deli & Bakery
1517 Lincoln Blvd., Santa Monica
310.395.8279, baycitiesitaliandeli.com
L & D Tues.-Sun. until 7 p.m. (Sun. until 6 p.m.).
Beer & wine. $
Any food establishment that's survived in this
town since the 1920s deserves applause.
Customers keep coming back for the
sandwiches pairing Italian cured meats with
legendary soft hoagie rolls baked on site every
day. The line can be daunting, and the staff
can be gruff, so when you finally make it to the
counter, be ready with your order. You can build
your own sandwich or go all out with the famed
Godmother, a massive heap of Genoa salami,
mortadella, coppacola, ham, proscuitto and
provolone. On your way out, pick up hard-to-find
Italian goodies from the grocery aisles –
imported pasta, anchovies, cheeses, cookies,
even wine – and you'll be set for dinner, too.

Cha Cha Chicken
1906 Ocean Ave., Santa Monica
310.581.1684
L & D daily. No booze. $
See listing page 150.

Le Marmiton
1327 Montana Ave., Santa Monica
310.393.7716
B, L & D daily until 8 p.m. No booze. $-$$
When you get a craving for an authentic cassoulet that's almost as good as the one you had
in France, head straight to Le Marmiton. The tiny
takeout café is packed with impossible-to-resist

pastel meringues, buttery croissants, glistening
fruit tarts, rustic quiches and fresh pâtés. If you're
not in a hurry, take in Montana's passersby at
one of the outdoor tables as you sop up steamed
mussels with your crusty baguette.

Marmalade Café
710 Montana Ave., Santa Monica
310.395.9196, marmaladecafe.com
3894 Cross Creek Rd., Malibu
310.317.4242
B, L & D daily (Santa Monica closes at 7 p.m.).
No booze (wine in Malibu). $
See listing page 146.

Reddi-Chick
Brentwood Country Mart, 225 26th St.,
Santa Monica
310.393.5238
L & D daily until 7:30 p.m. No booze. No credit
cards. $
Just try to make it to your picnic without ripping
into the steaming flesh of these savory, intensely
aromatic roast chickens. Typically served as a
half-chicken covered with a mountain of fries,
this westside staple is cherished by children,
their great grandparents and everyone in
between. You can eat at a picnic table in the
sunny courtyard inside the tony Country Mart, or
take your chicken and fries to go.

Santa Monica Seafood
1205 Colorado Ave., Santa Monica
310.393.5244, santamonicaseafood.com
L & D daily until 7 p.m.; closes earlier on
weekends. Beer & wine. $$
The deli cases at this busy seafood market
are packed with good stuff to take out: sushi,
chowders, ceviches, seafood salads, crab
cakes, crusty breads and more. It's also great
for party platters of smoked fish, sushi, shrimp
and crab. There's no place to eat – this is strictly
a market.

Stroh's Gourmet
1239 Abbot Kinney Blvd., Venice
310.450.5119
B, L & D daily until 7 p.m. No booze. $
Planning a beach picnic? Stop by Stroh's first for
some fabulous sandwiches: grilled turkey, brie
and avocado; roast beef and caramelized onion;
Black Forest ham with roasted red peppers
and mozzarella; and more. There's also a great
selection of artisanal cheeses and cured meats,
small-producer soda pops, gourmet chips and
little sweet things to top off your picnic basket.
The lucky snag one of the few tables on the
sidewalk; most take the food to go.

World Cuisine

Cha Cha Chicken

Santa Monica and environs are weak on some of the ethnic cuisine that lives in abundance further east, such as Chinese and Korean, and for the most part, its Thai food is just okay. But there's still some good eating from all over the globe. Please note that we don't consider Mexican restaurants to be exotic world cuisine, since tacos are to Californians what steaks are to Chicagoans; the same goes for Japanese restaurants and sushi bars, which are as plentiful as surfboards in these parts.

Cha Cha Chicken
1906 Ocean Ave., Santa Monica
310.581.1684
Caribbean. L & D daily, BR Sat.-Sun. No booze. $
The beach is around the corner, and $500-a-night hotels abound just up the street, which makes this cheap, lively, riotously colorful outdoor joint such a boon to the neighborhood. Jamaican jerk chicken, roasted and coated with an addictive sweet-fiery jerk sauce, is the staple, showing up in everything from enchiladas to wraps, but we're more partial to the pork stew with garlic and onion. Most dishes cost less than $8, and you can either take your order out or eat on the large shaded patio. Be sure to have water at the ready; some dishes have the spice turned up high.

China Beach Bistro
2024 Pacific Ave., Venice
310.823.4646, chinabeachbistro.com
Vietnamese. L & D daily; closed Wed. No booze. $
It's a shame that this place is so dinky (two tables inside, four on a parking-lot patio next to a liquor store), and it's particularly a shame that it has no bathroom – the food is deserving of a much better site. This is fresh, vibrant, authentic Vietnamese cooking: fragrant pho (noodle soups), slow-roasted five-spice chicken, a delicious baguette sandwich (bahn mi) and excellent Vietnamese egg rolls. Maybe by the time you read this it will have found a better home – call first.

Cholada
18763 Pacific Coast Hwy., Malibu
310.317.0025
Thai. D Mon., L & D Tues. Beer & wine. $
Good Thai food is hard to find in the Bay Cities,

and many locals despair that it simply does not exist. We bring hope. Not only does this tiny secret spot on PCH just north of the Palisades have good Thai food, but it also has a pleasant outdoor patio and, by Malibu standards, low prices. There's nothing innovative about the food, but the larb, tom kah soup, crispy catfish, curries and noodle dishes are better than at most any other Thai joint in Santa Monica. There's only one problem – this entire funky little neighborhood is slated to be torn down to revert it to parkland. So call first to make sure it's still standing.

Gaby's Mediterranean
20 Washington Blvd., Marina del Rey
310.821.9721
Lebanese/Mediterranean. L & D daily. No booze. $
The small inside room is rather grim, with too-loud music, but out on the sidewalk, with a constant parade of people headed for the sand and the Venice Pier a few doors away, it's the perfect beach café. This is the kind of food you want to eat on a sunny, salt-air day: fat, yummy pita bread, smooth hummus, fresh tabbouleh, excellent pita wraps, and long-roasted chicken. The dressing on the green salads can be tart to the point of misery, and food can emerge from the kitchen in a haphazard way, but in general, this is savory stuff, served outdoors by the beach at low prices. For that, we're grateful.

Gate of India
117 Santa Monica Blvd., Santa Monica
310.656.1664
Indian. L & D daily. Beer & wine. $-$$
This place is so close to the Third Street Promenade that it must be a tourist trap, right? Wrong. For years now Gate of India has been

a secret escape from the Promenade hordes, serving good Indian food in an ideal location between Ocean and Second Street—and there's even validated parking next door. Best bets are the coconut curry, ginger chicken and the "Top of the World" appetizer. The dining room is serene, but the service is inconsistent, sometimes friendly and sometimes barely cordial.

Sham
716 Santa Monica Blvd., Santa Monica
310.393.2913, sham.la
Syrian. L & D Tues.-Sun. No booze. $
Syrian cooking is similar to Lebanese, with some Turkish and Armenian influences; the best bets in this surprisingly fancy storefront joint are the rich hummus, the savory lamb dishes, the delicious arice sandwich (made with ground lamb and fresh pita) and the "baba ghannouj," which is a salad of eggplant, tomatoes and bell peppers, not the dip-like baba ganoush Angelenos are used to eating. Watch out for the occasional nights featuring live music and belly dancers – they can be fun, but they're also really loud, and the prices go up. Sham doesn't serve alcohol, but you can bring your own wine with no corkage fee.

Tongdang Thai
Brentwood Gardens, 11677 San Vicente Blvd., Brentwood
310.820.3200, tongdang.com
Thai. L & D daily. Beer & wine. $
If you're in Brentwood or north Santa Monica and don't have the energy to drive to Hollywood's Thai Town, you could do worse than this friendly Brentwood Gardens place near CPK – in fact, what CPK is for gourmet pizza, Tongdang is for Thai food. The dishes are classics (panang, pad Thai, barbecue chicken, tom kah soup), the seasonings are inoffensive, and the people are nice. You can ask for it spicier if you're used to the real thing.

Typhoon
3221 Donald Douglas Loop S., Santa Monica
310.390.6565, typhoon.biz
Pan-Asian. L Mon.-Fri., D nightly, BR Sun. Full bar. $$
This place is just plain fun. With a window-lined dining room overlooking retro Santa Monica Airport (where you might see a WWII-era plane take off), a chic Asian decor with aeronautical touches, a good bar and a fairly priced menu of dishes from Singapore, Korea, China, Thailand, Vietnam, the Philippines and Burma, Typhoon can't go wrong, and it's a great place to take out-of-towners for an experience they won't have anywhere else. The adventurous or the drunk dare each other to try the deep-fried Thai white sea worms or Singapore-style scorpions; everyone else shares small plates of such good stuff as siu mai, Vietnamese egg rolls, Korean-style short ribs, deep-fried whole catfish with black-bean sauce, vegetable curry and Thai river prawns with a cilantro-garlic-peanut paste. Upstairs is Hump, an affiliated sushi bar with even better views.

Warszawa
1414 Lincoln Blvd., Santa Monica
310.393.8831, warszawarestaurant.com
Polish. L Sun.-Fri., D nightly. Full bar. $$
This stick-to-your-ribs Polish food – pierogis, beef stroganoff, strangely delicious hot dried plums wrapped in crispy bacon – goes down great on a cold winter night (and it can get chilly in Santa Monica). In the summer, there's a pretty patio, interesting salads and the best cold borscht you've ever had, at least in Southern California. The old house has a warren of rooms that are cozy and romantic in any season.

World Café
2828 Main St., Santa Monica
310.392.1661, worldcafela.com
International. L& D Tues.-Sun., BR Sat.-Sun. Full bar. $$-$$$
The lush enclosed patio is a hidden oasis, the perfect spot to refuel after a day of Main Street shopping. Take in a leisurely brunch – be sure to sample the fresh scones and mini muffins in the bread basket – or get a glass of wine and a grilled pizza in the late afternoon. "World" is taken literally here, with a menu that's broad and unfocused (ahi tartare, hummus, spring rolls, tostadas, Italian pastas, American steaks…), but with a patio like this, who cares? If you can't get a table outside, grab a drink in the bar and wait. It's worth it.

Burgers, Burritos & Barbecue

Baby Blues BBQ
444 Lincoln Blvd., Venice
310.396.7675, babybluesbarbq.com
Barbecue. L & D daily. No booze. $-$$
Memphis-style dry-rub ribs are the focal point of this funky barbecue joint. Slow-cooked without sauce (though you can fire 'em up with a bottled XXX sauce or milder Carolinian red sauce), the ribs come either in the baby-back cut or the meatier Memphis "long-bone" cut, and both are fabulous. Also authentically good are the North Carolina pulled pork, the stewed tomatoes, the crisp slaw, the pork 'n' beans (made from that aforementioned pulled pork) and the Key lime pie. We know of only two disappointments: the unpleasant cornbread and the continuing lack of a liquor license, so you can't have beer with your barbecue – unless you order takeout and provide your own, which many locals do.

The Counter
2901 Ocean Park Blvd., Santa Monica
310.399.8383, thecounterburger.com
American/burgers. L & D daily. Beer & wine. $
The folks behind this new-era burger joint figure that it's possible to order some 312,120 variations on a hamburger: beef, turkey, chicken or veggie, topped with everything from roasted red peppers to guacamole to ginger-soy glaze – or plain old American cheese. You can even have it served as the centerpiece of a carb-free salad. The burgers are hearty, messy and delicious, the shakes are the real thing, and the sides are good, particularly the crispy onion rings and salty sweet-potato fries. The always-crowded Counter is going nationwide as a fast-growing franchise, and it all started in 2003 in this ultra-modern concrete space in Ocean Park.

Father's Office
1018 Montana Ave., Santa Monica
310.393.2337, fathersoffice.com
American/burgers.
D nightly. Beer & wine. $-$$
Is this the best burger in America? Some say it is, and now it's a challenge to get in the door to find out for yourself. When Sang Yoon, formerly chef at Michael's, said goodbye to haute cuisine to open a pub, a serious burger was probably inevitable, and Yoon became dead serious about creating a world-class hamburger. It's a rare, dry-aged beef patty topped with Maytag bleu cheese, smoked applewood bacon and caramelized onions. Don't bother asking for substitutions – the servers will simply ignore you. And expect to wait – the dark, shotgun bar has only a few bistro tables, with the line often out the door. Not to miss is the ever-changing selection of boutique beers that Yoon, a self-proclaimed beer sommelier, selects each season. This is a pub first, burger-joint second, so leave the kids at home: The over-21 rule is strictly enforced.

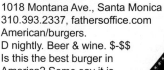

Howdy's Taqueria
3835 Cross Creek Rd., Malibu
310.456.6299
Mexican. L & D daily. No booze. $$
Locals line up out the door at Howdy's Taqueria, located in the ever-so-chic Cross Creek shopping center. It's the perfect antidote to Nobu, which is just across the parking lot – prices are low, only some of the patrons have had boob jobs, and the Mexican food is better than you'd expect in such a white-bread neighborhood. Try the grilled mahi mahi tacos, tacos al pastor, black-bean-and-cheese burrito or grilled turkey chopped salad.

No frills, just great food, at La Playita

La Playita
3306 Lincoln Blvd.,
Santa Monica
310.452.0090
Mexican. B, L & D daily. No booze. $
To the nattering nabobs of negativity who say that Santa Monica doesn't have good taquerias, we say get to La Playita, and then we'll talk. This is the real thing, a divey stand with nowhere to sit but wonderful taqueria chow: shrimp ceviche, carnitas tacos, carne asada burritos and so forth. Sure, the tacos cost a quarter more than on the eastside, but even taco-stand real estate is pricey around here.

Mr. Cecil's California Ribs
12244 W. Pico Blvd., West L.A.
310.442.1550
Barbecue. L & D daily. Beer & wine. $$
The operative word in the name of this place is California – if you don't come expecting authentic smoked barbecue, you'll be perfectly happy with your tender baby-back ribs, dry-rub St. Louis ribs and tasty hush puppies. The faux roadhouse shack is small, parking is an issue, and prices are high for what you get, but given the scarcity of good barbecue in these parts, Mr. Cecil's is worth knowing about when you need a rib fix. Good for takeout, too.

The Shack
2518 Wilshire Blvd., Santa Monica
310.449.1171, shacksm.com
American/burgers. L & D daily. Full bar. $
The Shack is a hard-core Philly hangout, with Eagles games blaring overhead and a rowdy game crowd on weekends, so consider yourself forewarned. But even the sports-phobic should slip into a booth (weekday lunches are quieter) for the Shack Burger, a charbroiled beef patty topped with a spicy, chin-dribblin' split sausage link. Heartburn never tasted so good.

Snug Harbor
2323 Wilshire Blvd., Santa Monica
310.828.2991
American/burgers. B & L daily. Beer only. $
Snug Harbor is the kind of diner-counter hole-in-the-wall that looks as if it's been around for at least 30 years. It has, plus another 30. The grill gets going at 6 a.m. sharp, firing out hungry-man breakfasts and, at lunch, the famous Zweibel burger, an onion-smothered, juice-dripping, pan-fried delicious mess. Regulars go straight for the sausage biscuits, drenched in a sausage-speckled gravy that's almost thick enough to stand your spoon upright. The coffee – black – is darned good, too.

Tacomiendo
11462 Gateway Blvd., West L.A.
310.481.0804, ta-comiendo.com
Mexican. L & D daily. No booze. $
Handmade tortillas are the draw at this friendly strip-mall taqueria, and they are indeed fat, warm and delicious. As for the meats that go in them – carnitas, carne asada, adobado – they're perfectly fine, if nothing to drive across town for. The salsa bar is varied and fresh, and the agua frescas are good. A reliable taqueria for eastside Santa Monicans.

Tacos Por Favor
1406 Olympic Blvd., Santa Monica
310.392.5768
Mexican. B & L daily, D Mon.-Sat. (closes at 8 p.m.). Beer only. $
This friendly, capacious taqueria manages to be both healthful (fresh tomatoes, lean meats, no lard) and authentic – the weekend menudo is restorative, the birria (baby goat) is tender, and the soft tacos are meaty and delicious. Also notably good are the chorizo-cheese tacos, the fresh chips, the guac and the pico de gallo. Watch out for the salsas, which can sizzle.

Jin's heavenly Louvres, made of milk chocolate and ginger

Good Eats:
Bakeries, Caterers & Specialty Markets

Bakeries

A La Tarte
1037 Swarthmore Ave., Pacific Palisades
310.459.6635
This sweet little café is also a great bakery, with pain au chocolat that would do Paris proud, as well as dreamy pains aux raisins, scones, chocolate cakes and baguettes. The coffee's good, too.

Angel Maid
4542 S. Centinela Ave., West L.A.
310.915.2078
This is the only place in these parts to find good tres leches cakes, birthday cakes (try the chocolate mousse cake), cupcakes, cinnamon rolls and cookies. It's an old-fashioned, family-run bakery in West L.A.'s Japanese-American community with a longstanding and loyal clientele, and we love it.

Belwood Bakery
11625 Barrington Ct., Brentwood
310.471.6855
Belwood is a hot spot for kids from the nearby Brentwood School and Archer School for Girls; the parents and the locals like it, too. It has exceptional morning coffee and lattes, as well as good bakery items, from mini baguettes to brioche to croissants. Baguette sandwiches are made daily and scarfed up quickly. Good star-spotting, always.

The City Bakery
Brentwood Country Mart, 225 26th St., Santa Monica
310.656.3040, thecitybakery.com
This chic transplant from New York, which is part bakery, part high-end salad bar, offers the pretzel croissant, a hybrid locals go ape for. It is indeed irresistible, somehow managing to be as flaky as a plain croissant but with the substance of a pretzel. But that's not the only baked thing worth the calories – make sure to try the "melted" chocolate-chip cookies (the cookie platters are great to take to a party) and the muffins. As for the salad bar, it's a good one, but pricey at $12 a pound – not that high prices deter anyone who hangs out at the faux-rustic Brentwood Country Mart.

Jin Patisserie
1202 Abbot Kinney Blvd., Venice
310.399.8801, jinpatisserie.com
Closed Mon.
Former flight attendant turned pastry chef Kristy Choo's artful chocolate creations are as decadent as they are gorgeous. Chocolates filled or flavored with jasmine, bergamot, lychee and chrysanthemum beckon from chic blond-wood display cases. If chocolate isn't your thing (shame on you), try the delicate sesame-peanut butter cookies or the mascarpone-tangerine macaroons. And don't miss the full-service afternoon tea on the serene walled patio. Pastry fiends will think they died and went to heaven.

Mani's Bakery
2507 Main St., Santa Monica
310.396.7700, manisbakery.com
The retail outlet of the original Mani's Bakery & Café on Fairfax sells "healthier" pastries, a word they use to encompass varying degrees of fat-free, all-natural and wheat-free baked goods. If you've been desperately searching for a vegan German chocolate cake or a wedding cake sweetened with agave syrup, come here. Is a chocolate-truffle "brick" really healthy? Probably not – but who cares? It's chocolate, and it's pretty darn good.

Marmalade
710 Montana Ave., Santa Monica
310.395.9196, marmaladecafe.com
3894 Cross Creek Rd., Malibu
310.317.4242
Famous for birthday cakes, these two branches of the locally grown chain are also gifted with tarts, bars and pies; heck, even the bran muffins are terrific.

Caterers

Jennie Cooks, A Catering Company
9806 Washington Blvd., Culver City
310.815.8273, jenniecooks.com
This busy caterer handles a lot of Bay Cities wrap parties, weddings, bar and bat mitzvahs and casual business functions. What's notable about Cooks, beyond the savory homestyle food, is the commitment to use local, organic products and to recycle. It has a lot of great choices for vegetarians and vegans. But if you want to build your party around a tenderloin of Niman Ranch beef, that's embraced, too.

Marmalade
710 Montana Ave., Santa Monica
310.395.9196, marmaladecafe.com
3894 Cross Creek Rd., Malibu
310.317.4242
Founded on Montana Avenue by a couple of local gals, this café, caterer and gourmet deli now has nine locations. It's one of the most popular caterers on the westside, handling every sort of event and doing a brisk business in catering to go – party dishes that you pick up yourself or have delivered sans staff. They make everything imaginable, including Korean tacos and Southwest empanadas, but it really shines with its Franco-Californian-Mediterranean fare. Great desserts.

Heavenly tarts at Marmalade

New York Food Co.
2320 Alaska Ave., El Segundo
310.643.6151, newyorkfood.com
Why a locally grown caterer would name itself the New York Food Company is a mystery, but it worked – what started as a deli in Hermosa Beach is now one of L.A.'s top caterers, feeding elegant people at many large-scale events.

Specialty Markets

Bay Cities Italian Deli & Bakery
1517 Lincoln Blvd., Santa Monica
310.395.8279, baycitiesitaliandeli.com
If it's Italian, Bay Cities has it: imported pastas, oils, vinegars, olives, cheeses, deli meats, even wine. Okay, so the bread baked on site isn't as good as eating a crusty loaf in Florence, but it's a lot cheaper than a plane ticket.

Brentwood Gourmet Market
11725 Barrington Ct., Brentwood
310.476.0565
More an upscale deli than a full-fledged market, this place caters to locals who like French wines, Russian caviars and Italian cheeses and don't mind paying handsomely for them. The deli makes excellent sandwiches – this is a good place to pick up a posh picnic. It's great for gourmet gifts, too.

Mitsuwa Marketplace
3760 S Centinela Ave., West L.A.
310.398.2113, mitsuwa.com
With the dozens of hard-to-find noodles, seaweed, Asian produce, tofu, sauces and prepared foods it offers, it's easy to spend hours perusing this Japanese market. When the kids get bored, drop them at the food court to snack on tempura and play Japanese video games. Most of the staff speaks limited, if any, English, so if you're not well versed in Japanese, be content to fill your cart with surprises. Figuring out what to do with them is half the fun.

Robins Nest
68 N. Venice Blvd., Venice
310.821.7281, robinsnestmarket.com
Thanks to Shari Robins, the westside finally has its own San Francisco–style gourmet grocery, stocking breads from Oliver's and the Bread Bar, Cowgirl Creamery cheeses, farmer-direct honeys, Kenter Canyon Farms field greens, Giorgio Baldi's sauces and more. There's even a small selection of household staples (toothpaste, toilet paper, pet food).

Sanchez Meat Co.
4525 Inglewood Blvd., Culver City
310.391.3640
This carniceria has some of the best carne asada in town. On weekends, fans line up for marinated meats to grill (during holidays, call ahead to order or you might leave empty handed). Grab a juicy taco while you contemplate whether to tackle the tripe for that menudo recipe, or pick up a pint to go and call it your own – no one will ever know.

Santa Monica Seafood
1205 Colorado Ave., Santa Monica
310.393.5244, santamonicaseafood.com
One of the leading seafood retailers in the state, this store has whatever's in season, from wild king salmon to Pacific swordfish. The freezer's full of calamari, cod, shrimp, lobster, crawfish, crab cakes and more. You'll also find fixings for a seafood-based meal: produce, salads, pasta, rice, wine and La Brea Bakery breads.

The Lowdown on the Farmer's Markets

Farmer's market expert Amelia Saltsman with farmer Alex Weiser

The very first certified farmer's market in Southern California may have been in Gardena, but for the last couple of decades, it's the Santa Monica Farmer's Market that has become the favorite of A-list chefs, serious home cooks and those obsessed with produce. Now held twice a week, the market also has stellar competition from other markets in Ocean Park, Virginia Park, Venice and the Palisades. To get the lowdown on the local market scene, we went to the woman who wrote the book: *The Santa Monica Farmers' Market Cookbook,* that is. Author and longtime Santa Monican Amelia (Millie) Saltsman has been a market habitué and serious cook for two decades.

Why is the Arizona market the queen of them all?
The large Wednesday market is almost exclusively farm produce, including eggs, meats and cheeses, making it perhaps the largest year-round market of its kind in the country. Laura Avery, the supervisor of all the Santa Monica markets and the manager of the Wednesday market, has done an exceptional job of bringing in talented farmers with a great diversity of crops, which in turn attracts the best chefs in Southern California and beyond. In fact, there are many restaurant foragers who shop there and ship unusual items to high-end restaurants all over the country. It's amazing that the center for all this is our small beachside city.

Why does farmer's market produce taste so much better than supermarket produce?
Because it's locally grown (anywhere from a 10- to 300-mile radius), picked fully ripe and brought to market within 24 hours of harvest, which lets flavors develop fully on the vine. That's a very different scenario from crops that must be picked early, stored and shipped before being distributed to supermarkets. Farmers who sell direct can grow varieties chosen for flavor first rather than sturdiness, and since they plant in small quantities, they can experiment with interesting varieties, so even ordinary crops – carrots, potatoes, onions – are worth writing home about.

When did you start frequenting the Santa Monica market?
Soon after I moved to the Santa Monica/Palisades area in 1985. At some point in the 1990s, I realized it was a core experience for me and my family. My shopping revolved around the market, and my cooking inspiration came totally from there – it's as though the produce was speaking directly to me. Wednesday and Thursday dinners are particularly special at our house – they're market feasts.

So did shopping the markets change the way you cook?
Completely. I look first at what's in season, and then I look at a cookbook – if I look at a book at all. Market ingredients are so delicious on their own that they need very little adornment.

You are friends with farmers, but are they friends with each other? Or are they competitors?

The markets are amazing communities. Farmers are often neighbors at home as well as at the markets, and they learn from one another as well as from their customers. For instance, a stone-fruit farmer will see that another has had great success growing a temperamental but incredibly delicious old apricot variety and have the courage to shift from growing a bland commercial variety. Because flavor is such an important criterion at the market, this learning exchange keeps improving the quality of our produce. Sure there's some competition, but most of it is friendly.

A Guide to the Markets

Millie Saltsman gave us the straight scoop on the best of the Bay Cities' farmer's markets.

Santa Monica: Arizona
On Arizona St. between 2nd St. & 4th St.
Wed. & Sat. 8:30 a.m.-1:30 p.m.
The original Santa Monica farmer's market, the Wednesday one is a hard-working operation – chefs wheeling carts and dollies piled high with crates; home cooks laden with baskets and bags; and office workers on lunch breaks. Every nationality is represented (so it seems), and it's very much a village square. This is also the market for celebrity chef sightings and media action. Saturday is a smaller version, with a weekend feel.

Santa Monica: Main Street
In the parking lot off Main St. between Ocean Park Blvd. & Hill St.
Sun. 9:30 a.m.-1 p.m.
This market very definitely has a weekend, family-festival vibe. Alone among the Santa Monica markets, it has an entire section of prepared foods, as well as live music and children's activities (including pony rides and a chess club). There's even a bustling (and free) bicycle check area. It's a lot of fun.

Santa Monica: Pico
At Virginia Park, Pico Blvd. at Cloverfield Blvd.
Sat. 8 a.m.-1 p.m.
Set up more as a square than an *allée*, the Pico market occupies renovated Virginia Park. Aficionados are deeply loyal to this topnotch market, which (along with the Saturday downtown market) is perfect for the market novice or those who want a lower-key experience.

Pacific Palisades
Swarthmore Ave. at Sunset Blvd.
Sun. 8 a.m.-1 p.m.
Thanks to its strong sense of community and good vendors, this is the market of choice for many Palisadians. It boasts a warm, small-town, meet-and-greet vibe.

Venice
Venice Way at N. Venice Blvd.
Fri. 7-11 a.m.
This intimate, high-quality market is tucked into the median parking strip that separates North and South Venice boulevards. Don't expect the boardwalk carnival – this is just about good vegetables, fruit, herbs, plants and flowers.

Strawberry queen Molly Gean of Harry's Berries at the Santa Monica market

11 Coffeehouses That Aren't Starbucks

Abbot's Habit
1401 Abbot Kinney Blvd., Venice
310.399.1171
Daily from 6 a.m.
The few sidewalk tables are highly coveted at this funky place (think Berkeley in the 1970s) in the heart of ultra-hip Abbot Kinney. Inside are two good-size rooms filled with tables topped with red-plaid tablecloths; you can sit down for a quick sandwich, salad or coffee, or you can settle in for an afternoon with your laptop or sketchbook. The people-watching is amusing, the vibe is mellow, and the coffee is good.

Café Bolivar
1741 Ocean Park Blvd., Santa Monica
310.581.2344
L & D daily
A real find in a sleeper Ocean Park neighbor-hood, Café Bolivar is a friendly, relaxed place with an open, modern look and warm Latin music on the stereo. The coffee is excellent, the lunches (grilled chicken sandwich with roasted pepper pesto, a true Spanish jamon serrano, a vegan torta) are delicious, and the WiFi is free. Art openings and poetry readings liven things up from time to time, but mostly this is a relaxed place to meet friends for coffee or lunch, or sit with the novel you're reading or the novel you're writing.

Caffe Luxxe
925 Montana Ave., Santa Monica
310.394.2222, caffeluxxe.com
Mon.-Fri. from 6:30 a.m., Sat.-Sun. from 7 a.m.
These folks are dead serious about their coffee – only espresso drinks are served (no brewed coffee), and each cup is a work of art, the espresso creamy and almost sweet, the milk steamed with precision. This is without a doubt the best latte (and cappuccino) in town. A few high-quality baked goods (croissants, baguettes, cookies) serve as accompaniments. The setting is serene and European, with high ceilings, framed mirrors and roomy tables. Our only complaint: not enough seating. But that well may be fixed by the time you read this.

Latte as art at
Caffe Luxxe

18th Street Coffee House
1725 Broadway, Santa Monica
310.264.0662
Mon.-Fri. from 7 a.m., Sat.-Sun. from 8:30 a.m.
In an adorable historic brick building with a homey out-door patio, 18th Street has a folksy, Berkeley/East Village vibe (maybe that's why the rumor mill says it's owned by Bob Dylan, which seems to be untrue). A mix of young moms, students and writers hangs out for hours, sipping coffee while noshing on bagels, sourdough sandwiches and homemade rugelach. The strict no-cell phone policy (outdoor calling only) allows for a respite from the normal coffeehouse chatter. Be sure to hold onto your cup – refills are only 50 cents, a little-advertised bonus.

Infuzion Café
1149 3rd St., Santa Monica
310.393.9985, infuzioncafe.com
Mon.-Fri. from 6:30 a.m., Sat. from 7 a.m., Sun. from 8 a.m.
This tiny coffeehouse does a strong and steady business all day long. Just north of the Promenade, it attracts local office workers and shoppers instead of tourists, and its free WiFi is a draw, too, even though the tables are too wee to allow for hours of leisurely e-mailing. But the coffee is fine, the "infuzions" (fruit-based iced-blended drinks) are delicious, and the people are friendly.

The Legal Grind
2640 Lincoln Blvd., Santa Monica
310.452.8160, legalgrind.com
Mon.-Fri. from 9 a.m., Sat. from 10 a.m.; closed Sun.
Corporate law seemed like a grind to Jeff Hughes, so he combined his desire to be a "people's lawyer" with his love of a good coffeehouse to create this groundbreaking place. Either on a drop-in basis or by appointment, you can get legal help with your latte – anything from forming an LLC or living trust to filing for bankruptcy or divorce. The $30 "coffee & counsel" gets you a java and twenty minutes of legal consultation on any issue. The idea was so brilliant that Legal Grinds are starting to pop up around Southern California.

Newsroom the Espresso Café

530 Wilshire Blvd., Ste. 102, Santa Monica
310.319.9100
Mon.-Fri. from 8 a.m., Sat.-Sun. from 9 a.m.
Well located in central Santa Monica, a short
walk from the Promenade, is this friendly café,
where the coffee drinks are carefully made
and the food is good for you: yummy oat-bran
muffins, veggie burgers, quesadillas and organic
salads. Try to score a table on the outdoor patio.

Novel Café & Bookstore

212 Pier Ave., Santa Monica
310.396.8566, novelcafe.com
Mon.-Fri. from 7 a.m., Sat.-Sun. from 8 a.m.
In this book-lined haven, you can spend
an afternoon or a month writing your novel,
especially if you head for one of the quiet
lofts, where you can sit with your laptop for
hours unnoticed. But you, of course, being a
considerate sort, will make yourself noticed by
ordering regular goodies – coffee drinks, bagels,
spinach Caesars, turkey quesadillas – from the
large-for-a-coffeehouse menu. The used books
are all for sale. Night owls, note that it's open
until 1 a.m. every night but Sunday.

Peet's Coffee & Tea

2439 Main St., Santa Monica
310.399.8117, peets.com
Mon.-Fri. from 5:30 a.m., Sat.-Sun. from 6 a.m.
1401 Montana Ave., Santa Monica
310.394.8555
Daily from 5:30 a.m.
Yes, it's a chain, but now that Starbucks has
seen fit to start producing music CDs, this is the
chain to head for. The coffee drinks are robust
and made by actual baristas, and both locations
have outdoor tables in lively, people-watching
neighborhoods. You can hang out as long as
you like, starting at the ungodly hour of 5:30 a.m.
And the baked goods are delectable.

UnUrban Coffee House

3301 Pico Blvd., Santa Monica
310.315.0056
Daily from 7 a.m.
This neighborhood fixture looks like the first
apartment for a bunch of theater majors: walls
painted red and purple, thrift-store tables and
chairs, old movie-theater seats and velvet
drapes in bold colors. Death Before Decaf is
the motto, and the baristas deliver the goods,
making an excellent double-shot cappuccino.
The WiFi is free, the tables are plentiful, and the
evening music and spoken-word performances
can be highly entertaining.

Velocity Café

2127 Lincoln Blvd., Santa Monica
310.314.3368, velocity-café.com
Daily from 5:30 a.m.
Crammed with folk art and little tiled tables,
Velocity is notable for its loaner computers and
relaxed atmosphere. The coffee could improve,
though. There's often something interesting
going on, from poetry reading to art opening.

On the menu at the Legal Grind

The Pub Crawl

Britannia Pub
318 Santa Monica Blvd., Santa Monica
310.458.5350, britanniapub.com
L & D daily, B Sat.-Sun. Full bar.
By day, Britannia is a friendly English pub where regulars saddle up to the bar for a snakebite (half Guinness, half cider) and tourists settle at a table outside for a traditional English lunch. By nightfall, it morphs into half karaoke club, half traditional pub – an odd combo that works well for the youngest imbibers.

Father's Office
1018 Montana Ave., Santa Monica
310.393.2337, fathersoffice.com
See listing on page 162.

Finn McCool's Irish Pub
2702 Main St., Santa Monica
310.452.1734, finnmccoolsirishpub.com
L & D daily. Full bar.
You can't get much closer to the real deal without crossing the Atlantic. Chef/owner Gerri Gilliland shipped her father's Northern Ireland pub to Santa Monica, timber by timber: intricately carved wooden booths, a classic bar and Irish memorabilia cluttering every cranny. On tap you'll find the standard pub beers and an even better whisky collection. We come on Sundays for the live traditional Irish music and the classic Irish roast served with horseradish crème fraiche (how thoroughly French). It's those unexpected culinary touches that make Gilliland's pub fare so easy to wash down with a pint.

O'Brien's Irish Pub
2226 Wilshire Blvd., Santa Monica
310.829.5303
L & D daily. Full bar.
The TVs are always tuned to sports and the pool tables are rarely empty at this comfy, brick-walled pub. It's the type of place where regulars hang out with a pint, give a nod to a newbie, then hunch back over their beer. The menu touts traditional Irish and English pub fare that's better than average, such as the banger (grilled sausage) sandwich with caramelized onions – it's the perfect halftime snack.

O'Brien's Irish Pub & Restaurant
2941 Main St., Santa Monica
310.396.4725, obriensonmain.com
L Sat.-Sun., D nightly. Full bar.
More a late-night bar scene than a low-key watering hole, the other O'Brien's draws a young crowd with its live music nightly. As befits many music venues, the drinks are overpriced and the food is mediocre, but no one seems to mind as they sip their American beers and tap their toes on the outdoor patio. Sunday afternoons are pleasantly mellow, with Irish or American folk music usually on offer.

McCabe's Bar & Grill
2455 Santa Monica Blvd., Santa Monica
310.264.9704
L & D daily. Full bar.
This vast commercial space turned bar is technically a Scottish pub, but the menu is average all-American fare, heavy on the burgers and fries – and no one seems to mind. They're mostly here to hang out at the bar, play a little pool, watch a little TV and down a few beers before heading home. Or maybe take in one last game of shuffleboard first.

Sonny McLean's
2615 Wilshire Blvd., Santa Monica
310.449.1811, sonnymcleans.com
L Tues.-Sun., D nightly. Beer & wine.
If you love all things Boston, this is the pub for you. Named after owner Jim Conner's Boston-Irish grandfather, Sonny McLean's is a dark, cozy place with a decent selection of everyday beers on tap, as well as beer-friendly chow. Insider's tip: If you're not a Red Sox or Patriots fan (worse still if you root for the Yankees), stay away on game days.

Ye Olde King's Head
132 Santa Monica Blvd., Santa Monica
310.451.1402, yeoldekingshead.com
L & D daily. Full bar.
Ex-pats, tourists and beer-loving locals flock to this famed English pub to take in a soccer match, compete in a friendly game of darts or discuss the merits of pasties. Bartenders are friendly and chatty, offering advice on what to order (the fish and chips) and what to drink (English beer, of course). If you've got the little ones in tow, the dining room next door is a popular family spot, especially the coveted outdoor tables on a sunny weekend afternoon.

The Drinking Life

Bodega Wine Bar

The Arsenal
12012 W Pico Blvd., West L.A.
310.575.5711, arsenalbar.com
Small and dark yet inviting and familiar, this is a favorite "I know a place" meeting spot for westside young and singles. The food isn't bad for a joint that might make you picture only french fries – in fact, they also carry the sweet-potato variety, as well as very good steaks and drinks that come as close as possible to being worth eight bucks. Two divided rooms and an outdoor patio create a downtown atmosphere that would make a New Yorker feel at home. (We're not sure who's supposed to be made to feel at home by the weaponry-decked walls.)

Beechwood
822 Washington Blvd., Venice
310.448.8884, beechwoodrestaurant.com
This bar has it all: plenty of room to sit and talk (on low-slung, 1950s-modern upholstered furniture or at the sleek wooden bar), a large walled patio with a firepit, a great bar menu (croque madames, steamed mussels, sweet-potato fries) and people who are attractive in a normal way. Most are in their 20s and 30s, but boomers will fit in, too.

Bodega Wine Bar
814 Broadway, Santa Monica
310.394.3504, bodegawinebar.com
Closed Mon.
The gimmick here is to make wine accessible to everyone, so every variety is priced the same: $8 for a glass, $20 for a carafe and $30 for a bottle. The list comprises small-producer, lesser-known varieties from around the world, and it's matched with a friendly collection of small-plate dishes. As for the bar itself, it's spare, chic and as dark as a coal mine, with a young crowd (lots of 20-something women meeting friends after work) that appreciates the lack of oenophile pretension.

The Brig
1515 Abbot Kinney Blvd., Venice
310.399.7537
This newly remodeled, Venice-chic, one-room lounge is a great place for weeknight drinks and a game of eight-ball on Abbot Kinney. The concrete and metal decor makes this place feel bigger (and draftier) than it is, but don't be fooled: It does fill up, so arrive early and stake out a place to sit.

The good life at Shutters on the Beach

Busby's West
3110 Santa Monica Blvd., Santa Monica
310.828.4567, busbysonline.com
Not quite as clubby as its Miracle Mile counterpart, Busby's West has more of a pub feeling – but it still has the sexy singles you've come to expect from the Busby's name. Artful brick walls and dark stained archways accent the X-Box 360–connected plasma screens and foosball tables.

Cameo Bar
Viceroy Hotel, 1819 Ocean Ave., Santa Monica
310.260.7511, viceroysantamonica.com
You can have your fifteen minutes of fame, or at least a sip of the good life, at the Viceroy's elegant bar. As befits a posh hotel, the cocktails are pricey, averaging $15, with the clientele to match. Specialty drinks tend toward the sticky sweet, like the Key lime martini with a graham-cracker-dusted rim. Opt instead for a classic cocktail or a glass of wine, then settle into one of the high-back vinyl lounge chairs to take in the glossy international clientele. Locals come for the high-class bar food, such as truffled grilled cheese or crab cakes with citrus confit from Whist chef Warren Schwartz, at a fraction of the price of dinner next door.

Chez Jay
1657 Ocean Ave., Santa Monica
310.395.1741, chezjays.com
Set just off the Promenade and Ocean Avenue restaurant chorus line, this little freestanding dive with red-vinyl booths and year-round Christmas lights has developed a deeply faithful clientele over the past half century. Some even say this includes famous faces, but you didn't hear it here. Come early for the surf and turf, or replace the dinner crowd at around 10 p.m. for solid drinks and wonderfully audible conversation. Eyes off the corner booth – that's our spot.

Circle Bar
2926 Main St., Santa Monica
310.450.0508, thecirclebar.com
Whoever called this place a dive was sorely mistaken. The drinks are pricey and the women all dolled up; squeeze your way around the center bar to the dance floor and let the DJ spin while you brush with Main Street's sexiest. Rose-colored glasses are doubly unnecessary – the place radiates a red-and-black glow that screams the pleasures of devilish sin.

Father's Office
1018 Montana Ave., Santa Monica
310.393.2337, fathersoffice.com
Things sure have changed since a volleyball player known as Dad opened this beer-and-wine tavern in 1953. Sang Yoon, today's chef/owner, has turned it into a foodie destination and global beer garden in one (tiny) spot. Yoon tastes hundreds of beers before settling on the 30 drafts, with even more in bottles. New arrivals are scribbled on a chalkboard beside the bar. The beer isn't cheap, but these are meant for sipping, not chugging. Unfortunately, the hamburger's fame means there's a line out the door almost every night, but if you're not in a rush – and what true beer drinker is? – the beers (and burger) are worth the wait.

Gas Lite
2030 Wilshire Blvd., Santa Monica
310.829.2382
Tuesdays and Thursdays are karaoke nights, and this place has found a loyal following among Santa Monicans looking to show off their high school choir skills or just embarrass themselves (is there any difference between the two?). On weekends you'll find dancing, and on Mondays live blues bands. Or come at high noon on Saturday for a weekly town hall meeting with SaMo city council members. Forget the Expo line – there's free pizza!

The Hideout

112 W. Channel Rd. (at PCH), Santa Monica
310.429.1851, santamonicahideout.com
Coming off a 68-year run as the Santa
Monica Canyon homosexual hangout called
the Friendship, the Hideout now serves as
neighborhood bar for laidback locals and surfers.
Familiar faces line the patio that once heard the
conversations of Christopher Isherwood and his
friends. Upstairs is an almost-private party room
for those who want to take the hideout theme
a step further. Reasonably priced cocktails,
attentive bartenders and a genuinely welcoming
atmosphere make this a great place to grab a
drink after a fancy Channel Road dinner or a day
on the sand.

Library Alehouse

2911 Main St., Santa Monica
310.314.4855, libraryalehouse.com
With 30 rotating, hand-selected beers on tap,
a charming wooden bar and knowledgeable
bartenders keen to chat about the finer points
of hops, this place is a beer aficionado's dream.
Beer not your thing? No problem. Choose from
more than fifteen wines by the glass or enjoy
lunch on the lovely garden patio out back. The
Library might just put an end to the quintessential
Saturday dilemma: beer and hearty grub, or
wine and a lovely lunch? How about Alehouse
BBQ ribs and a stout for you, and wild-salmon
enchiladas with chipotle cream and a pinot noir
for your guest. You say potato....

Liquid Kitty

11780 Pico Blvd., West L.A.
310.473.3707, thekitty.com
Lap up martinis with trendsetters at this
New York–hip bar that deserves its cool-cat
reputation. The Kitty draws a decidedly vodka
(not gin) martini crowd that chatters away on
teetering bar stools as rock tunes blare through
the sound system.

Lobby Bar

Shutters on the Beach, 1 Pico Blvd., Santa
Monica
310.458.0030, shuttersonthebeach.com
Some time ago we were here to meet a
business contact who was running late. Who
cared? We ran into friends, sipped champagne
and watched the sparkling ocean, content to
linger in this lovely locale. This swank hotel bar
boasts a rich, Ralph Lauren–like decor, with
comfy sofas and a roaring fire. The scene also
includes a piano man and smashing ocean
views. Other than the equally dreamy lounge
at the Casa del Mar next door, there's no better
place in town to meet and greet.

The Shack

2518 Wilshire Blvd., Santa Monica
310.449.1171, shacksm.com
The Shack is dubbed Eagles' Nest West for a
reason. Don't enter on game days if you aren't
a Phillies or Eagles fan. This burger joint by day
turns into a crowded sports bar at night and on
weekends, bursting at the seams with diehard
fans tossing back pints.

The Veranda

Casa del Mar, 1910 Ocean Way, Santa Monica
310.581.5503, hotelcasadelmar.com
A cold martini, a table by the window, an
interesting person to talk to ... it can't get much
better than in this casually elegant oceanview
hotel bar, at least until the check comes. (If you
have to ask, you can't afford it.) The large lobby
bar encompasses three areas: tables near the
expansive oceanfront windows, sofas and comfy
chairs around the fireplace, and a TV-equipped
library nook equipped with comfortingly dorky
tufted chairs, expensive versions of the kind in
your dad's den. It's relaxed during the week –
producers and business folk come here to close
a deal or impress a date – but more of a scene
on weekend nights.

5 Hot Happy Hours

Border Grill

1445 4th St., Santa Monica
310.451.1655, bordergrill.com
Happy hour Mon.-Fri. 4-7 p.m., Fri.-Sat. after
10 p.m., Sun. 11:30 a.m.-4 p.m. (drinks only)
Happy hour on the border translates to $3 house
margaritas, mojitos and imported beers, but
those in the know come for the same deal on the
addictive, inventive appetizers, including green
corn tamales and plantain empanadas, normally
$5 to $9. Go easy on the premium margaritas –
they're still full price ($10 and up), which is too
bad, because they're so good they make the
house version taste like lemon-lime soda. But
better happy-hour bargains are hard to find at a
restaurant that easily tops $75 for two at dinner.
Plus, there's no need to raid the fridge: Late-
night weekend snackers get the same deal.

Chaya Venice

110 Navy St., Venice
310.396.1179, thechaya.com
Happy hour nightly 5-7 p.m.
Bargain-basement prices on sushi rolls and
designer nibbles are the draw at this mod Cal-
Asian hot spot. For $3 and $4 you get sushi
standards, such as spicy shrimp and tuna rolls,
and chef-inspired dishes, from potato-leek miso
soup to the special roll of the hour. Wash it down
with choice sake, beer from around the globe
or, if you're feeling racy, a tangerine martini.
A little-known secret: Late-night revelers can
order sliders, mini versions of the full-size burger
topped with aged cheddar, mango chutney and
grilled onions, for $8.50 (after 10:30 p.m. on
weeknights and 11 p.m. on weekends).

Ocean Avenue Seafood

1401 Ocean Ave., Santa Monica
310.394.5669, oceanave.com
Oyster hour Mon.-Fri. 4-6:30 p.m., Sat.-Sun.
11:30 a.m.-6 p.m. (bar only) & 3-6 p.m.
Ocean Avenue Seafood's daily oyster hour is a
slurper's dream. Sample oysters from the Atlantic
to the Pacific and every riverbed in between
for half price – $6.50 per half dozen for most.
Or try the oyster sampler, a half dozen oysters
paired with three wines. If bivalves aren't your
thing, you can enjoy other half-price appetizers –
perhaps a little smoked trout or tuna tartare –
with suggested wine pairings.

Sushi Roku

1401 Ocean Ave., Santa Monica
310.458.4771, sushiroku.com
Happy hour Mon.-Fri. 5-6:30 p.m., Sat.-Sun.
4-6:30 p.m.
At this sushi haunt known for its sky-high prices,
we did a double take when we saw the prices
during Red Sun Hour: $5 for six-piece cut rolls,
$3 for hand rolls and $3 for hot appetizers.
Portions are generous, and there's hardly a
happy-hour fill-in to be found (except perhaps
the ubiquitous California and spicy tuna rolls).
The albacore-garlic and shrimp-jalapeño rolls
are plump and packed with flavor; the crispy
chicken kara age with cilantro sauce and
rock shrimp tempura from the hot menu are
downright addictive. All are $10 to $15 during
peak hours, so grab a seat at the bar during
happy hour and find out for yourself whether this
popular sushi bar is worth the hype.

Violet

3221 Pico Blvd., Santa Monica
310.453.9113, violetrestaurant.com
Happy hour Tues.-Thurs. 6-7 p.m.
Violet's young chef/owner, Jared Simons,
knows how to woo westsiders to his casual
neighborhood bistro. Sure, during lunch and
dinner he serves sophisticated food at affordable
prices, but nothing beats the seven happy-hour
dishes for $7 each before 7 p.m. Violet's menu
is seasonal, so go with an open palate. Dishes
might include classic duck confit one night, trout
with brown butter and golden raisins the next.
Wash it all down with a bottomless glass of wine
for $10. But eat and drink quickly. You've only
got an hour!

Wine Shops We've Known & Loved

Briggs Wines & Spirits
13038 San Vicente Blvd., Brentwood
310.395.9997, briggswine.com
Have you been searching high and low for a 2000 Chateau Haut Brion? At Briggs it can be yours… for $750. You know you're dealing with a high-end wine shop when caviar is an impulse purchase. Big spenders drop upwards of $100 per bottle at this 1940s institution. Amid the hard-to-find French and California boutique wines are affordable vintages from the same producers. The savvy staff is happy to help, but with bottles arranged alphabetically (what a novel concept!), it's just as easy to snoop around on your own.

The Duck Blind Fine Wine & Spirits
1102 Montana Ave., Santa Monica
310.394.6705, ducksblindswineandspirits.com
For years we drove past this 50-year neighbor-hood favorite without a second glance. But what looks like a standard grungy liquor store is actually a perfectly fine wine shop with lots of $10 to $15 bottles. There's plenty of variety, in breadth if not depth. Check out the specials, where you might luck into a $15 wine for $5. You'll find lots of good local and international brews, too.

Fireside Cellars
1421 Montana Ave., Santa Monica
310.393.2888, firesidecellars.com
If hearing names like Cakebread and Stag's Leap causes you to pull out the stemware, then head over to the Fireside. The tiny shop looks like a cozy home cellar filled with boutique wines, especially those from California and France: a Languedoc here, a Sonoma there. If you're a bargain shopper, Fireside probably isn't for you. Sure, there are good $12 selections, but it's almost impossible to resist that $45 cabernet you haven't had since your last trip to the Alexander Valley. Good selection of specialty beers, small-producer Scotch and hard-to-find liqueurs.

Los Angeles Wine Co.
4935 McConnell Ave., West L.A.
310.306.9463, lawineco.com
Located on the edge of Marina del Rey, this wine merchant has spent the last 25 years scouring the world for bargain-basement deals on wines, and it's damn good at it. Its motto – "every wine in stock, always sale priced" – isn't just a gimmick: A $95 Burgundy is $80, a $65 Sonoma cabernet is $50, and a $40 Italian Sangiovese is $30. Many come here for the Under $12 Club, a penny-pincher's dream with more than 100 selections, several at $5 or less – even if they're not all perfect for sipping, they'll make one hell of a sangria.

Moe's Fine Wines
11740 San Vicente Blvd., Ste. 114, Brentwood
310.826.4444, moesfinewines.com
Scott "Moe" Levy loves wine. So in 2004, the Palisades software engineer quit his day job to open this high-end neighborhood shop. With its stained-wood wine racks, Riedel stemware and temperature-controlled reserve room, the place looks like a dream home cellar, and it's stocked with a carefully chosen selection of $8 to $800 wines, many from small California producers, with a healthy dose of international heavy-hitters. Levy believes you have to taste to learn what you like, so don't miss the tastings on Saturday afternoon. While you're at it, ask to taste the delightful house chocolates and nuts.

Wine Expo
2933 Santa Monica Blvd., Santa Monica
310.828.4428
We love Wine Expo. Sure, it's got a vast selection of interesting wines, most notably from Italy, but it's the clever descriptions posted beside the cases haphazardly strewn around the store that keep us coming back. Ditto the newsletter, which is a hoot. What started as a champagne specialty shop (as evidenced by the Champagne World Headquarters sign out front – and yes, it still has gobs of champagne) turned into the westside's Italian-wine headquarters when the owner, Ali Biglar, turned Italophile. He travels there often, frequenting both tiny vineyards as well as highly coveted (and highly priced) wineries. He befriends the winemakers and strikes good deals. Then he ships cases back via his own import business – no distributor required – to keep prices low. The educated staff is far from perky, but they're refreshingly honest – ask for a $20 wine to use as a hostess gift and they'll tell you about the $14 one that tastes like it's $35. Or the $7 prosecco that's perfect with barbecue. Try something new, and if you like it, buy a case the next day, because they may never have it again. Ever. And that's the fun of it. A tip: One of the staffers is a fan of tequila, another of beer, so there is an interesting, prime selection of both.

Q & A: Josie Le Balch

Longtime Santa Monica restaurateur Josie Le Balch started wielding a kitchen knife as soon as she could reach the countertops at home with her father, French chef Gregoire Le Balch. She's been at the helm of Saddle Peak Lodge, Remi and the Beach House. Now she's turning out her own amalgam of California cuisine at Josie, the celebrated restaurant she opened with her husband, Frank Delzio, in 2001 on a sleepy Pico corner. Jenn Garbee chatted with Josie about life in the Santa Monica restaurant world.

You're a Valley girl – how did you end up at so many Santa Monica restaurants?
The first was Remi back in 1990, and that was just by chance. It was Venetian, and Venetians use a lot of game, and I was at Saddle Peak, which specializes in game. The owner asked me to cook for him. I said I didn't know much about Venetian food, and he said, "I can teach you, and you'll learn my way!" I was looking for something different. As they say, all roads lead to Santa Monica.

So what inspired you to pick Santa Monica for your own place?
We looked all over L.A. for a space, but we had a limited budget, and most places were much more than we could manage. Then this location came up. It was a real diamond in the rough, so it was less expensive, but once we got inside we realized why – everything had to be replaced. It was a risk because it's in a bedroom community – much of Pico is still building up – but it worked. We're fortunate to be in Santa Monica, because of all the produce coming to the Farmer's Market – the best, really – and people here like to eat out.

Growing up, did you flee the Valley for Santa Monica often?
Oh sure, we went to the beach all summer. Now we live in my dad's old house, so we have a nice bit of property that we didn't want to give up. When we opened Josie we thought about buying the tiny house next door, but we couldn't believe how expensive it was, so we stayed put. Of course, it was half of what it costs today!

What do you like to do when you have a day off?
My husband and I love to ski, and I like to go on beach picnics with my pastry chef, Jonna. But I really like to work in my father's old garden. Right now I'm growing wild arugula that we use at the restaurant. In the summer it's tons of tomatoes, salad greens – anything, really.

What's your favorite dish to make at home?
I married my husband because he loves to cook! I tend to not cook at home, unless chopping and dicing count. Well, I do cook one thing – my daughter loves an old-fashioned French roast chicken, and my family thinks I'm a rock star when I make it. They don't realize how easy it is – you just throw it into the oven.

Santa Monica is...
Entertaining

Creative people flock to the beach towns, so it's no wonder that Santa Monica and her sister communities are so rich in the entertaining arts: music, dance, film, theater, comedy and festivals. From outdoor summer concerts to church-housed chamber music, edgy film festivals to mainstream community theater, this place has it all.

Fresh-Air Fun

What better way to take advantage of the sun, sea and wide-open beaches than with outdoor celebrations? Santa Monica and Venice provide plenty of choices to enjoy music, dancing, movies and festivals in the great outdoors.

Surf-guitar king Dick Dale wows the crowd at a Twilight Dance Series concert on the Santa Monica Pier.

Abbot Kinney Festival
Abbot Kinney Blvd., Venice
310.396.3772, abbotkinney.org/festival
Late Sept.; free
This annual all-day weekend block party hosted by the Abbot Kinney District Association draws tens of thousands of revelers to Venice each year. Kick off the festivities by marching in the morning parade, then stroll along Abbot Kinney to experience the live music, street dancers, food courts, arts and crafts vendors, performance stages and, in true Venice style, the Spirit Garden. At the Family Court there's plenty to keep the kids occupied, from old-fashioned mural painting to cutting-edge X games.

Earth Day on the Promenade
3rd St. Promenade, Santa Monica
earthdayla.org
On Earth Day (mid-April); free
The Promenade, with its bevy of chain stores and tourist-friendly food, might seem like an odd choice for the green-centric Earth Day L.A. festival. But when planet-conscious folks and good-time seekers converge for a day of music, family activities, organic munchies and the latest solar-powered gadgets, fun times are had by all.

Santa Monica Drive-In at the Pier
Santa Monica Pier Parking Lot (south side)
310.458.8900, santamonicapier.org
Tues. nights Aug.-Oct.; free but tickets required (check web site for ticket locations)
BYO picnic dinner and settle in for the movie du jour at this popular Tuesday-night outdoor film series. Watch from your car or bring a chair for an al fresco pier seat (they're also available for rent). The movies are free, but space is tight, so advance tickets are required.

Santa Monica Pier Twilight Dance Series
Santa Monica Pier Central Plaza
twilightdance.org
Thurs. nights June-Aug.; free
Who needs *Dancing with the Stars* when you can dance under them? In a nod to the historic ballrooms that once graced the pier, the city of Santa Monica hosts evenings of live music and dance. These days you'll find swing, reggae, folk and rock bands entertaining a lively crowd of amateur and professional dancers.

Sunday Concert Series at the Santa Monica Pier
Santa Monica Pier Central Plaza, Santa Monica
310.458.8900, santamonicapier.org
Sun. afternoons March-May; free
Taking in a Sunday-afternoon waterfront concert really is as lovely as it sounds – only don't expect to hear classical music lilting over softly crashing ocean waves. This series features quality party bands: soul, R&B, classic rock and modern Latin, all the better for tossing off your flip-flops and doing a jig in the sand.

Classical & Modern Music & Dance

Gordon Getty Concert Series
The Getty Center
1200 Getty Center Dr., Brentwood
310.440.7300, getty.edu
You may not be able to travel the world on the Getty's dime, but you can get a taste of world-class music right in our own backyard. In conjunction with exhibitions, the Getty brings international performers to Brentwood, such as Paris-based L'Ensemble Pennetier and, closer to home, the New York Chamber Soloists.

Jacaranda: Music on the Edge of Santa Monica
First Presbyterian Church
1220 2nd St., Santa Monica
310.451.1303, jacarandamusic.com
$25 ticket donation ($10 students)
Think classical music can't be experimental, innovative and new? Jacaranda, an avant-garde ensemble, recasts classical selections in a modern light. Don't worry, we're not talking techno-funk – it's still classical music, just rediscovered.

Musica Angelica in action

Musica Angelica
First Presbyterian Church
1220 2nd St., Santa Monica
310.458.4504, musicaangelica.org
Tickets $12-$25
Famed organist and composer Martin Hasselbock leads what many regard as Southern California's premier Baroque music ensemble. In 2007, the group signed its first recording deal and began touring, so keep an eye out for other concerts by this hometown group. Tip: Arrive 45 minutes early for the free pre-concert lecture.

Santa Monica College
1900 Pico Blvd., Santa Monica
310.434.4323, smc.edu
Indecisive listeners will find a little of everything at Santa Monica College, where students, faculty and community musicians perform in the SMC Symphony Orchestra, SMC Concert Band, Chamber Choir, solo classical concerts, jazz quartets and opera theater. It's one of the best deals in town, with many shows free, and others just a ten spot.

Santa Monica Symphony
Santa Monica Civic Auditorium
1855 Main St., Santa Monica
310.395.6330, smsymphony.org
Driving downtown at rush hour to catch the LA Phil can be a real drag, so why not stay a little closer to home? Going strong since 1945, the SM Symphony is a homegrown orchestra with an ever-changing cast of college students and community musicians, peppered with professionals. Okay, so you probably won't see internationally acclaimed musicians here. But who cares when the concert is free (parking is $8), and you actually have time to go to dinner before – or after – the show?

Donna Sternberg & Dancers
911 9th St., #206, Santa Monica
310.260.1198, dsdancers.com
Donna Sternberg founded her small, progressive dance company in 1985, before collaborative ballet projects were cool. Her troupe performs all over Southern California, bringing modern ballet, poetry and music together on stage. Check the online calendar to catch local performances.

The Verdi Chorus
First United Methodist Church
1008 11th St., Santa Monica
310.826.8309, verdichorus.org
Tickets $10-$25
After Santa Monica's Verdi Ristorante di Musica closed in 1991, the professional opera singers who belted out songs for customers reorganized as the Verdi Chorus under artistic director Anne Marie Ketchum. Today the more than 50 members perform opera solos and chorus pieces, with frequent guest soloists. And this is one opera concert where kids are welcome.

On Stage & Screen

On Stage

City Garage
1340 1/2 4th St., Santa Monica
310.319.9939, citygarage.org
Tickets $20, $10 seniors/students; Sun.
"pay what you can"
Even the sign out front of this old city police
garage turned experimental theater gives off a
dissident vibe; inside, the edgy performances
are polished and professional. You'll leave
here pondering the social and political themes
explored in City Garage's contemporary, often
international plays.

Getty Villa Theater Lab
The Getty Villa, 17985 Pacific Coast Hwy.,
Pacific Palisades
310.440.7300, getty.edu
Free (reservations required); parking $8
Et tu, Brute? If you think classic plays are
sleepers, get thyself to the Getty Villa.
Each season guest troupes reinterpret Greek
and Roman plays and literature, such as
Euripedes's *The Bacchae,* a celebration of the
wine god through dance set to the beat of a
Brazilian percussion ensemble.

The Miles Memorial Playhouse
Emerson Reed Park, 1130 Lincoln Blvd.,
Santa Monica
milesplayhouse.org
The city-owned 1929 theater-for-hire has long
been home to many of Santa Monica's oldest,
and newest, theater companies. The menu of
performances varies from David Mamet's latest
work to modern dance theater. Check the online
calendar for the lineup.

Pacific Resident Theatre
703 Venice Blvd., Venice
310.822.8392, pacificresidenttheatre.com
Tickets $12
Rediscover rarely performed classics, lesser-
known works and modern plays at this theater-
lover's theater. Productions are refreshingly
more about exploring the craft of theater than
selling seats, thanks to Pacific's primary mission
as an artist's cooperative between actors,
directors, playwrights and designers.

Powerhouse Theatre
3116 2nd St., Santa Monica
310.396.3680, powerhousetheatre.com
Originally a Santa Monica trolley powerhouse,
this theater's intimate 75-seat space is home to
Shakespeare Santa Monica, a roving company
that performs in parks, parking lots and public
spaces throughout Santa Monica in July. Also not
to miss is the Late Night performance series, for
which $5 gets you a drink and a virtual guarantee
of wacky, experimental Friday-night fun.

The Promenade Playhouse
1404 3rd St. Promenade, Santa Monica
323.656-8070, ext. 17,
promenadeplayhouse.com
Tickets $12-$20
Tongue-in-cheek performances at this conserva-
tory and theater space are the specialty –
Bunny Tales Episodes IV: Bunny Wars, a modern
tale of Peter Rabbit as he saves the cabbage
patch from foes, among them. An ever-changing
menu of solo performances and stand-up comedy nights are also on tap.

Ruskin Group Theatre Co.
3000 Airport Ave., Santa Monica
310.397.3244, ruskingrouptheatre.com
Tickets $10-$20
Those of us with a love-hate relationship for
project deadlines appreciate the Ruskin Group's
monthly L.A. Café Plays – they give a playwright
ten and a half hours to unleash a firestorm of
creativity for a sold-out audience. If fast-food
theater isn't your speed, try one of the avant-
garde plays on the main stage.

Santa Monica Civic Light Opera
601 Pico Blvd., Santa Monica
310.458.5939, smclo.org
Tickets $20 each or $50 for all 4 shows
This community-sponsored conservancy for the
Santa Monica-Malibu Unified School District
presents classic musicals and plays, such as
My Fair Lady, Guys and Dolls and *Romeo and
Juliet.* Before you decide these are torturous
parents-only gigs, know that recent shows have
been nominated for national awards alongside
plays performed in the biggest theaters in town
(take that, Geffen!). And with so many famous
alumni – including Sean Penn, Robert Downey
Jr. and Charlie Sheen – you might have a saw-
them-when story for the grandkids someday.

Rehearsal under the oaks at Topanga's
Theatricum Botanicum

Santa Monica Playhouse

1211 4th St., Santa Monica
310.394.9779, santamonicaplayhouse.com
Tickets $11-$16
For almost half a century, the SM Playhouse has
been training actors, developing school curricula,
organizing theater workshops for kids and adults
and putting on two dozen plays, musicals and
family shows a year. Weekends are packed with
several matinees and evening shows. Kids are a
focus here, so bring the family.

Santa Monica Theater Guild

Morgan-Wixson Theater, 2627 Pico Blvd.,
Santa Monica
310.828.7519, morgan-wixson.org
Tickets $15-$23 ($5-$7 for youth shows)
Santa Monica's only volunteer community
theater has been going strong since 1946,
turning out upbeat musicals and popular plays.
It's an open-audition format, so dust off those
vocal cords and give it a whirl. Hey, James Dean
graced the stage here in 1947, so you never
know what might happen.

Sight Unseen Theatre

844 17th St., Ste. 105, Santa Monica
310.315.1477, sightunseentheatre.com
Tickets $15-$20
For five years and counting, Sight Unseen
has been quietly building a reputation as the
place for alternative contemporary plays. The
founders, three twentysomething theater and
film actors, have a fresh eye for offbeat theater.
The secret's out.

Will Geer Theatricum Botanicum

1419 N. Topanga Canyon Blvd., Topanga
310.455.3723, theatricum.com
A marriage of two of Southern California's
greatest assets – the Santa Monica Mountains
and gobs of talented people – results in one
glorious place to enjoy theater. Shakespeare
is the stock in trade, but you'll also encounter
such classics as *Blithe Spirit* by Noel Coward
and *Dracula* by Bram Stoker, as well as new

works from local playwrights. Staged outdoors
under oaks and sycamores, the productions
are typically lively, engaging and fun; it's a great
place to introduce kids to Shakespeare. Founded
by actor Will Geer back when he was blacklisted
by Hollywood, it benefitted greatly from his later
success as Grandpa Walton on TV; today it is
one of the treasures of California theater.

On Screen

Art-House Theaters

Aero Theater

1328 Montana Ave.,
Santa Monica
310.260.1528,
americancinematheque.com
American Cinematheque, a
nonprofit devoted to promoting
classic and art films, runs this
meticulously renovated, not-
to-miss 1940s theater. It's got
that Old Hollywood vibe but in
a friendly neighborhood way,
with screenings several nights
a week.

Laemmle's Monica Fourplex

1332 2nd St., Santa Monica
310.394.9741, laemmle.com
Very viewable independent films – the kind you
want to watch on a Saturday, not just in film
class – are plentiful at Santa Monica's largest art
theater. The multiscreen theater can get busy on
weekends, evenings and during film festivals, so
give yourself plenty of time to snag an aisle seat.

Landmark NuArt Theatre

11272 Santa Monica Blvd., West L.A.
310.281.8223, landmarktheatres.com
Okay, technically it's not in Santa Monica (though
it is west of the 405), but we couldn't leave out
L.A.'s favorite *Rocky Horror Picture Show* venue.
Every Saturday at midnight you can do the Time
Warp with like-minded fans, or if you're lacking
a Frank-N-Furter costume, choose from the
progressive menu of independent films on view.

Landmark NuWilshire Theatre

1314 Wilshire Blvd., Santa Monica
310.281.8223, landmarktheatres.com
This intimate, two-screen theater dating back
to 1931 may not be glam, and it doesn't
get the press of the bigger art houses, but
the independent foreign and American film
screenings are worth checking out.

Mainstream Theaters

AMC Loews Broadway 4
1441 3rd St. Promenade, Santa Monica
310.458.1506, amctheatres.com

AMC Loews Marina 6
13455 Maxella Ave., Marina del Rey
310.578.2002, amctheatres.com

AMC Santa Monica 7
1310 3rd St. Promenade, Santa Monica
310.289.4262, amctheatres.com

Hollywood Theaters Malibu Cinemas
3822 Cross Creek Rd., Malibu
310.456.6990, gohollywood.com

Mann Criterion
1313 3rd St. Promenade, Santa Monica
310.395.1599 manntheatres.com

Film Festivals

Inspiration Film Festival
877.874.4576
April, Laemmle's Monica Fourplex,
Santa Monica
Santa Monica's fairly new Inspiration Film
Festival features narrative films, documentaries,
shorts, animated works and children's films
that promise to lift your spirits, transform lives
and inspire. Okay, so maybe the theme is a bit
cheesy, but the films are top-notch.

Malibu Film Festival
310.452.6688, malibufilmfestival.com
April, various locations in Malibu & Santa Monica
Producer David Katz's Malibu Film Foundation
organizes its annual festival with the hopes that
new filmmakers' work will be seen, and picked
up, by industry players. Kick off the weekend at
the Bergamot Station opening party, then settle
in for a marathon of weekend screenings.

The Other Venice Film Festival
othervenicefilmfest.com
March, various locations in Venice
Not to be confused with the Venice Film Festival
in Italy, this art-film festival is centered on
its Abbot Awards for the best in low-budget,
maverick filmmaking. Take in a few of the 75-
plus films over four days and cast your vote for
the Audience Choice Award, or check out the
individual screenings held throughout the year.

Pacific Palisades Film Festival
310.459.7073, friendsoffilm.com
May, various locations in Pacific Palisades
Friends of Film organizes this May festival.
Heart-wrenching documentaries are often the
focus, with screenings and readings over a
three-day weekend. Check back throughout the
year for screenings and the popular outdoor
Movies in the Park, which screens family-friendly
features in August.

PXL This
310.306.7330, indiespace.com/pxlthis
Nov., various locations
Since 1981, Gerry Fialka's quirky PXL
festival has developed a cultlike following. All
submissions must be shot with the 1980s-era
Fisher-Price PXL 2000 (yes, it's a toy camera),
so you'll be watching lots of raw, grainy and very
personal films. After making the festival rounds,
some of these even have turned up in top
museums, including the Whitney and MoMA.

Santa Monica International Film Festival
smfilmfestival.com
August, various locations in Santa Monica
If you're not sure what to call the Santa Monica
International Film Festival, or where to find
information about it, join the crowd. Since it
began in 1996, the SMFF (or the SMIFF as it's
known these days) has experienced more than
its share of growing pains, including a black
curtain in 2002 followed by a 2003 reopening
under a Dallas-based organizer. (If we're going
to farm out our film festivals, couldn't we at least
have it be Austin?) No matter – as of press time,
the festival was back – or at least the moniker
was. This time around it's known as the Santa
Monica International Film Festival, it occurs in
August not February (maybe a little sun will do
it good), and it's produced by filmmakers who
reside in Santa Monica (how revolutionary).
A slew of independent short films are on the
weekend lineup, and tickets are a bargain at $10
for a general screening pass. Hopefully the third
(or fourth) time around really is a charm.

Santa Monica Teen Film Festival
310.458.8634, smgov.net/smtff
June, Main Library, Santa Monica
Budding filmmakers can get their first films
screened at this new teen-only festival sponsored
by the city. Short live-action and animated films
are eligible, with all-day screenings and juried
awards for the top two films in each category.

The Gig Guide

Comedy & Spoken Word

Beyond Baroque Literary Arts Center
681 Venice Blvd., Venice
310.822.3006, beyondbaroque.org
Readings & workshops several times weekly;
cover free-$7
This bookstore dedicated to emerging, overlooked
and out-of-print poetry puts on a progressive menu
of readings and workshops. At Poets Beyond the
Half Shell, hang with contemporary poets as they
read and discuss their work, then come back for a
workshop to hone your own voice.

The Talking Stick
1630 Ocean Park Blvd., Santa Monica
310.450.6052, thetalkingstick.net
Open daily; events select evenings; no cover
A cozy coffeehouse by day, the Talking Stick
turns into a bohemian lounge at night. Open-
mike Wednesdays lure comedians, musicians
and poets working out kinks; weekends bring
solo guitarists, singer-songwriters and acoustic
bands belting it out on the tiny stage while
patrons sip soy lattes and nosh on hummus.

The Westside Eclectic
1323-A 3rd St. (alley between 3rd & 4th),
Santa Monica
310.451.0850, westsideeclectic.com
Shows Tues.-Sun.; cover free-$10
Husband and wife duo Marc and Ali Campbell
are so keen on comedy that they opened the
Westside Eclectic in 2005 as a teaching studio
and performance venue for emerging comics
and sketch and improv groups. The loft-like
space, friendly staff and laid-back vibe have
made it a favorite among performers and their
supportive fans alike. Look out, Hollywood;
Santa Monica is hitting the comedy scene.

Dancing

Air Conditioned
2819 Pico Blvd., Santa Monica
310.829.3700
625 Lincoln Blvd., Venice
310.230.5343, airconditionedbar.com
DJ music nightly; no cover except special events
Young, trendy westsiders who want to avoid the
drive to Hollywood grind it out on the dance floor
at the Santa Monica and Venice locations of this
popular San Diego club. A rotating staple of guest
DJs spin hip-hop, soul and fusion funk each night.
Insiders hang out on Sunday nights, with laid-back
tunes and drink specials in Santa Monica, and
unplugged live bands in Venice.

Circle Bar
2926 Main St., Santa Monica
310.450.0508, thecirclebar.com
DJ music nightly; no cover
This neighborhood spot has been around for
more than 30 years – eons in nightclub terms –
and it's still bringing in the crowds. Post-
collegiate singles toss back a few cocktails in the
crimson-walled lounge before hitting the dance
floor to shark for a date.

Club Twenty Twenty
2020 Wilshire Blvd., Santa Monica
310.829.1933, clubtwentytwenty.com
DJ music Thurs.-Sat., cover $5-$10
Everything at this über-cool Santa Monica club
is white hot: the sleek decor, the sunken dance
floor and the pretty young people drinking pretty
martinis. College types flock here on Fridays for
'80s night to sing along to Madonna tunes that
they're too young to remember.

Isabelle's Dance Academy
1334 Lincoln Blvd., Santa Monica
310.392.3493, isabellesalsa.com
Salsa fiestas Fri. & Sun. nights;
no cover; day & evening classes
Salsa is the specialty at Isabelle Pampillo's
studio, where she ignites dormant libidos with
social sambas, women-only pole dancing and
couples' lap-dancing classes (bring your own lap).
Friday and Sunday nights are the late-night Salsa
Fiestas, with drinks and free open-floor dancing.

Dance Doctor
1440 4th St., Santa Monica
310.459.2264, dancedoctor.com
Day & evening classes, private parties
Not sure which moves to launch when club
DJs start spinning hip-hop (or when you're
chaperoning the high school dance)? John
Cassese, aka the Dance Doctor, to the rescue.
While the standards are here – salsa, swing,
ballet – Cassese also covers hip-hop, jazz/funk
and capoeira (16th-century Brazilian sparring
dance which the winner takes home a partner),
so you can get down with the cool kids.

Mor Bar

2941 Main St., Santa Monica
310.396.6678, themorbar.com
DJ music nightly; cover $2-$5
Bring your harem to this bohemian lounge bedecked with draping canvas and plush red velvet. The music changes from rumba and mambo on Salsa Mondays (with free lessons early in the evening) to funk classics and honey cocktails on Honey Wednesdays. Space is tight, so get there early.

Rusty's Rhythm Club

Elks Lodge, 8025 W. Manchester Ave.,
Playa del Rey
310.606.5606, swingshiftontap.com
Open Wed. nights; cover $8 first Wed. of the month (DJ), $12-$15 live band nights
Cut a rug at the Elks Lodge? You bet. Since 2001, professional tap/swing dancer Rusty Frank has hosted a Wednesday-night swing club, and this is one dance club that's actually about dance. The 2,800-square-foot dance floor, lessons from Rusty herself (or one of her many students) and stellar live bands are the draws.

217 Lounge

217 Broadway, Santa Monica
310.394.6336, lounge217.com
DJ music Wed.-Sat.; cover $5-$10
The music at this funky new dance club/cocktail bar is light on hip-hop, heavy on pop, which is how this late-20s to mid-30s crowd likes it. The rhythm phobic can sip cocktails at one of the candlelit lounge tables, or head to the back bar.

Zanzibar

1301 5th St., Santa Monica
310.451.2221, zanzibarlive.com
DJ music Tues.-Sun.; cover $5-$20
The cozy nooks with pillow-strewn couches and bamboo-covered everything make for an intimate, mellow island feel at Temple Bar's hybrid dance-lounge cousin. Rotating DJs who spin according to theme – Afro funk, bossa nova or a little Brazilian cool – fill up the dance floor.

Rock, Pop & Folk

14 Below

1348 14th St., Santa Monica
310.451.5040, 14below.com
Music nightly; cover varies, usually $10
Hang with indie hipsters at this local hole-in-the-wall to scope out the latest rock bands. The club tends to book several bands a night – good if you have a short attention span, bad if you came to

Rusty Frank and Giovanni Quintero lead the swing dancing at Rusty's Rhythm Club.

see one favorite band – but you can always play a round of pool in the back while you wait one out.

Friday Nights at the Getty

The Getty Center, 1200 Getty Center Dr.,
Brentwood
310.440.7300, getty.edu
Bimonthly concerts; free (reservations required), but parking $8
This museum concert series is surprisingly cutting-edge. One week it's Vashti Bunyan, aka "the female Bob Dylan," the next it's alt-country band the Knitters. Tickets are free, but competition for the hottest shows can be fierce, so check the web site for call-in release dates.

McCabe's Guitar Shop

3101 Pico Blvd., Santa Monica
310.828.4497, mccabes.com
Music Fri.-Sun.; tickets $8-$30
Unless you've turned your garage into a practice studio, it's hard to get much more intimate than an acoustic gig at McCabe's. The performance space is every bit as grungy and musician-friendly as the famed guitar shop below, with a roster of humble greats and the occasional kids' concert for tomorrow's Lou Reeds.

Rusty's Surf Ranch

256 Santa Monica Pier, Santa Monica
310.393.7386, rustyssurfranch.com
Music Fri. & Sat.; cover free-$10
Smack in the middle of the Santa Monica Pier, this restaurant/bar is lined with dozens of 1960s-era surfboards and even more tourists. But don't let that keep you away on weekends. Grab a drink on the patio, then head inside for an evening of live rock, blues or folk music. The Beach Boys would be proud.

Santa Monica Folk Music Club
Sha'Arei Am Synagogue, 1448 18th St.,
Santa Monica
Music 1st Sat. of each month; $5 donation
Since 1978 these folk-loving folks have been
strumming and singing for a hootin' good time
every month. If you play an instrument, bring it.

Temple Bar
1026 Wilshire Blvd., Santa Monica
310.393.6611, templebarlive.com
Music most Tues.-Sun. nights; cover $5-$20
Even the red-paper lanterns and smiling
Buddhas get into the groove at Temple Bar,
where you'll find an eclectic mix of live world
music (African funk to indie rock). The young,
mojito-sipping crowd doesn't like to slow down,
so DJs get busy spinning funk tunes between
sets to keep the party going.

UnUrban Coffee House
3301 Pico Blvd., Santa Monica
310.315.0056
Events Fri.-Mon. nights; no cover
Grab a cup of coffee and settle into one of the
comfy couches for an offbeat night of live music,
poetry and comedy. You never know what you're
going to get here, but that's half the fun of this
local-as-it-gets boho hangout.

Jazz & Blues

Hal's Bar & Grill
1349 Abbot Kinney Blvd., Venice
310.396.3105, halsbarandgrill.com
Music Sun. & Mon. nights; no cover
Listening to jazz and sipping martinis on Sunday
night – when the well-behaved are resting
up for the workweek ahead – is deliciously
indulgent. Grab a seat at the bar to hear such
accomplished musicians as blues guitarist Phil
Upchurch and experimental sax player Cal
Bennett. And no cover and no drink minimum
(yes, you heard that correctly).

Harvelle's Blues Club
1432 4th St., Santa Monica
310.395.1676, harvelles.com
Music nightly; cover $5-$12
Established in 1931, Harvelle's is the westside's
oldest live-music venue. Inside you'll find a dark
and stormy shotgun-style lounge with a classic
supper-club vibe. The low-key crowd comes for
the music – internationally acclaimed and local
blues and jazz musicians – not for the cutesy
cocktails named for the seven deadly sins.

Monsoon Cafe
1212 3rd St. Promenade, Santa Monica
310.576.9996, monsoon-cafe.com
Music Wed.-Sat. nights; cover free-$9
Craving modern jazz, a martini and pad Thai?
No problem. Look for the eerie painted blue eyes
out front and head past the bamboo-bedecked
restaurant and into the seductive lounge above.
Check the music calendar or you could wind
up on the dance floor with free salsa lessons
instead of tapping your toes to conga drums.

The Veranda
Hotel Casa Del Mar, 1910 Ocean Way,
Santa Monica
310.581.5533, hotelcasadelmar.com
Music Mon.-Sat. nights; no cover
You don't have to book one of the high-dollar
suites at this meticulously restored 1920s hotel
to enjoy the good life. The hotel bar is a secret
hangout for locals in the know, with live music
nightly, good (but pricey) cocktails and great
service. Special libations are paired with the
music – classic cocktails with jazz, for instance,
or Spanish wines and charcuterie with Spanish
guitar – except on weekends, when the creativity
is kept to a minimum.

The Vic
The Victorian, 2640 Main St., Santa Monica
888.367.5299, thevicforjazz.com
Music Thurs. nights; tickets $10-$20,
reservations required
Entering through the back door of the 1894 Kyte
House to get into this speakeasy lounge is so
underground cool that we'll forgive them for the
hokey cocktail names (like the Ella Fizzgerald).
Grammy-winning artists stroll onto the stage
every so often, so keep an eye on the calendar.

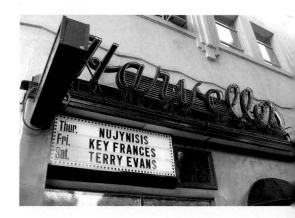

Q & A: Luciana Souza

Brazilian jazz singer, composer and three-time Grammy nominee Luciana Souza is a newcomer to Venice, having moved there in 2006 with her music-producer husband, Larry Klein, from New York via Boston and São Paulo. Souza never imagined she'd end up in a California beach town, but with a tour schedule that takes her back to Manhattan regularly for a taste of the city (and a pizza fix), she's found happiness in her almost-perfect new hometown. In between world tours, Souza chatted with Jenn Garbee about life in Venice.

What brought you here?
I got married, and I was dragged here! No really, I'm very lucky that my husband lives here. I moved here a year ago when we got married. We love being close to Abbot Kinney because it has such a sense of community. You can walk everywhere, into a little café or a shop, just like the neighborhoods in New York. The feeling in Venice is so unique for Southern California, or so I hear – I haven't lived in L.A. proper. There are so many diverse people – artists, musicians, writers – all struggling, but all doing what they want to do. It gives Venice real character.

How is living here different from the East Coast?
I lived in Boston for twelve years, then New York for nine. I had forgotten how happy sunshine makes me. Waking up every day, hearing birds, watching our cats sleep in the sun all day, or just bathing in the sunlight – I had forgotten how great that feeling is.

Do you miss New York?
I miss the pizza! But really, I just miss my friends. I'm lucky because I get to go often for work, and New York is always so easy to step right back into. Then I get to come home to the sunshine.

When you're not touring, what do you like to do on your time off?
We love to go bike riding, down to the beach and around Venice. Or to the farmer's market in Venice to get things like bok choy and other vegetables you don't usually see in the supermarket. And we like to eat at the little dives – the ones with a creaky door that are all grungy inside, but they serve up good, simple food.

What about at night?
For fancier restaurants, we love Axe. It's got good, natural, organic food – really good. And my husband took me to Mélisse the other night for the first time. It was fantastic, but you have to be ready for a meal like that, with all the courses – it was quite an event! For a quiet weeknight dinner, we like to go to Locanda Portofino on Montana. It's a small Italian place, not fancy, just really good homestyle Italian, and it feels like you're in Italy. I travel to Italy a lot, and this is the place that takes me back there.

Santa Monica is…
Outdoorsy

It's no wonder everyone looks so fit, tan and healthy in the Bay Cities – how could you not be, when you have so many extraordinary places to hike, jog, walk, cycle and ride? From our favorite campgrounds and Santa Monica Mountains trails to great in-city walks and even a driving route, we share our outdoorsy secrets in the pages that follow.

7 Great Hikes in the Santa Monicas

What, do you think we're dumb enough to claim there are only seven great hikes in the Santa Monica Mountains? No, we're fully aware of the bounty that lies within this vast wilderness in the midst of a vast metropolis. But to cover all that the Santa Monicas have to offer would fill – and has filled – several books. So the hikes that follow are some of our greatest hits. Try them all, and when you're ready for more, get a good map and go exploring. The Santa Monica Mountains National Recreation Area TopoMap from National Geographic Trails Illustrated is the definitive resource, a water- and tear-proof wealth of information that fits in your pocket. Pick it up at the Park Service Visitor Center or any local outdoor retailer, such as REI in Santa Monica. You can also find a plethora of free maps at the Visitor Center and on the park's web site. These are much less detailed but will get the average hiker in and out just fine. To get these maps, contact the Santa Monica Mountains National Recreation Area (401 West Hillcrest Drive, Thousand Oaks, 805.370.2301, nps.gov/samo) or REI (402 Santa Monica Boulevard, Santa Monica, 310.458.4370).

Inspiration Point Loop at Will Rogers State Historic Park
2 miles round-trip; easy
Alternate: Bone Canyon Trail is a quick way down once past the halfway point

Will Rogers knew what he was doing when he bought this patch of country just north of Sunset in the 1920s. With equal wisdom, his wife Betty deeded the 186 acres to the state for public use in 1944. Now, Will Rogers State Historic Park is home to a preserved ranch house, the last remaining polo field in L.A. County and possibly the most awe-inspiring vista on the westside. As its name suggests, this well-traveled trail forms a loop around the property, summiting about halfway through at Inspiration Point. (The park is also home to the southern terminus of the nearly completed Backbone Trail, which stretches about 70 miles through the Santa Monicas.)

From the park entrance, the Inspiration Point Loop trailhead is straight in front of you, just to the left of the restrooms (last chance!). After a few short switchbacks, it opens into a wide, dusty path that rises gently into the Palisades to reveal a marvelous southwesterly view of the coastline. About a mile in is Inspiration Point, a bare, flattened ridge top that affords views of not only Santa Monica and the coastline but back east to the San Gabriel and Santa Ana ranges. On a clear day, Catalina Island might appear through the haze just around the Rancho Palos Verdes point. Bring a camera and someone to take a picture of you perched over seemingly all of creation.

Driving Directions: From PCH, take Chautauqua (inland) and turn right on Sunset. Will Rogers State Park Road will appear on your left after less than a mile. As you turn in, watch closely for deer grazing in the small field to your left. Continue up the access road to the entrance gate. A ranger will take $7 from you in exchange for some literature and the assurance that you won't get a parking ticket.

The inspiring vista from atop Inspiration Point

Santa Monica is Outdoorsy

Temescal Canyon Loop
About 4 miles round-trip; moderately strenuous

If you're looking for the views of the city and coast offered by the Will Rogers trails but are keen to avoid cell-phone-yammering people in flip-flops, the short but relatively demanding Temescal Canyon Trail and adjoining Temescal Ridge Trail offer relief from the hustle, and they're just steps from Sunset.

North from the Temescal Canyon parking area and just past the gate you will find the trail, which heads to the left and up the hill. For about a mile and a half the trail follows a rising ridgeline that runs parallel to Temescal Creek, after which there is a thin waterfall. It won't impress Yosemite regulars, but it can become intense after a winter rainstorm. At this point, the trail crosses the creek by way of a bridge, then makes a turn back to the left while climbing steeply along a canyon wall. We're now just steps from our return route, the Temescal Ridge Trail. This narrow trail runs along a western ridge at a steadily declining pace for most of the way but declines more significantly near the end. Soak in the views of the Santa Monica coastline, and don't forget to relish the time you're not spending in the intense afternoon traffic below.

Driving Directions: Temescal Canyon Road intersects both PCH and Sunset just west of Chautauqua. Take it north, above Sunset, to the parking lot, where you can leave you car for a small fee.

Crags Fire Road to Lake Malibu
3 miles round-trip; easy
Alternate: Bulldog to Tapia Park

Malibu State Park headquarters is the nexus of a number of trails connecting the park to other parts of the Santa Monicas, and its central location makes it a vital artery for the whole system. Despite this fact, the park is usually not nearly as crowded as Topanga, which lies just to the east.

Following the signs toward the trailheads will land you on Crags Fire Road, a wide dirt road straight up through the canyon along the banks of Malibu Creek. Signs mark the way as numerous intersecting trails suggest roads less traveled. Nonetheless, stay on the fire road to take in the majesty of the canyon, which this Little Creek That Could has hollowed out over the millennia. Notice the chiseled rock walls that have left scientists puzzled as to why the creek chose to dig its way to the sea by this route rather than through softer terrain to the east. Indeed, it's this odd occurrence that allowed for the freshwater Malibu Lagoon to develop and for earlier, Porsche-less human settlements to thrive here.

The gentle, only occasionally upward-sloping walk meanders through the canyon lowlands and meadows, with views to the fore and rear that sometimes make the whole place seem like a rough draft for Yosemite Valley: all the inspired rhyme and turns of phrase without the polished gravity and refinement of the final manuscript.

Follow the road on foot or on a bike, and look for the burned-out jeep on the left side of the road. That's a remnant from television's *M*A*S*H,* which was filmed

Malibu Creek, en route to Lake Malibu

here for years. Trudge on under the blazing sun, shielded by that sunscreen that you always remember to wear, until you reach the southern end of Lake Malibu, and let out a perturbed "hmmpf" when the trail abruptly ends at a private residence, which is guarded by a fence that was quite possibly purchased from the set of *Mad Max*. Avoid eye contact with the stately cabin looming overhead and make your way back out the way you came.

Driving Directions: Take Malibu Canyon Road north from PCH until you see the sign for the State Park headquarters to the left, just before the intersection with Mulholland. Parking is plentiful and free for day use, but head out by sundown lest you be charged as a camper.

California Coastal Trail

Spanning fifteen California counties and 1,200 miles, the work-in-progress CCT is a network of trails and walkways hugging the coastline from Mexico to Oregon. While the trail is said to be just over halfway complete, this doesn't mean you'll face troll-guarded bridges. Because the trail uses existing paths, walkways and roads, it is largely navigable, even if many parts are not properly marked or commonly trod. All the better for the would-be Kerouacs among us.

You can hop on the trail at the Santa Monica Pier (walk to beach, turn left or right on bike path), then saunter on up to San Francisco or down to San Diego (taxi ride to TJ optional). Either way, the California Coastal Trail is the quintessential manifestation of the state constitution's guarantee of public access to shorelines, and yet another shining example of California's dedication to not only preserving but enjoying our well-endowed land.

Wait! Before you set off for the border, pick up *Hiking the California Coastal Trail* (two volumes, divided north/south at Monterey) from Bored Feet Press. The word "essential" does not do these books justice. You'll also find a wealth of knowledge at californiacoastaltrail.org.

Eagle Fire Road

Santa Ynez Canyon Trail to Eagle Rock

About 5 miles round-trip;
moderate to strenuous
Alternate: Musch Trail Loop

Cruising through Pacific Palisades, you might think that the wooded areas behind all those houses and condos are nothing more than land yet to be developed. Indeed, some do see it this way. Thankfully, this land is protected as part of Topanga State Park, and it provides some surprisingly wild escapes from the neatly manicured community it adjoins.

For this hike, take the well-marked trailhead at the end of Vereda de la Montura, heading north through dense vegetation and across a damp creek. The trail weaves back and forth across the stream for a while and can become confusing at times. Continue along the streambed, and watch those ankles on the water-rounded stones that pave your way. A little over half a mile in, you'll encounter a fork in the trail marked by a sign pointing the way to the waterfall up the right-hand trail. Ignore that and stay left – we've got bigger plans. (Besides, it probably hasn't rained in weeks.)

As the trail gains altitude along a rocky ridge, the ocean rises in the south, framed by mountains capped with Palisadian mini-palaces. Forge onward to the wide intersection with the Santa Ynez fire road and turn right. To the left is a stately set of oak trees, and the curved bough of one seems eerily suitable for an inquisitive, opium-smoking caterpillar. Follow this road northeast along a ridge that forms the watershed point between Topanga Canyon and Santa Ynez Canyon, which drains to the Pacific Ocean. Another mile or so of easy hiking up the fire road takes you to Eagle Junction, the Musch Trail intersection and the last way-point before the top of Eagle Rock, not more than half a mile away. Keep going and scramble to the top of Eagle Rock for some spectacular views all the way to the ocean. Make sure to notice the cave cut through the eastern side of the rock; brave souls can crawl through it to reach a lower, more private viewing platform. Take the same trail out, or loop around to the Musch Trail by turning right at Eagle Junction on the way down. The difference in scenery is well worth the slight gain in overall distance. Mind that just when you see Trippet Ranch below and to the right, make a hard, uphill left and scurry back up to the fire road/Santa Ynez Canyon Trail intersection. From here it's straight out the way you came.

Driving Directions: From PCH take Sunset to Palisades Drive and head north. At 2.4 miles turn left at Vereda de la Montura. You'll find the trailhead on the right side of the road just near the dead end. Park anywhere along this fairly steep street, and make sure to turn your wheels toward the curb to prevent a runaway car.

Sandstone Peak
3 miles round-trip; strenuous
Alternate: Mishe Mokwa Trail

For those seeking superlatives, this hike takes you to the highest point in the entire Santa Monica Mountains National Recreation Area. But don't worry — although you might think this fact portends a swarm of hikers, bikers and camera-wielding tourists, the trail is blessedly quiet, presumably because the trailhead is a bit of a drive from civilization. But hey, after a week of creeping along the freeways, a bracing mountain drive makes a welcome beginning to a mountain escape.

Step for step, this is one of the most rewarding hikes in the Santa Monicas. The trail, formerly a jeep-accessible fire road, is wide and well trodden. In less than 1.5 miles, you will gain more than 1,000 feet in altitude, which will please your cardiologist and clear any smog from your lungs. From the parking lot, head north up a steep incline hugging the right side of the mountain. You'll see the jagged summit of Sandstone Peak towering overhead to the northwest; it will continue to rear its head now and again as you wind up the ascending trail. Less than half a mile in, just about when you're starting to regret that midnight slice of pie, the trail levels out into an intersection with the Backbone Trail. Suck it up, turn left and trudge onward up a steep grade that swings around the back side of the craggy ridge we're headed to.

By now you will be privy to some amazing rock formations on an opposing ridge that (thankfully) blocks the view of the encroaching Conejo Valley. The trail then

The Channel Islands from atop Sandstone Peak

slants downward through a tunnel of evergreens and spills out onto a wide landing. Follow the sign to the left and scramble up toward the antennae just ahead. See that peak to your left, the one noticeably taller than the one you're on? That's where you're headed. Yeah, seriously. Look for the discernible trail that cuts left at the large boulder in your path. The vegetation is thick for a hundred feet or so until it opens wide onto the scree-covered rock face that makes up the final ascent. Leave behind anyone silly enough to have worn sandals and climb until you run out of mountain. Look southwest on a clear day and there's a stellar view of the Channel Islands. It gets pretty windy up here at 3,111 feet, so throw on another layer if you plan on staying a while, and don't forget to sign the register. Leave the way you came, or continue west on Backbone and pick up the Mishe Mokwa Trail, which loops back around to the first intersection just near the parking lot.

Driving Directions: Take Mulholland northeast from PCH at Leo Carrillo State Beach for 7 miles to Little Sycamore Canyon Rd. Turn left, go a little over a mile, and turn left again on Yerba Buena Rd. The second marked parking lot on your right is the Sandstone Peak Trailhead.

La Jolla Canyon Loop/Ray Miller Trail
7 miles; easy to moderate

Named for the park service host who tended it for many years, this trail marks the western terminus of the Backbone Trail and stands as a fantastic example of the sublime intersection of land and sea for which coastal California is known. From the parking-lot trailhead in Point Mugu State Park, head north on the La Jolla Canyon Trail. (This hike is a loop, so technically you could take the Ray Miller Trail, though we usually prefer to save that section for the end.) Throughout the course of the hike you'll face a number of trail intersections, but since you'll be traveling clockwise, just make a right turn every time the opportunity presents itself. You'll face about two miles of moderately strenuous hiking before the intersection with the La Jolla Valley fire road, a broad, dusty thoroughfare for hikers, trail runners and the occasional fluorescent mountain biker chugging uphill in low gear.

Turn right on the fire road, then take another right a few hundred feet up onto the overlook fire road. The gentle upward slope, wide track and wonderful scenery make this a great time to bump on up to a trot, a gallop or even a slight jog. Less than two miles later, bear right onto the Ray Miller Trail, which winds its way back down into the La Jolla Canyon parking area and a sweet, sweet reunion with your car's air conditioning. Just make sure to savor some of the amazing views of Big Blue before you lose too much altitude.

At 15,000 acres, Point Mugu is the largest state park in the Santa Monica Mountains, and because the vegetation is mostly short shrubbery and chaparral, the vistas are endless. But beware – summer temperatures can easily jump into the 100s, and shade is scarce. Wear plenty of sunscreen, bring plenty of water and take the open-flame warnings seriously; they don't call them fire roads for nothing.

Driving Directions: Take PCH toward Oxnard until you see the sign for La Jolla Canyon/Ray Miller Trailhead on the right, just past Thornhill Broome Beach Campground, and drop your parking fee in the collection box.

Solstice Canyon Walkabout
2 miles round-trip; easy to moderate
Alternates: Many, many

This is a great light-duty outing that the whole family will love, unless you come from a family of Sherpas. The paved trails are ideal for cyclists (mountain or road), leisure walkers and stroller pushers. We call this one a walkabout because the area boasts such a great selection of alternate routes around the main trail.

Once a private zoo, home to giraffes, camels, deer and exotic birds, this swath of parkland still holds remnants of historic structures. About halfway up the main Solstice Canyon Trail is a stone cabin erected in 1865 and named for its builder, Matthew Keller; it is believed to be the oldest stone building in Malibu. Almost a century later, a more extravagant home, named Tropical Terrace, was built just up the way, and its ruins are where most hikers are headed. The ruins come complete with a gurgling stream and gentle, picturesque waterfall; take a load off on the stone steps and marvel at the steep, cradling canyon walls. In fact, this blend of canyon isolation and relative convenience to the city made Solstice Canyon the testing ground for early satellite technology used in NASA space missions, including the Pioneer missions, which sent the first man-made object beyond the known solar system.

To do the basic two-mile trek, turn around here and head back to your car. But for more adventure, set off from Tropical Terrace on the Rising Sun Trail back toward the coast. This slightly more difficult trail will take you along a ridgeline that provides great views of the canyon below and the majestic Pacific to the south. We highly recommend picking up a free map of the park at any National Park Service outpost (or online at nps.gov/archive/samo/maps/solstice.htm), not because you'll get lost without it, but because we just don't want you to miss anything.

Driving Directions: Take PCH north to Corral Canyon Rd. in Malibu and turn right. The parking lot is just ahead.

The ruins of Tropical Terrace

On the Road: A Classic Mountain Drive

The relatives are in town and want to see what all this California fuss is about. Or maybe you just finished a screenplay and want to look for the perfect Malibu mountain retreat, just in case it sells. Either way, the canyon roads stretching through the Santa Monicas from PCH to the 101 are just what Dr. 90210 ordered. Everyone knows Mulholland Highway as the beautiful SoCal mountain throughway, and we also highly recommend a trip along both Kanan Road and Las Virgenes. But if we had to pick one favorite, it would be this loop through Sotheby's paradise into unspoiled inland Malibu wilderness for a glimpse of how things used to be, and how they could be for you if your agent would just call you back.

From Santa Monica, take Pacific Coast Highway north to El Pescador State Beach and turn right on Encinal Canyon Road, which winds inland past Malibu mansions perched on crumbling cliffs that ominously, sublimely loom over the road ahead. Take a few minutes at one of the southeast-facing turnouts to let your relatives take their "Our Trip to California" Christmas-card photo, or just to let that tailgating motorcycle go by.

The first intersection is Lechusa Road. Bear left ever so slightly (you may feel like you're merely continuing straight), then take the next right onto Decker Road. This connects to Mulholland in a little bit. Hang a left on Mulholland, then a right onto Little Sycamore Canyon Road, which becomes Yerba Buena Road. Now you're headed toward Circle X Ranch. Swing past the campground and down through a few gorgeous private properties set off in spring by fields of yellow wildflowers. Watch for Cotherin Road to sneak up on the right, then downshift and swing gently around alongside a white picket fence. The split ahead gives a choice between dead-end Serrano Road and Pacific View Road, which will become Deer Creek Road and take you down, down, down to PCH. This is the stuff hot-rod dreams – and nightmares – are made of. Stay in low gear, keep your eyes on the narrow, winding road, don't answer your cell phone, and let your passengers gaze at the Pacific abyss.

One of the extraordinary rock
formations on the Yerba Buena drive

5 Walks Around Town

Palisades Park to Adelaide
Route: Level footpaths through the park, paralleling Ocean Ave., and a slight uphill on Adelaide, a residential street
Parking: In local pay structures or along Ocean Ave.

Palisades Park

The city of Santa Monica was smart enough to figure out that one of its best assets – the bluff above PCH, overlooking the sweep of Santa Monica Bay – was worth investing in. The result is one of the most beautiful city-bound walking routes in the world. Start at the pier and head north along one of the several cushioned, packed-sand paths (they zigzag and mingle often). The ocean will be on your left and grassy areas on your right, with a stately façade of apartments and hotels across Ocean Avenue. You'll pass all sorts of people, from wealthy elderly women walking their shih-tzus, to young couples holding hands, to intense runners, to homeless folks sleeping. (This is, as Harry Shearer always says, the home of the homeless, but the homeless here rarely bother passersby – they're just enjoying the park like everyone else.) Especially in the early evening, it has the feel of an Italian *passeggiata*, except for the occasional jocks blowing past the more leisurely strollers.

You'll pass sculptures, a lovely Arts & Crafts pavilion, the Camera Obscura, picnic areas, gorgeous landscaping and always that grand view of the vast Pacific.

At the end of the park, cross Ocean and head up the one-way street on the high end of the road split. This is Adelaide Drive, home of Santa Monica's finest Craftsman and other traditional houses, all overlooking Santa Monica Canyon. Midway along Adelaide you'll see wheezing, sweaty people clinging to their knees for dear life – this is the top of the two famous Santa Monica Canyon stairways, the workout spot of choice for hard-training athletes and those looking to meet equally buffed hard-training athletes.

Continue on Adelaide until 7th Street, then reverse your course and go all the way back to the pier. This is a four-mile, one-hour walk; if you have less time, you can just revel in a 40-minute Palisades Park jaunt.

San Vicente Greenway

Route: Along San Vicente Blvd. from Bundy in Brentwood to Ocean Ave. in Santa Monica
Parking: The intrepid can usually find street parking on either end of this route

Broad San Vicente connects dense West L.A. with the Pacific Ocean, and from its Brentwood edge until it hits Ocean Avenue, it is divided by a huge, well-maintained grassy meridian. This is a favorite of walkers and joggers who like to move on grass; there are only a couple of traffic signals on the whole length, so you can usually run up to six miles round-trip with nary a stop. Traffic can get dense, especially during rush hour, so this route isn't for those who fear car fumes. But the grass and gorgeous coral trees (which are Historic Cultural Monuments) do a pretty good job of absorbing them, and it is a long, lush stretch with a beautiful nexus at Palisades Park. From Bundy to Ocean it's a 6.2-mile round-trip trek; from 26th to Ocean it's about four miles.

Palisades Hill Climb

Route: Sunset Blvd. up Chautauqua Blvd. until it ends
Parking: On Chautauqua just north of Sunset Blvd.

One of the views from atop Chautauqua

Sometimes you want a stroll in a pretty neighborhood. Other times you want to get your heart rate going. When you want both, consider this uphill walk, which pays off in both cardiovascular vitality and dazzling views.

Start at the bottom of the north leg of Chautauqua, just above Sunset. For the first half-mile or so, the upslope is gentle; you'll be walking on a good sidewalk past well-groomed Palisades family homes. Then the road narrows and gets considerably steeper, but not to fear – it's only this steep for a half-mile or so, and you can handle it! You can stop to catch your breath about ten minutes' walk up, when fabulous views of the ocean, the coastline and east into Westwood appear around every bend.

The road will split a few times, but just stay on the Chautauqua side of each split. At the very top, the road dead-ends into a chain-link fence, but clever locals take the unofficial trail that skirts the right side of the chain link to access the dirt road that heads up to a reservoir and points beyond... as far beyond, in fact, as your legs will take you.

But if the hike part is too much, just turn around and head back down Chautauqua, enjoying the views all the more on the way down. It's a 2.3-mile trek round-trip, more if you keep going on the trail.

Rustic Canyon Idyll

Route: Along Latimer Rd. and Brooktree
in Rustic Canyon, between Santa Monica
and the Palisades
Parking: On Mesa Rd. at the base of Latimer

It would be difficult indeed to find a lovelier urban hideaway than this lush canyon lined with sycamores, eucalyptus, oaks, redwoods and one fantastic house after another. If you live here, you're not allowed to complain about anything, ever, as long as you live. If you don't live here, the best way to experience it is on foot. Start at the corner of Mesa and Latimer and walk up Latimer's gentle slope into the cool, shady canyon. After a third of a mile, you'll come across Rustic Canyon Park, a jewel-like enclave that was once the home of the Uplifters social club, where Aldous Huxley, Will Rogers and the more bohemian of L.A.'s business elite came to

No sidewalks, lots of trees: in the heart of Rustic Canyon

bend an elbow during Prohibition. The tile-roofed former clubhouse now houses a co-op nursery school and art classes; elsewhere in the park are tennis courts, a playground, an unofficial dog park, a pool and more.

Continue up Latimer to revel in the fabulously diverse architecture: a Cotswold-style cottage, its window boxes spilling over with flowers; a 1970s modern, all wood and sideways angles; a gorgeous shingled Craftsman; a redwood cabin; a true California ranch; a Moorish fantasy; a brand-new architectural statement. The narrow road is rich with trees, vines (great wisteria in spring) and birds chirping. Take the detour on the right up Haldeman, which winds above Latimer and then drops back down. Turn right on Latimer, walk to its dead end, then double back and turn right on Brooktree, which crosses over Rustic Canyon's creek and holds more dreamy houses. When Brooktree ends on Sunset, reverse your course, turn right on Latimer and return to your starting place.

This route is about 3.5 miles, and you'll encounter more dogs being walked than cars being driven.

Abbot Kinney & the Canals

Route: Along Abbot Kinney Blvd. and through the walking paths along the Venice canals
Parking: Around Brooks and Abbot Kinney; if you can't find street parking, several $7 beach-parking lots are nearby

To solve the mystery of why anyone would pay $1.2 million for a 750-square-foot house in a densely packed neighborhood with bad parking and crime issues, take this wonderful walk through the heart of Venice. By walk's end, you just might put an offer in on one of those tiny houses yourself.

Start on the beach-adjacent end of Abbot Kinney, perhaps the hippest main street in Southern California. Named for Venice's founder, Abbot Kinney is lined with one fabulous boutique, gallery, bistro, coffeehouse and bookstore after another, all of them unique (there's not a single Starbucks!) and most of them housed in funky old buildings. If you want to keep up a heart-rate-inducing pace, you'll be able to, thanks to the scarcity of traffic signals – but it will take an iron will to resist poking through a fetching shop or stopping for lunch at Hal's, Lilly's or Joe's.

At three-quarters of a mile you'll reach broad Venice Boulevard; turn right and walk a short distance along North Venice. On your left will be the Frank Gehry–designed Abbot Kinney Memorial Library. Turn left to cross Ocean Avenue in front of the library and walk a couple of short blocks through a modest residential neighborhood. Turn right on Carroll, and you'll enter the public walkway that zigzags through the Venice canals. Built as resort property in 1906 by real-estate mogul Abbot Kinney, these six canals were part of a nineteen-mile network of waterways; in 1929, as automobiles began to dominate life in L.A., most of the canals were filled to make streets.

But enough of the canals survive to make for a blissfully quiet neighborhood of markedly eclectic waterfront homes. As you wander the canal walkways, you'll pass within a few feet of people sitting on their front porches; residents give up a lot of privacy to live in such a charming spot. Houses range from tiny, shabby-chic Craftsman cottages to looming modernist visions shoehorned onto skinny lots. Everywhere are gardens, window boxes, bougainvillea, ducks, geese and wee little boats tied to wee little docks.

You can wander at will through the canals, or take this route: straight from the Carroll entrance, turning right when you're forced to; left at Venice Boulevard, and left again along the Grand Canal walkway, which goes straight all the way to Washington Boulevard. If you're ready for a lunch break, head right for a brief detour to the cafés that huddle where Washington meets Oceanfront Walk. To stay on the canals, turn left on Washington and left again onto the next canal walkway. Zigzag back to where you started, jogging right on Sherman Canal or Howland Canal.

Retrace your steps along Abbot Kinney, walking on the opposite side of the street for a different experience. This is a three- to four-mile route, depending on how much you wander the canals.

Serenity along the Venice canals

Our 3 Favorite Campgrounds

A number of tent-camping options exist in the Santa Monicas, most requiring reservations and charging fees. In return, you and yours get to experience first-hand the sublime wilderness that's just around the corner – not to mention amenities not found in more remote parks, such as fire rings, trash receptacles, drinking water, toilets and even showers. Yes, showers. The three campgrounds that follow are our faves. For a full list of campgrounds with all the information you need to plan a getaway, visit the National Park Service web site at nps.gov and search for Santa Monica Mountains campgrounds.

Life is good at Leo Carrillo.

Malibu Creek Family Campground
Malibu Creek State Park
1925 Las Virgenes/Malibu Canyon Rd., Calabasas
818.880.0367, reserveamerica.com
$9-$25 per night; reservations required (accepted up to 7 months in advance)

A house around here will cost you several million, but for just $25 a night, you can have one of 62 campsites set in a gorgeous 7,000-acre park a few miles inland from Malibu's lovely beaches. Originally a Chumash paradise and later a much-used 20th Century Fox filming location, the land is now owned by the state and protected from further development. You enter the park from Malibu Canyon Road just south of Mulholland and continue straight for a few hundred feet, past some ranger buildings on the left.

Leo Carrillo State Park Campgrounds
35000 Pacific Coast Hwy., Malibu
818.880.0350, reserveamerica.com
$9-$25 per night; reservations required (accepted up to 7 months in advance)

On the beach and up into the mountains at the intersection of PCH and Mulholland lies this hugely popular park, famed for its tidepools, sycamore groves, surf break and, in winter, the arrival of the spectacular monarch butterflies. The "Hike & Bike" campsite is first-come, first-serve and charges $3 per person; space is limited, so arrive early to stake your claim. Otherwise, you can make reservations at the larger Canyon Campground, and make them early – weekend and holiday spots are usually booked seven months in advance.

Circle X Ranch
Yerba Buena Rd., about 4 miles inland from Pacific Coast Hwy., Malibu
805.370.2300, ext. 1702
$2 per person per night, with a 10-person minimum; reservations required (accepted up to 3 months in advance)

A Boy Scout camp for many years, this group-camping gem just inland from the Malibu coast nearly fell prey to development when the scouts moved south and put the property on the block. Luckily, our friends at the Conservancy snatched it up long before anyone began planning block parties. Follow the signs to the Sandstone Peak Trailhead and go a few hundred feet farther to the next parking area. This one is a well-kept secret, so don't tell anyone else about it, okay?

On 2 Wheels & 4 Legs: Cycling & Horseback Riding

Mountain Biking

A debate continues between hikers, equestrians and mountain bikers about trail usage in the Santa Monicas, but fortunately, there's room for everyone. Cyclists, you just need to make sure that the trail you're heading down is approved for bikes – not just for environmental reasons, but for your safety and everyone else's. Signs mark trail-usage rights throughout the park system, so keep an eye out. We also recommend checking the National Park Service web site at nps.gov/archive/samo/brochure/biking/biking.htm – it's a great resource for safety tips, trail etiquette and trail routes. Maps of the mountain areas, keyed to show bike-approved trails, are also available at the NPS visitor's center.

Nearly all of the Backbone Trail allows bicycles, but it's a good idea to check a map to make sure. Running over a hiker on a narrow stretch of trail just isn't good for anybody.

Just north of the Ray Miller Trailhead in Point Mugu State Park is a great stretch of the Backbone where two-wheelers go to kick up some dust. This wide-open trail allows for some thrilling downhill runs, as well as long, low-gear stretches on the way back up. Conversely, the eastern end of the Backbone Trail at Will Rogers State Park offers rides through Topanga that will put hair on your backbone. Watch out for that limb!

Road Riding

We discuss the famed bike path in detail in the Beachy chapter; here we're talking about road riding. Santa Monica and the Palisades are full of cyclists clinging to the side of the road in designated (if sometimes dubious) bike lanes. These lanes stretch down major thoroughfares and all around town; you can find a great map online at smgov.net/isd/gis/map_catalog/csm_map_catalog/bikemap.jpg.

Road riding in Santa Monica... with a buddy

In addition, cyclists meet up for group rides with a message; exercise your right to ride at the Santa Monica Critical Mass group ride, held the first Friday of every month as a show of solidarity against evil car drivers. Check out its other events, such as the "Bad Idea Ride: 66 Miles on Route 66," at santamonicacriticalmass.org.

Horseback Riding

Even considering the decline in popularity of polo playing and *Bonanza* watching, both English and Western equestrian sports are alive and well in the Santa Monica Mountains, particularly in Topanga.

Fair Hills Farms
2735 Santa Maria Rd., Topanga
818.347.5049, fairhillsfarms.com
A beautifully sited ranch that focuses on polo and pleasure riding; no guided rides, but lessons in both polo and English-style riding are offered.

Los Angeles Horseback Riding
2661 Old Topanga Canyon Rd., Topanga
818.591.2032, losangeleshorsebackriding.com
The place for small-group or private guided rides on the Santa Monica Mountains Backbone Trail; the full-moon rides are fantastic. Reservations are essential.

Mill Creek Riding School
1881 Old Topanga Canyon Rd., Topanga
310.455.1116, millcreekequestriancenter.com
Dressage, horse training and competitive equestrian events are the name of the game here. Excellent lessons for kids and adults, but no trail rides.

Q & A: Joe Edmiston

Palisadian Joe Edmiston has been the executive director of the Santa Monica Mountains Conservancy since its inception in 1980. The son of two active members of the Sierra Club, Joe grew up to become a Sierra Club lobbyist to the state legislature. In 1977, he was appointed to the Santa Monica Mountains Comprehensive Planning Commission, a forerunner to the Conservancy. A friend of the woods as well as an avid reader, Joe was kind enough to sit down with John Stephens to discuss the finer points of wildlife management, outdoor education and Malibu land deals.

What's the biggest problem facing the Conservancy right now?
We're always battling someone in Malibu about beach access, or dealing with some outside would-be investor about proposed development. And these are no Hatfield-and-McCoy-style battles – everyone involved has downtown lawyers. We've even been hassled about using our piece of land in Ramirez Canyon after a few noisy events we've had.

Sounds like the entertainment business. Say, didn't Barbra Streisand give you guys that property?
Yes, she gave us 22 acres in 1993.

So you throw better parties than Streisand?
Well, it certainly didn't seem like it was a problem until we moved in. In fact, in 1990 the Malibu Times *voted me "Man of the Year." Now I sometimes think I might be public enemy number one.*

What about the Palisades? Have you ever had to squash the development dreams of one of your neighbors?
As with Malibu, most of the pressure for development comes from outsiders. Palisadians are on our side, even though they all live in homes that they would object to someone else building.

So what do you do when you're not safeguarding our natural treasures from tyranny?
I have a number of rather esoteric reading interests that I satisfy at Village Books here in the Palisades. My wife would probably say that I buy more books than I have time to read.

To return to the threat of development in the Santa Monica Mountains – how do you think we can best protect them?
Their proximity to the city means that the mountains are always under the threat of urban encroachment, but it also means that they're that much easier for all of us to enjoy. Too many Angelenos are unaware of the nature found right in their backyard. I think widespread, responsible enjoyment is the key to ensuring a green future for the range.

Santa Monica is…
Athletic

In many towns, being athletic means playing (or watching) football or baseball. Out here at the beach, it means playing beach volleyball, going surfing, running the Santa Monica stairs, cycling the bike path and, when it's time to get out of the sun, hitting one of the serious gyms or Pilates studios. Here's how to get in touch with your athletic side, Santa Monica-style.

Working Out: Gyms, Yoga & Pilates

Don't believe for a second that good genes are behind those bulging muscles and bikini bods you see on the beach, bike path and boardwalk. It's the gyms, yoga and Pilates studios, and Spinning and fitness classes that created those perfect – and perfectly gorgeous – bodies.

City of Santa Monica Community Classes

310.458.8300, smgov.net/seascape
Every season the city offers all sorts of very inexpensive classes taught at municipal parks and rec rooms. There's a dance, kickboxing, jujitsu, walking, yoga, tai ch'i or slim 'n' trim class (to name but a few) for every level, from beginner to advanced. Sessions run eight weeks, with one class per week, and cost from $50 to $70 per session for residents (nonresidents pay more).

Easton Gym

1233 3rd St. Promenade, Santa Monica
310.395.4441, eastongym.com
This is the local no-nonsense gym. The original Easton opened in Hollywood in 1938 – it's now the oldest in the city – and served such celebs as Cary Grant, Gregory Peck, Kirk Douglas and Robert Mitchum. At this second Easton Gym, opened in 1993 on a Promenade second floor, you'll find solid equipment, no crowds and a breezy (i.e., not stuffy) weight and aerobics room.

Equinox

201 Santa Monica Blvd., Santa Monica
310.593.8888, equinoxfitness.com
More like a spa than a gym, this luxe club offers all the state-of-the-art equipment you'd expect, along with yoga, Pilates, Spinning and a full-service spa (from pregnancy massage to sea-glow body polishes). Day passes ($25) are obtainable only if you come in with a member or stay in a local hotel. Membership has its privileges – and a hefty price tag: $400 to $500 to join and monthly dues of $130.

Gold's Gym

360 Hampton Dr., Venice
310.392.6004, goldsgym.com
Best known as the location where *Pumping Iron* was filmed, this gym is still called the "mecca of bodybuilding." But even if you're not Arnold or Angela Bassett (both past members), you'll find Gold's to be welcoming. New members get a one-on-one tour of the gym and equipment along with body-fat measuring and diet advice. First-time visitors should check the web site: There's usually a free one-day pass available.

Revolution Fitness

1211 Montana Ave., Santa Monica
310.393.6399, revolutionfitness.net
For those who like going nowhere really fast, this is your gym. You can burn 500 calories in 40 minutes in the Spinning class, which will have you ascending steep mountain trails without ever leaving the room. You'll work up an even bigger sweat in the Indo Row class, a 45-minute strength and aerobic rowing workout complete with a simulated "crew." On another day, you can slow down – and slim down – in one of the Pilates classes. (Located through the courtyard behind the café that fronts Montana.)

Santa Monica Family YMCA

1332 6th St., Santa Monica
310.393.2721, ymcasm.org
This is the people's gym of Santa Monica. Most families join for the Olympic pool and kiddie swim program, then end up sticking around for years, taking advantage of the racquetball, Pilates and yoga classes, exercise machines, weights, martial-arts programs and babysitting. Reasonably priced day passes are available.

Santa Monica Power Yoga

1410 2nd St. & 522 Santa Monica Blvd., 2nd Fl.,
Santa Monica
310.458.9510
At this no-pressure yoga, school you don't have
to worry about personal-best posing or stylish
clothing. And true to the spiritual origins of yoga,
prices aren't listed – a box provided at the end of
class is for donations ($12 is suggested, but you
can simply give from your heart).

Spectrum Athletic Club

17383 Sunset Blvd., Pacific Palisades
310.459.2582, spectrumclubs.com
A tony club for the uber-tony Palisades, the
Spectrum overlooks the Pacific – the stunning
view enlivens your Pilates session, yoga class or
jog on the treadmill. After your strength workout
or outdoor rock-wall climb, you can take a
steam, get a massage or enjoy a healthy lunch
at the café, which is operated by the Palisades's
much-loved Café Vida.

Turning Point Pilates

648A Venice Blvd., Venice
310.217.7630
It's ironic that today's most fashionable workout
had its beginnings as a rehabilitation method for
injured World War I soldiers. Now far removed
from the sanatoriums, Pilates builds core
strength and creates graceful-looking limbs
in well-lighted boutique studios like this one
in Venice. Newcomers can take three private
introductory 55-minute sessions for $125.

YAS

1101 Abbot Kinney Blvd., Venice
310.396.6993, go2yas.com
Though YAS stands for "yoga and Spinning,"
there's nothing meditative about the classes
here. In fact, the studio's signature class is
tagged "yoga for athletes: no chanting, no gurus,
no Sanskrit." Be prepared for a tough workout –
Spinning or yoga or a combo thereof – and lots
of schvitzing

Yoga Works

2215 Main St., Santa Monica
310.664.6470
1426 Montana Ave., Santa Monica
310.393.5150
15327 Sunset Blvd., Pacific Palisades
310.454.7000, yogaworks.com
The Santa Monica studio that started the
westside's love affair with yoga two decades ago
is now a franchise with a cult-like following. If
you notice a preponderance of lithe, mat-toting
ladies around, you're not far from a Yoga Works,
where you too can breathe through the poses
from such schools as Ashtanga, Iyengar and
Viniyoga. It's $18 a class, and there's Pilates,
too, at $180 for three sessions.

The YWCA Santa Monica/Westside

2019 14th St., Santa Monica
310.452.3881, smywca.org
Forget about Curves – this is the most
comprehensive, affordable gym in town for
women's fitness. To wit: karate, 8 classes for
$40; ballet, 4 classes for $38; belly dancing,
8 classes for $80; aerobic, weight-training
and stretch, 10 classes for $60; even Mommy
and Me Pilates, $64 per session. Plus, there's
an array of youth classes (dance, soccer,
gymnastics) to occupy your kids while you
work out.

The Stairs & Other Outdoor Workouts

The more forgiving wooden stairs in Santa Monica Canyon

Perhaps the gnarliest workouts in the city take place on what's known as the **Santa Monica Stairs** (off Adelaide Drive near 4th Street). Built many decades ago so people on the palisades could access the beach below, the stairs are now tramped up and down, day and night, by serious fitness buffs. Beginner's advisory: Bring lots of water and head to the more forgiving wooden staircase located a block north of the cement stairs – your knees will thank you.

Those who want a little more Zen in their physical activity head to the three-mile loop trail at **Temescal Gateway Park** (Sunset Boulevard at Temescal Canyon, Pacific Palisades). This hike has everything: a waterfall, magnificent ocean views, streams (after a wet winter), oaks, sycamores and a few steep inclines. To keep your workout tranquil, visit during the week; weekends tend to draw 405-like hiking traffic.

At the **Original Muscle Beach** (just south of the Santa Monica Pier), you can test your strength and agility on the swinging rings, climbing ropes, parallel bars, chin-up bars and balance beams. From the 1930s to the '50s, this was where such famous bodybuilders as Jack La Lanne and Steve Reeves strutted their stuff in competitions. When the circus atmosphere got to be too much for Santa Monica, the action moved two miles down the coast to **Venice Muscle Beach** (1800 Ocean Front Walk), where the best and the biggest still lift barbells and dumbbells for crowds. (Years ago, you could have caught Arnold and Franco Columbu pressing and grunting.) For regular-size exercisers, paddle tennis, basketball and handball courts are located alongside the muscle-bulging show.

The quintessential Santa Monica workout, however, is a ride along the **Beach Bike Path**. You can speed and sweat through the north-of-the-Santa-Monica-Pier straightaways or cruise slowly through the s-curves of the Venice Boardwalk. From Temescal Canyon to the Venice Pier, it's 8.5 miles; ride till the path's end in the South Bay and it's a 22-mile workout. Journey back the way you came, and you'll have a 44-mile ride to brag about.

Playing Around

Beyond the gyms and yoga studios, here's how Santa Monicans recreate and stay in shape.

Basketball

You've seen *White Men Can't Jump.* You know not to get into a pickup game in Venice (where the movie was shot) unless you are very, *very* good. So what's an ordinary basketball player to do? Look for more relaxed games at parks around town. The games are good at Barrington Park in Brentwood and in the Palisades Rec Center (Monday, Wednesday and Friday during the day); the latest hot spot is the relatively new courts at spiffy Virginia Avenue Park, on Pico and Virginia. There's a game there pretty much every evening after 5 p.m., and the vibe is more relaxed than over in Venice – though last time we checked it out, the fellas were looking really, really tall.

The volleyball action north of Back on the Beach Café in Santa Monica

Beach Volleyball

For decades Santa Monica was the holy land for this sport, which was pretty much invented here. The big tournaments and a lot of the training has moved to the South Bay, but there's still plenty of serious play on our beaches. Expert players use the free courts south of the Santa Monica Pier and at State (Will Rogers State Beach), from Back on the Beach Café running north for a mile or so. (Wilt Chamberlain could be seen spiking and blocking at both locations when he was alive.) If you're not Olympic-caliber but would still rather play than observe, you can try to join a pickup game on any of the courts located near equipment-rental shops along the bike path in both directions from the pier. Newcomers may find some courts to be cliquish with regulars who've been playing in long-established games. In that case, your best bet is one of the city's beach volleyball classes offered in two- or four-person play. Classes are held at 1550 PCH (south of the pier) and 2030 Barnard Way (just north of Ocean Park Boulevard) and focus on movement, body control, jumping and running for all levels of experience. After class, the beach court will be yours for a pickup game with players of your choice! (For info call 310.458.2239 or visit smgov.net/seascape and click on "RecScape" for a list of beach volleyball classes.)

Bowling

The secret to a good bowling alley is its bar – and the one at the **Bay Shore Lanes** (234 Pico Boulevard, Santa Monica, 310.399.7731) doesn't disappoint: It's a dark, small honky-tonk, with a pool table, juke box and reasonably priced drinks. The coffee-shop fare is surprisingly tasty, and its arcade has air hockey – what more could you want from a bowling alley? The **Mar Vista Lanes** (12125 Venice Boulevard, Mar Vista, 310.391.5288) offers much the same "bowling" experience – down to the air hockey and pool table – plus, its coffee shop serves pretty decent Mexican food. No need to mention the spares, strikes or smelly shoes – you know what to expect.

At Penmar Golf Course, it's easy to forget that the city is just beyond those trees.

Golf

This being a prime-real-estate section of town, there's room for only one public golf course – and a small one at that. (In fact, the city's beloved oceanview pitch-and-putt course was razed and replaced by luxury beach condos some years ago.) **Penmar Golf Course** (1233 Rose Avenue, Venice, 310.396.6228) is a small nine-hole course, great for practicing your short game. For a good walk unspoiled, attend the **Nissan Open at Riviera Country Club** (1250 Capri Drive, Pacific Palisades, 310.454.6591) and watch Phil Mickelson, Tiger Woods or Vijay Singh spoil his own walk on this ultra-tough course. This famed PGA event held every February attracts tens of thousands – many of whom have never teed off themselves – thanks to the tournament's lovely setting and party atmosphere.

Hiking

It's really not fair. In addition to its glorious beaches, Santa Monica also has an eponymous mountain range. How much ecological serenity can we stand? But you don't have to explore these vast wildlands on your own: Bird-watching walks, moon-rise hikes, wetlands walks, garden tours, bluff explorations and the standard-issue kick-your-ass conditioning hikes, all led by rangers or experienced hikers, take place practically every day of the year. Visit the web sites of the Santa Monica Mountain Fund (samofund.org) and the Sierra Club, Angeles Chapter (angeles. sierraclub.org) for activity schedules. *(See Outdoorsy, page 178, for more on hiking.)*

Horseback Riding

Three nights a month, **Los Angeles Horseback Riding** (2623 Old Topanga Canyon Road, Topanga, 818.591.2032) offers a 90-minute trail ride under the full moon. If your eyes can't adjust to falling stars and nocturnal wildlife, try the daily sunset rides, with gorgeous views of canyons and mountain chaparral during the twilight "magic hour." Or you can simply take a ride under the light of day – this ranch will saddle you up anytime, whether you're a novice or Gene Autry.

Sailing

You're right here "on" the Pacific anyway, so why not get even closer? Don your skipper's cap and head to Marina del Rey, where the following schools promise to keep your three-hour cruise safe, little buddy: **California Sailing Academy and Coast Guard School** (310.821.3433) for lessons; **Bluewater Sailing** (310.823.5545) for rentals, cruises and instruction; and **Marina Sailing** (800.262.7245) for charters and instruction.

Surfing

Saturday is Ladies' Day on the waves – Mary Setterling's **Surf Academy** (310.372.2790, surfacademy.com) will provide the board, wetsuit, rash guard and all the expertise you'll need for a successful ride. You bring only your BFFs and sunscreen. You'll learn to paddle, pop and safely navigate and read waves with an instructor alongside you. If your gal pals don't want to surf, they can cheer you on from the sand. Sunday lessons are coed and open to everyone. Other schools open to all wanna-be wave riders in Santa Monica and Malibu are **Learn to Surf L.A.** (310.663.2479, learntosurfla.com), **Santa Monica Surf School** (santamonicasurfschool. com), **Malibu Longboards Surf School** (310.467.6898, malibulongboards.com) and **Aqua Surf School** (310.452.SURF, aquasurfschool.com).

Surf's Up!

Even nonsurfers can enjoy the sport by spending a day on the beach at a surf contest, watching the pros (or really good amateurs) rip it up. You won't find a more profoundly California activity on a sunny summer weekend. Here are some local faves.

Call to the Wall, in July at Surfrider Beach, Malibu (malibuboardriders.com). A terrific two-day longboarding contest sponsored by the Malibu Boardriders Club; proceeds from the event fund a day at the beach for kids from Camp Ronald McDonald.

MSA Classic, in September at Surfrider Beach in Malibu (malibusurfing.com). The first televised surf contest in the 1960s, this classic is still going strong. The invitational longboard competition benefits such beach-protecting groups as Heal the Bay and the Surfrider Foundation.

WSA contests, dates and locations vary (949.369.6677, surfwsa.org). The Western Surfing Association, a nonprofit aimed at giving amateur surfers a fun way to compete, sponsors contests up and down the coast. Many tend to be located at such famed breaks as San Onofre or Huntington Beach, but Malibu and Topanga also host events. You haven't lived until you've seen a 9-year-old rip it.

Swimming

The **Santa Monica Swim Center** (2225 16th Street, 310.458.8700) is the best addition to the city this century. A *community* pool in every sense, the center has two Olympic pools – one a splash and teaching pool for families, the other for adult lap swimmers – and lots of deck space for sunning and kibbutzing with friends (who you'll run into all summer long). With its high-dive boards, wet-aerobics classes, swim lessons for adults and kids, locker rooms, tanning decks and Fosters Freeze right across the street (for post-swim munchies), this a full-service water-workout center.

For a quieter vibe, take a dip at the **YMCA Aquatics Center** (15601 Sunset Boulevard, Pacific Palisades, 310.454.3514). It's located in Temescal Canyon State Park, where you can hike up a sweat first, then cool down your overheated body in the Olympic pool. And if you have very young ones who need lessons, check out **Family Life Aquatics** (310.264.SWIM, familylifeaquatics.org), a friendly outfit that teaches swimming to even the very young, using its "Gentle Touch" method, in hotel and private pools.

Tennis under the sycamores at Rustic Canyon

Tennis

Rally Around: Santa Monica and the Palisades have 39 courts at nine different parks, some better maintained than others. *(See court rundown below.)* Most are free and available on a first-come, first-served basis. The lighted courts at Reed Park and the unlighted courts at Ocean View Park are operated on a reservation basis. Santa Monica residents can purchase an annual reservation card for $10 and book these courts up to three days ahead. (Call 310.394.6011 for details.) The Palisades Park courts rent for $8 an hour, but the lovely Rustic Canyon courts are free. Here's a rundown of all the courts:

Clover Park: 2 lighted courts at 25th and Ocean Park Blvd.

Douglas Park: 2 lighted courts at 25th and Wilshire Blvd.

Los Amigos Park: 1 lighted court at 6th and Hollister Ave. (open only on weekends and weekdays after 6 p.m.)

Marine Park: 3 lighted courts at 17th and Marine Ave.

Memorial Park: 4 lighted courts at 14th and Olympic Blvd.

Ocean View Park: 6 unlighted courts at 2701 Barnard Way, south of Ocean Park Blvd.

Palisades Park: 8 lighted courts at 851 Alma Real Dr., Pacific Palisades

Reed Park: 7 lighted courts at Wilshire Blvd. and 7th St.

Rustic Canyon: 6 courts at 601 Latimer Rd.

Lessons and organized play: Whether you're a beginner, advanced, junior or senior player, the City of Santa Monica has lessons for you, year-round. They're cheap, too: around $9 to $10 per class (310.458.2239, smgov.net/seascape).

The **Santa Monica Tennis Club** is a public club at Reed Park open to all adults, aces and klutzes alike (310.281.3196, santamonicatennisclub.com). Further north, the **Palisades Tennis Center** (851 Alma Real Drive, Pacific Palisades, 310.573.1331) is paradise for tennis buffs, offering lessons, daily workouts and a full-service pro shop. At the **Santa Monica Senior Tournament** (310.208.3838), high-caliber players compete in singles and doubles on two successive weekends in late January/early February. "Senior" has a broad definition here: Players range from 30 to 70 years old. Finally, the nearly 80-year-old annual **Santa Monica Open Tennis Championship** (310.394.6011) at Reed and Ocean View parks every August is open to juniors and adults.

The Sports Shopper

Benton's Sport Shop
1038 Swarthmore Ave., Pacific Palisades
310.459.8451
This beloved, family-owned, longtime Palisades institution has it all: shoes for every sport and the balls, bats and rackets to go along with them. Beach life is also well represented in the stock of boogie boards, flip-flops, paddle-tennis gear, volleyballs, hats, bikinis, board shorts and Quiksilver casual wear. And that's not even covering the sports bras, Speedo swimsuits, Roxy girls' clothing, sunglasses and more, all crammed into about 1,600 square feet.

Doc's Ski Haus
3101 Santa Monica Blvd., Santa Monica
310.828.3492, docskihaus.com
Since 1958, Doc (yes, there is a Doc) has been fitting ski boots, tuning skis and helping people get the right gear. Doc and his team are just as knowledgeable about board gear, too. Boot-fitting is a particular specialty; it's worth a trip here to get it done right. Note that this Ski Haus is open in summer by appointment only.

Helen's Cycles
2501 Broadway, Santa Monica
310.829.1836
2472 Lincoln Blvd., Marina del Rey
310.306.7843, helenscycles.com
Helen's succeeds (and this is no easy task) in being a bike store for everyone, from the most serious gearhead to the 6-year-old dreaming of her first two-wheeler. Road bikes, mountain bikes, BMX bikes, tandems, beach cruisers, helmets, neon Spandex… you name it, they've got it, along with a savvy and helpful staff.

Kramer's Sporting Goods
1727 Ocean Park Blvd., Santa Monica
310.452.6266
A friendly little storefront specializing in team sports: uniforms, balls, cleats and gear for baseball, basketball, soccer and the like.

REI
402 Santa Monica Blvd., Santa Monica
310.458.4370, rei.com
This massive, relatively new branch of the outdoors-as-lifestyle chain is the sort of place that local hikers, bikers, campers, kayakers, climbers, skiers and cyclists visit on their lunch hour just to dream. If you look forward to your next backpacking trip the way some people look forward to their next spa day, then you already know about REI.

Rip City Skates
2709 Santa Monica Blvd., Santa Monica
310.828.0388, ripcity.net
Serious skateboarders head for this totally awesome place, which calls itself "Home of the $99.95 complete skateboard since 1978." No clothes, no "lifestyle" stuff, just quality custom skateboards built by skaters.

Sport Chalet
13455 Maxella Ave., Marina del Rey
310.821.9400, sportchalet.com
This homegrown California chain is large and well stocked, particularly with equipment for ball sports, skiing, snowboarding, diving, gym-going and running. The camping and fishing gear is good, too, though not as comprehensive as at REI. Skiers, watch for the excellent sales, and clothes hounds, note the good and fairly priced selection of workout wear and beachy casual clothing.

Q & A: Dane Selznick

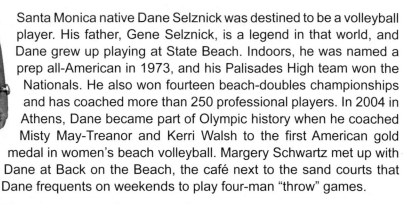

Santa Monica native Dane Selznick was destined to be a volleyball player. His father, Gene Selznick, is a legend in that world, and Dane grew up playing at State Beach. Indoors, he was named a prep all-American in 1973, and his Palisades High team won the Nationals. He also won fourteen beach-doubles championships and has coached more than 250 professional players. In 2004 in Athens, Dane became part of Olympic history when he coached Misty May-Treanor and Kerri Walsh to the first American gold medal in women's beach volleyball. Margery Schwartz met up with Dane at Back on the Beach, the café next to the sand courts that Dane frequents on weekends to play four-man "throw" games.

Who are you currently coaching?
A lot of amateur U.S. players, as well as the Chinese national (beach doubles) team – the Chinese are hosting the next Olympics, so this is huge for them. And this is a qualifying period for the Olympics, so it's a busy time for me.

Does it help as a coach to have been a player?
It helps me: You have the insight that comes from real game experiences, you recognize tendencies of your opponents, and you see situations where adjustments need to be made. Also, I'm a very technically oriented person regarding skills and translating them to my students. We work a lot on skills – that's my forte.

What stands out as your coaching high point?
The Olympic gold medal.

How else are you involved in the game?
Right now my focus is on youth development in the U.S. – and searching for our next gold medalists. I'm also the head coach for the Under 19s and Under 21s for the FIVB (Fédération Internationale de Volleyball).

Have the changes in beach volleyball – scoring, court size, etc. – improved the game?
No, they're really all about entertainment value because of television. The court got smaller, which made the game easier for bigger players who don't have to cover as much territory. The ball changed to accommodate a sponsor. And the scoring system has made games much faster, so the endurance part has been taken away. But everybody has to adapt to these changes. And it's still a great game.

Do you ever get nostalgic for the old days of competitive beach volleyball: summer weekend tournaments, playing in the finals in the dark, everybody knowing everybody else? No crazy crowds, no bleachers, no fake sand?
Of course. It was a great time – such a different lifestyle and way of thinking. Nobody goes to the beach like we used to. Now you have to make an appointment for a game. People go down for two hours; we went down at 9 a.m. and stayed till the sun went down. Pro volleyball is not a lifestyle anymore. Today a beach player doesn't even have to be a beach person.

Santa Monica is...
Materialistic

New York may be the fashion-design capital of America, but when it comes to setting the trends for what stylish Americans really want to wear, Santa Monica is where it's at. And clothing is just the beginning. From Venice to Malibu, Santa Monica to the Palisades, L.A.'s coastal towns host a wallet-busting bevy of one-of-a-kind shops that sell everything from fabulous gifts to quirky collectibles to high-fashion surfwear.

3 Main Streets to Wander

Stroller's heaven: on Main Street

The Bay Cities provide residents and visitors with some of the most rewarding shopping experiences in Southern California. Each town has at least one enchanting, walkable shopping district, from Swarthmore in the Palisades Village and Barrington Court in Brentwood to the Malibu Country Mart in Malibu and, of course, the famous Third Street Promenade in Santa Monica. But before we give you the lowdown on these hot spots, we need to showcase the three "Main Streets" that really stand out, not just for their historical importance, but for their neighborhood character, seaside locations and fabulous shopping, eating and people-watching (and yes, we mean star-watching) opportunities.

Main Street, Santa Monica

In the heart of Ocean Park, Main Street's commercial district runs from Strand to Rose. Not only is it a choice shopping/dining/drinking street, with a plum location two blocks from the beach, but it's also a street with a lot of historical significance. On this five-block stretch, you'll find not one but two buildings designed by Frank Gehry (the Edgemar Building and the Chiat Day-Mojo Building), one of the oldest and last Carnegie libraries in Southern California (Main Street Branch Library) and a landmark Victorian structure, which now houses the Heritage Square Museum. And let's not forget the wacky half-man, half-woman "Ballerina Clown" by artist Jonathan Borofsky that looms over the Renaissance Building at Rose and Main. It all adds up to a neighborhood that is edgy, artsy, open-minded, historic, colorful and a lot of fun. And because of its proximity to the Venice Boardwalk and Abbot Kinney, Main Street has become a hugely popular tourist attraction. It has a great assortment of one-of-a-kind shops, worthy art galleries and an appealing diversity of restaurants, from Wolfgang Puck's much-adored Chinois on Main (French-influenced Asian cuisine) to the fresh, healthy café fare at the Urth. Shopping is upscale and eclectic. From surfwear (ZJ's Boarding House) to party dresses (Blonde) to quirky gifts (Homeworks), there's something for everybody. The Sunday farmer's market (known for its valet bike parking and lively music and children's amusements) is terrific, too.

Abbot Kinney Boulevard, Venice

Named for the tobacco millionaire who founded Venice, Abbot Kinney is the increasingly upscale heart of this funky beach neighborhood. But Venice being Venice, as expensive as some of the shops are, there is always an element of eccentricity that negates poshness. That's why people like it. The street is crammed with art galleries, tiny

Abbot's Habit is the funky heart of Abbot Kinney's shopping district.

boutiques stuffed with goods from both acclaimed designers and local up-and-comers, kitschy vintage shops, lots of antiques stores, one-of-a-kind gift shops and great eating for any budget. The vibe is artsy, cutting-edge and beachy; the people range from hemp-wearing neo-hippies, to pink-haired sales girls, to the Palisades bourgeoisie. Specialty boutiques include Brick Lane, housed inside a tiny Craftsman-style bungalow, which sells products from the U.K., including cashmere sweaters, metro-friendly T-shirts and British flag-themed messenger bags. Strange Invisible is a botanical perfume shop that will conjure up an all-natural signature scent just for you. Firefly is a bookstore/boutique that carries handmade journals by local artisans and clever thank-you notes and birthday cards. Tortoise carries products only from Japan. And Bountiful is a gorgeous, densely packed antiques shop that will elicit a gasp as you enter its garden gates. For a snack, head to the local coffeehouse, Abbot's Habit, or to Abbot Kinney Pizza for a slice of bagel-crust pizza. For a fancier meal, the choices are fantastic: Our favorites are Hal's Bar & Grill, Joe's, Lilly's and, for sushi, Wabi-Sabi.

Montana Avenue, Santa Monica

On Montana Avenue everything is upscale, ever-so trendy and downright beachy, thanks in part to ocean breezes blowing in off the nearby coast. It represents Santa Monica's more genteel side. The shopping part starts at

Café Montana's walls of glass bring in the neighborhood's chic street life.

7th Street and continues east ten blocks to 17th Street. It's the best place to outfit your baby like royalty; at last count we spied at least five high-falutin' stores for tots. You'll also find plenty of luxury shopping for the rest of the family: designer clothing, antiques, home decor, jewelry, even three stores just for dogs. Shopping on Montana says you've arrived. Who cares if that bath towel at Waterworks costs $40? It's got that darling blue starfish on it, and you deserve a whole set. And only Planet Blue will do for your daughter's prom dress. For jewelry, check out Moondance, where you'll find many of the same lines that Neiman Marcus carries. Mixed in with all the fab shops are two yoga studios, two massage centers, multiple coffee venues (try Caffe Luxe) and a couple of needlepoint shops. The restaurants are good, too, especially Blue Plate for breakfast, 17th Street Café for lunch and Café Montana for dinner – and all are choice for star-spotting.

Where the Locals Shop: The Neighborhoods

Happily, most of the communities around the Santa Monica Bay have their own "villages," which the locals frequent day in and day out. All these shopping areas are outdoors, pedestrian-friendly and charming. Here's the rundown.

3 Places to Consume in Brentwood

The "stables" in this barn are filled with $200 T-shirts and glamorous tchotchkes.

Barrington Court, just off Sunset Boulevard near the 405 Freeway, is a collection of shops suitable for both westside trendsters and members of the old-money L.A. elite, many of whom reside in Brentwood. The area also attracts students from the nearby Archer School for Girls and the Brentwood School; they head to Belwood Bakery for a croissant or sandwich, to Market and Yellow Dog for clothes, and to Maria's Italian Kitchen for a slice of pizza. The older crowd likes Gloria S. for classic women's clothing, Brentwood Gourmet Market for caviar and cheeses, and Brent-Air Pharmacy for a pharmacy where everybody knows your name. For babies, tots and kids, check out Ruby Slippers and Star Toys.

Brentwood Gardens on San Vicente Boulevard is a glitzy three-story mini-mall, with upscale shopping and valet parking, as well as some good yuppie eats at such places as the Daily Grill, CPK and the Japanese restaurant Taiko. At the Gardens you'll find such ultra-trendy shops as Theodore, Ron Herman, Madison, BCBG and Boulmiche. There's an imaginative children's store called Pumkinheads, and the home-furnishing stores carry imported tablecloths from France, gorgeous faux flower arrangements and stylish antiques.

Finally, there's the **Brentwood Country Mart**, the big red barn at 26th and San Vicente (technically in Santa Monica) that's famous for Reddi Chick, the greasiest, tastiest roast chicken and spicy fries in town. It also houses some great shops, including Calypso, Jigsaw, Jigsaw Jr., Post 126, Marie Mason Apothecary and Flora and Henri for the pampered tot. Other than Reddi Chick, try the mac and cheese at the City Bakery and the gourmet burger from Barney's.

The Palisades's small-town charms include a much-frequented village square.

Pacific Palisades

In the Palisades, most locals stick to the stores in the **Village**, which runs along Sunset Boulevard from Carey Street to Via de la Paz. Swarthmore Avenue is the Main Street; that's where you'll find Benton's Sports Shop, an excellent all-around sporting-goods shop; the much-beloved Village Books, which has a caring sales staff who actually read; Intima for incredibly cute lingerie; Booa for trendy women's clothes; Whispers for that last-minute date outfit; and Paliskate for the skating/surfing crowd. Side streets feature such shops as Elyse Walker, whose haute couture has gotten hotter and hotter, and Black Ink, a stationery and gift shop that features some of the most original invitations and cards we've ever seen. For food, try a yummy *croque monsieur* at A la Tarte, an authentic French bakery and café on Swarthmore – *c'est très bonne*!

Venice: Bargain-Hunting on the Boardwalk

If you ever pine for the street vendors of New York, look no further than the circus that is the Venice Boardwalk. The goods are all cheap, all fake and all touristy... but the intrepid shopper can root out some worthy buys. And for a retreat from the boardwalk nuttiness, duck into Small World Books, a fine place to pick up a good read.

Malibu

Malibu-ites do their local shopping mostly at the **Malibu Country Mart**, located on Cross Creek Road and PCH. Not only will you find movie stars there, but also Planet Blue for amazing body products, James Perse for $80 T-shirts, Laura M. for beautiful custom jewelry (she also has a shop in the Palisades), Madison, which teenage boys call "hot-girl heaven," and 98% Angel for the most adorable and softest babywear ever. For the home, check out Rachel Ashwell's Shabby Chic for divine comfy sofas and chairs that are just perfect for that beach house on Malibu Road.

Everything but cars on the Promenade

The Lowdown on the Third Street Promenade: We Love It!

The Third Street Promenade, located on 3rd Street between Wilshire and Colorado, is the most popular shopping, eating and entertainment venue on L.A.'s westside. Formerly a severely depressed strip of distressed stores that served as command central for the homeless, the Promenade was completely overhauled in 1989 and is now hailed as one of the most successful retail endeavors in Southern California. It's got everything going for it: a seaside location (it's two blocks from Palisades Park, overlooking the Pacific), outdoor, ocean-breezy, year-round shopping, and street performers who sing, juggle, tell jokes, bang plastic bins and break dance. Thanks to the Promenade, Santa Monica now has the big chain stores: J. Crew, Victoria's Secret, Sephora, Restoration Hardware, Pottery Barn, Barnes & Noble, Borders, the Apple Store and American Eagle, to name just a few. (The downside is a lack of unique shops, but those are plentiful on the surrounding streets and on Main, Abbot Kinney and Montana.) It's vibrant and crowded all the time, especially on hot summer nights and weekends, when inlanders yearn to escape the heat. Other amusements include three movie-theater complexes (plus the art-house Laemmle around the corner on 2nd Street) and scores of restaurants, including Bravo Cucina, Broadway Deli, Houston's and Johnny Rockets. Longtime locals who were skeptical and didn't think it would fly are now saying, "How did we ever survive without the Promenade?"

The Goods

Antiques

We've labored to winnow down the vast array of antiques merchants in the Bay Cities. In the stores that follow you'll find not just pricey pieces from the 19th century, but also elegant chandeliers from Italy, the first "modern" furniture from the '50s and '60s, collectible vinyl albums, British war memorabilia, quirky, colorful beachy accessories and much more.

Please note that antiques stores often have limited and fickle hours, so in most cases we don't list hours; call before you visit.

Bountiful is packed to its high ceilings with antique accessories and small pieces, as well as flowers, shells and all sorts of wonderful *objets d'art*.

Bountiful
1335 Abbot Kinney Blvd., Venice
310.450.3620, bountifulhome.com
Sue Balmforth's sprawling store is renowned as a source for the best and most unique blend of American country charm and European elegance. Enter through its garden gates and discover a world of 19th-century American and French painted furniture, chandeliers from Italy and Southern farm tables covered in fine linens from Europe. The spectacular shells from around the world make great gifts.

British Collectibles (Militaria) Ltd.
1727 Wilshire Blvd., Santa Monica
310.453.3322, britishmilitaria.com
If you're looking for, say, a British officer's shako plate (circa 1855) to add to your collection of British war memorabilia, including Zulu War artifacts (1869-1876), Royal Air Force aviation uniforms and caps (early 1900s) and officers' shoulder belt plates (1950s), do check this place out. Visit the web site for detailed information on inventory.

Detelich Arts & Crafts Gallery
1654 Ocean Ave., Santa Monica
800.595.8192
Detelich Gallery has many fine examples of antique furniture from the Arts & Crafts movement, including pieces by Gustav Stickley, Stickley Brothers, Roycroft, JM Young and Shop of the Crafters. It also carries some Handel lamps and other lighting fixtures from the period.

Equator Vinyl is found in back of the gallery-like Equator Books.

Equator Vinyl
1103 Abbot Kinney Blvd., Venice
310.399.5544, equatorbooks.com
Equator Vinyl, located in back of the famous Equator Books, is dedicated to the survival of the vinyl record. In addition to vintage concert posters and music artifacts, it has stacks of classic and collectible music of all varieties, from jazz to blues to R&B and classical, and there's not a CD in the bunch.

French 50s and 60s Vintage Furniture
1427 Abbot Kinney Blvd., Venice
310.392.9905, french50s60s.com
This store really lives up to its name – it showcases midcentury furniture from the '50s and '60s, with all pieces found in France: furniture, art, lighting and accessories.

Also in the neighborhood:
Neptina
1329 Abbot Kinney Blvd., Venice, 310.396.1630
Glassware from the 1950s and '60s.

Gift Garden Antiques
15266 Antioch St., Pacific Palisades
310.459.4114
While other antiques stores have come and gone, Gift Garden Antiques endures as the best antiques shop in the Palisades, featuring furniture from many periods, sterling silver collections, vintage clothing, china, crystal and other pretty artifacts for the home and garden.

Historia Antiques
1322 2nd St., Ste. 2, Santa Monica
310.394.3384, historia-antiques.com
Historia specializes in Spanish Colonial art, folk art, ceramics, furniture pieces, dance masks and textiles, with an emphasis on 19th- and early-20th-century Mexican devotional and folk art.

Rosemarie McCaffrey Antiques
1203 Montana Ave., Santa Monica
310.395.7711
For those of you with very deep pockets, check out these European antiques from the 17th, 18th and 19th centuries. The store specializes in French country furniture, paintings, tapestries and 18th- and 19th-century mirrors.

Santa Monica Outdoor Antique Market
Santa Monica Airport
Airport Ave. & Bundy Dr., Santa Monica
323.933.2511
1st & 4th Sun. of the month, 8 a.m.-3 p.m.
Much smaller than the big daddies in Pasadena and Long Beach, this flea market is a lot less exhausting to negotiate. You can find great stuff here, especially collectibles and small pieces.

Surfing Cowboys
1624 Abbot Kinney Blvd., Venice
310.450.4891, surfingcowboys.com
They call themselves "the purveyors of California lifestyle and beach culture," specializing in midcentury furnishings, vintage surf clothing, surf-themed paintings, posters and photos, and antique fireplaces and lighting.

Also in the neighborhood:
The Perfect Piece
1216 Abbot Kinney Blvd., Venice, 310.581.1002
Very strange artifacts and furnishings made from old movie-set pieces.
Venice Vintage Paradise
144 Abbot Kinney Blvd., 310.452.0733
Beachy, kitschy.

Wertz Brothers Antique Mart
1607 Lincoln Blvd., Santa Monica
310.452.1800, wertzbrothers.com
Unlike Wertz's furniture store *(see below)*, this place is really an antiques mall, where many vendors offer furniture, "smalls," lamps and pillows. It's the perfect place to find something for the beach house or cabin.

Wertz Brothers Furniture Store
11879 Santa Monica Blvd., Santa Monica
310.477.4251, wertzbrothers.com
This huge warehouse is packed to the brim with

furniture and accessories galore from the 20th century. It's all used, and it's all old – doesn't that make them antiques?

Threads of many colors at Aristeia

Arts & Crafts

Aristeia
141 S. Barrington Pl., Brentwood
310.476.6977
Even though it's hard to spell, this fantastic needlepoint and knitting store has a devout following, because it's intimate, friendly and rich in materials, supplies and classes.

Artful
1726 Ocean Park Blvd., Santa Monica
310.581.5150
Artful sells arts and crafts supplies, provides quality arts and crafts instruction, and also carries gifts for all occasions.

The Clayhouse
2909 Santa Monica Blvd., Santa Monica
310.828.7071
For pottery equipment, clay and pottery instruction, everyone in Santa Monica goes to the Clayhouse.

Color Me Mine
1109 Montana Ave., Santa Monica
310.393.0069
What fun to take a shaped piece of dried clay and decorate your own vase, platter, frame, class gift, whatever! Kids love it, too. You apply the paint to whatever object you choose, and Color Me Mine applies the glaze. The results can be extraordinary.

The Goddess
1507 Abbot Kinney Blvd., Venice
310.314.1494, thegoddessstudio.com
Wow, this place is amazing! The beads are gorgeous, and the variety and abundance are remarkable. The Goddess also makes its own jewelry, including the dazzling "Wedding" necklaces, and it sponsors jewelry-making workshops, classes and creative outdoor gatherings, such as Bead and Breakfast on the first Sunday of the month, 10 a.m. to noon.

Hiromi Paper International
Bergamot Station, 2525 Michigan Ave., G9, Santa Monica
310.451.4015, hiromipaper.com
Hiromi Paper is the west coast's link to the centuries-old art of Japanese papermaking. In addition to selling exquisite Japanese papers in all varieties, beautiful stationery and gifts, it offers workshops in paper- and print-making. Call for workshop schedules – spaces are limited.

Jo-Ann Fabrics & Crafts
1637 Lincoln Blvd., Santa Monica
310.450.6441, joann.com
This vast place houses every kind of fabric – from flannel to silk – and every kind of craft supply – from sequins to fake flowers. It also carries patterns from many manufacturers, as well as the gamut of sewing supplies.

L'Atelier on Montana
1202 Montana Ave., Santa Monica
310.394.4665
Let's face it, at one time or another, every woman goes through a knitting phase, and this is the perfect place to start, from getting all the supplies to attending highly personalized classes. Before you know it, you'll have knitted a cap, a scarf and half a sweater (but will you ever finish it?). If you join the "L'Atelier SOTM Club," you'll get discounts on patterns and yarns.

Also in the neighborhood:
Needlepoint on Montana
625 Montana Ave., 310.451.3393
Beautiful and beloved.

Michaels Art & Crafts
1427 4th St., Santa Monica
310.393.9634
It's a chain, but it's the only one we've got for miles around, so it's essential to know about, especially if your kid has to make a diorama. It's got tons of art supplies, fake flowers, holiday items for Christmas to the 4th of July, beads, T-shirt-making supplies, doll-making tools, frames and so very much more. If you're not the crafty sort, you'll probably break out into hives.

Also in the neighborhood:
Mittel's Art and Frame Center
2016 Lincoln Blvd., 310.399.9500
Heavy on the arts supplies.

Nina at Fred Segal
420 Broadway, Santa Monica
310.458.8820
A good source for beads on the funkier, trendier, pricier side, Nina also carries jewelry.

Polished stones are among the thousands of lovely, tiny things at Ritual Adornments.

Ritual Adornments
2708 Main St., Santa Monica
310.452.4044
Bead enthusiasts love this place for its walls of hanging strands of beads, trays of semiprecious gems and bowls of beads made of ceramic, glass, metal, wood, shells and crystal. The staff is friendly and helpful.

Semi-Precious
1021 Montana Ave., Santa Monica
310.899.0910
This tiny shop on Montana is packed to the brim with glittering, dazzling beads, including an array of semiprecious gems, turquoise, coral, chalcedony and freshwater pearls, hanging in strands and displayed in bowls.

Sewing Arts Center
3330 Pico Blvd., Santa Monica
310.450.4300, sewingartscenter.com
Quilters and seamstresses convene at the Sewing Arts Center, which offers the finest selection of high-end sewing machines (Husqvana Viking and HandiQuilter), as well as more than 3,000 bolts of quilting cottons (including hand-dyes and batiks), sewing classes and supplies.

Stitches from the Heart
3316 Pico Blvd., Santa Monica
866.472.6903
This organization sends handmade clothing and blankets to premature babies across the country, and the effort is funded by this nonprofit store, which sells yarn, knitting and crochet tools and patterns. It also offers knitting and crochet classes.

Wildfiber
1453 E. 14th St., Santa Monica
310.458.2748, wildfiber.com
Located in the old Laundry Building at 14th and Broadway, Wildfiber provides an expansive space for customers to linger and examine yarns and knits in many vibrant colors and varieties, as well as take classes and connect with other knitters.

Clothing & Accessories

Blonde
2430 Main St., Santa Monica
310.396.9113, blondla.com
Beachy but refined, Blonde carries styles that range from Rebecca Taylor party dresses to Cheekey Puella lingerie. In between you'll find a good assortment of Nicole Miller bikinis and stacks of the newest, hottest jeans.

Canyon Beachwear
106 Entrada Dr., Santa Monica
310.459.5070
"We suit everybody" is the motto of this longtime swimsuit store, strategically located across the street from State Beach. Bikinis, trunks, Speedo suits, one-pieces… they've got ' .em all, along with sunscreen, hats and other sand staples.

Elyse Walker
15306 Antioch St., Pacific Palisades
310.230.8882
When Elyse Walker first opened its doors about ten years ago, everyone said, "Duh, it's about time a designer high-end clothing store came to the Palisades." It took off, and the emphasis

went from hot to haute. The store features Marc Jacobs everything, $3,000 cocktail dresses, pricey Tsubi jeans and $100 camisoles. In other words, this place ain't cheap, but fashionistas love it.

European Equestrian
18820 Pacific Coast Hwy., Malibu
310.456.1454, europeanequestrian.com
Come in here for equestrian clothing for men, women and children: horsey vests, pants, jackets and hats. Lots of people shop here who don't ride – they know a good look when they see one!

Foot Candy
11934 San Vicente Blvd., Brentwood
310.820.4800
This elegant shoe store carries a slew of high-end designers: Jimmy Choo, Manolo Blahnik, Christian Louboutin, Narciso Rodriguez. Enjoy the serene, gallery-like space while you peruse the latest footwear fashions.

Fred Segal
420 & 500 Broadway, Santa Monica
310.458.9940, fredsegal.com
This world-renowned Fred Segal complex houses some 25 Fred Segal vendors in two buildings across the street from each other, showcasing the hippest, trendiest clothes for men, women and children, lingerie, body products, jewelry, hats, shoes, gifts and stationery. Jewelry stores include Fred Segal Sparkle, Fred Segal Tiara and Fred Segal Nina; cutting-edge, fashion-forward clothing is at Fred Segal Fun, Fred Segal Man, Fred Segal and Fred Segal Street, to name a few. Body products and cosmetics are at Fred Segal Essentials.

Hidden Treasures
154 S. Topanga Canyon Blvd., Topanga Canyon
310.455.2998
Housed inside an enchanting cottage decorated with sparkling lights and a welcoming mermaid, this three-room store is filled with vintage Hawaiian shirts, prom dresses, bedspreads and hand-embroidered sheets and throw pillows.

Intima
1027 Swarthmore Ave., Pacific Palisades
310.573.3794
Intima is the best place in the Palisades to grab the cutest lingerie: Cosabella and Hanky Panky undies, bras by Chantelle and really sexy teddies and nightgowns. The staff is vigilant about making sure what you buy really fits. Guys come here for great "Mom" gifts, like pretty pens, jewelry, candles, slippers and ultra-soft robes.

Lisa Kline Men
23410 Civic Center Way, Malibu
310.456.2439, lisaklinemen.com
A man could outfit himself for decades at this stylish store that features suits, casual wear, board shorts, T-shirts, shoes and accessories – including Lisa Kline Men's private label.

London Sole
1331 Montana Ave., Santa Monica
310.255.0937, londonsole.com
You'll find only flats here, but they are all exquisite and beautifully made. Kate Moss, Nicole Kidman and Calista Flockhart are devotees.

Also in the neighborhood:
Souliers Shoes
1205 Montana Ave., 310.393.0460
Very comfy designer shoes from Europe.

Madison
Malibu Country Mart
3835 Cross Creek Rd., Malibu
310.317.9170
Brentwood Gardens
11077 San Vicente Blvd., Brentwood
310.820.2300
Madison has shoes and clothes that all the girls love, including adorable pieces by Chloe, Theory, Marc Jacobs and Dianne Von Furstenberg, as well as from up-and-comers. For shoes, count on hip styles from Miu Miu, Dolce & Gabbana and Sigerson Morrison.

Candy-colored bras at Intima

Claudia Milan

1350 Abbot Kinney Blvd., Venice
310.581.2964, claudiamilan.com
If you need something very, very special – say a dress for a big night out – then head to the shop run by Milan, a stylist with 20 years of experience. Her "closely edited" collections for men and women will give you a put-together look. She's also got fantastic accessories.

Also in the neighborhood:
Pamela Barish
1327 Abbot Kinney Blvd., 310.314.4490
Edgy, flattering fashions.

Only Hearts

1407 Montana Ave., Santa Monica
310.393.3088 onlyhearts.com
Everything in here is sweet, frilly and pretty, with heart-themed packaging. The store features top designer intimates, slips, sleepwear, leggings, tops, jeans and dresses. A favorite of the college-girl crowd.

Also in the neighborhood:
Lisa Norman Lingerie
1134 Montana Ave., 310.451.2026
Ritzy lingerie for the more mature woman.

California chic at Planet Blue

Planet Blue

800 14th St. (at Montana), Santa Monica
310.394.0135
2940 Main St., Santa Monica
310.396.1767
Malibu Country Mart
3835 Cross Creek Rd., Malibu
310.317.8566
The clothing at Planet Blue, from pretty party dresses to high-end sweats, is what's new right now. The stores have a few finds for men, too. These are fashions mostly for the skinny and fit; 17-year-old girls armed with a parent's charge card love it.

Also in the neighborhood:
Rita's Rags
1211 Montana Ave., 310.393.4588
Velvet T's, great jeans, cashmere.
Three Bags Full
716 Montana Ave., 310.395.5559
"The sweater store."

Principessa

1323 Abbot Kinney Blvd., Venice
310.450.6696
Princepessa stocks the best and most interesting pieces from the collections of designers Ella Moss, Milly, La Rok and many other modern classicists.

Savannah

706 Montana Ave., Santa Monica
310.458.2095
Known as the place for high-end, spare designer clothing, including pieces from Jil Sander, Yohji Yamamoto, Issey Miyake, Etro and Maxfield Parish, Savannah is a fashionista's sanctuary.

Sequins

3101 Ocean Park Blvd., Santa Monica
310.452.5006
From the former owner of Sara's on Montana, Sequins features the same great styles, including Sara's signature Balinese shoes, clothes, jewelry and gifts.

Tortuga

23410 Civic Center Way, Malibu
310.924.9749
For bikinis you might see on the cover of *Sports Illustrated*, don't miss this one-of-a-kind Malibu swim shop. The fabrics are unusual, the styles minimal.

Undefeated

2654-B Main St., Santa Monica
310.399.4195
Teenage boys with style love this sneakers store because they can find popular brands (Nike, Adidas, Converse, Vans) in styles you don't see anywhere else. The limited editions make this place really cool.

Also in the neighborhood:
Boca & Boca for Men
15300 Antioch St., 310.454.3891
Chic clothing for men and women.
Whispers
1014 Swarthmore Ave., 310.454.5581
Hip classics for women.

Pirate central at Make Believe

Costumes

Make Believe
3240 Pico Blvd., Santa Monica
310.396.6785
If you need a Sgt. Pepper's costume or a medieval wench getup, you'll find it at this serious costume store. It supplies local theater companies, so its inventory is vast.

Ursula's
2516 Wilshire Blvd., Santa Monica
310.582.8230
When it's Halloween and you need to outfit the whole family, Ursula's will set you up with costumes and accessories.

Weathervane
1209 Montana Ave., Santa Monica
310.454.5582
Rich, crisp, sophisticated clothing for women who can tell their Commes des Garçons from their Yohji Yamamoto is showcased in an architecturally beautiful space. Good service, loyal customers and beautiful pieces for grown-ups.

Also in the neighborhood:
Weathervane for Men
1132 Montana Ave., 310.395.0397
Handsome, rich clothing.

Furniture & Housewares

Rachel Ashwell Shabby Chic
Malibu Country Mart
3900 Cross Creek Rd., Malibu
310.317.9750
1013 Montana Ave., Santa Monica
310.394.1975, shabbychic.com
Designer Rachel Ashwell coined the term "shabby chic" to describe her relaxed but elegant style, a California blend of beauty, comfort and function, and it went on to become part of the interior-design vocabulary. She opened her first store on Montana Avenue in 1989, and before long her slipcovered sofas, chairs and ottomans in soft, warm fabrics were popping up in fashionable houses all over the country. She also carries bedding, fabrics, knickknacks, antiques and precious items for baby.

Baldwin & Company
1021 Montana Ave., Santa Monica
310.899.0655, baldwinandco.com
Check out this beachy cottage-style shop filled with new and vintage accessories for the home, including clapboard signs proclaiming: "My Garden," "Gone Surfin" or just "Beach." You'll also discover great garden accessories and whimsical gifts.

Casa Allegra
2714 Main St., Santa Monica
310.396.7978
At Casa Allegra you'll find a fantastic collection of imported vintage and new furniture, richly colorful tableware, household linens, handmade gifts and artsy home decor items, all with Mexican flair. There's even a nifty toy store.

Color is the watchword at Casa Allegra.

Digs
1118 Abbot Kinney Blvd., Venice
310.450.3072, digsak.com
Craftsmanesque furniture is featured here, as well as pieces that blend American classicism with a bit of Asian flair. Digs aims to provide solid, well-built furniture with clean, handsome lines that doesn't cost an arm and a leg. It does a lot of custom work, too.

Hemisphere
1627 Montana Ave., Santa Monica
310.393.1845, hemisphereonmontana.com
Since 1985, this store has specialized in California Monterey furniture, beautiful rugs and antiques and home accessories from China.

Malibu Colony Company
Malibu Country Mart
3835 Cross Creek Rd., Malibu
310.317.0177
There are two Malibu Colony stores at the Malibu Country Mart – one carries extravagant accessories for the home, including sterling-silver frames, fancy candles, lush pillows and luxe bed linens, and the other sells highly desirable furniture.

Oasis
3931 S. Topanga Canyon Blvd. (at PCH),
Pacific Palisades
310.456.9883, oasisfurniture.net
For exquisite outdoor patio furniture, as well as indoor furniture, you've got to see this place. The teak and aluminum sets are quite handsome.

Ponte Vecchio
702 Montana Ave., Santa Monica
310.394.6038
This place looks like it belongs in the Italian countryside, with its huge Mediterranean vessels, Venetian glass, Florentine leather and handmade Tuscan wood furniture. Tableware and ceramic vases are also available.

Room with a View
1600 Montana Ave., Santa Monica
310.998.5858
This store specializes in luxurious items for the home: furniture, china, sterling frames, fine linens, lamps, tables and sumptuous chairs.

3 Hometown Hardware Stores

Busy Bee Hardware
1521 Santa Monica Blvd., Santa Monica, 310.395.1158
Now, this is an old-fashioned hometown hardware store, small but jam-packed with everything a good hardware store should have, including replacement parts for older, discontinued products. It does a brisk key and locksmith business, too.

Malibu Lumber & Hardware Company
23419 Pacific Coast Hwy., Malibu, 310.456.9031, malibulumber.com
The locals love this place, because it's filled with everything a handy person will ever need, from lumber and tools to plumbing supplies and wheelbarrows.

Topanga Lumber
506 S. Topanga Canyon Blvd., Topanga Canyon, 310.455.2047
In addition to having everything under the sun for home-improvement enthusiasts, this place is known for its high-quality lumber. Contractors come from far and wide to stock up.

A room to view in Rooms & Gardens

Rooms & Gardens
1311A Montana Ave., Santa Monica
310.451.5151, roomsandgardens.com
Reflecting a colonial West Indies-British style, this ultra-charming store, operated by Jami and Eric Voulgaris in partnership with actress Mary Steenburgen, offers not just exquisite antique furniture, lamps and porcelain, but also comfortable custom-made sofas, chairs and pillows. The Voulgarises also operate two stores of the same name in the Santa Barbara area.

Jewelry & Gifts

Cabachon Fine Jewelry
1426 Montana Ave., Santa Monica
310.576.2455
This lavish store specializes in dazzling handmade platinum engagement rings – they're to die for. In addition, it showcases eighteen- and fourteen-karat-gold jewelry by 50 designers, and does custom jobs and appraisals.

Laura M. Fine Jewelry & Diamonds
15310 Antioch St., Pacific Palisades
310.459.9666
Malibu Country Mart
3835 Cross Creek Rd., Malibu
310.456.3123, lauramjewelry.com
Laura M's designs are modern, pretty and one-of-a-kind. Check out the teardrop sapphire earrings lined with pearls, dazzling diamond rings and dainty necklaces in gold mixed with gemstones. It's hard to pick a favorite – we want it all!

Firefly
1413 Abbot Kinney Blvd., Venice
310.450.6288
You won't find a better spot for the perfect gift with Venice style: candles by Votivo, baby clothes by Dean, leather bags by Dean, handmade journals, a clever selection of art, interior-design and surf books, handmade jewelry and lovely little Mimi & Coco sweaters, all tidily tucked into a three-room cottage.

The Gallery of Functional Art
Bergamot Station
2525 Michigan Ave., E3,
Santa Monica
310.829.6990
This extraordinary gift store has items ranging from $10 to $1,000 – each one worth a careful ponder. Most are artist-made, some are just plain artistic, and there's something for everyone: a chair made out of wine corks, a gorgeous polished-aluminum table, handmade jewelry, handblown glass, folk art, clever boxes woven from recycled magazines and newspapers, sculpture, books and more. Lots of fun to browse.

From the entrance, there's a prevailing sense of wit and whimsy at the Gallery of Functional Art.

Hey Kookla
1329 Montana Ave.,
Santa Monica
310.899.9499, heykookla.com
This personality-rich store in a charming little cottage carries gifts, personal accessories, home decor and beauty items with an edgy style. It's a good place to get attention-getting corporate and personal gift baskets.

Homeworks
2923 Main St., Santa Monica
310.396.0101
These wacky gifts will put a smile on your face: Ouija Boards, vintage lunch boxes, clever T-shirts, sardonic refrigerator magnets and all sorts of *objets d'amusement*. The greeting-card selection is fantastic (some are pretty crude), and kids love the gag gifts, especially those of the fake-vomit variety.

Moondance Jewelry Gallery

1530 Montana Ave., Santa Monica
310.395.5516, moondancejewelry.com
Contemporary handcrafted jewelry and
accessories from more than 60 designers,
including Gabrielle Sanchez, Me & Ro, Dana
Kellin and Anthony Nak. Think pieces that
Rachel from *Friends* would wear – it's hot stuff.

The Nest Egg

15241 Sunset Blvd., Pacific Palisades
310.573.9777
This delightful shop is the perfect combination
of beach kitsch and elegance, featuring sparkly
jewelry, sterling frames, deliciously scented
candles and items for every holiday. There's no
way you can't find the perfect gift here.

Sculpture to Wear

808 11th St., Santa Monica
310.260.1957
This establishment offers fine contemporary art
jewelry made by international artists. It's very
artsy and very different.

Tibetan Arts

704 Santa Monica Blvd., Santa Monica
310.458.6304, tibetan-arts.com
Tired of the same old silver frames for gifts?
Then head here to explore gorgeous handmade
arts and crafts from the Himalayan countries of
Tibet and Bhutan, including pashminas, Buddha
statues, handmade bags, pillowcases, wall
hangings and banners.

Tortoise

1208 Abbot Kinney Blvd., Venice
310.314.8448, tortoiselife.com
Everything in this sleek, minimalist store hails
from Japan or was made by Japanese artists.
The kitchen items, tableware, books, jewelry,
stationery and furniture make unique gifts.

23rd Street Jewelers

2319 Wilshire Blvd., Santa Monica
310.828.0833
Owned by two sisters, this premier jeweler
goes back more than 25 years. It carries a
beautiful selection of bespoke jewelry, as well
as sophisticated designs by Diane Allen, Mary
Kelley and Norma B. Jewels of all kinds are set
in platinum and gold.

Personal Care

Apothia at Brentwood Gardens

11677 San Vicente Blvd., Brentwood
310.207.8411
You'll get blissed out at Apothia, where you'll find
the Bliss line of body products, as well as such
chic personal-care essentials as Caitlin, the red-
hot fragrance that all the actresses are wearing.
A high-end body-shop experience.

Marie Mason Apothecary

Brentwood Country Mart
225 26th St., Santa Monica
310.394.5710
At Marie Mason you'll discover the finest luxuries
for body, bath and home, in addition to richly
scented candles, elegant robes and hard-to-find
skin-care items. Marie is famous for her custom-
blended scents.

Palmetto

1034 Montana Ave., Santa Monica
310.395.6687
Step inside and you're immediately overwhelmed
by a million different fragrances. That's because
Palmetto features a huge variety of upscale
soaps, lotions, hair products and perfumes, in all
shapes and sizes. You can even get black-and-
pink poodle soap for that canine-loving friend.

Planet Blue Essentials

Malibu Country Mart
3835 Cross Creek Rd., Malibu
310.317.8566
This Planet Blue branch has a small inventory of
adorable clothing and lingerie, but the emphasis
is on things that smell good – for your face, body
and aura. It's jam-packed with scrubs, scents,
soaps, candles, oils and hair products. We love
the big supply of Kai, including the hard-to-find
body wash and yummy candles.

Strange Invisible Perfumery

1138 Abbot Kinney Blvd., Venice
310.314.1555
If you want to create a signature fragrance, this
is the place. Strange Invisible is a botanical
perfumery, so it eschews synthetic ingredients
for natural flower and plant extracts. Explore the
scents of jasmine, orange blossom and pink and
blue lotus to discover what's right for you.

Stationery

Arts & Letters on Main
2665 Main St., Santa Monica
310.392.9076
Great, high-quality custom invitations and announcements, handmade papers, art cards, Mont Blanc pens and fine stationery are all part of the extensive inventory at this quality shop.

Black Ink
873 Swarthmore Ave., Pacific Palisades
310.573.9905
We love Black Ink for its adorable, original invitations for everything from cocktail parties and beach barbecues to Christmas open houses and, yes, divorce parties. It also does a brisk holiday-card business, with a huge variety of custom cards. Great gifts, too: frames, photo albums and wonderful stationery.

Embrey Papers
11965 San Vicente Blvd., Brentwood
310.440.2620
This stationery store has been serving Brentwood's elite for decades, and though the vibe is staid and old-fashioned, you won't find a more appropriate place to get engraved wedding invitations, high-end stationery (Crane, of course) and lots of Vera Bradley products, from checkbook covers to little quilted cosmetic bags.

Brenda Himmel Stationery
1126 Montana Ave., Santa Monica
310.395.2437
Not only is this a fine place for traditional wedding invitations, it also carries more modern designs using specialty and handmade papers. Himmel also has useful gifts, such as leather photo albums, frames, clocks and agendas.

Pulp & Hide
13020 San Vicente Blvd., Brentwood
310.394.0700
The name alludes to where paper comes from, and inside you'll find a good selection of fine stationery, the ability to procure engraved invitations and cute stuff for kids. All the holidays are highlighted with special gift items and papers.

Thrift & Resale

The Address Boutique
1116 Wilshire Blvd., Santa Monica
310.394.1406
Here you'll find everything from J. Crew argyle sweaters to couture by Valentino. The inventory of high-quality, gently used clothing changes constantly, and the prices are exceptional.

Great Labels
1126 Wilshire Blvd., Santa Monica
310.451.2277, greatlabels.com
Almost next door to The Address Boutique is Great Labels – and they mean great labels: Fendi, Gucci, Chanel, St. John, Missoni, Prada and more. It specializes in gently worn clothing "from the best closets in Tinsel Town."

PJ London
11661 San Vicente Blvd., Brentwood
310.826.4649
You'd think one of the richest neighborhoods in L.A. would have a great resale shop, and it does! This is truly one of the best resale and consignment shops anywhere, featuring pieces by Armani, Calvin Klein, Jil Sander, Alaia and many, many more. In stock at any time could be an orange Chanel suit, a red Versace party dress or a like-new Louis Vuitton wallet.

St. Matthew's Thrift Shop
2812 Main St., Santa Monica
310.396.9776
An outreach program of the Episcopal parish of St. Matthew's in the Palisades, this shop uses its proceeds to reach out to locals in need. It carries used clothing, housewares, luggage, toys and useful items. Donations are most welcome and can be dropped off behind the store.

A sense of humor makes shopping at St. Matthew's fun.

Q & A: Karyn Craven

Ever since she left UCLA armed with a fine-arts degree, L.A. native and longtime Venice resident Karyn Craven kept creating: collages, photographs, hand-painted T-shirts, fashion designs for international companies and, since 1999, clothing for her fast-growing company, Burning Torch. Originally a line made from recycled vintage garments, Burning Torch now produces diverse collections known for their lush colors, custom embroidery and quality fabrics. Her clothes appear in all the hot fashion magazines and sell in chic boutiques around the world and close to home (including Planet Blue, Fred Segal and Minnie T's). Karyn and her old high-school-era pal Colleen Bates talked over tapas at Primitivo, not far from the house she shares with her longtime partner, ceramic artist Luis Bermudez.

Why Venice?
I love being by the ocean. I love the spirit and the diversity of lifestyles and interests, which brings the quality of the unexpected. Because of the close quarters of our neighborhoods, you get to know people you never thought you would.

Has Venice influenced you as a designer?
That's a chicken-and-egg thing – when we first moved here, I was naturally drawn to living among other creative types. I will say that a sense of freedom is really important to the creative process, and I have that in Venice. Your neighbors don't judge you by the car you drive or what you do for a living.

How do Venice style and Santa Monica style differ?
Ten years ago, there was a greater difference, but now with the real estate getting so crazy, it's less so. But still, Venice style is more edgy.

Do you go to the beach much?
Not like when we were in high school, when we'd slather on the baby oil and lay in the sand at Zuma! Now I walk on the beach, either first thing in the morning or in the evening, and look for dolphins. There have been so many more in the last few years. I avoid the boardwalk – I'm not so good with crowds – except to go to Small World Books.

Do you think Abbot Kinney can escape the generic-mall fate of the Third Street Promenade and Old Town Pasadena?
Yes – there's just not enough square footage to put in a Gap.

What's your perfect Sunday?
I love Sundays! First, I'd go to yoga at Exhale, then to the farmer's market on Main Street for breakfast and our weekly produce. Then my girlfriends and I would hike the trail at the end of El Medio in the Palisades; our motto is, "What gets said on the mountain, stays on the mountain." Later Luis and I would go to the sushi happy hour at Chaya Venice, and if I'd picked up some fish from Santa Monica Seafood, we'd go home and cook it up and chill out. Sometimes I go to the Rose Bowl flea market, and on the fourth Sunday of the month, I go to the smaller flea market, at the Santa Monica Airport.

Santa Monica is…
Childlike

With 40 miles of beaches and their accompanying waves, surf camps, piers, aquarium, whale watching and sand, Santa Monica and its neighbor towns are kid heaven. But the beach is just the beginning – from skateparks to pizza parlors, theaters to art museums, playgrounds to the Promenade, there's enough here to engage the most active kid for a lifetime… without ever setting foot into a McDonald's.

10 Fun Parks

Beach Playground
2600 Barnard Way (at Ocean Park Blvd.),
Santa Monica
310.458.8974
santa-monica.org/osm/beach_facil.htm

Though it's small, you can't beat the location of this park: alongside both the Strand and beach bike path, and right next to restrooms and a food stand (so if you forget to bring noshes for the kiddies, you can always pop for a pizza, burger, veggie sandwich or smoothie). Weekdays, you'll find nannies tending to their adorably dressed charges on the slides, space shuttle, swings and climbing equipment. On weekends, it's moms, dads, their Blackberries and their 6-month- to 9-year-old kids enjoying the ocean breezes and fabulous view.

Clover Park
2600 Ocean Park Blvd., Santa Monica
310.458.8974
santa-monica.org/osm/park_facil.htm

At eighteen acres, Clover is one of the largest parks in the city. Located right next to the Santa Monica Airport, the park can be noisy – but what other playground boasts its own kid-style air-traffic-control flight tower, complete with "communications center" (i.e., kids at the top can talk to parents/friends on the ground through pipes)? Soccer and baseball fields and tennis, volleyball and basketball courts will keep the older kids amused while you barbecue the burgers.

Crestwood Hills Park
1000 Hanley Ave., Brentwood
310.472.5233
laparks.org/dos/parks/facility/crestwoodHillsPk.htm

Run by the city of L.A., this hillside haven serves as a hub for Brentwood family life. It offers everything from T-ball and sports camps to art classes and summer camp, and it has good play equipment, basketball courts, a community center, hiking trails, soccer fields and more. It's a great place for birthday parties, too.

Rustic Canyon Park

Douglas Park
2439 Wilshire Blvd., Santa Monica
310.458.8974
santa-monica.org/osm/park_facil.htm

Too hot in the 'hood? With this park's three man-made reflecting pools (including fish, ducks and lily pads), a fly-fishing area and streams, the family will cool off in no time – as well as forget that Wilshire Boulevard is just beyond those bushes. Kids love the seesaws, tire swings and oval cement track for riding trikes and scooters. Mom and Dad can watch the kids play as they swing away on the lighted tennis courts located right next to the playground. Bring the grandparents, too, who can enjoy a mean game of lawn bowling on the park's immaculate bowling green.

Joslyn Park

633 Kensington Rd., Santa Monica
310.458.8974
santa-monica.org/osm/park_facil.htm

Bring your kids and your dogs! In addition to its gated playground for toddlers and younger kids, you can let your pooch loose in the large, fenced, off-leash dog area. Older kids can play hoops on the basketball court or tag on the big lawn area. The community center, with a craft room and kitchen, is available for birthday-party rentals.

Malibu Bluffs Park

24250 Pacific Coast Hwy., Malibu
310.317.1364, ci.malibu.ca.us

Okay, so there's no actual playground. But we defy you to find a more spectacular setting for a city park in the state. Spread over six acres of jaw-dropping real estate on a bluff overlooking the Pacific, with views to Catalina and Santa Monica, this is the most beautiful place imaginable to play catch with your kids. The two baseball fields and soccer field are well used by local kids' leagues; you'll also find picnic tables, a jogging path, a whale-watching station (they swim right by from January through March) and a community center.

Marine Park

1406 Marine St., Santa Monica
310.458.8974
santa-monica.org/osm/park_facil.htm

Hidden in a residential neighborhood a few blocks east of Lincoln, Marine Park is a much-loved retreat for weekend barbecues and birthday parties, especially for Ocean Park residents. In addition to the playground, there are lighted baseball and soccer fields and tennis and basketball courts. Get there early (before 10 a.m.) to claim a picnic table and barbecue grill for your day in the park – they're available on a first-come, first-served basis only.

Reed Park

1133 7th St., Santa Monica
310.458.8974
santa-monica.org/osm/park_facil.htm

Known to locals as "Lincoln Park" (it's located at Wilshire and Lincoln), this is more of a cultural center than a park. Sure, there's a great – and shaded – playground, but there's also tennis *(see Athletic chapter)*, basketball, croquet and horseshoe courts. Plus, the park's Miles Memorial Playhouse presents dance, theater and musical performances that appeal to kids... of all ages. *(See Kids & Culture, page 226.)*

Rustic Canyon Park

601 Latimer Rd., Santa Monica
310.454.5734
laparks.org/dos/parks/facility/rusticcynpk.htm

Rustic Canyon is what you dream about when you envision a park. It has everything: playgrounds, sandlots, a pool (open in summer only) baseball, tennis, volleyball, swimming, basketball, even art and ballet classes and a wonderful co-op nursery school. All this is set in a lush, perpetually green site dotted with giant sycamore trees – a few are perfect for climbing and hanging.

Virginia Avenue Park

2200 Virginia Ave., Santa Monica
310.458.8688
santa-monica.org/osm/park_facil.htm

Located in the Pico Neighborhood, this park has just undergone a much-needed renovation. Now there are two playgrounds – for younger and older kids – with "space-age" equipment (replacing the beloved rocket ship) – basketball courts, fitness gyms and the Beach Blanket, a new water patio for splashing, spraying and squirting all summer long. Parent tip: Bring a change of clothes and towels.

Plein-air Shakespeare at Theatricum Botanicum

Kids & Culture

The beach is hardly Santa Monica's only contribution to local family-friendly culture. Check out the city's other engaging and enriching experiences.

Theater

The **Miles Memorial Playhouse** in Reed Park (1130 Lincoln Boulevard, 310.458.8634) is a mission-style edifice constructed in 1929 as a "public recreation hall for the young men and women of the city." Today, the Miles still presents dance, theater and musical performances that appeal to kids of all ages. On weekend days at the **Morgan-Wixson Theatre** (2627 Pico Boulevard, 310.828.7519, morgan-wixson.org), children are the performers as well as the target audience. Its Youth Education/Entertainment Series offers five youth productions each year, as well a holiday musical in November and December. For a summertime drama-in-the-wilds experience, nothing beats Topanga Canyon's **Will Geer Theatricum Botanicum** (1419 North Topanga Canyon Boulevard, Topanga, 310.455.3723, theatricum.com). The Theatricum's Family Funday presents performances of such children's classics as Aesop's Fables, Legends of King Arthur and stories by Hans Christian Andersen, and its kid-friendly Shakespeare performances are typically fantastic. On a much smaller stage, at the **Santa Monica Puppet & Magic Center** (1255 2nd Street, 310.656.0483, puppetmagic.com), *Puppetolio* has been charming fans of marionettes and hand puppets for almost a decade. You and your 3- to 5-year-old are the show at the "Enchanted Lunchtime Theater" in the **Santa Monica Playhouse** (1211 4th Street, 310.394.9779, santamonicaplayhouse.com). Members of the Actor's Repertory Theater help the audience enact a fairy tale, legend or folk story in a 90-minute performance on weekdays. If you prefer to escape reality entirely, visit **Magicopolis** (1418 4th Street, 310.451.2241, magicopolis. com), where illusion, levitation and sleight of hand are the stars of the staged magic-and-comedy shows.

Music

Beach culture meets music culture at the Santa Monica Pier every spring and summer. At the pier's **Sunday Concert Series**, kids and adults dance the afternoon away to R & B, Latin rock, oldies and swing music from 2 to 4 p.m. every Sunday from late March through May. (It's free; visit santamonicapier. org for schedule of performers.) Come summer, the pier's **Twilight Dance Series** draws thousands of fans from around Southern California to its celebrated Thursday-night concerts. From zydeco, African, soul and reggae to good old rock 'n' roll, there's a free show for every taste – and if your kids get bored with the music, there's always the dulcet tones of the carousel. (See twilightdance.org for concert schedule.) Another outdoors, but often overlooked, musical event takes place every Sunday morning at the **Main Street Farmer's Market** (corner of Main Street and Ocean Park Boulevard). An eclectic array of musicians – klezmer, marimba, jazz, brass bands, vocal groups – entertains families as they eat, drink coffee and make merry. (See santa-monica.org/farmers_market/sunday. htm for performance schedule.)

For almost 60 years the Santa Monica-Malibu Unified School District has presented **Stairway to the Stars**, a musical extravaganza spotlighting the most talented students in the district's orchestras, symphonies, jazz bands, choirs, wind ensembles and madrigal groups. It's a hot ticket, so call the Santa Monica Civic Auditorium a month before the annual March show dates (310.458.8551, santamonicacivicauditorium.org).

Literature

The Santa Monica Public Library sponsors readings and storytelling for babies, toddlers and older kids at all four of its branches. A few branches offer the **Preschool Twilight Story Time**, at which tots are introduced to folk tales and fables. Older kids and teens can sign up for the library's **Summer Reading Program**, in which kids track the books they've read (magazines, comic books and graphic novels count, too!) and are rewarded with book bags, T-shirts and paperback books (visit smplkids.org for details).

original art from children's books

Art

The **Santa Monica Museum of Art** (2525 Michigan Avenue, 310.586.6488, smmoa.org) is downright cool. It's located at Bergamot Station, which was once a stop on the Red Line trolley running through Los Angeles and ending at the beach in Santa Monica. Not a museum in the traditional sense, it's a complex of small galleries that house big, colorful

paintings and sculpture. If your youngster gets bored, you simply move on to the next gallery – or walk over to the outdoor café for a snack and some hot chocolate. The museum offers children's contemporary art classes as well. **Every Picture Tells a Story** (1311 Montana Avenue, 310.451.2700, everypicture.com) is a gallery specializing in the art of illustration. Exhibitions include signed artworks from such kiddie classics as *Cat in the Hat*, *Where the Wild Things Are* and *Curious George*. It's a wonderful place to browse and for kids to get inspired.

And then, of course, there are the Gettys. Every weekend at the **Getty Villa** (17985 Pacific Coast Highway, Pacific Palisades, 310.440.7300), kids and their parents can romp through the 45-minute Art Odyssey, designed to engage kids as young as 5. And every day in the Family Forum room, kids get to do hands-on activities that get them in touch with their inner (and ancient) artist. At the **Getty Center** (1200 Getty Center Drive, Brentwood, 310.440.7330), there's always something great going on for kids, from storytelling to art-making workshops to the fun Art Detective Cards, which send kids on a whodunit quest through the gardens, galleries and buildings. (Go to getty.edu for details.)

Science

They swim, surf and splash in their beloved Pacific every summer, yet most local youth are unacquainted with what's underneath the waves they ride. At Heal the Bay's **Santa Monica Pier Aquarium** (under the pier at 1600 Ocean Front Walk, 310.393.6149, healthebay.org/smpa), kids get up close and very personal with urchins, crabs, sea stars, sharks, octopi, kelp – and everything else that lives in our local waters. Our skies, too, can be examined at the **Museum of Flying**, located in a hangar on the north side of the Santa Monica Airport. Kids can play pilot in the flight-ready World War II aircraft or watch real flyboys take off and land from the observation deck overlooking the runway. (At press time, the museum's new facilities were under construction, with a projected opening of early 2008; visit museumofflying.com to learn more.)

This way cool aircraft rescue truck lives at Fire Station #125.

Little Kids

Ya-yas – that special brand of energy in young kids that drives parents nuts – can be worked off in the gymnastic, tumbling or dance classes at **Kidnasium Children's Gym** (808 Wilshire Boulevard, 310.395.6700, kidnasium.com). For physical activity that's a bit more Zen, take your tots for a stroll through the bucolic grounds of the **Self Realization Fellowship Center** (17190 Sunset Boulevard, Pacific Palisades, 310.454.4114). The meditation center's ten-acre site features gardens, a spring-fed lake, swans, ducks, koi and a windmill – enough amusements for the kids and blissful relaxation for their parents. For Sunday-morning *shpilkes* (Yiddish for ya-yas), head to the **Main Street Farmer's Market** (corner of Main Street and Ocean Park Boulevard) for pony rides, face-painting, musical performances and tons of great fresh food.

More simple pleasures – like climbing into a big red truck and donning a big red hat – can be had at the city's fire stations. Free tours are available at **S.M. Fire Station #125** (2450 Ashland Avenue, 310.450.0911) and **L.A. Fire Station #63** (1930 Shell Avenue, Venice, 310.575.8563); call in advance and you just may get a ride.

Young animal lovers love the **Malibu Feed Bin** (3931 South Topanga Canyon Boulevard, Malibu, 310.456.2043), an historic feed store with a small petting zoo (bunnies, goats, chicks) in back – but be warned that this wonderfully funky neighborhood is slated for eventual demolition, so call before heading over there.

On one Wednesday afternoon a month, the **Creative Kids Club** at the Main Library (601 Santa Monica Boulevard, 310.458.8621, smplkids.org) regales 4- to 7-year-olds with stories and engages them with arts, crafts and treat-making and tasting; call or visit the web site for the schedule. Other creative outlets for youngsters include: **Color Me Mine** (1109 Montana Avenue, 310.393.0069), where kids create and paint ceramic pottery; **Crafts Around the Corner** (1716 Ocean Park Blvd., 310.452.8820, craftsaroundthecorner.com) for dancing, singing, painting, sewing, cartooning, candle-making and drawing; and **Santa Monica Mudd** (2918 Santa Monica Boulevard, 310.315.9155), which features parents-and-me pottery classes.

School-Age Kids

To keep your kids from climbing the walls at home, drop them off (or stick around) at **Rockreation's Kids Climb Time** (11866 La Grange Avenue, West LA, 310.207.7199), where experienced belayers teach beginners to climb in 9,000 square feet of indoor terrain. Or let the kids learn to use a racket – rather than make one at home – at the **Palisades Tennis Center** (851 Alma Real Drive, Pacific Palisades, 310.451.5445, palitenniscenter. com), where children from 4 to 14 learn strokes, play games and prep for match play.

After school, the library is the place to be – and not just for finishing homework. At the Main Library, young film buffs can join the monthly **Book to Movie Club for Kids**: Children discuss the book (such as *James and the Giant Peach*) on a Wednesday and watch the movie on a Friday (visit smplkids. org for schedule). **Marvelous Mondays** at the Montana Avenue Branch Library (1704 Montana Avenue, 310.829.7081) feature crafts and other activities for 3rd to 5th graders at 3:45 p.m. once a month; call for schedule. Also on Mondays – and equally as marvelous – is the Fairview Branch Library's **Kids' Craft Club** (2101 Ocean Park Boulevard, 310.450.0443), where 6- to 10-year-olds share books, create art projects and enjoy snacks from 4 to 5 p.m. every week. The **Youth Technology Center**, also at the Fairview Branch Library, has a computer center for students (grades 4 to 12) with supervised assistance; it's open during the school year on Thursdays from 3:30 to 9 p.m.

Come evening, enjoy a night under the stars at **Temescal Gateway Park's Campfire Programs** (15601 Sunset Blvd., Pacific Palisades, 310.454.1395 ext. 106, lamountains.com). Naturalists tell stories, lead sing-alongs ("Kumbaya," anyone?) and help the kids roast marshmallows. Don't forget the Hershey bars and graham crackers.

Middle School & High School Kids

Santa Monica's version of the mall – that traditional teen hangout – is a lot cooler than the typical suburban indoor marketplace. The **Third Street Promenade** (3rd Street between Colorado and Wilshire) entertains older kids with street performers, relatively inexpensive eats, hip (if chain) stores and movies, easily eclipsing the malls of the 'burbs.

Fluorescent lights and ultra-loud music accompany the strikes and spares during **Extreme Bowling Nights** at Bay Shore Lanes (234 Pico Boulevard, 310.399.7731). A great coffee shop serving such teen staples as burgers, fries and quesadillas, along with an arcade (featuring air hockey and Dance Dance Revolution) make Bay Shore the perfect adolescent hangout.

PAL (1401 Olympic Blvd., 310.458.8988), as the Santa Monica Police Activities League is affectionately known, is a drop-in rec center. Teens ages 14 to 17 can participate in PAL's sports leagues, field trips and computer classes – or simply have fun using the gym, basketball court, crafts room, pool table, teen lounge with big-screen TV, workout room and video games. PAL is open until 1 a.m. on Friday nights and is located in Memorial Park, which also boasts the Cove, a superb skatepark. *(See Surf and Skate, page 231.)*

If video controllers give you carpel-tunnel syndrome, show your tween/teen you've still got game at **Youth and Family Chess Wednesdays** at the Ocean Park Branch Library (2601 Main Street, 310.392.3804), where all levels of play are welcome.

Kayaking is hot now, and kids ages 10 to 18 are welcome on the monthly **Harbor Kayaking** or **Surf Kayaking** outings sponsored by L.A. County Parks & Rec. The cost for the two- to three-hour sessions is $25, and that includes equipment and instruction; the adventures depart from Burton Chace Park in Marina del Rey. Call 310.822.8530 for details.

In Santa Monica, parents don't even need to do the schlepping: The **Tide Shuttle** runs every fifteen minutes, seven days a week, from Ocean Park to the Promenade – and many points between – for just 25 cents. The **Big Blue Bus** (bigbluebus. com), Santa Monica's own municipal line, has 210 buses that run all over the city's 51 square miles; students with a "Little Blue Card" bus pass ride for just a quarter.

The historic carousel on the Santa Monica Pier

For Kids of All Ages

Fishing

Marina del Rey Sportfishing
Dock 52, Fiji Way, Marina del Rey
310.822.3625, marinadelreysportfishing.com
Give a kid fish for dinner and he says, "Yuck."
Teach him to fish and you have a pal for life.
This well-established outfit offers year-round
fishing trips for all ages and experience levels.

Santa Monica College Fireworks Show
1900 Pico Blvd., Santa Monica
310.434.3000
Unlike other July 4th celebrations around the
county, this one begins at 5 p.m. with musical
performances, exhibits, watermelon, corn and
hot dogs. Spread out your beach blanket on the
college's Corsair Field and enjoy a picnic dinner
(bring your own or buy goodies there) until the
big sky show begins after dark.

Santa Monica Pier
Colorado at Ocean Ave., Santa Monica
310.260.8744, santamonicapier.org
From the 'coaster to the carousel, the concerts
to the arcade buzzers and bells, the pier has
been delighting the young and old since 1909.
*(See Pacific Park on the Pier in the Beachy
chapter, page 51, for more info.)* If you have little
ones, don't miss the small playground just south
of the pier, complete with a misting Viking ship.

The Swim Center
Santa Monica College
Pico at 16th St., Santa Monica
310.458.8700, santa-monica.org/aquatics
Open year-round, the Santa Monica Swim
Center has two Olympic-size pools, with
lifeguards at both. Kids can frolic in the 84-
degree splash pool or swim laps with you in
the 80-degree fitness pool. The fitness pool's
deep end is thirteen feet – perfect for flips or
cannonballs off the high-dive board. *See Athletic
chapter, page 202, for information on swimming
and diving lessons.* The pool is also home to an
excellent swim team for kids and has become
a thriving center of water fun for Santa Monica
families. Local kids pay just $1 to swim, adults
$2.50; inexpensive residents' passes are also
available. The fare is equally reasonable for
nonresidents: $2 for kids and $5 for adults.

Whale & Dolphin Watching

Marina del Rey Sportfishing
Dock 52, Fiji Way, Marina del Rey
310.822.3625, marinadelreysportfishing.com
On weekends from January through March,
view the gray whales up close as they
migrate from the chilly Arctic waters to
the more tropical waters of Baja. Dolphin-
watching outings depart year-round.

Surf & Skate

Skateland

Decades before Santa Monica became known as today's liberal enclave for the privileged, some scraggly kids who surfed the Cove – a dodgy surf spot under the abandoned P-O-P amusement park pier in "Dogtown," aka Ocean Park – brought their renegade surf style to skateboarding, and a new school of skating was born. Skateboarding on sloping concrete banks and in empty swimming pools became the new wave of the 1970s. This radical manner has been revitalized in the 21st century by myriad *Dogtown* films. Here's where kids can show their own Dogtown stuff.

The Cove Skatepark

Memorial Park, 1401 Olympic Blvd.,
Santa Monica
310.458.8228, smgov.net/ccs/skatepark
This superb park has 20,000 square feet of concrete bowls, stairs and rails for skating and biking (bikers get their own times; call for details). Local kids pay $3 a day, and visitors pay $5, plus an annual registration fee; good-value quarterly passes are also offered. A new lighting system has brought night skating.

Papa Jack's Skate Park

23415 Civic Center Way, Malibu
310.456.1441, skateboardpark.com
This 10,000-square-foot collection of powder-coated metal ramps and obstacles is run by the city. It costs just $2 for a two-hour skate session.

Santa Monica Boys and Girls Club Skateboard Park

1238 Lincoln Blvd., Santa Monica
310.393.9629, smbgc.org
A good collection of ramps and rails fills a former parking lot next to this very fine nonprofit community center. It's typically open after school and on Saturdays.

Venice Pit Skatepark

Venice Boardwalk near Venice Blvd. (north of the outdoor gym), Venice
No phone; sk8parklist.com/ca_venice.html
It's not fancy, but it's free, and it's in the old Dogtown neighborhood.

The Cove is one of the finest skateparks in SoCal, as befits the town that spawned the Z-Boys.

Surf City

You can't call yourself a true beach kid if you haven't at least tried surfing. Thanks to today's soft foam boards and comfortable wetsuits, it's a lot easier to get the basics than it used to be. It'll take more than a few lessons for a kid to really shred – surfing has one of the highest learning curves of any sport – but all of the schools that follow can give any kid the thrill of riding a wave.

Aqua Surf School

310.452.SURF, aquasurfschool.com
This small, locals-run surf school hosts day camps and lessons on the beach in Ocean Park. It's the coolest of the local programs, with way-cool instructors, and is particularly recommended for teenagers.

Learn to Surf LA

310.663.2479, learntosurfla.com
This large, well-established company runs good summertime and spring-break camps in Santa Monica and at Dockweiler in Playa del Rey. It also offers group and private surf lessons in Ocean Park (lifeguard tower 24), Venice (just north of the pier) and Manhattan Beach.

Surf Academy

310.372.2790, surfacademy.org
Former pro surfer Mary Setterholm runs this terrific organization, which offers lessons for all ages in Santa Monica and the South Bay. The small-group lessons run $185 for a series of four classes, but it includes boards and wetsuits. Offered in conjunction with the city of Santa Monica, its summer surf camps are safe, quite reasonably priced and lots of fun – kids learn bodyboarding, surfing, paddling skills and ocean safety; worth noting is the camp just for 5- to 7-year-olds, offering age-appropriate, safe water fun. Call 310.458.2239 for camp details.

A new surfer is born at Learn to Surf L.A.

Swings and tables on the sand at Back on the Beach

Eating Like a Kid

Pizzerias and burger joints are included in our list of favorites, of course. But at many of these eateries, you too can enjoy the food and the ambience – perhaps even a nice glass of pinot noir.

Back on the Beach Café
445 Pacific Coast Hwy., Santa Monica
310.393.8282
American. B & L daily, D nightly in summer. Beer & wine. $
Bring the beach toys! The outdoor tables at this daylight café are plopped right into the sand, so kids can swing on the beach swingset and play with their shovels and pails as you finish your spinach-and-Swiss omelet.

Benihana
1447 4th St., Santa Monica
310.260.1423
Japanese. L & D daily. Full bar. $$-$$$
Benihana's chefs are skilled child entertainers who create steaming volcanoes out of onion rings and toss bowls of fried rice gleefully into the air while making your dinner right in front of you. The grilled steak and seafood are tasty, too. A good place for a big-kid birthday dinner.

Bravo Cucina
1319 3rd St. Promenade, Santa Monica
310.394.0374
Italian. L & D daily. Beer & wine. $-$$
Before or after a movie, this is a great spot for quick, inexpensive *real* food on the Promenade. Satisfying pastas and Italian sandwiches – or burgers and PB&Js – are a welcome alternative to the Promenade's pre-film fast-food eateries and movie-theater junk food.

California Pizza Kitchen
210 Wilshire Blvd., Santa Monica
310.393.9335
American/Italian. L & D daily. Beer & wine. $-$$
You know what to expect: fresh, hearty pizza, pasta and salads that appeal to everyone. But this CPK also provides a community service: It's a popular destination for local elementary school field trips, where kids get acquainted with a restaurant behind-the-scenes – and make and eat their own pizzas, natch. Room parents, take note! The location is ideal, just off the Promenade and two blocks from the bluffs.

The Cheesecake Factory
4142 Via Marina, Marina del Rey
310.306.3344
American. L & D daily, brunch Sun. Full bar. $
The oversize burgers, salads, desserts, et al. are the same here as they are in every CF. So what's so special about this one? Beachfront service with a view of the Marina and all its glorious boats. While waiting for your food, you can nurse your martini with the blue-cheese-stuffed olive on the deck while your kids play on the beach or in the playground below.

Coogie's Beach Café
23755 Malibu Rd., Malibu
310.317.1444
American. B, L & D daily. Beer & wine. $-$$
Okay, it's not really on the beach, it's in a shopping center just off PCH, but the vibe and menu are beachy – and kid-friendly. It's lively and casual, with outdoor seating, a kids' menu and a perfectly decent roster of egg dishes, burgers, sandwiches and salads.

The Counter
2901 Ocean Park Blvd., Santa Monica
310.399.8383
Burgers. L & D daily. Beer & wine. $
At this always-crowded, ultra-modern burger spot, kids can have it their way, *any* way. A clipboard-style menu lists the overabundance of ingredients from which you can build your burger. Parents get to have it their way, as well, with a beer to boot – and *without* a drive-through window. It's pricier than most burger joints, but the quality is worth it.

Di Dio's Italian Ices
1305 Montana Ave., Santa Monica
310.393.2788
Italian ice. Daily. $
This brightly colored shop gets high marks from kids and parents alike for its vibrant ices. Kids' perennial flavor favorites: Blue Raspberry and Green Mystery (don't ask, we don't know either).

Enterprise Fish Co.
174 Kinney St., Santa Monica
310.392.8366
Seafood. L & D daily. Full bar. $$-$$$
You can enjoy a healthy, grown-up fish dinner while the kids order a burger, fish and chips or pasta off the kids' menu. Plus, you'll even be able to sip a glass of wine in peace at the bar while the kids busy themselves in front of the aquarium and lobster tanks--in your sightline.

Fosters Freeze
1530 Pico Blvd., Santa Monica
310.452.0996
American. L & D daily. No booze. $
The classic soft-serve heaven also dishes up scrumptious burgers, fries, onion rings and chili-cheese fries. Bring your vanilla malt or chocolate-dipped cone across the street to the Swim Center *(see page 202)*, and you've discovered the equation for a perfect summer's day.

Hot Dog on a Stick
1633 Ocean Front Walk, Santa Monica
American. L & D daily. No booze. $
Now found in malls everywhere, this is the original (and beloved) Hot Dog on a Stick. Though the staples at this 60-year-old Muscle Beach food stand (just south of the pier) are corn dogs and fresh lemonade, even mom and dad will appreciate its simplicity… and the goofy, 1960s-pop-style uniforms of its employees.

Joe's Diner
2917 Main St., Santa Monica
310.392.5804
American. B, L & D daily. Beer & wine. $
Exactly what you'd expect from a joint called Joe's Diner: hearty breakfasts, tasty burger and sandwich lunches and comforting meatloaf – all served at a counter or in red vinyl booths.

Kaiten! Sushi
1456 3rd St. Promenade, Santa Monica
310.451.8080
Japanese/sushi. L & D daily. Beer & sake. $$
Though the food here is nothing extraordinary, the way it's served is. Sushi is placed on a conveyor belt that winds through the restaurant, and customers pick their ono and yellowtail right off the belt. If your child freaks when he finds out that the plate he's chosen is really eel, you can order some tempura or teriyaki chicken to calm him.

La Cabaña
738 Rose Ave., Venice
310.392.7973
Mexican. L & D daily (to 3 a.m. nightly). Full bar. $
Featuring homey Mexican food and a kids' menu (burritos, tacos, quesadillas), La Cabaña has been a Venice institution for almost 50 years. Kids love watching the senorita make thick tortillas at the brick stove as much as eating them. Parents like the margaritas and, when they have a babysitter, the 3 a.m. closing time.

Michael D's Cafe
234 Pico Blvd., Santa Monica
310.452.8737
American. B, L & D daily. Full bar. $
The only reason this coffee shop has a full bar is because it's located in the Bay Shore Lanes bowling alley. But that's the beauty of this surprisingly good restaurant. When the kids get bored, send them to the arcade or have them bowl a few games. You can even bring your tuna melt to the lanes and watch them bowl.

Palisades Garden Café
15231 La Cruz, Pacific Palisades
310.459.6160
American/bakery. B & L Mon.-Sat. No booze. $
This is the place to be for Palisades kids after school – they love the doughnuts, croissants and muffins, not to mention the really good burgers and fries. And many local parents have figured out that the coffee is much better here than at Starbucks and Coffee Bean.

Perry's Café, Bike & Skate
2400 & 2600 Ocean Front Walk, Santa Monica
310.452.7609 & 310.458.3975
American. B & L daily. No booze. $
At two locations right on the beach, Perry's is the place to nosh for beachgoers, bikers, skaters and Segwayers. The burgers, tuna sams, smoothies, fries and hot dogs are substantial – so much so that you'll consider renting a few of Perry's bikes for a family workout afterward.

Typhoon
3221 Donald Douglas Loop S., Santa Monica
310.390.6565
Pan-Asian. L Sun.-Fri., D nightly. Full bar. $$-$$$
You'll find unusual – and unusually good – Chinese/Thai/Vietnamese/Korean food along with a wide selection of Asian beers at this restaurant, located on the south side of the Santa Monica Airport. The draw for kids? The observation roof to watch single-engine and light-jet aircraft land and take off over the Pacific. It's particularly beautiful at sunset.

A wooden-toy wonderland at the Acorn Store

Shopping Like a Kid

Here's a collection of stores at which the kids have a lot more fun than the adults who schlep them there. *Ed. note: For surf and skate shops, see Surf Shops We Love in the Beachy chapter, page 54.*

Acorn Store
1220 5th St., Santa Monica
310.451.5845
Walking into Acorn is like walking into a toy store from the turn of the century (the 20th, that is). This old-fashioned shop specializes in wooden, tin and fabric toys (no plastics!). Kids are encouraged to play with everything. And they do.

Crafts Around the Corner
1716 Ocean Park Blvd., Santa Monica
310.452.8820, craftsaroundthecorner.com
At this friendly store/community center, you'll find enough crafty stuff to keep your kids busy for days. It also offers all sorts of classes and workshops.

EB Games
1910 Lincoln Blvd., Santa Monica
310.399.5444, ebgames.com
This 21st-century place is the store of choice for gamers of all ages. Test your Super Paper Mario skills on the in-store Wii or pre-order the hot PS3 and Xbox360 games before they come out.

Forever 21
270 Santa Monica Pl., Santa Monica
310.458.0533, forever21.com
Racks upon racks of colorful, trendy, cheaply made but bargain-priced clothing keeps teenage girls coming back — constantly.

Hi De Ho Comics

525 Santa Monica Blvd., Santa Monica
310.394.2820, hideho.com
A vast selection of vintage and new comics, books, toys and collectible cards live at Hi De Ho. If your kid is into this stuff, you'll never get him out of there.

Homeworks

2923 Main St., Santa Monica
310.396.0101
Kids love the whoopie cushions, fake dog poo (or vomit) and bug-laced plastic ice cubes at this 25-year-old novelty and gag shop; you'll love the provocative greeting cards and postcards – many of which are in questionable taste.

Ivy Greene for Kids

1020 Swarthmore Ave., Pacific Palisades
310.230.0301
This swank boutique draws in the grade-school set with such hard-to-find candies as Zotz and mega Pixy Stix. Their moms love the chic clothing and don't object to the high prices.

PacSun

330 Santa Monica Place, Santa Monica
310.451.8891, shoppacsun.com
Plenty of teens and preteens who don't surf or skate buy beach fashions that make them look like they do. Prices here are moderate, and the names kids care about (Hurley, Roxy, Volcom, Lucy Love) are in evidence.

Planet Blue

800 4th St., Santa Monica
310.394.0135
3835 Cross Creek Rd., Malibu
310.317.8566
High-end clothing for high-end teenage girls well armed with their parents' credit cards. Jeans, T-shirts and dresses from the likes of Splendid, Rich and Skinny, Ella Moss and J. Brand are the mainstays. Britney Spears has been known to shop at the Malibu store. 'Nuff said.

Puzzle Zoo

1413 3rd St. Promenade, Santa Monica
310.393.9201, puzzlezoo.com
When you need a break from strolling the Promenade, step into the Puzzle Zoo, where kids and parents can play with the magic tricks, remote-control vehicles and train sets on display, and you can browse the collectible aisles in search of the *Star Wars* action figure you need to round out your set. Naturally, you'll find a cornucopia of puzzles, too.

Tales & Toys

1140 Abbot Kinney Blvd., Venice
310.396.6909
A personal, hands-on toy store with a play-with-me train table and a fun, thoughtful selection of books, Brios and children's art supplies. You'll find great toys here that you won't find at Target. Heaven for toddlers to 7-year-olds.

This Little Piggy Wears Cotton

309 Wilshire Blvd., Santa Monica
310.260.2727, littlepiggy.com
You can pick through the store's unique clothing and gifts while your child munches on candy and tries on the Bob Marley wigs. Great for jammies, boxers, T-shirts and colorful layettes.

Q & A: Jerry Harris

Jerry Harris started teaching in the Santa Monica public schools in 1967, and since 1982, he's been at Roosevelt Elementary. During his tenure as principal, Roosevelt earned the title of a California Distinguished School; its test scores are consistently high, its parents are involved, and its children have thrived. During that time, Jerry's own son thrived, too; Evan attends Harvard University, where he plays power forward on the varsity basketball team. Alongside the 2007 graduating class of fifth graders, Jerry graduated into retirement. Nancy Gottesman talked to Jerry about education, life in Santa Monica and kids today.

Why is Roosevelt such a successful school?
There are several reasons. It works collaboratively and focuses on results; we believe that all children can learn, and we work hard to make that happen; parents, staff and community work well together; students come to school well prepared by parents who are actively supportive; and its environment is warm and supportive. Roosevelt is a happy school.

Now that you're retired, what do you miss most?
I miss all the wonderful people, and the children, of course – their smiles, laughter, hugs and honesty. And their energy. I don't miss the rainy days, when we had to keep 800 energetic students in the cafeteria and auditorium during the lunch hour.

Is a 6-year-old today different from a 6-year-old 30 years ago?
Yes. Today's 6-year-olds are more independent and much busier. Children are scheduled (piano, soccer, tutoring, etc.) much more heavily than they were when I first came to Roosevelt. The demands on them are also greater – they go to school for a longer day, with no nap time, and they have homework, even in kindergarten. Children seem to be more rushed today to grow up.

When your son Evan was younger, what were your favorite things to do here?
Go to the pier, ride the roller coaster and then go to the beach.

Is Santa Monica a good place for kids?
It's a great place for kids. Our schools are among the best in California, and kids and their families can use school playgrounds for recreation after school. And organizations like the Y, the Boys and Girls Club, AYSO and others offer excellent programs for children. Basically, this is a great place for kids because of its deep commitment to children and deep sense of community.

What is retirement bringing?
I am a part-time consultant, and I plan to travel to places that I've always dreamed of seeing, including Brazil, Italy and Africa. Consulting is keeping me involved in education and allowing me to share my experience with others. As Jackie Robinson once said, "A life is not important except in the impact it has on other lives." I want to have an impact on other lives.

Santa Monica is…

Home Away from Home

In the pages that follow you'll find everything you need to make Santa Monica and environs your home away from home: welcoming hotels, a guide to getting around, a calendar of events, and all sorts of useful places to know about, from a dry cleaner to a florist to an emergency vet.

A Comfortable Bed

The Ambrose
1255 20th St., Santa Monica
310.315.1555, 877.AMBROSE,
ambrosehotel.com
$210-$230
This serene, sweet boutique hotel is pure Santa Monica – it is certifiably green (having won the city's Sustainable Quality award), its continental breakfast (including fair-trade coffee and organic fruit) comes from Urth Café, and the WiFi, of course, is free. The residential neighborhood is quiet, central and particularly great for business travelers, shoppers (chic Montana Avenue is close by) and visitors to St. John's hospital, but you won't be strolling to the beach – it's twenty blocks away. Not to worry – you're not paying oceanfront rates, and you're getting a lot of comfort and Asian-Craftsman style for your buck. Rooms vary in size (ask for a larger one), and they're all handsome, with wood floors, soothing earth tones and comfy upholstered furniture. And unlike at most stylish hotels, the parking, internet access and breakfast are all free. Extras include a small fitness center, a lovely Japanese garden and, in proper Santa Monica fashion, on-site hybrid-car rental. For peace, quiet and comfort, the Ambrose is the best deal in town.

Casa del Mar
1910 Ocean Ave., Santa Monica
310.581.5533, 800.898.6999,
hotelcasadelmar.com
$485-$775, suites $1,075-$3,360
This beautiful Italianate-style hotel sits next door to its sister, Shutters. Built in the 1920s as an exclusive beach club, the Casa had many incarnations before $50 million brought it back as a luxury hotel. Rooms have a seaside Victorian theme, with wicker headboards and chaise lounges; bathrooms open onto the bedrooms via glass louvers; and there are even some split-level suites. The Casa has all the high-end amenities of its sister property but is far more old-world elegant (while Shutters is more seaside cottagey), and that should govern your choice between the two. The Casa also boasts its own spa, which uses Dr. Murad's products and has oceanview treatment cabanas. Other extras include an excellent seafood restaurant, Catch, a posh workout room, and the lovely pool area in the center of the U-shaped building, which helps protect it from the wind.

Channel Road Inn
219 W. Channel Rd., Santa Monica
310.459.1920, channelroadinn.com
$215-$310, suites $325-$415
A short walk from the beach, this fourteen-room bed and breakfast is in a historic (1910) house that's had a third floor added. The gardens are tranquil, full of jasmine, roses and citrus trees, and you just may encounter a duck or two paddling around the Jacuzzi. The breakfast room is bright, the library flooded with light and decorated in white wicker and chintz, and the living room has a Batchelder tile fireplace. There's always something out to munch on, and in addition to breakfast there's a wine and cheese hour in the evening. Rooms have flat-screen TVs, and one suite has a day bed in the bathroom, along with a two-person spa tub. Here's the clincher: Parking is complimentary.

Fairmont Miramar Hotel
101 Wilshire Blvd., Santa Monica
310.576.7777, 866.540.4470,
fairmont.com/santamonica
$349-$379, suites $419-$1,100
This hotel has the prized spot on the corner where Wilshire Boulevard ends at Ocean Avenue; its impressive driveway encircles a massive and historic Moreton Bay fig tree. The Miramar has had many incarnations, and at the moment, though rooms have everything you need in a luxury hotel – from Italian linens to Bose clock radios and coffeemakers – it seems to be slumbering in wait for that kiss from a prince. It was recently sold to the founder of Dell computers, so the kiss may be coming. For the time being, the deadly Musak in the lobby is the giveaway that the decor lingers in the '90s. That said, this is the only hotel near the beach with bungalows, and the grounds are lovely. There are two sections, one six floors, the other a newer ten-story tower with dramatic ocean views. The older Palisades section is mostly large suites. There's a spa and a big, new gym.

Huntley Santa Monica Beach
1111 2nd St., Santa Monica
310.394.5454, thehuntleyhotel.com
$429-$499, suites $650-$1,500
The once-aging Huntley has been reborn to the tune of $18 million and is now one of the most stylish hotels in Los Angeles. How many hotel lobbies have strips of stingray skin on their

The historic Casa del Mar

reception counters, or a wall of white-ceramic-dipped piranhas as a backdrop to the lounge? The decor is elegant enough but cheeky to the core, thanks to German designer Thomas Schoos, who uses beautiful natural elements but isn't above throwing in a shag rug. Rooms are serenely modern, with beige tufted headboards, 42-inch plasma TVs, sleek DVD/CD players and, in the suites and some rooms, red window seats. The Penthouse restaurant is a date-night hot spot, thanks to its elevated white leather banquettes and tables along the windows, which bring in dazzling ocean views; skylights open during warm weather, and pretty people sip cocktails next to a fireplace. While there's neither pool nor spa here, the hotel is only a block from the top of the California Incline, which leads down to the beach, and it's strolling distance from the Third Street Promenade.

Inn at Playa del Rey

435 Culver Blvd., Playa del Rey
310.574.1920, innatplayadelrey.com
$195-$290, suites $325-$385
This sister B&B of the Channel Road Inn has beautiful views of the Ballona Wetlands, with Marina del Rey in the distance; on clear days you can see all the way to the Hollywood sign. An attractive living room with a fireplace overlooks the wetlands, and a courtyard patio holds lounge chairs that beckon readers (and nappers). Consider splurging on the Romance Suite – the bedroom fireplace is double sided, so it can also be enjoyed from the two-person spa tub, which also boasts views of the wetlands. Even the shower in this bathroom has a porthole view. This inn has all the features of its sister, along with complimentary parking and bicycles, which will ride you to the Santa Monica bike path.

Le Merigot Beach Hotel & Spa

1740 Ocean Ave., Santa Monica
310.395.9700, 888.539.7899,
lemerigothotel.com
$320-up, suites $449-$1,200
Next door to the Loews is Le Merigot, a JW Marriott property. Due to an apartment building smack in front, it bills its premium rooms as partial ocean views, though rooms on the upper levels actually have great views. To reach the beach, you go down the steps by the pool, cross Ocean Way (little more than an alley) and you're on the sand. The Mediterranean theme includes pergolas around the pool, murals on the walls and cobalt glasses in the restaurant, Cezanne. Rooms are modern but warm, with blond wood desks and coffee tables, pale gold walls and beige and brown easy chairs. Bathrooms include rubber duckies and oversize showerheads. Le Merigot feels more personal than most 175-room hotels – it even welcomes dogs of all sizes.

Loews Santa Monica Beach Hotel

1700 Ocean Ave., Santa Monica
310.458.6700, 800.235.6397,
santamonicaloewshotel.com
$309-$489, suites $625-$1,750
This eight-story hotel feels like a ship with its prow pointed straight toward the Pacific. An airy atrium lobby ends in a fireside lounge with ocean views; next door, the swank restaurant Ocean and Vine pairs wines with California cuisine and offers an extensive menu of artisanal cheeses. Rooms are modern and comfortable, as are the bathrooms, which are equipped with TVs and separate tubs and showers. Newly redecorated premier oceanfront rooms have large patios, and even the cityside rooms have attractive park views. Once home of the Pritikin center,

the hotel retained the large exercise room and now runs the spa in-house. There's nothing quite like having a cocktail on the restaurant's terrace (warmed by fire pits) and watching the sun set as the pier's Ferris wheel lights up for the night.

Everybody in the pool at the Loews

Luxe Hotel Sunset Boulevard Bel-Air
11461 Sunset Blvd., Brentwood
310.476.6571, luxehotelsunsetblvd.com
$330-$380, suites $430-$700
Set on seven acres on the hillside just below the Getty Center (and right beside the much less glamorous 405 Freeway), this newly redecorated 161-room complex is the perfect plush hideaway for art lovers. Even the entry-level rooms here are more than 500 square feet, and all have WiFi, iPod docking stations and flat-screen TVs, and many have lanais or balconies. Extras include tennis courts, a large pool on the upper level, a restaurant and a spa. Rooms are in two complexes connected by shuttles.

Oceana
849 Ocean Ave., Santa Monica
310.393.0486, hoteloceanasantamonica.com
Suites $450-$2,700
The Oceana was still under construction when we went to press, undergoing a remodel that took the building down to the bones. This former courtyard apartment complex on the quiet, residential end of Ocean Avenue has rooms full of vibrant colors, each with a red game table, a green couch and walls in splashes of gold or aqua. All the suites have lanais opening onto the courtyard – and the pool below – with yellow Adirondack chairs; inside are 42-inch plasma TVs, iPod docking stations, big desks and (a legacy of the apartment days) real walk-in closets. The oceanfront suites look across gorgeous Palisades Park to blue, blue ocean.

The Ritz-Carlton Marina del Rey
4375 Admiralty Way, Marina del Rey
310.823.1700, 800.241.3333, ritzcarlton.com
$339-$619, suites $489-$3,500
If you'd rather view sailboats than sand, this is the spot for you. This beautiful 304-room hotel has all the five-star bells and whistles (including a spanking-new spa), as well as impeccable service. Its formerly staid, Ritz-Carlton-standard

public rooms have been remodeled, and the restaurant, Jer-Ne, is elegantly trendy. Locals come here on weekend nights, when DJs spin in the lobby lounge, and on Sundays for the fabulous brunch. Decorated in gold and deep-blue fabrics, the rooms boast feather-top beds and 42-inch flat-screen TVs; on the down side, bathrooms have single sinks and combo tub-showers. The pool is saline – not chlorinated – which is so much kinder to the skin, and the air in the hotel is lightly perfumed with White Tea and Ginger by Bulgari. It's worth it to pay extra for a club room – the club has five food services during the day, as well as complimentary cocktails and its own concierge.

Sea Shore Motel
2637 Main St., Santa Monica
310.392.2787, seashoremotel.com
$95-$135, suites $140-$260
One of our friends always puts up her family in this cheerful pink motel smack on Main Street amid the shops and restaurants, with the beach an easy walk away. At press time, rooms were undergoing a transformation from some kind of dude-ranch fantasy to a more beachy decor, but, thankfully, prices were not expected to rise significantly. The real deals are the one-bedroom suites with full kitchens (even dishwashers) and comfortable living rooms with balconies, in their own building a couple of doors down, with complimentary parking. There's a charge for parking in the motel itself. An excellent value for the location.

Sheraton Delfina Santa Monica
530 W. Pico Blvd., Santa Monica
310.399.9344, 800.325.3535,
sheratonsantamonica.com
$259-$419, junior suites $359-$560, club floor $40 surcharge
People who walk into the lobby expecting a standard Sheraton gasp in surprise – it's been completely remodeled by the Kor Group, using its distinctive Hollywood Regency/modern style. Starting with the lobby in its dramatic tones of chocolate, cream and gray-green (which at night is lit with candles), the effect is one of being in an ultra-chic boutique hotel – but it's a 308-room Sheraton, where you can use your Starwood points to your heart's content. Rooms on the sixth floor and up have ocean views; all rooms have fun faux-crocodile headboards and 27-inch flat-screen TVs, along with bathrobes and slippers. The hotel is four long blocks from the beach, but two electric cars are available to ferry guests around within a three-mile radius.

Shutters on the Beach

1 Pico Blvd., Santa Monica
310.458.0030, 800.334.9000,
shuttersonthebeach.com
$480-$775, suites $1,075-$3,000
By far the most celebrated hotel in Santa Monica, Shutters pops up year after year on all those "Best of" lists. Combining Craftsman and cottage-style architecture (and of course those white window shutters), the 198-room hotel manages to be both a beachside resort and a perfectly good choice for someone in town for business meetings. The list of the well-known who've stayed here is endless. What do you get? You can walk out the door, cross the busy bike path and be on the sand, just south of the Santa Monica Pier. At sunset you can enjoy cocktails on your balcony or in the lobby, which is filled with overstuffed couches surrounding a fireplace. Rooms have hardwood floors, four-poster beds and gleaming white shelving units with 32-inch flat-screen TVs and iPod docking stations. There are safes, robes, WiFi – all the rich-traveler amenities. Sliding shutters open the bedrooms to the bathrooms, where large, inviting soaking tubs and an array of spa goodies lurk (but watch out – those spa goodies are for sale, not a wild gesture of goodwill). The fine-dining restaurant One Pico has beautiful views – and reviews – and downstairs, casual Pedals offers an entertaining seat to watch the constant parade of people on the bike path. The spa uses Ole Henriksen products. Caveats? The pool is small and the deck always crowded, and it's often closed for weddings. Some oceanview rooms overlook an ugly rooftop with the ocean beyond, and the lovely beachfront rooms can be noisy. For quiet, request a room on an upper floor.

Travelodge Santa Monica Beach

1525 Ocean Ave., Santa Monica
310.451.0761, travelodge.com
$129-$199 summer, $89-$169 winter
This bare-bones motel desperately needs a remodel, but it's not going to get one – it's going to be torn down to build a bigger Travelodge some time in the next few years. That said, you can't beat the price for the location: right across the street from the Santa Monica Pier. There's a tiny pool, rooms have coffeemakers, and there's a suite with a fireplace. Parking is $10 per night extra. For these prices, just don't expect much. The same family owns the Best Western on the next block, where rooms are more plush and more expensive ($149-$289).

Beach-cottage chic at Shutters on the Beach

The Venice Beach House

15 30th Ave., Venice
310.823.1966, venicebeachhouse.com
$145-$235
This nine-room B&B is a short block from the sand, at the less raucous end of the Venice Boardwalk but close enough to amble down to the action within minutes. It has a few red flags: Four of the rooms share a bathroom, and the Olympic Suite has a dark-green bathtub that no amount of money would get us into. Otherwise, the building is attractive, surrounded by gardens, and the location is swell. The Pier Suite has a fireplace. There's an extra charge for parking.

Venice Beach Suites

1305 Ocean Front Walk, Venice
310.396.4559, venicebeachsuites.com
$107-$271
This budget hotel is right in the middle of the action on the boardwalk. Rooms are bare-bones but clean and equipped with kitchenettes; some have exposed-brick walls, pullout couches and a bar complete with barstools. If you're young and want to be where everything's happening, this is the spot for you. There's no parking.

Viceroy Santa Monica

1819 Ocean Ave., Santa Monica
310.260.7500, 800.670.6185,
viceroysantamonica.com
$380-$480, suites $600-up
When this stylish Kor Group hotel first opened, it was *the* spot to be on weekends for westsiders. Things have calmed down some, but it still costs an arm and a leg to rent one of those black-and-white-striped cabanas for an evening's festivities. The decor is Hollywood Regency as interpreted by Kelly Wearstler, now familiar to watchers of *Top Design*. You'll find everything a hipster could want, from WiFi to 27-inch flat-screen TVs. One-bedroom suites have oceanview balconies and whirlpool tubs (for oceanview rooms, you need to book on the higher floors). The restaurant, Whist, is justifiably popular.

Stuff You Need

Animal Care – Emergency

Pet Medical Center
1534 14th St., Santa Monica
310.393.8218, petmedical.com
A full-service animal hospital.

Westside Animal Emergency Hospital
1304 Wilshire Blvd., Santa Monica
310.451.8962
Open overnight and on weekends for
emergency care.

Churches
See Reaching Out chapter

Currency Exchange

A+ Currency Exchange/Western Union
1454 4th St., Santa Monica
310.394.7211

Dry Cleaners & Alterations

Ann Tailor
729 Broadway, Santa Monica
310.393.5756
Forgive the pun and enjoy the quality alterations
and tailoring.

Brown's Cleaners
1223 Montana Ave., Santa Monica
310.451.8531
If moths attacked your cashmere coat or your
ball gown needs cleaning, go to Brown's. You'll
part with some serious change, but the job will
be done right.

Cleaner by Nature
2407 Wilshire Blvd., Santa Monica
310.315.1520
Get with Santa Monica's green program and
check out this fine dry cleaner, which cleans
clothes without nasty chemicals. It's a little more
expensive, but it's worth it.

Dress Code
250 26th St., Santa Monica
310.656.9884
Excellent alterations; they'll hem your jeans so
they don't look hemmed.

Emergency Rooms

Centinela-Freeman Medical Center
4650 Lincoln Blvd., Marina del Rey
310.823.8911, ext. 5100, centinelafreeman.com

St. John's Health Center
1328 22nd St., Santa Monica
310.829.8212, stjohns.org

Florists

FloralArt
1338 Abbot Kinney Blvd., Venice
310.392.1633, floralartla.com
Dramatic, creative, make-a-statement
arrangements.

Scentiments
1331 Abbot Kinney Blvd., Venice
310.399.4110, scentimentsflowers.com
These gorgeous arrangements aren't cheap,
but they never fail to impress. The collection of
tabletop, gift and home-decor items is also great.

Hair Salons

Euphoria
1351 Abbot Kinney Blvd., Venice
310.399.2660
This excellent salon is hip without being freaky,
and the prices are very reasonable. Good cuts,
color and styling.

Mart Barber Shop
Brentwood Country Mart, 225 26th St.,
Santa Monica
310.394.9978
This 40-year-old classic barbershop is a
westside icon. Great for kids and no-fuss men,
but a number of stylish women get their hair cut
here, too.

Vidal Sassoon Academy
321 Santa Monica Blvd., Santa Monica
310.255.0011, ext. 2, sassoon.com
If you have more time than money, come to this
hair-care college and get a cut and blow dry for
$20 on weekdays, $25 on weekends. Teachers
watch over the students to make sure they don't
give you an inadvertent mohawk; the cuts are
usually very good. The downside: You may have
to wait two hours or more.

The timeless barber shop in the Brentwood Country Mart

Soshin Salon
1331 7th St., Santa Monica
310.393.6553
A serene spot with soothing music, good tea, and a lovely husband-and-wife team – she does skin care, he cuts and styles hair. It's well located in downtown Santa Monica near the new library.

Jewelers

Readers Fine Jewelers
331 Wilshire Blvd., Santa Monica
310.451.1349
When your pearl necklace breaks, your ring needs sizing or your earrings need re-setting, head to this excellent shop run by a fifth-generation Santa Monica family.

Libraries
See Smart chapter

Nail Salons

Dawn Dale
Sunset West Coiffeurs
15119 Sunset Blvd., Pacific Palisades
310.459.1616
Dale is a highly skilled manicurist with a devoted local clientele.

Lee's Nails
2307 Santa Monica Blvd., Santa Monica
310.828.1104
The Cambodian-French owners are gentle and skilled, and the massage chairs are heavenly. Also a good place to practice your French.

Main Attraction Nail Spa
2654 Main St., Santa Monica
310.450.1688
This large, clean, efficient and inexpensive nail parlor has really comfy chairs and offers good foot and neck massages for a buck a minute. It's always busy, so if you don't want to wait, make an appointment. Good waxing, too.

Pharmacies

CVS Pharmacy
2505 Santa Monica Blvd., Santa Monica
310.828.6456
It's not that we're CVS fans, but we're grateful that this one has a 24-hour pharmacy.

Long's
3202 Wilshire Blvd., Santa Monica
310.829.5513
Careful and quick, with personal service and plenty of underground parking.

Pharmaca
15150 W. Sunset Blvd., Pacific Palisades
310.454.1345
Natural remedies are celebrated here, but you also get a professional refilling of that Ambien or Lipitor.

Post Offices

Marina del Rey Post Office
4766 Admiralty Way, Marina del Rey
310.306.4533
This post office boasts parking and long hours: 8:30 a.m. to 7 p.m. during the week and 9 a.m. to 5 p.m. on Saturdays.

Santa Monica Main Post Office
1248 5th St., Santa Monica
310.576.6786
Open weekdays 9 a.m. to 6 p.m., Saturdays 9 a.m. to 3 p.m.

The fabulous streamline modern main post office

Public Restrooms

Restroom facilities are strategically placed along all the larger public beaches; they're basic but work just fine, and even the ones in the heart of the Venice Boardwalk aren't as gross as you might expect. You'll also find public facilities in Palisades Park and in the parking structures that serve downtown Santa Monica and the Promenade; if you're worried about safety, the two bathrooms between Arizona and Santa Monica Boulevard (in the alleys behind the Promenade, on both the east and west sides) have attendants.

Senior Services

Santa Monica Dial-a-Ride
310.394.9871, ext. 454
Santa Monica residents can get a ride to wherever they need to go, seven days a week, for just 50 cents; it's an extra quarter if a personal attendant comes along. You just have to enroll in the program – and enrollment is free.

Senior Recreation Center
1450 Ocean Ave., Santa Monica
310.458.8644
This fine center is beautifully sited in Palisades Park. It offers all sorts of classes (improv performance, dance, bingo), a lunch program, trips to Vegas, Palm Springs and the theater, and movie and dance nights.

Shoe Repair

Mart Shoe Repair
Brentwood Country Mart, 225 26th St., Santa Monica
310.394.1856
Excellent shoe repair, purse repair and leather restoration.

Spas & Massage Therapy

Kenneth George Sanctuary
1914 Wilshire Blvd., Santa Monica
310.453.0224, kennethgeorge.com
This spa and salon is known in particular for its facials, but it also offers the full range of body services, from peels and waxes to massages and pedicures. For a great massage, ask for Robert.

The Massage Place
625 Montana Ave., Santa Monica
310.393.7007, montanaave.com/themassage
No frills, no seaweed wraps, no posh environment – just first-rate massages from experienced therapists at unbelievable prices. A full-hour Swedish, deep-tissue, shiatsu, pregnancy, sports or reflexology massage is just $44. And that's in the heart of high-rent Montana Avenue. Go ahead, live a little and get the 90-minute massage – it's just $64. You can pay more than that for a T-shirt in one of the boutiques just down the street.

Nite Spa
490 Santa Clara Ave., Venice
310.396.5122, nitespa.com
Working too hard to fit in that desperately needed massage, waxing or facial? Nite Spa is your dream come true. Open from noon to midnight, with a DJ and cocktails to set the mood, this charming old bungalow just off Abbot Kinney is staffed with skilled people who have the energy to knead your sore muscles at 10 p.m. It's also a great place for a spa party.

Travel Agent

PNR Travel
2534 Lincoln Blvd., Marina del Rey
310.574.6800, pnrtravel.com
This good all-around travel agency is an American Express affiliate and offers all the AmEx services.

Visitor's Bureaus

Marina del Rey Visitors Center
4701 Admiralty Way, Marina del Rey
310.305.9545, visitthemarina.com
Open daily; hours vary
A full-service center that can help you with anything regarding Marina del Rey.

Santa Monica Visitor Information Center
1920 Main St., Ste. B, Santa Monica
310.319.6263, 800.544.5319, santamonica.com
Open daily 9 a.m.-6 p.m.
You can pick up maps, bus schedules and a good tourism magazine here, as well as make a hotel reservation and get your questions answered. The Santa Monica Convention and Visitor's Bureau also runs two information kiosks, one on the Third Street Promenade and another in Palisades Park near the pier.

Getting Around

Rental beach cruisers and mountain bikes are plentiful all along the bike path.

Airports

Long Beach Airport (LGB)
longbeach.gov/airport
A charming JetBlue hub that's easy to get into and out of; it's the Burbank Airport of the South Bay, and it's not too far from Santa Monica, unless it's rush hour on the 405.

Los Angeles International Airport (LAX)
lawa.org/lax
Take Lincoln, seriously.

Santa Monica Airport
smgov.net/airport
Great for a visit to the museum or a to watch the planes take off and land; not so great for flying into and out of, unless you've got your own Cessna or a bankroll for charters.

Airport Shuttles

Prime Time
310.536.7922
primetimeshuttle.com

Super Shuttle
310.532.5999

Bike & Skate Rental
The following are all in Santa Monica; there's also a good rental spot on Ocean Front Walk at the end of Washington in Venice.

Blazing Saddles
320 Santa Monica Pier
310.393.9778

Joey's Bike Rentals
1715 Ocean Front Walk
310.305.4740

Perry's Beach Club
2400 Ocean Front Walk
310.372.3138

Perry's Bike Rental
1200 Pacific Coast Hwy.
310.458.3975

Sea Mist Rentals
1619 Ocean Front Walk
310.395.7076

Spokes 'n' Stuff
1700 Ocean Front Walk
310.395.4748

Buses

The Big Blue Bus
310.451.5444, bigbluebus.com
An excellent, wide-ranging city bus system, the Big Blue links not just the various Santa Monica neighborhoods but also links Santa Monica to the wide world: the Palisades, Santa Monica College, UCLA, Culver City, downtown L.A., the LAX Transit Center and more. The fare is 75 cents (50 cents for students and 25 cents for seniors), and the buses are large and clean.

Getting you around between Wilshire and Marine Ave. in Venice for only a quarter, the Tide Shuttle is one of the best deals in town.

The Tide Shuttle

310.451.5444, bigbluebus.com
Buses run every 15 minutes
Sun.-Thurs. noon-8 p.m.,
Fri.-Sat. noon-10 p.m.;
additional lines for farmer's markets
These cute little buses link the most popular beach and downtown areas during the most popular times, and the fare is only a quarter. On the north end, it stops at the fabulous new library, the Promenade and up to Wilshire; it also hits the Pier, the south end of Palisades Park, several stops along Main Street, the Ocean Park beaches and, on the southern end, Venice Beach and the boardwalk. Many hotels are found along on the route. Wednesday and Saturday from 8:30 to 1:30, a special bus takes people from as far north as San Vicente down to the farmer's market on Arizona; on Saturday mornings, another shuttle takes shoppers from the middle part of town to the Pico Farmer's Market. Life in Santa Monica really is possible without a car!

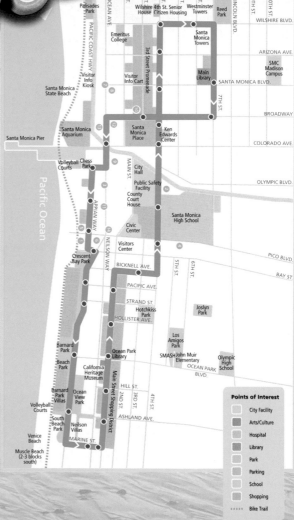

Points of Interest

- City Facility
- Arts/Culture
- Hospital
- Library
- Park
- Parking
- School
- Shopping
- Bike Trail

Car Rental

ALS Limousine
310.450.9988

Avis
310.453.4421

Avon
310.392.8618

Beverly Hills Rent-a-Car
310.829.9384

Dial-a-Ride
310.394.9871
Serving seniors and the disabled inside the city of Santa Monica for 50 cents a ride; you must first enroll for the service.

Enterprise
310.395.4941

Euro Taxi
310.020.4200, eurotaxiom.com

Hertz
310.451.3539

Limos & Taxis
Ace Limousine Services
310.452.7083

Taxi Taxi
310.828.2233, santamonicataxi.com

Segway Rental

Segway Los Angeles
1660 Ocean Ave., Santa Monica
310.395.1395
Good lord, these things are dorky, but people sure have fun riding them on the bike path.

Parking Dos & Don'ts

DO: If you're a regular beachgoer, get a parking pass from the city (parking.santa-monica.org, 310.458.8295); an annual pass is $130, semiannual is $88, and monthly is $22. They sell out, so get yours early. They're good at all beachfront lots except the top of the pier and in the two-hour spots.

DON'T: Park on the east side of PCH and try to cross the highway. People get killed doing this.

DO: Try the beach lot just south of Pico or at the end of Ocean Park on busy days; they are $6 for the day and usually have more room than the jam-packed Main Street lots.

DON'T: Make a U-turn on PCH to get into a parking lot. Again, people get killed doing this. A lot.

DO: Try to get a beach or pier parking space before 11 a.m. on hot weekend days – all the lots can jam up.

DON'T: Think you can outfox a meter maid (or mister). They'll get you. Trust us, we know.

Calendar of Events

January
Santa Monica Outdoor Antique Market. Santa Monica Airport, 323.933.2511. A fun small market (particularly good for collectibles) that happens the first and fourth Sunday of each month.

March
Santa Monica Pier Sunday Concert Series begins. 310.458.8900, santamonicapier.org. Runs through May.
Stairway to the Stars. Santa Monica Civic Auditorium, 310.458.8551, santamonicacivicauditorium.org. A hugely popular student concert benefiting local public schools.
CA Boom. 310.394.8600, caboomshow.com. A design exhibition that looks at what's next in how we live and how we work.

April
Earth Day on the Promenade. 888.295.8372, earthdayla.org. A large and vibrant street fair and environmental-education opportunity.
Celebration of the Arts. 310.396.4557, smmef.org/pier.html. Showcasing student work on the Santa Monica Pier, this is produced by the Education Foundation of Santa Monica-Malibu.

May
Santa Monica Festival. Clover Park, 310.458.8350, arts.santa-monica.org. A celebration with local artists, performers and environmentalists, with a focus on sustainable living.
Venice Art Walk. 310.392.9255, venicefamilyclinic.org. Studio tours, a silent auction and a food fair in support of the Venice Family Clinic.

June
Twilight Dance Series at the Pier. 310.458.8786, twilightdance.org. Ten weeks of popular (and free) Thursday-night concerts at the Santa Monica Pier.
Summer SOULstice Block Party. Main Street, Santa Monica, mainstreetsm.com. Lots of live music, arts and crafts, face painting and, of course, spoken-word performances.

July
Celebrate America Fireworks Show. Corsair Field at 16th & Pearl, 310.434.3000. Sponsored by Santa Monica College and the only fireworks display in the city proper; often happens a couple of days before the 4th.
Marina del Rey July 4th Fireworks. 310.305.9545, visitthemarina.com. Prime viewing spots between Fisherman's Village and Burton Chace Park.
Palisades Americanism Parade. Pacific Palisades, 310.459.7963. Small-town, hokey, wonderful fun.
Call to the Wall Longboard Contest. malibuboardriders.com. Longboarders put on a show at Surfrider Beach to benefit Camp Ronald McDonald.

August
California World Guitar Show. Santa Monica Civic, 918.288.2222. An annual buy-sell-trade show for more than just guitars: amps, banjos, mandolins, effects, memorabilia, records, violins, books, you name it.
Movies in the Park. Pacific Palisades, friendsoffilm.com. Free, family-oriented outdoor screenings at the Pali Rec Center.

September
Abbot Kinney Festival. Venice, 310.396.3772, abbotkinney.org. Abbot Kinney Blvd. is closed to traffic for live music, performance artists, a spectacular children's court, food areas, a "spirit garden," art pavilion and more than 300 vendors.
Coastal Cleanup Day. 310.451.1500, healthebay.org. Founded by Heal the Bay, this cleanup day stretches beyond Santa Monica to more than 90 countries and may be the largest volunteer day on the planet. Third Saturday of Sept.
Santa Monica Book, Print, Photo & Paper Fair. Santa Monica Civic, 209.358.3134. Antiquarian books, first editions, prints, autographs, maps, manuscripts and ephemera.

October
Santa Monica Symphony Orchestra season begins. 310.395.6330, smsymphony.org.

November
American Film Market. 310.446.1000, ifta-online.org. In just eight days, acquisitions execs, sales agents and producers close over $800 million dollars in deals, most of them at the Broadway Deli. Running in conjunction with AFI Fest in Hollywood, this annual scramble exhausts the inexhaustible.

December
Marina del Rey Holiday Boat Parade. 310.670.7130, mdrboatparade.org. Watch the twinkle-light action at Burton Chace Park.
Main Street Merchants Holiday Party. mainstreetsm.com. Caroling, a tree-lighting, eggnog, the works.
Santa Claus Come to Pacific Palisades. palisadeschamber.com. He's traded in his sleigh for a shiny red fire truck and he's coming to the Village Green in early December.

Index

Photography Credits

Photography: Paul Click, Colleen Dunn Bates & John Stephens, except as noted below.

7 Towns in Search of One: Mother's Beach by Robert Landau.

Historic: Ocean Park Bathhouse panorama by W.D. Lambert, 1908; Long Wharf, Gold Coast, P-O-P, North Beach Bathhouse, beach volleyball, Mrs. Muscle Beach courtesy of Santa Monica Public Library.

Beachy: Santa Monica beach and Muscle Beach by Greg Peterson; sailboats by Robert Landau.

Architectural: Santa Monica Library by John Edward Linden; Colorado Court by Marvin Rand.

Smart: RAND photos by Diane Baldwin/RAND; Natalie Crawford and Chloe Bird courtesy of RAND; LMU fans courtesy of Loyola Marymount University; Mount St. Mary's courtesy of Mount St. Mary's; Pepperdine by Ron Hall; Santa Monica College courtesy of Santa Monica College; Santa Monica Library by John Edward Linden.

Artistic: The Getty Center entrance hall by Marcelo Coelho, courtesy of J. Paul Getty Trust; Getty Center at dusk by Scott Frances/Esto, courtesy of J. Paul Getty Trust; Getty Villa by Richard Ross, courtesy of J. Paul Getty Trust; Santa Monica Museum of Art by John Linden; Bergamot Station gallery by Greg Peterson; Hamilton Galleries courtesy of the gallery.

Literary: Drawing of Christopher Isherwood by Don Bachardy, courtesy of the artist.

Reaching Out: Self-Realization Fellowship courtesy of Self-Realization Fellowship.

Hungry & Thirsty: Ivy at the Shore courtesy of the Ivy; Whist cabana courtesy of Whist; Bodega Wine Bar courtesy of Bodega; Shutters Lobby Bar courtesy of Shutters.

Entertaining: Dick Dale courtesy of the Twilight Dance Series; Musica Angelica by Paul Antico, Creative Antics; Theatricum Botanicum by Miriam Geer Photography; Rusty's swing dancers by Mary Ann Stuehrmann; Luciana Souza by Bob Wolfenson, courtesy of Sunnyside Records.

Athletic: WSA surfer and beach scene courtesy of WSA.

Childlike: Theatricum Botanicum actors by Miriam Geer Photography; carousel on the Santa Monica Pier by Greg Peterson; girl surfing courtesy of Learn to Surf L.A.; balloon man by Greg Peterson.

Home Away from Home: Casa del Mar courtesy of Casa del Mar; Loews pool courtesy of Loews; Shutters room courtesy of Shutters; Tide Shuttle map courtesy of Big Blue Bus.

Thanks to:

The design team: Production director Sally Pfeiffer, book designer James Barkley, production artists Kim Ennis and Katherine Hillseth

The artist: Ethel Fisher, creator of the cover painting

The photographers: Paul Click, Colleen Bates and John Stephens

The copy queen: Margery Schwartz

The assistant editor: John Stephens

The sales team: Sally Workman and John Stephens

The advisors: Dorothy Dunn, Penny Dunn, Judy Neveau, Ruth Subrin, Amelia Saltsman, Mira Velimorovic, Ann Vitti and Sally Workman

The families: Caroline, Max, Zach, Robbie, Addie, Kevin, Erin, Emily, Darryl, Sara, Kevin, Pat

Further Reading

An Architectural Guidebook to Los Angeles, by David Gebhard and Robert Winter (Gibbs Smith)

Hiking Trails of the Santa Monica Mountains, by Milt McAuley (Canyon Publishing)

Pacific Palisades: Where the Mountains Meet the Sea, by Betty Lou Young and Randy Young (Casa Vieja Press)

Santa Monica Bay: Paradise by the Sea, by Fred E. Basten and Carolyn See (Hennessey & Ingalls)

Santa Monica Canyon: A Walk through History, by Betty Lou Young and Randy Young (Casa Vieja Press)

Santa Monica Farmers' Market Cookbook, by Amelia Saltsman (Blenheim Press)

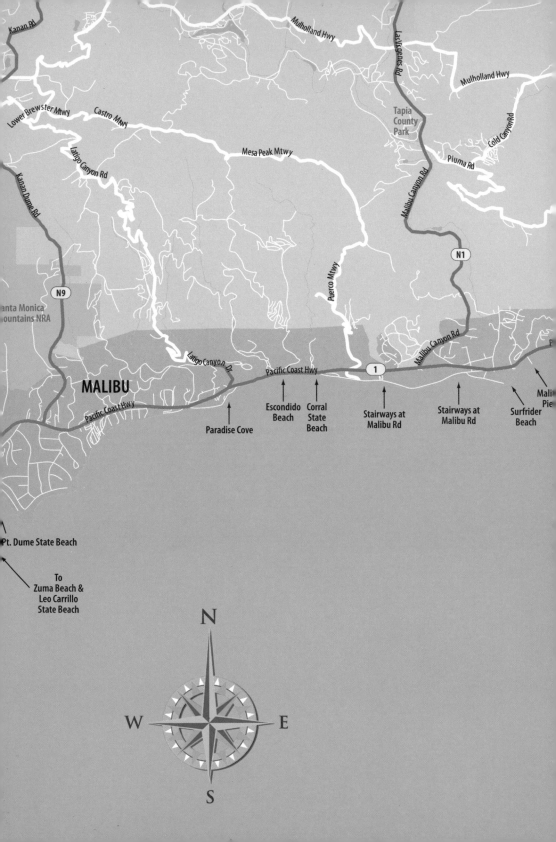